Edward Arthur Fitz Gerald, Stuart Vines

The highest Andes : a record of the first ascent of Aconcagua and Tupungato in Argentina, and the exploration of the surrounding valleys

Edward Arthur Fitz Gerald, Stuart Vines

The highest Andes : a record of the first ascent of Aconcagua and Tupungato in Argentina, and the exploration of the surrounding valleys

ISBN/EAN: 9783337156930

Printed in Europe, USA, Canada, Australia, Japan

Cover: Foto ©Andreas Hilbeck / pixelio.de

More available books at **www.hansebooks.com**

THE
HIGHEST ANDES

A RECORD OF THE FIRST ASCENT
OF ACONCAGUA AND TUPUNGATO IN
ARGENTINA, AND THE EXPLORATION
OF THE SURROUNDING VALLEYS

BY

E. A. FITZ GERALD

AUTHOR OF "CLIMBS IN THE NEW ZEALAND ALPS"

WITH CHAPTERS BY

STUART VINES, M.A., F.R.G.S.

AND CONTRIBUTIONS BY

PROFESSOR BONNEY, D.Sc., LL.D., F.R.S., G. C. CRICK, F.G.S.
R. I. POCOCK, G. A. BOULENGER, F.R.S.
I. H. BURKILL, PHILIP GOSSE

WITH TWO MAPS BY A. E. LIGHTBODY, A.M.I.C.E., F.R.G.S.,
FIFTY-ONE ILLUSTRATIONS, AND A PANORAMA

METHUEN & CO.
36 ESSEX STREET, W.C.
LONDON
1899

TO MY MOTHER

PREFACE

THIS book is the outcome of seven months' work by myself and my colleagues, Mr. Stuart Vines, Mr. Arthur Lightbody, and Mr. Philip Gosse, in the Andes of Argentina. My expedition had for its object primarily the triangulation of the country immediately surrounding the peak of Aconcagua, America's highest mountain; and secondly, the scaling of the great peak itself, which had up to that time defied the efforts of all who had attempted to gain its summit. The success that we met with was due to the unflagging help and splendid efforts of my companions, who in the face of many difficulties and hardships assisted me with unfailing cheerfulness and great courage. The delay in the appearance of this narrative is owing to a severe attack of typhoid fever as I was about to leave South America. No sooner did I become convalescent than my friend Mr. Vines was stricken by the same malady, with the result that it was not till January 1898 that we reached England.

The genesis of the expedition and the history of Aconcagua are set forth in the first chapter. It may be of interest, however, to reproduce here a short passage written in 1876 by the late Mr. T. W. Hinchliff, an ardent mountaineer of the early days of the Alpine Club, upon the prospect of an ascent of Aconcagua and Tupungato. He wrote :—

> "Lover of mountains as I am, and familiar with such summits as those of Mont Blanc, Monte Rosa, and other Alpine heights, I could not repress a strange feeling as I looked at Tupungato and Aconcagua, and reflected that endless successions of men must in all probability be for ever debarred from their lofty crests. When we used to look at the highest peaks and passes of the Alps the only question which suggested itself was 'Which is the best way to get there?' In the presence

of the huge peaks of the Andes I could but think of the great probability that no one would ever get to them at all. There they reposed in divine dignity, too great for mortal approach, and suggesting the abodes where the gods of Epicurus 'sit careless of mankind,' and careless of the tremendous calamities dealt out to men by the fires concealed beneath the feet of these glorified monsters. The Alps have been conquered, and Mont Blanc has been obliged to bow down to the monarchs of the Caucasus; but Nature proclaims the existence of an impassable limit somewhere, and the latest conquerors of even Elbruz and Kasbek have been compelled to admit the effects of the rarefaction of the air. Those who, like Major Godwin Austen, have had all the advantages of experience and acclimatisation to aid them in attacks upon the higher Himalayas, agree that 21,500 feet is near the limit at which man ceases to be capable of the slightest further exertion. Even this has only been attained by halting after a very few steps and lying down exhausted in the snow. Mr. Simpson, whose pictures of Himalayan scenery are so well known, tells me that he and his party suffered severely in crossing the famous Purung Pass, which is 19,000 feet above the sea; and that some of the natives from the plains declared they were not only dying but dead! None could advance without more and more frequent halts. There is reason to believe that from some climatal reason this difficulty of breathing, called *puna* in South America, is experienced with greater severity in the Andes than in other great ranges. When Mr. Darwin crossed the Portillo Pass to Mendoza at the height of 13,000 or 14,000 feet, he found that 'the exertion of walking was extremely great, and the respiration became deep and laborious.' With their 9000 or 10,000 feet above this, Aconcagua and Tupungato may probably defy intrusion unless through the medium of a balloon." [1]

Such opinions are familiar to all climbers. The impossibilities to one generation of Alpinists become the achievements of the next; and so, doubtless, it will continue to be until the summit of the Himalayas themselves is scaled, and the breaking of mountaineering records ceases for ever.

[1] *Over the Sea and Far Away*, p. 90.

PREFACE

One other matter that may be noticed here is the attempt that was made to climb Aconcagua while I was in South America. For a long time the members of the German *Turnverein* (or Athletic Club) of Santiago had cherished the idea of ascending Aconcagua, and thus completing the work begun by Dr. Güssfeldt, their countryman. During several successive years they made ascents in the Andes in order to gain experience and training. Maipo was climbed by them for the second time, as well as a peak to which the name of Bismarck was given, and the still higher summit of Plomo, 18,964 feet above the sea. When we arrived in South America in the autumn of 1896 the members of the Club were already contemplating an attack on Aconcagua, January 1898 having been provisionally fixed for the attempt. I was as unaware of these preparations as the members of the Club apparently were of mine, although the fact that I was organising an expedition to Aconcagua had been made known in the Press a year before we left England. Our arrival in South America, however, took the Club by surprise, and seemed to threaten the destruction of their plans and hopes. Nevertheless, in friendly rivalry which I gladly recognise, the members of the *Turnverein* gallantly resolved to attempt the ascent of Aconcagua that season, and after hurried preparations they left Santiago on January 9. The gentlemen who took part in the expedition were Messrs. Robert and Emil Conrad, Karl Greibel, Adolf Moser, Harold Wolff, and Gustav Brant, all members of the German colony in Chile. The route which they followed from point to point was that already explored by Dr. Güssfeldt through the Valle Hermoso and the Cañon del Volcan. Their base camp was pitched on the very spot where Dr. Güssfeldt's had stood fourteen years before. The whole mass of the mountain interposed between their camp and our own, and each expedition remained completely in ignorance of the movements of the other. Aconcagua was thus being attacked simultaneously from opposite sides, and neither party could tell what success the other had met with. On January 16th the Germans crossed the great ridge which Dr. Güssfeldt had called the Sierra del Penitente, and spent that night at the base of the mountain. Their ascent began on the 17th, three days after the summit had been actually reached by my guide Mattias Zurbriggen. The climb so far offered few difficulties, and towards evening they reached a height of about 19,000 feet, when they saw two men approaching along the side of the mountain. These were my porters Pollinger and Lanti, whose meeting with the Germans is described elsewhere. From them the party received the news of Zurbriggen's ascent to the summit. That night they reached an elevation of 20,670 feet, where they were compelled to stop, as the feeble moonlight was insufficient to light them over the rocky ground in front. They bivouacked as well as circumstances permitted, and passed an exceedingly trying night. The thermometer sank to 12° cent. below freezing, and they had no covering whatever except a few shawls.

On the morning of the 18th the Germans reached their highest point, which they estimated to be at an altitude of 21,326 feet. They were now suffering from exhaustion and mountain sickness, and a mist suddenly enveloped them, so dense that although only a few yards apart they could scarcely see one another. The weather became more and more threatening, and it was absolutely necessary to turn back. They spent that night on the Sierra del Penitente, and descended into the Cañon del Volcan next morning. For some days they hoped that a change in the weather might allow them to make a second attempt, but it continued to rain, and thick clouds surrounded Aconcagua. On the 21st they abandoned the enterprise.

I have to express my sense of deep obligation to Professor Bonney, D.Sc., LL.D., F.R.S., Mr. G. C. Crick, F.G.S., Mr. R. I. Pocock, Mr. G. A. Boulenger, F.R.S., and Mr. I. H. Burkill for their invaluable technical contributions to this volume; and to thank my friend Mr. Henry Norman for his help in preparing my proofs for the press.

EDW. A. FITZ GERALD

SAVILE CLUB, LONDON,
September 1899

CONTENTS

CHAPTER I
INTRODUCTORY .   PAGE 1

CHAPTER II
TO MENDOZA AND VACAS   15

CHAPTER III
GENERAL ASPECTS OF THE ANDES   29

CHAPTER IV
UP THE VACAS VALLEY   38

CHAPTER V
FIRST ATTEMPT ON ACONCAGUA   45

CHAPTER VI
THE ATTACK RENEWED .   59

CHAPTER VII
THE ASCENT ACCOMPLISHED .   72

CHAPTER VIII
BEATEN BACK BY SNOW AND COLD   84

CHAPTER IX
FURTHER ATTEMPTS ON ACONCAGUA .   94

CHAPTER X
THE SECOND ASCENT OF ACONCAGUA .   105

CONTENTS

CHAPTER XI
TWENTY-THREE THOUSAND FEET ABOVE THE SEA . . 118

CHAPTER XII
A TRIP TO CHILE . . 127

CHAPTER XIII
THE FIRST ASCENT OF THE CATEDRAL . . 133

CHAPTER XIV
WORK IN THE HORCONES VALLEY . 146

CHAPTER XV
HEADING FOR TUPUNGATO . . . 153

CHAPTER XVI
THE FIRST ATTACK ON TUPUNGATO . . . 166

CHAPTER XVII
MORE ATTEMPTS ON TUPUNGATO . 175

CHAPTER XVIII
TUPUNGATO ASCENDED . . 190

CHAPTER XIX
THE SUMMIT AND THE DESCENT . 203

CHAPTER XX
THE LAST OF ACONCAGUA . 220

CHAPTER XXI
A LOST VOLCANO . 228

CHAPTER XXII
THE HORCONES VALLEY IN WINTER . . . 241

CHAPTER XXIII
THE POSADA AT INCA 258

CONTENTS

CHAPTER XXIV
THE PASS IN WINTER . 267

CHAPTER XXV
LIGHTBODY'S CROSSING OF THE ANDES . 281

CHAPTER XXVI
WE LEAVE THE ANDES . . 289

CHAPTER XXVII
CONCLUSION 298

APPENDIX A
NOTES ON ROCK SPECIMENS COLLECTED IN THE CHILIAN ANDES BY MR. FITZ GERALD'S EXPEDITION . 311

APPENDIX B
NOTES ON THE FOSSILS FROM THE CHILIAN ANDES COLLECTED BY MR. FITZ GERALD'S EXPEDITION . 333

APPENDIX C
NOTES ON THE NATURAL HISTORY OF THE ACONCAGUA VALLEYS . 338

APPENDIX D
THE BOUNDARY DISPUTE BETWEEN CHILE AND THE ARGENTINE REPUBLIC . 377

INDEX . 385

LIST OF ILLUSTRATIONS

	PHOTOGRAPHED BY	FACING PAGE
ACONCAGUA FROM HORCONES LAKE	A. E. LIGHTBODY	*Frontispiece*
THE TRANSANDINE PASS ROAD	,,	16
THE POSADA, LAS VACAS	,,	25
ACONCAGUA FROM HORCONES VALLEY	THE AUTHOR	30
AT THE HEAD OF THE VACAS VALLEY	A. E. LIGHTBODY	38
LOOKING DOWN THE VACAS VALLEY	,,	40
ACONCAGUA FROM VACAS VALLEY	,,	43
HORCONES LAKE LOOKING TOWARDS CUEVAS VALLEY	,,	49
THE HORCONES VALLEY	,,	52
LOOKING DOWN HORCONES VALLEY FROM GLACIER	THE AUTHOR	53
SADDLE ON WHICH THE 18,700 FOOT CAMP WAS SITUATED	,,	57
OUR HIGHEST CAMP ON ACONCAGUA (18,700 FT.)	,,	76
THE SUMMIT OF ACONCAGUA	A. E. LIGHTBODY	91
THE PASO MALO	,,	97
THE CAULDRON	,,	98
SERACS OF THE HORCONES GLACIER	,,	104
ACONCAGUA FROM THE PENITENTES. *Telephoto View*	,,	114
ON THE HORCONES GLACIER	THE AUTHOR	120
A TRIGONOMETRICAL STATION, NO. 8	A. E. LIGHTBODY	131
THE CUERNO	,,	143
K3 CAMP, HORCONES VALLEY (11,821 FT.)	THE AUTHOR	152
TUPUNGATO THIRTY MILES AWAY. *Telephoto View*	A. E. LIGHTBODY	157
THE GREAT TUPUNGATO VALLEY	,,	158
THE BASE CAMP, TUPUNGATO	STUART VINES	167

LIST OF ILLUSTRATIONS

	PHOTOGRAPHED BY	FACING PAGE
NIEVE PENITENTE ON TUPUNGATO	STUART VINES	174
TUPUNGATO FROM THE EAST	,,	186
THE WATER-PARTING BETWEEN CHILE AND ARGENTINA, FROM TUPUNGATO	,,	197
POLLERA FROM THE TUPUNGATO VALLEY	A. E. LIGHTBODY	207
IN THE TUPUNGATO VALLEY	,,	217
VIEW FROM THE SUMMIT OF TUPUNGATO, ACONCAGUA IN THE DISTANCE	STUART VINES	218
UNDER THE SOUTHERN PRECIPICE OF ACONCAGUA, LOOKING SOUTH	A. E. LIGHTBODY	222
GREAT PRECIPICE ON ACONCAGUA	,,	224
STRIKING CAMP IN HORCONES VALLEY	THE AUTHOR	226
SNOW PEAKS ON THE BOUNDARY	A. E. LIGHTBODY	240
THE TWIN PEAKS FROM THE PENITENTES	,,	252
DIGGING OUT OUR BASE CAMP NEAR INCA	,,	260
MULES ON THE CUMBRE PASS IN SUMMER	,,	267
A WINTER SCENE NEAR CUEVAS	,,	282
THE INCA LAKE AND PORTILLO		285
THE INCA VALLEY IN WINTER	,,	291
LIGHTBODY'S CAMP IN TUPUNGATO VALLEY	,,	298
TORLOSA FROM LAS VACAS. *Telephoto View*	,,	301
THE IGLESIA OR PENITENTES	,,	302
INCA CUTTINGS ON A ROCK	,,	304
PANORAMA FROM SUMMIT OF PENITENTES		308

LIOLÆMUS FITZ GERALDI	Page 354
NEW ANDEAN ARACHNIDA	Facing Page 360
VIOLA SEMPERVIVUM	Page 362
CALYCERA VIRIDIFLORA	,, 364
ACÆNA LÆVIGATA	,, 365
BLUMENBACHIA CORONATA	,, 366
ANEMONE MAJOR	,, 368

SKETCH MAP SHOWING ROUTES	End
MAP OF ACONCAGUA AND DISTRICT	End

THE HIGHEST ANDES

CHAPTER I

INTRODUCTORY

WHEN travelling in a remote part of the Tyrol, some years ago, I met an Austrian climber at the little inn where we were stopping. That evening, around a big log-fire, we talked long of the Alpine work we had been doing, and conversation turned to the Andes of South America. He had climbed there and had many surprising adventures, and these he narrated to me: how he had set out to climb and explore in the Cordilleras and those regions in Argentina that surround the great mountain Aconcagua—the highest peak of the two Americas; how he had then gone over into Chile, and been stopped by the insurgents, and forced to join their ranks and fight against the dictator, Balmaceda. These exciting narratives of experiences around the great mountains and in troubled times, made a vivid impression upon my mind. His stories of the vastness of the ranges and the beauty of the scenery left a lasting impression on me—so much so, indeed, that I then and there resolved to try my luck on this great mountain, as soon as a favourable opportunity should arise. To climb the giant peak of the Andes, that had so long defied the attempts of all who had tried to conquer its virgin snows, became henceforth one of the ambitions of my life.

At that moment I was planning an expedition to New Zealand, which I determined to carry out before I tried my hand in South America. I realised already that any attack made upon these ranges would be most difficult, and I wished to gain more experience in foreign travel before I set out on such a task. With these ideas in view I started for New Zealand a few months later, and my thoughts were fully occupied by my climbs out there. On my return to England, a year after, I found myself in the midst of the work of publishing my book on the New Zealand Alps, a task to me far more terrible and difficult than the climbing of the ragged cliffs of Mt. Sefton. It was, therefore, not until the spring of 1896 that my thoughts turned towards the highest Andes.

The great peak of Aconcagua naturally presents a most attractive field for the climber and explorer, partly because it is the highest mountain in the world outside the great ranges of Asia, and partly because it is a prominent feature seen from the coast, its lofty summit being visible thirty leagues inland from the harbour of Valparaiso. The spring and summer of 1896 I spent organising an expedition to these regions. I obtained the assistance and co-operation of Mr. Stuart Vines, Mr. de Trafford, and Mr. Philip Gosse, grandson of Philip Gosse, the well-known naturalist. My old guide, Mattias Zurbriggen, was to go with us,—he who accompanied me on my expedition to New Zealand,—and we secured five porters from Switzerland and Italy, by name the brothers Joseph and Louis Pollinger, Lochmatter, Nicola Lanti, and Fritz Weibel. Before starting, in order to make experiments in camping at high altitudes, we went to Switzerland, with the intention of camping as high up as possible upon the Dom, the highest mountain there. I also wanted to make the members of our expedition acquainted with heliography and flag-signalling. I had suffered so much in New Zealand from having to come down from high camps a whole day's journey for some small item forgotten, that I thought this method of communication from high camps to base camps would be invaluable to us. We spent this time in Switzerland in camping-out, testing our instruments and condensed provisions, and learning these methods of communication. Owing to remarkably bad weather, however,—the worst known for many years,—we were unable to do much, and only succeeded in pushing our camps some 13,000 feet up on the Hohberg Glacier. Here Vines and I spent a night in a storm, which, at the time, we thought unpleasant, but it was hardly even a suggestion of what we were to suffer later on in the Andes through wind and snow. Looking back upon it, I cannot but smile when I think what child's play it was in comparison to our 19,000 Foot Camp in a storm on Aconcagua. We were at least able to breathe comfortably, and were in excellent health and spirits, and that, in itself, means everything.

On returning to London we were busy packing the innumerable objects which constitute the equipment of a large party going to a country where little can be procured. One of the most difficult problems is what food to take, in order to combine lightness and variety, and at the same time to select those foods which give the greatest strength and health. The experiences of Dr. Nansen in equipment were exceedingly useful to us in many ways, but then a mountain expedition has to take into account great heat as well as Arctic cold. If has often occurred to me that Antarctic explorers must find their conditions very strange and unsuitable when they have to cross the Equator in a ship fitted out for the Polar regions. It is the contradictory nature of these demands that sets the mountain explorer so hard a problem. The various forms of surveying instruments, barometers, thermometers, aneroids, etc., are also a great question in such work. From what I had learned of the country from books, I gathered that most things could be carried on muleback. I therefore did not sacrifice everything for lightness, except so far as the equipment for the final climbs was concerned. Our surveying outfit consisted of 6-inch and 3-inch theodolites, and a sextant. When we were in the Andes, we had at work two 6-inch theodolites, one 5-inch, one 3-inch, a sextant, and a telemeter gradient level. These, with mercurial barometers, aneroids, and boiling-point thermometers, completed our surveying equipment. For food we provided ourselves with large quantities of the Bovril Blue and Red Ration, their dessicated vegetables, and their cocoa-and-milk, all of which we found excellent; also Brand's extracts of meat. For biscuits we took Kola, and a large supply of Garibaldi and cabin biscuits, which took the place of bread with us, thus saving us the labour of baking. Of photographic material we had an ample supply. Twenty pack-saddles were made for us, a large quantity of tents, and some eighty wicker panniers lined with macintosh, covered with Willesden canvas, and furnished with straps and hooks, two of them forming a light mule-load. For the clothing of the party we used, of course, wool, and our mountain clothes were made from Scotch homespun, covered with Burberry gabardine, which proved excellent for resisting wear and tear in rough work. Large quantities of woollen blankets and sleeping-bags formed an essential part of the equipment, but for the higher camps, where the cold would be intense, and weight a great drawback, we chose eider-down sleeping-bags covered with silk. These were exceedingly warm, and did not weigh four pounds. When all these things were collected, they filled no fewer than a hundred large crates, weighing in all nearly eight tons. Looking back upon it, I think we might have reduced the quantity of food that we took out; but going into a virtually unknown country, it is wise to err upon the side of more provisions than may be necessary, as one can never count beforehand upon the exact resources that will be at one's disposal. At the end of our work we had more than five or six hundredweight left over.

Of course before starting we made ourselves conversant with the literature of the subject. A great deal has been written on travel in the Andes, but with the single exception of Dr. Güssfeldt's interesting work, narrating his own plucky but unsuccessful attempt, there was nothing that dealt directly with Aconcagua. The passes and valleys near its base had been frequently described by travellers; but except Güssfeldt no one had actually attempted the great mountain itself. My intention was to approach Aconcagua through the Argentine, and by way of the Mendoza Valley, through which runs a well-known pass road that eventually crosses the Andes by a ridge known as the Cumbre, and descends

OUR PREDECESSORS IN THE ANDES 5

into Chile on the western side. This route, sometimes known as the Uspallata Pass, runs comparatively near to the base of Aconcagua, and is one of the best known ways over the Andes from one Republic to the other. Very many books have been written by travellers who have used it. One of the first scientific explorers to cross by the Cumbre was Darwin, and the chapter in the *Cruise of the Beagle*, in which his expedition is described, remains an important part of the literature of the Andes. The great naturalist landed at Valparaiso in March 1835, and after crossing to Mendoza by the Portillo Pass, which lies farther to the south, he made his way back into Chile by the Cumbre. He did not actually leave the frequented track known to thousands of passengers, but nevertheless his observations on the nature of the country, especially its geology, are still of the greatest value. In 1849-52 an American party, the "U.S. Naval Astronomical Expedition to the Southern Hemisphere," made the explorations which have been described by Gilliss, its chief. Stelzner, in the course of his prolonged geological explorations in South America, crossed the Andes by a more difficult route farther to the north, and recrossed on his return by the Cumbre and the Mendoza Valley.

With regard, therefore, to the frequented ways where travellers are led over the Andes by Chilian or Argentine guides, little remained to be seen that had not often been described before. The labours of the men I have named, and of others such as Pissis and Stübel, had been mainly in the direction of geology. Mountaineers had seldom thought of approaching the southern Cordilleras, and much of the ground there remains even yet virgin soil. Not that the Andes had never been climbed at any point, for they had often been successfully attacked; but with wonderful unanimity the mountaineers had passed by the southern Andes and had concentrated their energies upon the peaks in Ecuador, far to the north. Alexander von Humboldt set the example as long ago as 1802, when he made the first attempt to climb Chimborazo, and attained, as he believed, the height of over 19,000 feet, although the figures are thought to be open to doubt. Humboldt's attempt, and his frequent references to Chimborazo in his works, made the mountain one of the most celebrated in the world. It was long believed to be the highest in South America, and indeed the highest on earth, until the Himalayas began to be known.[1] Attention having thus been drawn to the Ecuadorian Andes, travellers turned eagerly in that direction. Another attempt on Chimborazo was made in 1831 by Boussingault, but the summit was reached for the first time on 4th January 1880, when Edward Whymper made his memorable ascent. Along with two Piedmontese guides whom he had taken out, he established a series of camps, one at 14,375, one at 16,624, and one at 17,285 feet. All three suffered from mountain sickness, and one of the guides had his feet badly frost-bitten. On the crest of the mountain they had to struggle through great fields of soft snow, in which it was necessary to beat down a path at every step they took. In spite, however, of all difficulties, Whymper reached the summit at 20,498 feet— the highest point attained by any climber up to that date. In July he made a second ascent of Chimborazo. Whymper also climbed Antisana, Cayambe, Sara-urcu, and Cotocachi, and made a remarkable ascent of the great volcano, Cotopaxi, where he encamped and spent the night on the summit close to the crater. Cotopaxi, which has an altitude of 19,613 feet, had already been ascended. The first to reach its summit was Dr. Reiss, who made the climb successfully in November 1872. After him came Stübel in 1873, Wolf in 1877, Freiherr Max von Thielmann in 1878. Whymper encamped near the top of Cotopaxi not only to get a view of the crater by night, but also to test the effects of the rarefied air at so high an elevation. During the twenty-six hours they spent on the summit, neither he himself nor his guides experienced any serious symptoms of mountain sickness. He had chosen the volcano for this experiment in order to eliminate the effects of cold,—the ground under their tent being so warm that it almost melted the india-rubber covering, —and thus to discover the influence of the rarefied air alone,

[1] Humboldt, *Aspects of Nature*, vol. i. p. 96.

GÜSSFELDT'S WORK

without other elements of hardship to aid it in lowering the vital powers.

The experiences of Whymper on this expedition could not but be of immense value to anyone contemplating an ascent in the Andes. But in the territory which I had chosen for myself Güssfeldt was my only predecessor. Disregarding the tradition which had led previous explorers in South America to turn their attention first towards the Andes of Ecuador, he set out from Europe with the intention of scaling the virgin mountains of the southern Cordillera. Although in his attempt on Aconcagua he failed to reach the summit, it is impossible to speak with too great admiration of the work he performed upon the mountain itself and in the valleys beside it, under exceedingly difficult and trying conditions.

Dr. Güssfeldt made his expedition practically alone. Even the guide he had taken out from Switzerland failed him. This guide had been specially chosen for his skill and knowledge, and had himself volunteered for the journey for South America, after a series of climbs in the Dauphiné Alps undertaken as a test under the conditions, so far as they could be secured, which Güssfeldt expected to meet with in the Andes. But on the voyage he fell ill; homesickness took possession of him, as it almost always does of the Swiss; and soon after landing in Chile he demanded his release from the engagement and returned to Europe, having attained no higher point on South American soil than the German hospital in Valparaiso. Güssfeldt was thus left without a single companion. There was no time to send to Europe for other guides without losing the summer season, and he was forced to go on with such assistance as he could find in Chile itself. The Chilian *huasos* whom he engaged knew nothing of mountaineering and brought no enthusiasm to the unaccustomed and dangerous work, so that the task of encouraging and inciting those awkward and timorous companions at every turn was not the least part of the undertaking which Güssfeldt had to face. This was a difficulty which seems never to have been absent from the Aconcagua expedition.

In the ascent of Maipo he was better served. One of his companions, however, broke down at a height equal to that of Mont Blanc, and the other, after a desperate struggle, collapsed at an altitude 1312 feet above. Güssfeldt was obliged to complete the ascent by himself, and reached the summit of Maipo, 17,448 feet above the sea, eleven hours after starting from his bivouac. No one had yet made so high an ascent alone.

In climbing Maipo, which till then was a virgin peak, Güssfeldt achieved one of the most striking successes of his expedition. He ascertained the mountain to be an extinct volcano. Under the topmost peak there was a huge crater several hundred feet deep, into which he was able to look, lying on the ground to escape the force of the wind. The depths of this abyss were filled with masses of snow. Nothing indicated recent volcanic activity, and a long time must have elapsed since the volcano was in eruption. Güssfeldt was free altogether from mountain sickness on Maipo, and breathed without difficulty, but in deep breaths. To such an experienced Alpine climber Maipo offered no serious difficulty from the nature of the ground, the chief obstacles being the long and laborious slopes, the high wind and the cold.

It was after his successful ascent of Maipo that Güssfeldt turned his attention towards Aconcagua. He was the first mountaineer that had ever penetrated into its neighbourhood. Everything had to be done from the start—the exploration of the territory, the examination of the approaches, and even, strange as it may appear, the finding of the mountain itself; for the first difficulty to be confronted was how to make one's way to the base of the giant through the perplexing labyrinth of valleys and gorges that surrounds it. Absolutely nothing was known about the mountain except its supposed position upon the map and the distant appearance of its western side. In this lack of all information, Güssfeldt determined to try approaching its base from a northern direction. All other things being equal, the north side offered, he believed, one advantage—there would be less snow upon it. In latitudes south of the Equator, the position of the sun, being inverted, is in the northern sky, not the southern, and the northern side of a mountain becomes the sunny side. Güssfeldt expected therefore that the northern slope of Aconcagua would be freer than any other from the obstructions which snow and ice might put in his way. This point would not have outweighed others of more importance, but he knew of no others, for nothing about Aconcagua was known. Should he find himself at last in the depths of a valley from which Aconcagua was inaccessible, he would have the long and wearisome task of retracing his steps and forcing his way into another which might lead to the mountain from a different direction. All that could be done was to trust to luck. In this respect fortune favoured him, for he actually discovered a route by which he gained the base of Aconcagua and was able to begin the ascent.

As will be seen in the sequel we ourselves did not make use of the route described in Dr. Güssfeldt's book. He approached Aconcagua through Chile, we through the Argentine. He came to Aconcagua from the west and the north, we from the east and south. It was only upon the actual slope of the mountain itself that our track at last crossed his.

In February 1883 Dr. Güssfeldt set out for Aconcagua. He was accompanied, rather against his own will, by a Chilian volunteer, Don Rafael Salazar, who turned back, however, ten days later, taking with him two of the *huasos*. With three *huasos* that still remained, Güssfeldt pressed forward resolutely towards the mountain. The route he had chosen led upwards from Chile through the valley of the river Putaendo, which he followed up to its source. Above that point, crossing a high ridge or pass, the Boquete del Valle Hermoso, where the two Republics meet at the parting of the waters, he descended into the Valle Hermoso on the Argentine side. Through this valley, which lies imbedded in the very heart of the Andes, runs a track by which travellers, after surmounting the Espinazito Pass at the other or lower end, can descend into the Pampas. It was when entering the Valle Hermoso from the west that Güssfeldt caught his first glimpse of Aconcagua, stern, forbidding, and, as it seemed for the moment, inaccessible. The Valle Hermoso, or "Fair Valley," lay in front, with its pleasant green pastures and craggy sides. The direction of the track down towards Espinazito was away from Aconcagua; but another valley entered almost at right angles and seemed to offer a way by which its very base could be reached. Up this valley or defile, to which he gave the name of Valle Penitente—the local name, it appears, is Cañon del Volcan—Güssfeldt made his way. He was now proceeding to his goal from the north, southward; fourteen years afterwards, far on the other side of the great mountain mass, we were toiling from the south, northwards, up the valley of the Horcones, with the same lofty summit for our destination which Güssfeldt then had before his eyes. In the upper part of the Valle Penitente, as far up as the limit of pasturage for the mules allowed, Güssfeldt fixed his base camp. It was of an extremely simple character. It does not even appear that he had brought a tent with him. The field-bed on which he slept stood in the open air, and the water was frozen hard every night. There was not the slightest shelter from rocks or boulders—not even a niche for the barometer. This camp stood at an altitude of 11,752 feet.

At first Güssfeldt seemed to have got into a hopeless *cul-de-sac*. In front of him, completely blocking the upper end of the valley, was a huge wall or palisade of rock, to which he gave the name of Sierra del Penitente. The name, like that which he gave to the valley itself, was suggested by the fields of *nieve penitente* which he saw around. Rising almost sheer to a height of 3000 feet above the floor of the valley, this immense barrier of stone appeared to make all access to Aconcagua impossible.

Riding forward to reconnoitre, Güssfeldt discovered with a shock that he was not the first wanderer to penetrate into that dismal defile. A few paces from him, lying against a rock, was a human skeleton, to which still clung a few wasted rags of clothing. Strange superstitions concerning Aconcagua are widespread amongst the ignorant Chilians. It is believed that somewhere about that mysterious mountain there is treasure. They seem scarcely to know themselves what treasure they look for; perhaps they hope to find gold in masses on the surface, or to penetrate, like Sinbad, into a valley of diamonds. Here some wretched treasure-seeker had perished, overwhelmed by sudden tempest and blinding snow. Within the next weeks, the struggle for Aconcagua still unended, Güssfeldt rode eight times past that ghastly figure, crouched by the wayside in dumb and significant warning. Fourteen years later, when the German expedition from Santiago tried to reach Aconcagua by Güssfeldt's route, they also came upon the skeleton of the dead Chileno. Doubtless at this moment, as I write these lines, that grim sentinel still keeps watch and ward in its silent valley, before the awful gate of the mountain.

The immense rocky barrier which interposed between the Valle Penitente and the base of Aconcagua proved on examination to be not insurmountable. In the middle of it Güssfeldt discovered a couloir by which it was possible to reach the top. This couloir led upwards to a notch or gap in the ridge, to which he gave the name of Portezuelo del Penitente, or "Büsserthor." From this gateway on the ridge a magnificent spectacle, never before seen by human eyes, presented itself. Aconcagua had been reached at last. Right in front, its base separated from him only by a hollow filled with last year's snow, rose its immense black slopes. Above was the summit in an unclouded sky. The surrounding mountains were covered with white; Aconcagua alone was bare, and dominated everything else. Although the explorer stood at an altitude of 16,500 feet, and the summit was therefore only some 6500 feet higher, the whole effect was one of overpowering immensity. The way for the ascent was now open, and Güssfeldt returned to his camp to prepare.

He made his attempt on the 21st of February 1883, accompanied only by two Chilenos, neither of whom, it is needless to say, had any experience of mountaineering, or indeed had ever given it a thought before Dr. Güssfeldt appeared and engaged them for his expedition. The attempt failed. Indeed, under all the circumstances, it could scarcely have been successful; but as a mountaineering feat it was distinguished by extraordinary daring.

Güssfeldt was unable to establish, as we afterwards did, a high camp on the slope of the mountain itself. He simply left his camp down in the Valle Penitente, rode with his servants to the foot of the rocky barrier, where they left their horses, scaled the huge cliff, crossed the snowfield to the base of Aconcagua, and attacked it there and then. It was four in the afternoon of the 20th when they left camp. Passing on their way the skeleton, now a familiar landmark, they reached the couloir, at seven, where they rested for an hour and a half. At half-past ten they had reached the top of the cliff. By the light of a brilliant moon they crossed the snowfield, and it was nearly two in the morning when they first set foot on the lower slope of Aconcagua and began the real ascent. As time went on, and the ascent became more toilsome and the cold winds keener, a spirit of something like panic came upon the two Chilenos. From time to time Güssfeldt had to add to the labours of the climb by delivering persuasive speeches in Spanish to his companions, in order to overcome their reluctance to proceed a step farther. Day broke. At ten o'clock one of the Chilenos collapsed. His feet were frozen, and it was absolutely impossible for him to proceed. Leaving him there, Güssfeldt pressed doggedly forward, having induced the other Chileno to continue the struggle. Together they reached a point about 1300 feet below the summit. It was now afternoon, and the question forced itself upon their minds whether the peak could be reached before sunset. They had with them the smallest supplies of food; their base camp was far away; and they had set out from it twenty-two hours before. Suddenly the sky clouded over, the summit became wrapped in mist, and sleet began to fall. A snowstorm was coming on. Unless other skeletons were to lie on the sides of Aconcagua, they must turn back at once.

Descending, they joined the unfortunate Chileno who had been left behind, and hurried down the slopes and across the snowfields. At the foot of the cliff the horses were waiting, and at eleven o'clock at night they reached the camp again, after an absence from it of thirty-one hours, spent without sleep and with little food, in almost continuous exertion.

Next day snow fell heavily in the Valle Penitente. Trigonometrical measurements had been begun, but the change in the weather made it impossible to remain on the spot. Grass for the mules was no longer to be had; in snow and ice the open unsheltered camp was uninhabitable. It was thereupon broken up, and the caravan withdrew on 24th February to the Valle Hermoso.

Güssfeldt was not, however, at the end of his resources. The time spent in that beautiful valley, among its green meadows and flocks of sheep, restored the spirits of his men. The weather improved; and the way seemed clear for another attempt on Aconcagua. Once more the caravan proceeded up the Valle Penitente, and he encamped a second time in view of the rocky barrier that closed it in. With great determination he proceeded with the preparations for the second attempt, although he suffered so severely from an abscess which had formed under a tooth that he could not sleep at night, even with the aid of strong doses of opium. The second climb took place on 5th March. This time a new plan was adopted. On the previous day he set out with two of his three men, crossed the Sierra del Penitente and the snow-field beyond to the slope of the mountain, where the night was spent, the three climbers huddling together for warmth in one sleeping-bag. In the morning, shortly before sunrise, the ascent began. Güssfeldt endured agonies from toothache and the pain of the abscess; the men also suffered greatly from fatigue. Snowflakes began to fall, and a storm came on. Although they had not yet reached so high an altitude as on the first occasion, it was found necessary to turn back. Even had the weather continued favourable it would hardly have been possible for them to reach the summit of Aconcagua that day. The explorer and his men, after all their heroic endeavours, were utterly worn out. There was nothing for it but to return as quickly as possible to Chile.

The labours of that courageous and energetic traveller

first made the world acquainted with the district round Aconcagua, which until his arrival was virgin soil, and with all the conditions of climbing upon the mountain. To such a pioneer those who follow in his steps and enjoy the fruit of his exertions owe a debt of gratitude which they can never sufficiently repay. Our obligation to Dr. Güssfeldt is none the less because we did not actually follow in his track. Although after his attempt on Aconcagua from the north, he crossed the Cumbre and arrived at Puente del Inca, he did not actually enter the Horcones Valley,[1] which was the chief scene of our labours in 1897, and the avenue by which we in our turn approached the mountain. It does not appear upon his map, and although he speaks of a valley entering that of the Rio de las Cuevas, which from its position must be the Horcones, I have not observed that he even mentions it by name. The first scientific exploration of the Horcones Valley was made by Herr Jean Habel in January 1895. In the course of his journey across South America, Habel spent a number of days up the Horcones, which he followed as far as the glacier and the sources of the river. A large collection of splendid photographs of the valley, some showing Aconcagua, were published in his *Ansichten aus Südamerika*. With Habel's results we were not acquainted at the time of our own exploration, as the work just mentioned was not issued from the press till a later date. Curiously enough, although Habel was the first scientific investigator who saw Aconcagua from the Horcones Valley, he was not aware of its identity, but speaks of the mountain which he photographed there as the Cerro de los Almacenes. Not until the investigations of our party, of which he has spoken with great kindness, were made known, did he identify this mountain with Aconcagua itself.

---

[1] Pronounced "Orŏcōnés."

CHAPTER II

TO MENDOZA AND VACAS

WE sailed from Southampton in the R.M.S.S. *Thames*, on 15th October 1896, and on 29th November we left Buenos Aires, *en route* for Mendoza and the mountains. The director of the Great Western Railway had very kindly placed a small sleeping-carriage at our disposal. This had been coupled at the end of the train, but as it was not swung on bogey trucks, an absolute necessity in these countries, where the permanent way is not kept in the best of repair, we were nearly rattled to pieces. Several times during the night I started up convinced that our carriage was off the line, so alarmingly did it swing from side to side, swaying and jarring as if it were bumping along the sleepers. The journey takes about thirty-six hours, and when we drew up at the terminus in Mendoza we were so shaken and fatigued, that we could scarcely stand up. The town as it now stands was built some thirty-five years ago on a new site not far from the old town, which was destroyed in 1861 by a terrible earthquake, being literally levelled to the ground. Not far from the Great Western Station lies the terminus of that little railway which styles itself "Il Ferro Carril Trasandino de Buenos Aires a Valparaiso." The original intention of the constructors of this line was to carry it through from Mendoza to Santa Rosa de los Andes, the nearest town on the Chilian State Railway, and thus to make a complete line from Buenos Aires to Valparaiso. On the side of Argentina there are, at the present time, some ninety miles of rail open, but on the western or Chilian side, only thirty miles have so far been constructed. At present, construction has ceased, owing to the bankruptcy of its former contractors. As the railway now stands, there remain some sixty miles to be completed, the difficulty of course being that these sixty miles include the tunnel under the Cumbre Pass, a long and costly operation. There is, near Las Cuevas, the beginning of a great tunnel, which was to have been nine miles long. The new construction plans of its engineers, who, I am told, still have hopes of completing the line, reduce the length of this tunnel considerably by the institution of a rack and pinion cog-wheel railway, much on the same principle as that now running up the Zermatt Valley in Switzerland. Already the last few miles of the line, on the Argentine side, are built in this fashion, starting from Zanjon Amarillo ("Yellow Gorge") to Punta de las Vacas. It is hoped that the Chilian and Argentine Governments will agree to raise and guarantee sufficient capital for the completion of this line. Could they find means to do so, it would form the first trans-continental route for South America, and the time saved in getting from England to the West Coast ports would be enormous. At present there is nearly a fortnight lost in taking the circuitous route by the Straits of Magellan. In summer it is possible to cross the ranges, but the transport of luggage is necessarily very expensive. In winter only strong men can force their way across through the deep snows, and even then with great danger. Many lives are lost yearly on this pass. At times it is impossible to get through at all, and the transport of luggage is out of the question. The postal service is so irregular during these winter months that none of the business houses in Valparaiso rely upon it, but send their letters by the longer and safer route of the Magellan Straits. The Transandine Railway could keep up a constant winter service by means of the help of snowsheds, as used on the Canadian Pacific Railway through the Rocky Mountains, and it would also shorten the route to New Zealand, for Buenos Aires can be reached in a fortnight from London by direct express steamers; three days more by rail would take one on to Valparaiso, whence by steamer one could reach Auckland in another fortnight. This would make four and a half weeks, as against six weeks by the Suez Canal or

THE ARGENTINE ARRIEROS

the Cape route. In a word, ten days would be gained in transit from London to New Zealand and the West Coast ports of South America, besides a new and quick route to Sydney—a route that could compete with the Suez Canal, as mails would be shipped direct from Liverpool or Southampton to Buenos Aires, the railway journey from there to Valparaiso corresponding roughly to the present journey from London to Brindisi.

We spent a few days in Mendoza, in order to hire mules for our work in the Andes. This was a troublesome business, but with the help of some kind friends we finally made a contract with one Tomas Sosa, a half-caste. It was arranged that he and his son should furnish us with twenty mules and a bell mare, and that they should also supply animals for their own riding. The bell mare is a necessity with a large troop of mules, for they will all follow her in single file without straying, while if driven by themselves, they are calculated to make the most patient man insane in a few hours. The mule-drivers, or arrieros, never set foot on the ground if they can help it. It would be a loss of caste to walk, and they would, I think, prefer to ride their horses over the edge of a sheer precipice rather than humiliate themselves by getting off and walking. Some of them wear soft slippers, made out of one square piece of raw hide, drawn round the foot by leather thongs, like the shoes often seen in Eastern Europe, which are certainly not suitable for walking on rocky ground. Their general get-up and demeanour are exceedingly picturesque, the costume they wear being very distinctive, and giving them a striking appearance. They ride, as a rule, on the old-fashioned Mexican saddle, with a number of soft sheepskins strapped over the top of it, quite hiding the original saddle from view. Their stirrups are formed from solid blocks of wood, carved in the form of a slipper, very heavy and clumsy. Their feet are so small that an Englishman can rarely get his feet into their stirrups at all. They are fond of silver trappings and gaudy accoutrements—the more noise of jangling silver as they ride, the more pleased are they. To this purpose they wear enormous clinking silver spurs, and when in full dress very light and high-heeled boots, the great height of the heel being necessary to keep the huge rowel of their spurs from catching in the ground when walking. Of late they have taken a great fancy to spurs made in Birmingham. These have been built for them upon the same lines as their ancient silver ones, but the rowel, frequently some five inches in diameter, is made of fine tempered steel. As they ride along, the vibration from this steel rowel causes a humming noise, which gives them great satisfaction, and also, they declare, encourages their horses. Their bits are exceptionally cruel, in fact, I cannot conceive of a more barbarous invention for torturing a horse's mouth. As, however, they seldom if ever use their reins, this is more barbarous in appearance than in practice. The men themselves always wear a "poncho," which consists of a blanket of many-coloured wools. The head is thrust through a hole in the centre, while the folds of the cloth hang about the man on all sides, completely covering him to his knees as he rides. These ponchos are often made of guanaco wool, while occasionally one sees more valuable ones made from the wool of the vicuña. The latter are very thin, yet most warm, for they are woven with extraordinary tightness and fineness, and they are handed down from generation to generation as precious heirlooms. When really good they are worth as much as £20 to £30, but the men would prefer to sell almost everything before parting with them.

Tomas was a venerable-looking old man. He whimpered bitterly, and assured us that he was going to be ruined if he supplied us with the mules at the price offered him, but he finally came to terms. He assured us that he was very old and infirm, and could do no work, so he said he must have his son with him. We suggested that he should stay at home altogether, and let his son take his place, but this he would not hear of. "No," he said, "I cannot be parted from my precious mules, all of whom are personal friends of mine, and know me intimately." Later on we found that he had gone round the corner, to a friend of his, and hired them all for the occasion, leaving his own animals at home, as he feared they might get hurt. During our subsequent work he complained very much of old age and infirmity, especially if anything had to be done early in the morning. I remember one day his hat blew off, and was rapidly being taken by the wind in the direction of the river, rolling with great speed. I then saw this old and infirm gentleman leap from the stone he was sitting on and sprint down the road after his hat, far faster, I am sure, than his son could ever have done. We were astounded at his tremendous agility and nimbleness, and after this episode he got little more sympathy from us on the score of infirmities and age.

We were obliged to remain several days making these bargains, for in South America nothing of this sort can be hurried. One day we took the opportunity of visiting the old Mendoza that had been levelled by the great earthquake of 1861. It lies about a mile from the new town, and is one mass of ruins, not a single house remaining intact. There is something sad and depressing about these white, plastered walls, relics of the old Hispano-Moorish church architecture, invariably seen in all old South American towns, and these heaps of fallen stones, broken arches, and sightless windows; and if you peer through the chinks you can see at the bottom of some cellar the bleached bones of the poor victims. The old city covered some two hundred acres, and contained seven churches and three convents. The earthquake took place on 20th March 1861. It was an Ash Wednesday, after sunset, when the churches were crowded with the pious population who had thronged by thousands to the solemn services of that impressive commemoration. The very first shocks levelled every building to the ground, and the greatest heap of the bones of the people lies under the ruins of the old abode of worship. A place of frequent pilgrimage is this to the friends of the poor souls who were thus hurled unshriven to their death, and hundreds of burning candles stand about in nooks and corners, lit by the devout for their friends and relatives who perished thus miserably.

You can see these candles and the guttered remains of them upon all the stones—pools, patches, splashes of votive wax. Surely purgatory cannot long retain its hold upon the souls of the unprepared, overtaken as they were at their worship. The very traces of the streets were obliterated, some trees of the Alameda and a fragment of a church alone remaining erect, and 13,000 souls perished while only 1600 were spared. For a whole week fires raged among the ruins, and the robbers at their work of pillage paid no heed to the cries of the wretches buried in living graves. There have been many earthquakes since 1861, though without great damage, but almost all the towns in these regions have been destroyed once or twice during the century.

It was at Mendoza that I first met Mr. Arthur Lightbody, who afterwards joined us, and became a member of our expedition. He gave us much useful information concerning the country and its people, and promised to come with us to Vacas and show us the best camping-ground. He was then engineer in charge of the permanent way of the Transandine Railway, a post involving great responsibility, as during certain parts of the year the terrible thunderstorms that rage in the little hills play havoc with the track. One night he was called up to a point where a large iron girder bridge had been carried away. It was some time before he found it, for it had been washed down the stream a long distance and piled up on the opposite bank.

Early on the morning of 7th December we left Mendoza for Vacas, which was the farthest point we could reach by rail. Having driven down to the station, we found that it would be a matter of some difficulty to settle with the numerous drivers who had brought us and our baggage. These gentlemen heartily despised us as "gringos"—a South American name for foreigners, which contains all the superiority on one side and abasement on the other that the Chinese imply when they talk of "foreign devils." The gringos were inexperienced; the gringos were rich; the

WE LEAVE MENDOZA

gringos must pay handsomely. Great was the drivers' disappointment when Dr. Cotton of Puente del Inca came to the rescue and kindly undertook the thankless task of settling with them. He tendered them their legal fare in the paper currency of the country. At first they refused it with disdain, then to our surprise and amazement they took the notes, tore them into small pieces, threw them on the ground, and spat on the fragments. Cotton signed to us that the matter was closed with this dramatic incident, and we turned into the station, but on looking back I beheld the heroes of this little tragedy on their hands and knees collecting the torn and dusty shreds of the fare, while their fellow-drivers stood round, greatly enjoying the joke. After an incident like this I found it less difficult to understand the patched and fragmentary condition of many of the notes that passed through our hands.

At last we got under way. Mr. Thornton, the chief mechanical engineer, very kindly had iron chains screwed on the front platform of the engine, so that we were enabled to ride in the open air in front of the smoke-stack and get a perfect view of the scenery without annoyance from cinders. For the first few miles we ran between mud walls enclosing vineyards and orchards, with the pampas on our left, and the Cerrillos, bleak-looking hills which hid the more rugged features of the higher Andes, on our right. Where there was no irrigation the country was an uncultivated wilderness. But for some distance the irrigation work was very extensive, its effect shown by rows of green meadows bounded by poplar trees. Mendoza is an oasis in the desert, made by the hand of man. There is hardly a drier climate in the world, and the annual rainfall is so slight, that where it alone waters the earth nothing will grow, and only bare stony soil is to be seen around. In and about Mendoza, where the water that descends from the Andes in the Rio Mendoza has been led in every direction by canals and rills, the desert has been turned into glorious green, and the vineyards of Mendoza become more flourishing every year.

The Cordilleras which we were now approaching are formed of three distinct ranges running north and south. The western range forms the watershed, and is the boundary between the Argentine and Chile, while the central range contains the highest peaks, Aconcagua and, to the north, Mercedario. The eastern range is divided from the central one by a wide plain or plateau some 6000 feet above sea-level, known as the Uspallata Pampa. In this region the most notable mountain is the Cerro de la Plata, which can be seen to great effect from Mendoza. This lower range conceals from view the higher Andine summits behind. We had been told, however, that at certain points on the line we should catch a glimpse of some of the great peaks, and we kept our eyes anxiously turned towards the Cerrillos on our right. At length we were rewarded by the sight of a great white dome appearing over the hills. It was the rounded summit of Tupungato, looking all the more grand and striking because of the bare and ugly foreground of the hills near at hand. Again and again we caught glimpses of it, but as we gradually turned into the barren valley of the Rio Mendoza it was lost to view.

The aspect of the country now changed considerably. Uncultivated land covered with brushwood lay far and wide around us. We had started from Mendoza at a height of 2700 feet above the sea, and had continued at that level for some distance. Now we began gradually to ascend the slopes connecting the pampas with the Cerrillos. Almost at the last edge of the plain a wide bridge spans the Rio Mendoza, which bursts away from the Cordilleras and spreads itself far over the plain, as if rejoicing to be free from the walls of rock that had imprisoned it for a hundred miles of its course.

Twenty miles from Mendoza we left the plains, almost without warning, and plunged in among the mountains. The change of scenery was as marked as it was sudden. High bridges and short tunnels followed in quick succession as we pursued the winding course of the Rio Mendoza gorge. Our first stopping-place after leaving the plain was Boca del Rio—

"the mouth of the river," or rather the spot where the river emerges from the hills. Our ascent had been rapid, for we had now reached a height of 3746 feet.

Twenty-four miles from Mendoza we stopped at Los Baños del Cachenta, famous in the Argentine for its hot springs and baths. Beyond Cachenta the valley widened somewhat, and to the southward there suddenly came full into view the magnificent peak of the Cerro de la Plata, 19,000 feet high, and covered with snow. But our thoughts were occupied with Aconcagua, and we eagerly inquired whether a glimpse of its summit could be obtained from the railway. Our fellow-passengers, although we plied them with questions, could tell us little about it. It had never been seen from the line; indeed none of them ever seemed to have seen it at all. Mystery and uncertainty hung over the great mountain. Not until afterwards did we learn something of the almost superstitious dread with which every native of these passes shrinks from admitting that Aconcagua is ever visible to the human eye.

As we went on, Lightbody pointed out to us the chief difficulties that had to be encountered in the construction of the line, and the still greater difficulties in keeping it open for traffic. From time to time he showed us places where the railway had evidently been lately rebuilt. Everything was new—embankment, brick-work, sleepers, and metals, while far below in the river lay scattered and sunken masses of earth and iron, the remains of what had been destroyed. Certain parts of the line are continually swept away by a "wash-out" after heavy storms of snow or rain, when whole hillsides seem to slip down upon it; for floods and avalanches of snow do less damage than the immense torrents of soft mud which the rain sets in motion. After bad weather these mud avalanches slide down into the valley, burying the whole track under masses of ooze, or carrying everything before them into the torrent below. The scars they had left were visible everywhere on the cliffs and slopes that overhung our route.

Mr. Dalton, the chief engineer of the line and one of its

directors, has now adopted the practice of replacing the iron girder bridges that span the usually dry side valleys down which these avalanches of mud flow, by embankments of stone—thus leaving the mud to flow over the rails. When these wash-outs occur, a gang of peons is sent to shovel away the debris, thus saving the expense of new girder bridges; for it is found that nothing can stop these huge masses of mud in their course.

Leaving this gorge behind us, we emerged from the outlying eastern range of the Andes, known as the Uspallata Range, and entered upon a high level plain, the Uspallata Pampa, by which the outlying mountains that we had traversed are separated from the great central chain of the Cordillera. It is about twelve miles broad, and stretches from the point where we crossed it for over 150 miles to the north. Without lakes or trees, and devoid of any trace of verdure, the shingly surface of this Pampa is one of the most desolate and uninteresting spots imaginable. I was struck, however, by the wonderful colouring of the stratification in the great wall of rock which bounded it to the south. We were now at a height of some 6000 feet above the sea.

After crossing this plain we again approached the river, and found ourselves running along the shelf overhanging it. Beneath us was a cliff some 250 feet high, and at its base the stream. The upper valley now began to close in upon us, and we were soon piercing the main range of the Cordilleras between walls of porphyry and granite. In traversing the pass one could see on the other side of the river the old mule-track by which it would have been our fate to ascend in days before the railway was so far completed. Sometimes it was close to the stream, sometimes far above it clinging to a tottering ledge of rock. It was by this rather perilous way that Darwin made his journey over the Andes.

Descending at last from the top of the cliff to the river bed, the train reached the Zanjon Amarillo. A few miles farther on, at the narrowest point on the river, the railway climbs once more to the top of the shelf that overhangs it. Here the "rack" system, without which

PUNTA DE LAS VACAS

the ascent would be impossible, begins, and by its aid the last climbs towards Punta de las Vacas are accomplished. We crossed the Tupungato River by a bridge, and knew that our destination was almost at hand.

On nearing the journey's end I began to overhaul some of the baggage, and Vines, who was helping me, discovered that his revolver, holster, pouch and cartridges had been removed from their case, together with everything in the way of gold and silver that he had brought with him. Joseph Pollinger, thoroughly convinced of the iniquitous character of the inhabitants of the country he was now entering for the first time, showed his sympathy by the startling suggestion that there was a wholesale conspiracy to disarm the expedition before it reached the mountains. But Lightbody, after a few questions on the subject, suggested that it must have been stolen in Mendoza, adding that a good revolver was too great a temptation for any native.

Punta de las Vacas is the highest point yet reached by the Transandine Railway. We alighted from the train, and looked around us, curious as to what we should find at the basis of our first operations. Vacas, as I shall henceforth call it, stands in a widening of the main valley, in which, flowing from opposite directions out of the heart of the Andes, the rivers Vacas and Tupungato converge and meet. The only building in the place, besides the station terminus, a small, low wooden shanty, is a little inn or house known as the "posada"—a common name in South America for a little drinking-house. There were also, it is true, a few sheds belonging to the Villa Longa Express Company, who run the coach service across the Andes. The posada itself, with which we were afterwards to become better acquainted, is formed of mud huts round a courtyard, the doors of all the rooms opening into the open air. In the wet weather during the winter there is about six inches of water in most of the rooms, and I have seen the "comedor," the bar and dining-room, with as much as two feet of water in it. For sleeping there are a few straw truckle-beds with blankets thrown over them. The only provision of which a large stock is kept in the place is Worcester sauce, a condiment very popular in South America. Even the poorest posada is provided with numerous bottles of it.

We did not intend, however, to throw ourselves upon the hospitality of this unimposing hotel. A site was promptly chosen for a camp about half a mile away in the most sheltered spot we could find, and we proceeded in all haste to unload our baggage from the train. Lightbody got us a cart, mules and peons from the Express Company's agent, and we set all hands to work to get as much of the baggage as possible to the camp before dark. Everything had to be unloaded and removed from the station that night.

Leaving Vines with Weibel to manage things at the station, I went on with everyone else to pitch and arrange the camp. We were at once struck by the dilatory habits of the peons engaged. They could not be got to understand that there was the slightest need for hurry. While Vines was superintending the loading of the cart, he found things went so slowly that, to encourage the men, he put a hand to the work himself. This arrangement suited the peons admirably. Hitherto they had lifted the luggage with all the slowness and deliberation possible, but now, when they found the work being done for them, they were entirely satisfied. They stood around in easy attitudes, doing nothing whatever, and watching him at the work, so that he was forced to adopt other means of encouragement. At last the cart was full, and the team was brought up and put to.

The journey to the camp was not accomplished without adventure, which gave Vines his first experience of what driving in the Andes is like. Between the shafts was a fine mule, and on each side of the mule two small ungainly horses were tethered to the cart, while two mules with a postillion went in front. Vines climbed up on the top of the luggage; the peons did the same, and off they went down the soft shingly road. Presently they came to a place where the track turned sharply to the left, while in front rose a steep hill. The postillion left the road with his two leaders, and drove straight up the ascent in front; but the driver, it appeared, preferred the road, and strove his hardest to turn the cart round the corner on the level ground. The leaders and the beasts yoked to the cart thus pulled different ways for the moment, but the driver gained the mastery. Round they went in the roadway, the cart rising high in the air on one side and tottering on two wheels. The instant was critical; for the cart was just on the point of upsetting and hurling out the baggage, with Vines and his companions, in utter smash. But with great coolness and quickness driver and peons threw their whole weight on the lifted side of the cart; it righted, and on they went. No one seemed in the least alarmed. At the time Vines conjectured that so many men had mounted on the heavily-laden cart in order to balance it promptly in case of tilting, but we were not long in learning that a peon will never set his foot to the ground if there is anything to ride.

Three cart-loads were brought up before dark, and everything was progressing merrily at the camp. Three tents had already been pitched when I missed one of the tent poles, which had somehow been left behind at the station, and sent Vines out at once to fetch it. It was now late in the evening, and darkness was coming on, so that no time was to be lost. Seeing a broken-down looking pony from which one of the peons had just dismounted, he jumped on its back and galloped off, without asking its owner any questions. There was no saddle but a loose blanket, and he had not gone far when it began to slip. Making a hasty attempt to catch it, he frightened the mild and apparently quiet little beast; it shied and bolted, trying to run up an ascent as steep as a rock wall. Vines threw his whole weight back, and pulled the pony's head. It reared, and both pony and rider fell backwards into the road, rolling over and over. When he collected himself and looked up, the terrified animal was off down the road at full speed, heading for Vacas. The peons, however, had watched the whole occurrence, and before he found his feet again a horseman dashed by, swinging his lasso. One dexterous throw and the pony was caught round the neck and safely brought back to camp. Vines had a very sore elbow for the next few days, but otherwise was none the worse for his dangerous spill. Both riding and driving in the Andes, as he had found that first evening, are very different from anything of the kind at home.

Lightbody stayed with us that night, and we were glad to have his help with the peons, who found our Spanish rather hard to understand. We ate a somewhat scrambling dinner, and sat long afterwards around a fire which burned brightly in the still mountain air. I shall never forget that first night in the Andes. The dark rocks towered above us into a cloudless sky. It was a magnificent starlight evening, and Lightbody, who had brought up a guitar with him, sang Spanish ballads until bedtime. By his advice we set a watch during the night, to guard against theft, for the arriero of the Andes, though he may resist many temptations, is not proof against good new trappings, and might have found some of our straps, saddles, and halters quite irresistible. We turned in with all our tents pitched and about half our baggage piled around us.

CHAPTER III

GENERAL ASPECTS OF THE ANDES

NEXT morning we resumed work early, and before midday brought up the rest of our luggage. At about eleven o'clock the wind sprang up, and we had the first taste of its real force in the Andes. We then found that our camp was very badly situated. We were practically on a sand-heap, and the clouds of dust were almost unendurable. The ground was not sufficiently solid to take tent-pegs, nor were the stones around us heavy enough to use as extra supports, so that the first few gusts blew all our tents down. A couple of tables that we had outside were blown away, and I saw Vines wildly chasing our aluminium cups and saucers for a hundred yards before he captured them. It was obvious that this place would not do for a permanent base camp. I decided therefore to ride up the Vacas Valley, taking Zurbriggen with me, and see if I could get a view of Aconcagua, and some information about the best place from which to approach it. I hired an arriero and some animals to go up this valley, at the same time leaving Vines, de Trafford, and Gosse to prospect up the Inca Valley, and look for possibilities of a better camping-ground there. Arrangements were accordingly made for a start next morning. But before I describe our first exploration trip, I think I had better give a slight sketch of the country that we were in, and the difficulties we were about to meet for the next seven months.

Aconcagua, the highest mountain in South America, rises some 23,080 feet above sea-level. It is situated more than ninety miles from the Pacific sea-coast, and from the harbour of Valparaiso on a clear day it can be distinctly seen raising its mighty head 4000 feet or more above its neighbours. It lies on the central range or rib of the Andes, its summit being some six miles from the water-parting, on the Argentine side. Yet though this great mountain can be seen so easily from the Pacific, all the ice and snow that melt on its flanks pour down to the Argentine pampas, and thence flow on to the South Atlantic Ocean. The mountain is so surrounded by winding valleys, by rugged and precipitous spurs and ridges that it is difficult of access, and indeed there are, I believe, only two points to the south from which a view of its topmost peak can be obtained. One of these views is from a little above Inca, where the Horcones Valley opens out into the Cuevas Valley. This view of the great peak is the one best known, as all travellers across the Cumbre Pass, from Argentina to Chile, gaze upon it. The other view is obtained some distance up the Vacas Valley. Aconcagua is often wrongly described by the Chilians as a volcano, and Güssfeldt speaks of the natives calling it "el volcan." The mountain is really built up by successive flows of lava and is composed of varieties of andesites. There is no sign of a crater on it, and traces of scoria were remarkably few. It is separated from the province of Ramada by the pass renowned in the history of Chile,—the Boquete del Valle Hermoso, some 11,700 feet above sea-level,—and from here the Penitente Valley leads straight to the northern glaciers which flank the mountain from this point. The Hermoso is also called, I believe, de los Patos, from the Argentine river of that name (Duck River). This pass is by no means easy of access, yet in 1817 General San Martin crossed it at the head of the army of Chile, for the purpose of out-flanking the Spanish forces which were then assembled to meet him at the Cumbre Pass.

San Martin's crossing of the Andes, one of the most famous events in South American history, has been compared to Hannibal's crossing of the Alps. The comparison is perhaps rather pretentious, when one considers the relative size of the armies that took part in those two expeditions, and the sum of the difficulties to be confronted in each case.

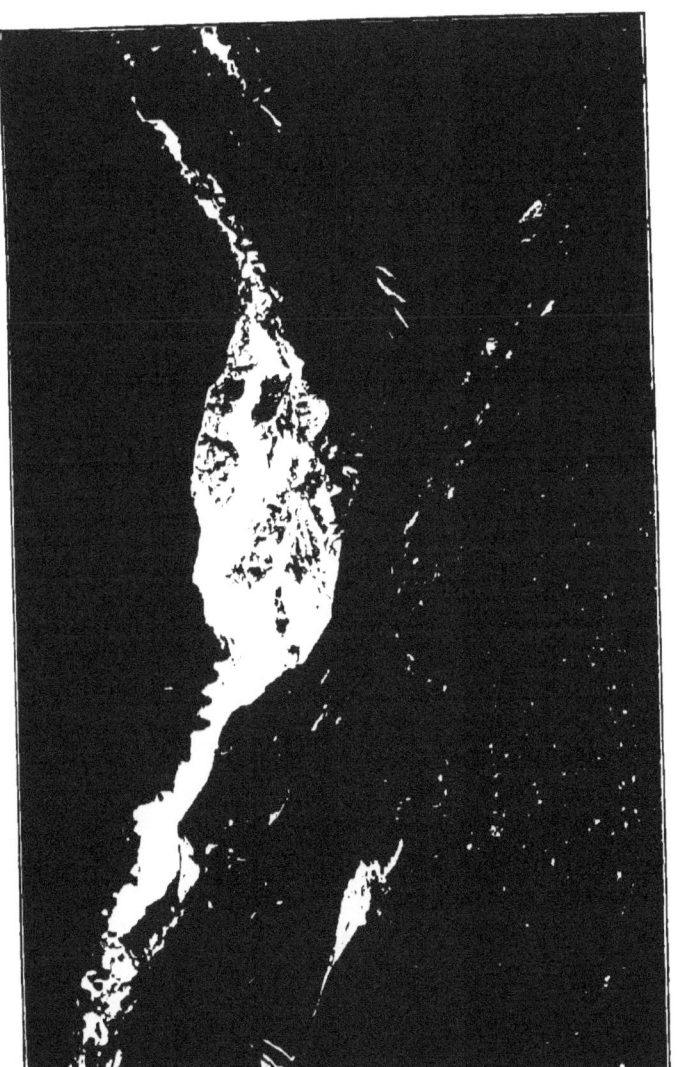

ACONCAGUA FROM HORCONES VALLEY

Nevertheless San Martin's feat was a wonderful example of enterprise, tenacity, and courage. Chile at that time was still in the hands of the Royalist troops, but Mendoza had already gained its independence, and San Martin was able to assemble an army there for the invasion. Having resolved to make the crossing by the Valle Hermoso, he took the most elaborate measures to divert the attention of the enemy in other directions and break up the Spanish force as much as possible into detachments. A small division of his soldiers was sent southwards to appear in the passes towards Talca, another northward towards Coquimbo. A battalion under Colonel Heras was sent over the Cumbre to make a demonstration in the direction of Los Andes. In order to complete the deception of the enemy, San Martin hit upon a further plan. He assembled the chiefs of the Indian tribes and took them into his confidence with a simplicity that seemed quite engaging. The plan of campaign which he imparted to those honest allies consisted of an advance of his chief force into Chile by the road of El Plancon. He then gave handsome presents to the Indians, and extracted from them the most solemn vows of secrecy. The result of this manœuvre was that the Spanish general, Marco, was speedily possessed of confidential information which led him to look for San Martin's arrival anywhere but in the direction of Aconcagua.

In January 1817 the crossing was made. San Martin had with him an army of about 3000 infantry, 970 cavalry, and artillery, with 1600 horses. They took with them provisions for fourteen days, and 9000 mules. Only 2000 of these were baggage animals, while 7000 were for riding, so it would appear that the whole army actually crossed the Andes on muleback. Fodder for these animals was carried into the passes, and to guard them against mountain sickness the extraordinary precaution was adopted of taking several loads of garlic, with which the noses of the animals were rubbed, for garlic, we are informed, was then thought to be a remedy against this disabling ailment. In spite of these precautions half of the beasts succumbed on the way. The men were also said to have suffered greatly from mountain sickness. The valleys which they traversed lie at a height of about 10,000 feet above the sea, and the highest point passed on the way, the summit of the Boquete, is estimated by Güssfeldt at 11,693 feet. These heights should be noted, but in this place I cannot well discuss the possibility of mountain sickness at so comparatively low an altitude. Certainly the men were not experienced mountaineers, and they were making a forced march under very trying circumstances. The weather also was exceedingly cold and stormy in those bleak valleys, although it was in the middle of the uncertain Andine summer. At one time it seemed possible that San Martin would lose the bulk of his force, but he triumphed over all obstacles. He descended safely into Chile, took the enemy by surprise, and on 12th February utterly defeated them in a battle fought with desperate courage at Chacabuco. From this blow the power of Spain in Chile never recovered.

To the north of Aconcagua lies the great peak of the Mercedario, over 22,000 feet in height, while on the Chilian side, near the Cumbre Pass, lies the mountain of Juncal, some 19,500 feet high. South from Juncal are the great peaks of Pollera and Navarro, till, finally, on the crest of the water-parting, we come to the great dome of Tupungato which rises some 22,000 feet above the level of the sea. To the south of this again is the great volcano of San José, and farther south Maipo. In 1843 a violent earthquake overthrew one of the adjacent peaks, filling the valley with heaps of rock and debris "for the space of over three leagues." The passage of the Cumbre Pass has been narrated by many travellers, and is well known to hundreds of people who have crossed it during the summer months. Later on I shall have more to say of the winter aspects of this pass, which, I believe, have not been so fully described. In summer the passage presents no great difficulties or risks, but in winter it is at times a terribly difficult and dangerous task, in attempting which travellers have frequently lost their lives. The time occupied in summer is a day and a night, the night being spent at the inn at Las Cuevas by those crossing to Chile, while for travellers going to Argentina the night is spent at Juncal. In winter the passage often takes over a week, and those who have crossed at this season, and who have not been obliged to spend the night in one of the *casuchas* or shelters that stand at easy distances along the route, may indeed consider themselves fortunate. These *casuchas* are built in the shape of a dome, reminding one slightly of the oven of a lime-kiln. They have a small door, but no windows, and they accommodate twenty people at a pinch. They are built mostly of brick, with a brick floor, the interior being absolutely bare. There is nothing to sit upon in them, not even a bench, and they are, in fact, nothing but gruesome black holes, filled with every conceivable form of filth, the stench emanating from them being overpowering.

One of the points that strike the visitor to these Andine valleys is the terribly bleak and desolate aspect that they present, with only blades of grass here and there, or perhaps a few stunted shrubs. Trees there are none, nothing but a huge expanse of yellow sand and stone, the peaks rising up on either side in extraordinary and rugged stratification, whose many-coloured hues are bewildering to the eye. Great torrents flow down the middle of these valleys, the water being of a dull, blackish hue. The fording of the rivers is one of the most dangerous tasks of explorers in this country. The torrents are exceedingly rapid, and full of deep, treacherous holes. The Andes abound in mineral springs, those at the Puente del Inca being, perhaps, the most remarkable. Here the water bubbles out of the rocks, at a temperature of about 91° Fahr., a clear, limpid stream, with a strong odour of sulphur.

The geology of the country has been treated separately and in detail from specimens brought home by us from the various valleys by Professor Bonney, whose profound knowledge and great kindness have laid me under a deep obligation.[1] Roughly speaking it is trachite, andesite, and basalt. The question of the snowline of these ranges is one very difficult

---

[1] Appendix A, p. 311.

to determine. When Zurbriggen made the ascent of Aconcagua he went to the summit of the mountain without placing his foot upon snow; the side of the mountain was bare to the top on the north-west slopes, yet the south slopes were massed with snow and ice and glacier. In places the snowline may be said to be between 17,000 and 18,000 feet, while in other places it is higher still. From seven months' observation in these ranges, I have come to the conclusion that there is no defined snowline as in ranges like the Alps, and that, according to the season, and year by year, great changes take place.

In the spring a very curious phenomenon is to be observed on the glaciers and snow-slopes. It consists of huge fields composed of cones or pyramids of frozen snow some four or five feet high, placed close beside one another, these cones narrowing up to a hook. This is known in the country as "nieve penitente," or penitent snow, so called from its quaint resemblance to the cowled "Penitent Friars." The effect is produced by the combined action of sun and wind upon the frozen mass of snowfield, the crystalline parts upon which the sun has little melting power remaining erect in this strange fashion; while frequently the ground is bare between these shapes of ice, and one is able to thread one's way through them as through a forest, their tops standing nearly as high as a man's head. A good idea of this formation is given in the illustration of the main range of Tupungato, p. 174.

The remoteness of Aconcagua was the first difficulty of our explorations. Though in actual distance it is not much more than a dozen miles from Inca, it is most difficult to get at, and when we first arrived we could not even get trustworthy information of its exact position. The native arrieros and people were inclined to say, when the summit was pointed out to them, "Ah yes, that is a range or spur of the mountain; behind that there is no doubt another peak, and I think that perhaps beyond, and out of sight, is the real and true summit of the mountain. But we do not know. No, that which you see cannot possibly be the summit—it is behind." No matter

CLIMATE

what the point of view, this is what they say. We never got any man to point out a peak, and say, "That is Aconcagua."

The greatest drawback, however, to the climber and explorer in these regions is the terribly uncertain weather. M. Elisée Reclus speaks most truly of the mountain when he says :

"Being surrounded by numerous rugged spurs, and everywhere furrowed by winding gorges, Aconcagua is of difficult access, although its upper section for a total height of about 6500 feet rises in a superb cone above the elevated pediment of the surrounding uplands. A broad snowfield, intersected by crevasses, is developed round the west and north-west slopes, but presents no great obstacle to the climber, nor would the higher and almost snowless escarpments be difficult to scale, but for the rarefied atmosphere and sudden snowstorms." In the summer months a terrible wind springs up soon after sunrise and usually blows the whole day. This wind renders all work of exploration difficult, and on the higher slopes, very dangerous. During the winter there is a deep snowfall, when the valleys are filled with snow, the drifts in places being of huge depth. When the spring sun clears this snow away, there is as a rule no more rainfall or snowfall till the next winter. The valleys are then like deserts, and the only place in which vegetation can be found is close beside some spring or stream, though even here the strong mineral quality of the water often destroys such vegetation. The result of this is, of course, a dust which is almost unendurable. Surveying in the upper valleys I have frequently been forced to wait for an hour before I could get a sight of a pole a thousand feet away, owing to tornadoes and eddies of dust. This dust penetrates everywhere—into food, into clothes, among books and papers, on the verniers of instruments, cutting and scratching them ; in short, making life miserable and work almost impossible. During the day the sun has great power, and I have known the thermometers to mark nearly 90° in the shade. We suffered severely from the absence of trees or shelter under which to pitch a tent. We had to live in the open, and the fierce rays of the sun beating down upon the canvas sides of our tent made the interior almost uninhabitable. Many a day have I spent, working out calculations, unable to go outside on account of the blinding dust-storm, while in the tent itself the heat was 110°. I cannot conceive of more miserable surroundings. We had to contend against temperatures and conditions that ranged between a Sudan campaign and an Arctic expedition. This, as I have said before, is perhaps the greatest difficulty in this country, for after some months' work, one's strength is exhausted, and there is no place to which to retire for a few day's rest under normal conditions. Storms spring up too with terrible rapidity. On the heights—that is to say above 16,000 or 17,000 feet—they often become veritable blizzards, though at a lower level they are as a rule only great gales of wind, with an occasional shower or flurry of snow. Lower down the ranges, between the Uspallata Valley and Mendoza, severe thunderstorms and cloud-bursts rage during the months of January and February. The lightning is especially vivid and dangerous. But these storms seldom extend to the higher Andes; upon two occasions only have I seen lightning at all near, though on a long summer evening, one can observe the bright flashes far over the ranges and pampas of Argentina. The prevalent wind during the summer is from the north-west, but I am told that this varies considerably from season to season. During our stay in these valleys the wind was particularly aggressive; in the following year there was scarcely any.

With irrigation the soil produces luxuriant crops. The proprietor of the posada at Vacas had a large field artificially irrigated by canals, where the grass grew with extraordinary abundance. On the Chilian side there is more vegetation in the valleys, and on going down some distance, large quantities of cacti are seen, and even small trees, though at no place in the valleys is there anything like the forests that are found farther south in old Patagonia.

Till last year there was some doubt as to which was the highest mountain of South America, but since Sir Martin Conway's triangulation of Illimani and Sorata or Illampu, it is

HIGHEST MOUNTAINS

admitted beyond question that Aconcagua overtops every other mountain there, and indeed every mountain outside the great ranges of Asia. There are still unmeasured mountains in Africa, such as the ranges of Ruwenzori, which are, I believe, estimated to be between 16,000 and 17,000 feet high. These, however, were measured from a great distance, and nobody knows what lies behind them. The expedition just starting for those regions will doubtless clear up the doubt, and settle these heights exactly. Tupungato rises above Chimborazo, Sorata, Illimani, and Sajama; it is still doubtful as to whether it exceeds the height of Mercedario. If Pissis' height of the Mercedario, viz. 22,315 feet, is correct, this would be the second highest peak in America. In any case it is now certain that Aconcagua, Mercedario, and Tupungato are the three highest mountains of the American continent.

CHAPTER IV

UP THE VACAS VALLEY

AFTER this historical and topographical excursion I return to our own story.

We were on foot at four o'clock on the morning of 9th December, Zurbriggen and I preparing for the trip up the Vacas Valley, of which I have already spoken. Our arriero and the mules we had hired at Vacas were late, as in these early days we did not know that it was useless to give an order to a native. The only way to get him to do anything is to send someone to make him do it about an hour before it has to be done. We intended to be up this valley only a few days, so we took a very small quantity of provisions, and told the arriero that he must supply himself with what he wanted. At about 5.30 we started, but we had not gone far before we suddenly remembered that we had not brought our binoculars with us, and so had to turn back for them. It is not until after several weeks of work that one gets into the way of remembering the hundred-and-one trifles necessary in an unknown country, even on a short journey. One can make oneself absolutely miserable for several days, for instance, by starting without, say, matches. One has to remember first and foremost what scientific instruments are required; secondly, note-books and pencils; thirdly, foods; then clothing and covering; besides which one must always be provided with extra pieces of string, straps, knives, etc. etc. To be fitted for this sort of work everyone must be a jack-of-all-trades, carrying a small but varied equipment for all purposes and all needs of repair. One must be ready at any moment to shoe a horse, mend a strap, or sew a patch on a coat; to estimate the distance between two points; to take

AT THE HEAD OF THE VACAS VALLEY

photographs when the sun is at impossible angles, and allign on peaks that are hidden behind other peaks. When one cannot see, one has to remember routes; to keep in one's head, more or less, all the various parts of the equipment, men and provisions, and what everybody is supposed to be doing. In fact, it is necessary to be a general compendium of knowledge, and a universal gazetteer of the locality.

Having fetched the field-glasses, we started out again, and were soon introduced by our arriero to a true Andine ford. The river which flows down the Vacas Valley is a large and deep torrent, fed in great part by the masses of snow in the valley at this season of the year. Early in the morning we found it in fairly easy condition, but later on in the day, when we had to cross and recross the river, to keep upon a path that could be followed by the mules, we had great difficulty. This was also my first experience of riding in what seemed impossible places. Later on we grew so accustomed to it that we thought no more of setting our horses at shocking slopes, or of galloping among huge rocks and boulders, than we should have thought of riding in a hansom down Piccadilly. During our stay we had innumerable falls, and though we were rolled over in almost every conceivable place and position, we were fortunately never hurt. An Andine pony is a delightful beast. He is exceedingly clever in keeping his feet and finding the way, and when he does fall he always manages to arrange not to hurt you. He is as gentle and nice-tempered as need be, and will follow you round camp like a dog, sometimes putting his head in at the tent to see what he can procure in the way of food. These ponies are always ready to do their best, and go on until they collapse from fatigue—an equine virtue of which we unfortunately had experience after the winter months came. They are always gay and bright, ready to gallop, and if there is pasturage about will remain by you during the night.

The Vacas Valley, perhaps one of the most fertile in the whole of these ranges, yet struck us then as the most desolate spot imaginable; nothing but great vistas of yellow sand, with here and there a stunted bush, and a little grass peering through the crevices of the stones and rocks. This vegetation, however, was really profuse in comparison with the Horcones Valley, which was the scene of so much of our labour in the following year.

Great mountains rose on either side of us, but we could see nothing, as we turned in and out along this valley, that resembled in any way even a buttress of Aconcagua. We cross-examined our mule-driver, but he was very reticent upon the subject. He told us he believed that there was once a man who had been up in these parts, and who had come back and told his wife's uncle that he had seen a high spur which might possibly be a part of the mountain, but he could not say for certain. His impression could be pretty well summed up in the fact that there was always a peak behind, reminding one of the White Queen's remarks to Alice, "Jam yesterday, and jam to-morrow, but never jam to-day."

We decided to go along as far as we could get that day, and then climb to the top of one of these peaks so as to get the view. We soon reached a place where the Vacas Valley branches off, the Rio del Peñon coming down to the east. We were obliged to ford the river here, and our arriero had to try several places before we could get one that was safe to cross. Twice he was nearly washed away by the current, and was obliged to turn back. Finally we got across, and dismounted in order to give our horses some rest. The sun was extremely hot, and it was impossible for us to get any shade. Zurbriggen and I lay down where we could get our heads in the shadow of a rock, the rest of our bodies grilling in the sun. In this way we obtained about half an hour's sleep. It was the first day of exercise in the mountains, and as we were naturally rather out of training, the long ride that morning had fatigued us unduly.

After we had started again we had an experience of the rubbishy South American saddles. They are strapped down by long girths of leather, tied and knotted together. The Andine muleteer knows nothing of buckles; he has never seen such things. He can only cinch an animal with these

long thongs, which he winds round and round, tying them in quaint and fantastic knots, very difficult for the uninitiated to untie. One has to dismount about every hour, or perhaps oftener, and resaddle one's horse, placing straight again the numerous sheepskins and cloths that form its rude equipment.

The valley mounted very much, and curved about here, while the scenery at every moment grew wilder and more barren; then the sides closed in to a deep sort of gorge, and we were surrounded by huge boulders. As the arriero kept on his horse I thought it best to do so too, but I could not imagine how he was going to avoid rolling over. His horse leapt from stone to stone, and the boulders would occasionally rock as if about to topple over. At about noon we reached a stream, where the horses were watered. They had been suffering from thirst for some time, and I asked the man why he had not watered them before. He explained to me that the streams we had passed were not wholesome, and I was initiated into the fact that the greatest care is necessary concerning the water one drinks, for the springs hold so many injurious substances in solution that to drink from them produces serious diarrhœa. Following the river bank we mounted hill after hill, which looked like the remains of ancient terminal moraines. The valley soon widened out again, and finally we reached a great plain. On either hand, where the side valleys open into this plain, are great heaps of rubbish in the form of a talus; they extend far out into the valley in a semicircular form, beautifully piled up and rounded off, some of them being nearly a mile in diameter. The route was fairly easy here, and we were able to gallop over the stunted snow-grass growing near the river, seeing as we passed several flocks of guanaco grazing on these mounds. About four o'clock in the afternoon we stopped and camped under a great overhanging rock, which gave us some shelter from the wind blowing down the valley. We had not brought a tent with us, but wrapping ourselves up in our blankets we got what rest we could.

Next morning I started with Zurbriggen to climb a hill

close by the camp, hoping that from the summit we should get a view of our mountain. We walked up one of the great slopes of debris, following the little paths that ran along the hillsides, made by the herds of guanaco that seemed so plentiful here. Upon turning the corner of a rib, we came upon half a dozen of these animals quietly grazing. The guanaco, like many timid animals, has a habit of stopping to look at any new sight before it runs away. We came upon them frequently, and they all turned and stared at us inquisitively, standing still for a few seconds, and then scampering away down the hillside, passing us not more than thirty or forty yards away. Zurbriggen, who was the Nimrod of his own valley of Macugnaga, stamped and growled in rage at being so near to game and having no gun. He sat down and positively beat his head in his despair, exclaiming, "Ah, if we only had a revolver we might have shot one!"

When we reached the summit of the peak we had set out to climb, we found to our disappointment it was only a rib of a very much higher peak. This being our first climb it had greatly tired us; we lay down in the sun to rest, and fell asleep. On awaking, I suddenly became aware that a huge bird was flying in small circles round us, not more than forty or fifty yards off. It was nothing less than a condor, which had evidently taken us for dead as we lay there sleeping and had come down to pick up a meal. As soon as I moved, the bird soared into the air and disappeared behind the ranges in the direction of Aconcagua, while Zurbriggen, as he watched it fly away, again gave utterance to his grief that we had no gun. "Stop!" he cried to it; "stop! I also want to see a view from up there. Wait for me!"

We were now at an altitude of about 16,000 feet, but we had not the energy to go on and climb the range above, which looked at least another 2000 feet. Besides, we were not at all aware that there was not a similar range behind that. Nothing is more discouraging to the mountaineer than to climb a peak in the hope of getting a view, and then to find still higher another peak beyond, which shuts off the view.

After we reached our bivouac at about eleven o'clock,

ACONCAGUA FROM VACAS VALLEY

Zurbriggen felt energetic enough to prospect on horseback, guided by the arriero, a little farther up the valley. They returned in a few hours, Zurbriggen having seen a great peak to his left. He did not know what it was, but he thought it was not Aconcagua. He described it as being similar to the Grande Jorasse near Chamonix. Whatever it was, he thought that it did not look very accessible from this side, so I determined to go down, rejoin our party, and try the next valley—that of the Horcones. The peak that Zurbriggen saw was, as a matter of fact, the highest point of Aconcagua, but as the arriero had assured him that it was not Aconcagua, and, in fact, nowhere near it, we naturally supposed that the man had some rough knowledge of the topography of the country, and believed him. We slept that night at our bivouac, and started again next morning before daybreak, thus fording most of the worst places before the great masses of water came down from the melting snows. The Vacas Valley is, in some ways, the most dangerous of all, on account of its fords, which have to be crossed six times. The last ford that we reached just before Vacas was in a very bad condition, as the water had risen rapidly during the last hour. We tried several times to get through, but our horses would not face the stream, and finally we were obliged to abandon the attempt. Our arriero, therefore, led us up some of the steepest slopes I have ever seen a horse ascend. Every moment I felt that the animal must topple over backwards and fall, so loose was the soil, and so steep the angle. We arrived, however, without accident at the top of this slope, and by climbing along the edge of a precipice succeeded in avoiding the ford. Zurbriggen had dismounted long before, and had been leading his horse. As the arriero, however, remained on his animal, I did not like to get off, but when we reached the edge of this precipice, I could stand it no longer. For fifty yards after I was out of the saddle the animal was tottering over the edge, while rocks and masses of earth rolled down from under his feet, falling from cliff to cliff, and dashing with alarming splash into the river below. With a great deal of scrambling he managed to get across. The arriero kept his seat the whole time. The worst part now over, we reached Vacas at about eleven o'clock. The rest of the party had had a very bad time of it during the previous two days, what with the heat of the sun, which had driven them out of their tents, and the wind and dust, which had half-blinded and choked them. They had unpacked all the equipment, and Tomas Sosa had arrived with his troop of mules, a fine lot of animals. At the time I could not understand how they managed to exist upon the meagre pasturage that surrounded the place, yet during all the summer months they kept themselves not only alive, but very well, some of them even being fat, and they were always in high spirits, for this dry snow-grass seems to stimulate them like corn. I was reminded of the snow-grass in the Mackenzie Plains of New Zealand, where horses can be taken in from the fields and driven eighty miles in a day.

CHAPTER V

FIRST ATTEMPT ON ACONCAGUA

AFTER my trip up the Vacas Valley, I had come to the conclusion that nothing could be done at present from that side. Although we had actually seen the mountain, we did not, of course, know that it was really the peak of Aconcagua; our arriero had been so positive in denying that we had seen the actual peak, that we were for the time convinced. There were several drawbacks to our camping-ground, too; in the first place, the water was bad, and we had to go a long way for it; it had to be very carefully filtered, for it was as black as ink and full of sulphur. In the second place, we were exposed to the terrible morning winds that blow in these parts. There was no place in which we could shelter ourselves, and our tents had all been blown down several times. Vines, who had been up to the Inca, reported there was an excellent camping-ground near the mouth of the Horcones Valley, fairly sheltered from the north-westerly gales, with spring water close at hand. In our present position we were camping at the junction of four valleys, which is always undesirable; I therefore rode up to Inca that night, after giving orders that the camp should be moved next morning. It was still early in the season; the trans-continental road that leads to Chile was being used for the first time for mules, having been blocked up until now by the winter snows. The next few days we spent in moving our luggage up to our new camp. We made ourselves as comfortable as possible there, and in fact used it for the next seven months, making it our headquarters.

Our chief difficulty in removal was with the mules, which were new to the military pack-saddles we had brought from

England, and did not take to them in a kindly spirit. Before packing the saddles, our arrieros made sure of the docility of the beasts during the operation by carefully muffling up their heads in their ponchos. But when the loads had been adjusted and these coverings removed, a new scene immediately opened. No mule cares for new straps with sharp edges at any time, and our beasts had been hitherto accustomed to saddles of a very different sort. The pack-saddle of the country is a crude affair. A pad is placed on the back of the mule; on the top of the pad goes a high wooden frame, somewhat similar to those used for camels in Egypt; the packs are then held on each side, and saddle, packs, and the mule's body are bound round together with leather ropes. No halter is used, but sometimes a rope is fastened round the animal's neck. The mules were accustomed to loads of this sort, but they quite failed to understand the new English equipment. Being chafed by the cruppers and halters, and frightened by the jogging of the panniers, which, instead of being bound on, were merely slung on hooks, they began to rub against one another, then to kick, and finally they stampeded. Off the whole herd galloped amongst the rocks and boulders, loaded and unloaded animals together. The panniers, heavy with photographic plates, many of them unhooked at one corner, were bucked into the air, or hurled amongst the rocks. It was a sickening sight for anyone who knew every detail of the contents of the panniers, and we were powerless to put an immediate stop to it. However, the most turbulent soon parted with their loads, and the rest were caught. No irreparable damage was done, but it taught us a lesson. Never load a mule too lightly; he is an animal who shows no gratitude. From this time forward four panniers instead of two was the load for each mule. We never had reason to regret our military pack-saddles again: far stronger and more efficient in every way for ordinary work than the clumsy contrivance used by the natives, they also adapted themselves much better to the difficult places we had to negotiate in the high valleys.

Before reaching the mountain we thought it advisable to have some horses as well as mules. During my experiences with Zurbriggen up the Vacas Valley we had proved what splendid goers and expert climbers the horses were, and I determined to buy some for our work, so Zurbriggen was sent down to Vacas to purchase three to start with. He found only three for sale, and was able to obtain two of them for one hundred dollars; but the third, a black horse with a sore back, they considered as valuable as the other two put together, and refused to sell the three for less than two hundred dollars. Zurbriggen beat them down to one hundred and sixty, and returned with his purchases. Now £12 for three horses is not a ruinous price, but I was not overjoyed at the bargain for the third horse, when I went and inspected the creature, and saw the open sore on his back. Zurbriggen had been assured that a week's rest would make this all right. We gave him three weeks with no result. The dryness of the air in the Andes is very unfavourable to the quick healing of sores. We followed the example of the natives and used him as he was, and he seemed none the worse for it. He was an invaluable animal for the work, he bore his many hardships with courage. I sold him for a good price before I left the country.

By the 14th of December we were fairly settled, and I determined to continue thirteen miles farther up the Inca Valley and ascend the Cumbre Pass, hoping that from there we should get a good view of our mountain, and be able to devise a plan of attack. We accordingly rode up early in the morning to Las Cuevas. Nothing in my experience of mountain passes compares with the hopeless and absolute dreariness of the scenes we passed through as we galloped along. Every few miles we passed the little round dome-shaped *casuchas*, with their doorways perched up high above the ground as a precaution against their being snowed up. In approaching Las Cuevas, some plateau land is passed, known as the Paramillos. It is one of the most dangerous parts of the Pass in winter, as a little graveyard by the roadside, with numerous wooden crosses in various stages of decay, eloquently testifies. Las Cuevas consists of two galvanised iron posadas or inns, and the stone-built

Argentine Custom-house. It is here that the coaches stop, travellers making the final ascent of the Cumbre Pass on horses or mules. Though the carriage road continues over the Pass into Chile it is seldom used, owing to the great difficulty and expense of getting the lumbering coaches over it. During the whole of our stay in these ranges, I saw only one carriage come all the way across. We stopped at Las Cuevas and had breakfast, while they saddled us fresh horses to take us to the top of the Pass. They were anxious to supply us with a guide, assuring us that we should undoubtedly be lost if we tried to find the passage alone. As the Pass was in plain view above us, we decided, however, much to their chagrin, to forego this luxury. We got off about ten, after the usual delay and attempts at extortion experienced in such places. Our line of direction lay straight up the steep slopes of the Pass, which we were obliged to climb in zigzags. The weather now began to change, and we had not gone far before we were overtaken by a tremendous snowstorm, accompanied by a blinding wind, but we were so near the top that I determined to go on, in the hope that we might at least catch sight of the surrounding mountains. In this, however, I was disappointed. Our horses seemed to suffer terribly during the ascent of the final slopes; we were obliged to stop every few minutes and let them stand, for it was with difficulty that they caught their breath. We did not succeed in getting even a glimpse of Aconcagua, still we were quite satisfied with our trip, as at times, through rents in the clouds, we saw many of the surrounding peaks. The view towards Chile was a magnificent one, the valleys all wrapped in black clouds. We came down as quickly as possible, leaving our tired horses at Las Cuevas, and galloped back to the Inca on our own animals. It was still snowing, even at the Inca, but towards evening the storm ended as quickly as it had begun. Next day I sent Zurbriggen down to Vacas to buy more horses, since we found the mules unsatisfactory for riding purposes, and meanwhile we gave up several days to astronomical observations to determine the precise latitude and longitude of the Inca. On 18th December I sent

HORCONES LAKE LOOKING TOWARDS CUEVAS VALLEY

ZURBRIGGEN'S STORY

Zurbriggen up the Horcones Valley to discover the best sides of the valley for riding, so that we might establish a secondary camp near Aconcagua, and while he was gone a new complication appeared, in the shape of a telegram, informing me that the German Athletic Club at Santiago was making arrangements to attempt the ascent of the mountain at once.

After an absence of four days Zurbriggen returned and reported. The following account of his journey, with which he has since furnished me, is characteristic and interesting. It has been translated, with due regard to style, from the original document in Italian.

"On 18th December I left Puente del Inca at seven in the morning with the young muleteer Tomas Sosa, in order to investigate the mountain Aconcagua from the Valley of the Horcones. I rode my own horse, the young man Tomas his mule, and we also had in our service another mule to carry the provisions.

"A little pathway traversed the fields and served as a road at the commencement; but after some three hours it disappeared, and a more different route presented itself over fields, stones, and moraines. I was compelled twice to cross the torrent of Horcones, which came down in great volume because of the thawing of the snow. I remember, and shall always remember, that day of days, the 3rd of January 1897, when I found myself hurled over and over in the cruel waves of that limpid stream. For no small time will the hideous remembrance remain imprinted on my heart." (The adventure to which Zurbriggen refers in these affecting terms will be found recorded in a later chapter.)

"When at last we reached such an altitude that I saw the front of the great mountain before me, I commanded the muleteer-fellow to prepare me a cup of tea, while I ascended the high ground to ascertain the route that it would be best to take.

"Before me I saw a precipice about eight or nine thousand English feet high, and I understood at once that it would be useless to attempt anything in *that* direction. The ascent must be tried from the rear.

"I turned back, and returned to the place where I had left the muleteer. The cup of tea that I had ordered was ready; a frugal meal restored me to vigour, and instantly I forced the muleteer-fellow in the best way that I could—for the poor man understood no language but Spanish—to prepare me the cavalcade. After journeying along for fully three hours, I planted the tent at the extremity of the pasturage. There was beautiful weather, but the wind was terrible.

"The morning of the next day came, refulgent in red. I commanded the muleteer to saddle my horse, and then to return homeward with the two mules. For many hours I rode along over moraine and stony gullies, where prodigious avalanches had fallen. The winds had driven the snow into enormous wreaths, over which the horse had great difficulty in passing. Thus I reached a place from which I could swear that it was possible to go up Aconcagua without much difficulty. It was now two o'clock; and, as I had with me none of the provisions necessary to sustain life, and the horse was equally destitute, for I had ridden many hours without finding a blade of grass, I was compelled against my will to turn back to the camp, or, to speak more accurately, to the place where I had pitched the tent.

"Next morning I rose at two, and at three saddled my horse, which had got rested and refreshed in the abundant pasture. This time I found a shorter and easier way, and in five hours reached the foot of the mountain, where I dismounted and tied up my horse lest perchance he should escape.

"Going forward on foot, I climbed along a gully amongst moraine, over rubbish and detritus of rocks. After six hours of these gymnastic achievements, I reached the summit of an eminence from which I saw, stretched out before me to the north, the valley that leads into Chile. On this site, which I then selected, was afterwards placed the general encampment of the entire caravan. The aneroid gave the height as 19,000 English feet, as was ascertained by Mr. FitzGerald after we had established ourselves there. I reposed myself on this spot, and examined the route thence to the summit of

Aconcagua. It appears to me now that the route which I marked out must have been the same as that followed in 1883 by Dr. Paul Güssfeldt, whose visiting-card we afterwards found about 2000 feet higher up. It did not seem at all difficult to ascend to the highest point in view, but naturally I could not tell whether it was the actual summit of the mountain or not. My respiration at this altitude was perfectly free, but I must admit that I felt heavy and tired. Accordingly I resolved to return instantly by the way I had come, and to lay before Mr. FitzGerald the results of my exploration.

"It was now late in the day, and I descended as quickly as possible to where I had left my horse.

"I had not been riding for more than an hour and a half when I came to a mass of snow, one of the fallen avalanches, on which my horse stumbled and fell. Both horse and rider rolled over and over together. One of my feet remained caught in the stirrup, and, strive as I might, I could not extricate myself, but unwillingly shared all the motions of the beast. Fortunately I was not hurt, but the horse was lamed in one leg, so that for the rest of the way I was compelled to lead him. In consequence of this incident it was impossible to reach the tent that night, and I had to sleep on the ground, half-way down the valley. It was bitterly cold, and I spent a terrible night in the open air without shelter of any sort. Not till late next morning did I reach my tent, suffering greatly from fatigue.

"I will not speak of the appetite I and the horse had. Suffice it to say that we had both been without food for twenty-four hours. There I rested all day, and did not set out for Inca till the following morning. On the way I met Mr. Vines and the muleteer-fellow, who had come to search for me, Mr. FitzGerald being solicitous about my long absence."

Zurbriggen had been absent four days. As he had taken provisions for exactly that space of time, I had sent Vines and young Tomas with three days' provisions to relieve him if necessary.

Vines rode up the main Inca Valley by the Pass road for a mile, and then ascended the grass-covered detritus, which in the shape of dunes vomited forth, so to speak, from the Horcones, almost blocks the entire Inca Valley at that point. Winding in and out amongst them, he crossed the wide marshy pasturages that surround the shores of the little Horcones lake, in whose waters are vividly reflected the great white walls of Aconcagua fifteen miles away. There he met Zurbriggen, who looked wonderfully well in spite of his four days and nights spent in the open air on the slope of the great mountain. He told Vines of the accident to his horse; his axe was broken, and his leg hurt. But he was in high spirits. He was sure he had found the way, and the only way, to get up. It must be the way by which Güssfeldt had ascended. He was told of the German expedition from Santiago. They must join the path he had just ascended, Zurbriggen thought, but if they came by the north it would take them a week or more to cross the huge mass of the Cordilleras from Chile, before they reached the base of the mountain. And once on the shoulder we should command the summit. He was certain that it was 6000 feet higher than the point he had reached, but he did not think the ascent would be difficult.

On hearing this report, I decided to make an attempt upon the mountain at once, and by way of the Horcones Valley; so two days before Christmas I set out, taking with me Zurbriggen, four porters, two horses, and ten mules. Though I roused the camp at four o'clock in the morning, I delayed starting until nearly half-past seven, as our Spanish drivers had great difficulty in collecting the necessary pack animals. We rode up towards Las Cuevas for about two miles, and then turned up the Horcones Valley, but we were soon obliged to ford the river to get on to the east bank, the west side being too precipitous to ride over.

The scenery here was exceedingly wild and picturesque. Along the edge of the stream were great tall pillars of conglomerate mud and stone similar to those in the valley of Evolène in Switzerland, while the mountains on either side

The Horrores Valley.

LOOKING DOWN HORCONES VALLEY FROM GLACIER

THE HORCONES VALLEY

showed in their stratification the most marvellous colouring. We soon reached a peak they call in this country the Almacenes, which is Spanish for a shop. It is built up by a most curious series of absolutely regular layers of rock of almost every conceivable hue and tint. Here we were obliged to make enormous detours, and ford the river again before we could reach the upper level of the valley. Our pack mules grew almost unmanageable, and we had to stop many times to reload them and adjust their packs. Having crossed over moraine slopes which seemed interminable, we at last reached the upper part of the western valley. Vegetation had ceased, and there lay before us great spaces filled with detritus deposit, perfectly level, and nearly half a mile wide. Soon after midday we reached the little tent that Zurbriggen had left there under a great forked peak. A halt was made for lunch, and we continued on. The valley now changed its aspect; once again, instead of the flat bed of snow, we had great mounds and bits of old, unmelted winter snow to traverse. The road was most difficult and dangerous for animals, and we had several nasty falls before we reached the head of the valley under the peak of Aconcagua, where we arrived at about four in the afternoon, fortunately without serious accident. As the lack of pasturage made it impossible to take the mules any farther, we unloaded our baggage and formed a camp, which we afterwards called the 14,000 foot camp; it was just at the snout of the Horcones Glacier. We made into a few packets the food we required, and started at once on foot to climb the north-western saddle of the mountain. An altitude of 16,000 feet had been reached when I called a halt on account of the lateness of the hour, and decided to spend the night there.

The sun was then just setting over the western hills towards the Pacific, and darkness descending rapidly on us. The cold was intense as soon as the sun went down, and being much fatigued, we decided not to pitch our tent, but simply to crawl into our sleeping-bags. No one had the energy even to make for himself a smooth place to lie down in. We sought shelter under a friendly over-hanging rock, where we huddled as close to one another as possible for the sake of warmth, and tried to get what rest we could. During the night one of my Swiss porters, a tall, powerfully-built man, Lochmatter by name, fell ill. He suffered terribly from nausea and faintness, which it seemed impossible to check. Towards morning, however, he was better. As soon as the sun tinged the peaks of the opposite mountains, we crept from our bags, miserable and cold, our attempts to sleep having been in most cases a failure. We tried to heat some water with spirits of wine, but our cooking apparatus struck work, and it was with great difficulty that we managed to melt some snow and prepare a lukewarm beverage we called coffee.

It was some time before the sun caught the slopes we were on. The giant cliffs and crags of Aconcagua towered above us to the east, a great mass of rock rising like the battlements of some stupendous castle. The many-coloured stratifications, running in straight and regular lines along its face, gave it the appearance of some structure piled up by the hand of man, but its vast proportions, bewildering to the pigmy onlooker, told infallibly of a mightier agency. More than once the thought passed through my mind, while amongst these mountains, that the masses of rock strata must have been actuated by living passions; must have fought and boiled, and torn one another in flame and lava, must have striven and writhed and crumbled along in frozen glacial majesty—true "dragons of the prime"; that here, in such places as the amphitheatre of peaks and valleys round Aconcagua, was one of the arenas of that early-world drama æons and æons ago,—here the scene of the tragedies and high moments of the great protagonists.

The sun was shining brightly over the hillside, warning us and encouraging us to further efforts. I determined to camp that night as high as we could get, but before starting I sent one of the men down to our lower camp by the snout of the glacier with orders to bring up a further supply of provisions, while the rest of us collected our luggage and pushed on. We were all feeling ill and weak in the morning, and I soon came to the conclusion that it would be impossible that day to reach the saddle which Zurbriggen had recommended as a camping-ground. We had here our first taste of one of those great slopes composed of small loose stones, of which we saw so much afterwards, and we were by no means pleased with our experience. Every step we took we slipped back, sometimes half, sometimes more than the whole distance we had originally risen. Up this slope we struggled, each man taking a line for himself, but I noticed that we were all steering straight towards a small patch of snow that lay above us. We were repeatedly obliged to make long halts, sometimes for as much as half an hour. Towards midday we reached the head of this gully filled with snow, and I saw, both from my own condition and from that of the men with me, that it would be unwise — if not impossible—to think of climbing higher that night. Lochmatter was growing pale and ill again, so I was obliged to send him down with another man by the glacier to our lower camp, telling him to remain there until he had perfectly recovered. We were eager to have our tent comfortably pitched, the recollection of the last night spent in the open being far from pleasant; so we set to work at once to make an encampment on a flat bit of ground, sheltered by a large boulder. Pitching the tent was something of an undertaking, for it had fourteen guy-ropes, all of which had to be fixed to large loose stones, the ground being too hard to admit of anything like a peg being driven into it. I had suffered acutely during the afternoon from nausea, and from inability to catch my breath, my throat having become dry from continual breathing through my mouth. At times I was obliged to cough; this momentarily stopped my breathing, and ended in an unpleasant fit of choking. There were now four of us sleeping in the tent, Zurbriggen, myself, and two porters. I was unable to sleep at all, partly because of the difficulty I had in breathing, and partly on account of the dreadful snoring of the men. They would begin breathing heavily, and continue on in an ascending scale till they almost choked. This would usually wake them up, and they were quiet for ten minutes or so, till gradually the whole performance recommenced with the regularity of clockwork. Our tent was a small one, about 6 ft. by 4, ending in a peaked roof 3 ft. 6 in. from the ground. The floor of it was securely sewn to the sides so as to prevent the wind from getting underneath. The drawback of this was that towards morning it got extremely stuffy inside, but the cold outside was so intense that we dared not open the flap.

On Christmas morning we crawled out after the sun was up. The day, in spite of its happy omen and crowded recollections of home, was not a promising one. Great clouds were banked up to the north-west, and the wind was blowing heavily. One of my men greeted me with a " Merry Christmas," but I said in reply that it was *not*. This ended the matter, for nobody was prepared to dispute the point. As we were unable to cook anything, we were obliged to fall back on some tins of Irish stew, melting the great white frozen lumps of grease slowly in our mouths, and then swallowing them. The natural result of this was violent fits of nausea. I now saw the hopelessness of any serious attempt being made till a suitable provision of wood was brought up, with which we could make fires, and cook our food. What one requires at these altitudes is light nourishment such as is given to invalids or people recovering from severe fevers. I was determined, however, to fix our camp on the ridge before turning back, so a couple of porters were sent down to bring up fresh provisions. In the afternoon, as we were beginning to feel slightly better, Zurbriggen and I started out to reconnoitre, and if possible to find a suitable camping-ground on the shoulder of the ridge above us. The weather had greatly improved since morning, the clouds dispersing as the wind subsided. We were feeling distinctly weak about the knees, and were obliged to pause every dozen steps or so to catch our breath, and frequently we sat down for about ten minutes to recover; but after about two hours and a half we reached the shoulder, and climbed to the top

SADDLE ON WHICH THE 18,700 ft. CAMP WAS SITUATED

of a small mound at about 19,000 feet, from which we got a magnificent view of what was practically the peak of Aconcagua. It was, as we afterwards discovered, a point only about 150 feet lower than the actual summit. Although some 4000 feet above us, it looked at the moment so close that Zurbriggen said he would walk up to it next day while the men were moving the camp up to the ridge and see what lay beyond, for we then thought that the peak must lie some distance beyond and reach a much higher elevation. Not until afterwards did we learn that it was a good eight to ten hours' climb; our idea then being that it could be reached in two or three hours. The view out towards the Pacific was obscured by clouds, and the wind had now sprung up again, and was blowing heavily from the north-west.

I was again attacked here with severe nausea, and as it was late and the weather threatening we thought it advisable to return at once. On the way down we noticed a suitable spot to pitch our camp at about 18,700 feet elevation. It was in the cleft of a great rock, more or less hollowed out in such a way that we could place our tents there comfortably and be sheltered from the north and west wind, while the mass of the mountain itself screened us somewhat from the south.

That evening I was completely done up. The men arrived after dark, bringing with them a fresh supply of provisions and a quantity of spirits of wine, with which, after a great deal of trouble, we succeeded in preparing for ourselves some hot coffee. We crept into our tent early, for the cold at this altitude seems absolutely unendurable after sunset. I have seen the men actually sit down and cry like children, so discouraged were they by this intense cold. Their circulation was so low that they were unable to resist its effects.

The nights that one spends at these altitudes are the worst part of the work. It is difficult to sleep for more than a quarter of an hour or twenty minutes at a time without being awakened by a fit of choking. Another discomfort, moreover, was that our tent was so small, and we were so tightly wedged in, that it was impossible to turn round without waking up everybody else.

On the morning of the 26th I decided to push our encampment up to the saddle, south-west of the peak of Aconcagua. Accordingly we spent the day in moving our tent and provisions up to the spot which Zurbriggen and I had selected the previous afternoon. The men made two journeys, and were utterly tired out by evening.

Zurbriggen went out to prospect some route towards the peak we had seen the day before. He started at nine o'clock in the morning and returned to our new camp late in the evening completely exhausted. He reported that he had gone about 2000 feet above our high camp, and that from here the mountain still looked as far off as ever. On returning he was attracted by a small heap of stones that had the appearance of having been built by someone. Upon a closer investigation he found a small tin box, and on opening this he discovered, to his great delight, Güssfeldt's card.

It was here then that the great German explorer, accompanied only by two Chilenos, found it necessary to turn back owing to the intense cold and to the fact that a storm was nearly upon him. He turned literally to save his life, and left this signal on the highest point that had been reached on his second attempt to climb Aconcagua. On the card was written, "A la segunda entirda del cerro Aconcagua, Maerz 1883."

I determined to beat a retreat next morning and to return to our camp in the Horcones Valley at 12,000 feet where there was plenty of wood, so early in the day I sent young Pollinger down with instructions to get to Inca as soon as possible, and return with a further supply of provisions, wood, and especially the best fresh meat he could procure, also, if possible, to bring some fresh vegetables, and to bring a small cooking-stove to burn wood. We followed directly afterwards, and as soon as we reached camp at the foot of the glacier, we felt completely restored, and were able to walk down to the camp at 12,000 feet. Here we were able at last to make once more a good fire and prepare a hot meal. We stood in much need of it.

CHAPTER VI

THE ATTACK RENEWED

WE were so overcome by fatigue after our last four days' work at high levels that we did not wake next day till the sun turned us out of the tent, beating down fiercely on its sides, and making the atmosphere within like a greenhouse. What a contrast to the morning before! Then the question was how to keep one's fingertips from freezing, with the mercury showing 25° of frost, while now the temperature inside our tent was 90°. We spent the morning basking in the sun, doing absolutely nothing. Soon after midday, Vines, accompanied by young Pollinger and Lanti, arrived with a lot of mules loaded with fresh provisions. He reported that they had made a road through a bad defile, which would save us a long detour of about two hours and at the same time afford us a better place for crossing the river. This was on the west bank of the stream, at the junction of the two upper Horcones Valleys. I gathered that they had had a bad time with the heliographs, on account of the wind. The sandstorms down at Inca had been unusually violent, and they were at times nearly blinded in their attempts to watch the summit of the mountain through the dense clouds of whirling dust that blew round them. We spent the afternoon in taking a series of readings with the mercurial barometer to determine the height of this camp. Vines spent the night with us, returning to the Inca next afternoon. During the morning I employed the men in collecting as much firewood as they could bring together. Firewood is scarce in these valleys, and it is frequently necessary to go miles and miles to collect a few mule-loads.

Towards evening they returned with three large loads, but

I did not like the appearance of this wood, and as a matter of fact it proved nearly useless to us. On the following morning we made an early start with all our pack-mules to reach our 14,000 foot camp. This time we had an entirely fresh supply of food, and plenty of warm blankets; we arrived at the old camp at about 9.30, and at once prepared the baggage the men were to carry up to 19,000 feet. The selection proved a difficult one, for there were many things we wanted, and yet I did not like to give the men more than about 30 lbs. apiece. On account of their weight we had to keep rejecting things that we really had considerable need of. We finally settled on a load of wood and blankets, and some fresh food. With these we started about eleven o'clock in a cutting wind, though the sun was shining brightly, This time we chose a different route, and followed a steep couloir or gully filled with *nieve penitente*. We found it extremely steep climbing, even difficult in places, though it was a distinct relief from the monotony of the long slopes covered with rolling stones across which we had threaded our way before. We reached our camp at 17,000 feet where we had spent Christmas Day. At about 4.30,—as the men were suffering considerably from the effects of the heavy loads they had carried so far,—we decided to leave a certain number of things at this old camping-ground. We were all experiencing severe thirst, but as the day was extremely cold and cloudy there was not a drop of water to be had; everywhere we had found the streams frozen. We tried laying snow on a large flat rock upon which the sun had been shining all day, in hopes that the heat absorbed by the stone would melt it. This plan was a failure, and we had to proceed thirsty. The upper camp was reached at six o'clock, and we tried at once to make a fire with the wood we had brought; it would not burn, however, and we were unable to cook anything. We managed to thaw some water and even to prepare tepid soup, but we could not produce sufficient heat to boil water. The night bade fair to be a bitterly cold one, so as soon as the sun set we crawled into our tents thoroughly benumbed by the sharp wind. We had been sitting round the fire trying to absorb some of its warmth, but though we scattered the embers and positively sat amongst them we were unable to warm ourselves. What we needed was light pine kindling-wood to start with. Later on we used to have splendid fires, but we were always obliged to choose our firewood with the care a gunner bestows upon his powder or an angler upon his lines.

31st December.—We rose early this morning and cooked some meat before dawn, and also prepared coffee; the morning was exceedingly cold, the mercury standing at only 6°; but the day looked promising, though there was a cold wind from the west. We left our camp at 5.45, and as the dawn came we were all quite cheerful, feeling certain of success. At that time we little knew what lay before us; the summit looked so very near that we even talked of five or six hours as a possible time in which to reach it. We set out towards our peak over the loose, crumbling rocks that covered the north-west face; the steepness was too great for a direct line of march, and we were obliged to twist and zigzag, so as finally to gain our point. We were anxious also not to exert ourselves more than was absolutely necessary, knowing well that on these occasions one must husband one's strength in the early part of the day. It was after about half an hour of this work that I noticed Zurbriggen was going very fast; I was obliged to call to him several times, and ask him to wait for me, as I did not wish to exhaust myself by pressing the pace so early. I was surprised at his hurrying in this way, as it is generally Zurbriggen who urges me to go slowly at first. However, I soon discovered the reason for this; he was suffering bitterly from cold. Seeing that his face was very white, I asked him if he felt quite well. He answered that he felt perfectly well, but that he was so cold he had no sensation whatever left in his feet; for a few moments he tried dancing about, and kicking his feet against the rocks, to get back his circulation. I began to get alarmed, for frozen feet are one of the greatest dangers one has to contend against in Alpine climbing. The porters who had been lagging behind now came up to us; I at once told Zurbriggen to take his boots off, and we all set to work to rub his feet. To my horror I discovered that the circulation had practically stopped. We continued working hard upon him, but he said that he felt nothing. We took off his stockings, and tried rubbing first with snow, and then with brandy; we were getting more and more alarmed, and were even beginning to fear that the case might be hopeless, and might even necessitate amputation. At last we observed that his face was becoming pallid, and slowly and gradually he began to feel a little pain. We hailed this sign with joy, for it meant of course that vitality was returning to the injured parts, and we renewed our efforts; the pain now came on more and more severely; he writhed and shrieked and begged us to stop, as he was well-nigh maddened by suffering. Knowing, however, that this treatment was the one hope for him, we continued to rub, in spite of his cries, literally holding him down, for the pain was getting so great that he could no longer control himself, and tried to fight us off. The sun now rose over the brow of the mountain, and the air became slightly warm; I gave him a strong dose of brandy, and after a great deal of trouble induced him to stand up. We slipped on his boots without lacing them, and supporting him between two of us, we began slowly to get him down the mountain side. At intervals we stopped to repeat the rubbing operation, he expostulating with us vainly the while. After about an hour and a half, we succeeded in getting him back to our tent, where he threw himself down, and begged to be allowed to go to sleep. We would not permit this, however, and taking off his boots again we continued the rubbing operations, during which he shouted in agony, cursing us volubly in some seven different languages. We then prepared some very hot soup, and made him drink it, wrapping him up warmly in all the blankets we could find and letting him sleep in the sun. In the afternoon he seemed quite right again, and was able to walk about a little, though he was very much depressed, and kept muttering to himself that now for twenty years he had been climbing mountains, and that this was the first occasion upon which his party had been compelled to turn back owing to illness on his part. I narrate this

FOOD DIFFICULTIES

incident at length as an example of what Aconcagua does to even the most hardy and experienced of mountaineers. He got so well towards the evening that I decided to make another attempt next day, but this time I determined to start a little later, and not till after the sun had risen. At these altitudes the cold before sunrise is really unendurable. With the barometer standing at fifteen inches (which is half pressure compared to its height at sea-level), the rarefied atmosphere lowers all the vital organs to such an extent, that 20° of frost feel more like 60, and one does not have the usual power to fight against the temperature. Almost all the time we had a cold biting wind, which, no matter how thickly we clothed ourselves, seemed to penetrate to our very marrow. In the afternoon we had a fine view of the Pacific Ocean, the clouds which so often hung to the west of us having been dispelled by a heavy gale of wind.

Another of our great difficulties (as we discovered later), was that the food that we were eating at this time was not of the right sort. The digestion is so weak at these altitudes that the ordinary kind of camp food is quite unsuitable; afterwards, when we brought up eggs and port wine and condensed beef-teas, we suffered less than we did in these first attempts. We also found that the tinned foods did not agree with us, and it was not till we had fresh meat, and plenty of wood to cook it with (as spirits would not burn), that we were able to fortify ourselves sufficiently to fight against the combined effects of cold and physical depression.

1st January.—The night had been warm for this altitude, 10° being the minimum temperature registered. We tried heating coffee in the morning on a Russian furnace. This machine looks exceedingly like the "blowing lamps" most of us have seen painters use to remove coats of old paint from wood by scorching. It consists of a boiler containing a quantity of spirits of wine, which is warmed by a flame from beneath, the heated spirits being forced through a tube in the lower end, from which they emerge in a glowing flame. I had already had some experience with this machine, and discovered that although it worked admirably when tested in London before starting, it was by no means reliable in the rarefied atmosphere of the mountains. The pressure on the boiler varies, of course, according to the altitude, and the thing was exceedingly hard to regulate. When it would not burn at all, we tried heating the boiler by burning under it cotton which had been well saturated with spirits, with the result, as might have been expected, of a tremendous explosion. The pressure of the air up here being only half what it is at sea-level, the force of the spirit when made to boil in this way caused it to blow up, and although we had been complaining for some time that spirit would not burn properly there, on this occasion we were surprised to find how well it would burn upon our hands and faces. Zurbriggen got the lion's share of the scalding, and was proportionately furious. He hurled the machine down the hill, cursing the man who invented it. This little episode delayed us considerably, and it was not until eight o'clock that we managed to get under way. The sun had now risen over the northern ridge, and the temperature rose to 26°,—a very warm morning for these regions.

Once more we set out to make the ascent, and made directly for the summit, keeping a straight line of march up the great slope of loose rolling stones that covers the northwest face of the mountain. We soon reached the place where the day before we had to turn back on account of Zurbriggen's frost-bite. The height of this spot was about 20,000 feet, and up till now we had advanced without difficulty, as the route lay chiefly over great reefs of solid rock. But here all these conditions suddenly changed. In place of the firm footing we had hitherto enjoyed, was a great and steep slope of loose rolling stones, which extended right up to within a few hundred feet of the actual peak. Looking at it from below it seemed the easiest kind of going; one would say that an hour's good walk should take one over it. We were soon, however, to be undeceived. The first few steps we took caused us to pause and look at one another with dismay. Every step we made, we slipped back, sometimes the whole way, sometimes more, but never less than half of what we had gone up. We continued plodding on in this manner for some time, our breath getting shorter and shorter as we struggled and fought with the rolling stones in our desperate attempts not to lose the steps we gained. The monotony of the work began to have its effect on us. There was nothing to fix our attention upon except the terrible, loose round stones, that kept rolling, rolling as if to engulf us. After a while we grew giddy, and it seemed as if the whole mountain were rolling as well. Then we were obliged to stop and look out at the view in order to steady our nerves and rest our eyes. As we gradually moved up, the horizon widened out. We looked across the great expanse of the Pacific Ocean which lay glittering and rippling in the brilliant sunlight; the coastline, some hundred miles away, seemed gradually growing nearer and nearer, as our view of the ocean expanded, while the horizon was lifted in the air higher and higher. We now were obliged to change our tactics, for this breathless struggle was getting more than we could bear, so we tried making zigzags on the slope, hoping thus to rest ourselves by changing first on one side, and then on the other. In this manner we kept on, falling down, and barking our hands and shins against the sharp stones. Zurbriggen seemed in fairly good condition, but I noticed that Louis Pollinger was turning a sickly, greenish hue. All the colour had left his lips, and he began to complain of sickness and dizziness. A cold wind sprang up from the south-west, which considerably impeded our progress. It blew thousands of small particles of rock and sand, cutting our faces cruelly, and at the same time nearly blinding us. We were now at about the same elevation as the spot where Zurbriggen had some days before discovered Dr. Paul Güssfeldt's card, but about a mile or more to the west of it. The wind by this time had increased to a gale, and seeing that it would be hopeless to reach the summit by this direct but laborious route, I told Zurbriggen to cut off to the North Ridge. This we accordingly did, making for it at an angle, so as to continue our upward progress. It was nearly midday when we reached the first rocks on this ridge, and the sensation of standing on firm ground again was a great relief to us. We got into a sort of small amphitheatre partially sheltered from the wind on two sides, where we sat down to rest, and tried to cook some warm food. Unfortunately, like so much of our cookery at high levels, this was a failure, and we were reduced to eating cold soup in the form of an almost frozen jelly. I soon discovered that we were not in reality well sheltered from the wind, and started off to find another place. Pollinger, however, was feeling very ill, and did not wish to move. I looked about for some time for shelter, but was forced finally to give up the search. It was too cold to remain sitting, so we got little rest. After about an hour we started again, Pollinger seeming better, though the colour did not return to his face. This time the climbing over rocks was not so satisfactory, but as we were very cold we pressed the pace, until we were finally obliged to stop and lie down from sheer exhaustion. The route was extremely steep, which made things worse. The wind had now risen almost to hurricane force, and, weak as we were, it seemed positively to blow the breath out of our bodies. We would gasp after strong gusts as a man does after an ice-cold plunge into water. We were therefore reluctantly compelled to turn back at about 2.15; Zurbriggen, I think, could have gone a little farther, but even he admitted that he did not think he would be capable of reaching the summit. The wind that day must have been appalling on the exposed places. The temperature had now dropped to 17°, and the sun gave us no warmth to speak of. Coming down was almost worse than going up. Fatigued as we were, and chilled and numb to the bone, we constantly fell down, and it was four o'clock before we reached our encampment, so cold and tired that we just rolled into our sleeping-bags, and closed the door of our tent. Owing to our Russian furnace having blown up that morning, we were unable to cook anything for ourselves, and our stomachs revolted at the cold and frozen food we had in camp, so we were practically compelled to

SICKNESS

go supperless to bed. We were all of us suffering from splitting headaches, the feeling being as if one had an iron band shrunk on to one's head. That night we got very little rest. There were four of us in the tent, and packed so close that each time one of us turned over, he was obliged to wake the rest. Next morning we were still suffering acutely from the altitude and cold. The temperature went down to 5° during the night. The maximum temperature in the sun had only been 47° during the last three days, and it had barely reached 29° in the shade. This, taken in conjunction with the poor circulation of the blood, made our suffering intense, and it was all that we could do to keep from getting our extremities frost-bitten. Several times during the night we had to rub each other's hands to restore the fast-failing circulation.

A terrible and stunning depression had taken hold upon us all, and none of us even cared to speak. At times I felt almost as if I should go out of my mind. All this was, no doubt, due in part to our want of suitable nourishment, but it must also have been caused to some extent by anæmia of the brain, the heart beating too feebly to nourish our extremities properly with blood. All ambition to accomplish anything had left us, and our one desire was to get down to our lower camp, and breathe once more like human beings. Every time I got up suddenly my head swam, and I nearly fell fainting to the ground, while great black blotches floated across the retina of my eyes, obscuring sight completely for the moment. I realised now the absolute necessity of bringing up proper wood for cooking purposes. Nothing more could be done at the time; the weather looked very threatening; and I decided to turn back to our base at the Inca, and get thoroughly well before making another attempt. I took some sphygmographic pulse tracings, which showed an enfeebled circulation; they registered from 130 to 140 beats per minute. Our water was frozen now, and we had nothing to drink but snow slowly dissolved in the mouth.

At an early hour I made everything fast about the camp, and we turned our faces towards the valley. After coming down some two thousand feet our spirits seemed to return, and also our hunger, for we had practically been on starvation diet for the last three days. When we arrived at our 14,000 foot camp we were positively in the best of spirits. The day turned out a fine one, in spite of the threatening bank of clouds towards the west that had so depressed us in the morning. As we got lower and lower, the weather became much warmer, and we had repeatedly to stop to strip off various articles of clothing. We hurried along, however, knowing well that this hot sun would mean rivers greatly swollen and bad fords. At the camp Tomas Sosa was waiting for us with the horses; he had seen us coming down the mountain side, and had cooked us an excellent meal. I decided to leave Pollinger and Lanti here. Though we were all suffering more or less from acute sore throat, brought on by the excessively rapid breathing we had done the day before in the cold air, we did not wait long, but jumping on our horses, pressed on as rapidly as possible. In about three hours we reached the first ford, our arriero being the first to cross. The torrent was thundering down in immense volumes, and I could see that the passage was very dangerous, for the water was passing completely over the back of his horse, and several times as I watched him, I noticed that it was practically swimming. I followed next, and was fortunate enough to get across without an accident, though how my little horse managed to steer through that wild torrent remains a mystery to me. Zurbriggen came next. He started well, mounted on one of our most powerful mules, but when he got to the middle of the river I was startled and horrified to see him turn his mule's head down stream. This was fatal: the animal at once lost its balance, and rolled over, precipitating him into the raging water. In crossing these streams it is necessary to keep the horses' heads well up against the current, for should they get sideways, and the water strike them with full force, they invariably lose their footing. Poor Zurbriggen, the instant his mule rolled over with him, was swept rapidly down the stream, turning over and over with the animal, so that at times he and at times the mule was uppermost. He could not swim, but even had he been able to, I doubt whether it would have availed him much, the force of the water being so great. In another moment they both struck on a great boulder, Zurbriggen underneath. The force of the water held the mule tightly jammed against the rock, effectually pinning his rider underneath. In a moment I was alongside of him, the arriero close behind invoking all the saints to our assistance. I noticed that he was engrossed solely with the welfare of his animal; the fact that a man was rapidly drowning before his eyes was an unimportant detail to him. It was necessary to move the mule first before we could help Zurbriggen; so we plunged into the torrent, and tried to dislodge the unwieldy beast. Tomas wanted to haul him towards the bank; I, on the contrary, wished to shove him into midstream again, as I saw it was easier to accomplish, and would therefore release Zurbriggen sooner. I seized him by the head, and tried to press him away, while Tomas in a wild frenzy of excitement clung to his tail. This man's idea in life, when he was in trouble with animals, was to twist their tails. The unfortunate creature was far too terrified to move, so I was reduced to pushing him bodily. I got my back against the stone, and pushed with all my strength; slowly he gave back a few inches, and the water, rushing in between him and the rock with great violence, swept him out into midstream again, Tomas being reluctantly compelled to let go his tail. At once I grabbed Zurbriggen's arm and dragged him on to the bank; he was almost unconscious, and had swallowed considerably more water than was good for him. I laid him down on the grass, and with the help of a little brandy succeeded in restoring him to life. Meanwhile Tomas had been flying after the mule as it swept along in midstream. After several failures, owing to his excitement, he succeeded at last in throwing his lasso round the beast's neck, and bringing it to shore, where it arrived in a most pitiable condition, trembling all over, and covered with blood. While the arriero busied himself in attending to his mule, I took off Zurbriggen's wet things and wrung them out, wrapping him up in our dry ponchos, which we had flung off when we started to his rescue. I now learned for the first time that he had seriously injured his shoulder. It gave him great pain, and he was generally much shaken.

Zurbriggen has a fixed idea in his head that he is to die by drowning, so that little episodes of this character have a most distressing and demoralising effect on him. He very nearly lost his life in a New Zealand ford when with me some years ago, and had some narrow escapes when he was in the Karakoram Himalayas. On this occasion, when I saw him pinned under his mule, I thought there was no hope of saving him from the fulfilment of his premonition. It was more by good fortune than by skill that I was able to do so, and had I found it impossible to dislodge the mule, he would assuredly have been drowned in a few minutes more.

Zurbriggen would not trust himself to a mule again for a long time. He was far too much shaken to walk, however, and as he was wet to the skin I naturally wanted him to press on as fast as possible. We finally got him on Tomas's own animal, but though I did everything to cheer him, he was inconsolable. He said to me, "I know I do get killed to-day," and as luck would have it, we had not gone more than a mile when he and his mule quietly rolled over the edge of a rock precipice. The mule was not hurt, but Zurbriggen had fallen on his bad shoulder again. This was a finishing blow to his nerves. When I ran and picked him up, he turned to me, and said slowly, "You see, I do get killed to-day." I did my best to encourage him by pointing out that he was still alive, but he shook his head sorrowfully and said, "I cannot smoke, thank you," when I eagerly pressed my tobacco-pouch on him as a remedy against all evils.

At length we got under way again. Tomas was much disconcerted by this last accident, for Zurbriggen after his first adventure had muttered something forbidding to the effect that people who kept mules which could not stand up ought to have their necks wrung. About sunset we reached the next and last ford. This time Zurbriggen remarked, "It is all over, I do die now." The ford was certainly in a very bad condition, and the water was rushing white with foam. Tomas tried it first, but as he was riding the mule that had been so nearly drowned before, he was obliged to turn back almost at once. The beast had lost its nerve, and was trembling again pitifully. Tomas said he thought there was a better place higher up, and accordingly we galloped up the river bank some distance, till at last we did indeed find a spot where the river was wider and shallower. It was not until the arriero and I had crossed and recrossed several times that I could induce Zurbriggen to face the passage. He wanted to sleep there, and wait till the night-frosts had reduced the flow of water, but we persuaded him to come, as of course with his injured shoulder and wet clothes such a night in the open would have been most dangerous. In spite of all our precautions his mule stumbled at the worst spot. This time, however, he was not greatly disconcerted, for he had made up his mind to be drowned, and was resigned to his fate. In the end, however, we got him over without mishap, and riding on we reached our base camp in about an hour and a half, having come down all the way from 19,000 feet since morning.

CHAPTER VII

THE ASCENT ACCOMPLISHED

ZURBRIGGEN'S injuries proved to be somewhat serious, and for the next few days we had to keep him quiet. There was nothing broken, but he had sustained a severe sprain, and he had also taken cold in it, which brought on rheumatic pains, so we were compelled to give up further attempts on Aconcagua for the time. I gave my whole attention, therefore, to the survey of the country around us. We had just begun a long serious of simultaneous readings with mercurial barometer and boiling-point thermometer, in conjunction with the Argentine Government's meteorological observatory at Mendoza. We hoped thus to settle accurately the height of Inca, and, making that our point of departure, to measure our mountain. At the same time we commenced a careful triangulation of the surrounding country during the day, while at night we carried on astronomical observations for latitude and longitude.

A theodolite needs for its operation two strands of spider's web, stretched crosswise behind the lens, upon which any exact point may be observed. Anything else, even the finest hair, would appear in the magnifier like a ship's cable. Lightbody sent me up a box of spider's web to replace those in our six-inch transit instrument. When I opened the package I thought they must have been broken, for I saw nothing. The Argentine spider, however, spins fine, and with the help of a magnifying-glass I did at last succeed in finding them. It took two days to adjust these webs in position, as the smallest current of air striking them during the operation would blow them into shreds. This trifling detail of surveying work may interest the non-technical reader, and the expert is begged to overlook it.

Gosse had now established himself in a separate tent full of unpleasant insects in bottles. He had rather an exciting chase one day after an eagle. I give the account in his own words :—

"At 5 a.m. I got up, and by 6 a.m. was half-way up the mountain behind Inca. At a spot where I suspected that a pair of Chilian sea-eagles had a nest I hid myself and watched. After three-quarters of an hour of sitting perfectly still, there was a noise of screaming on the precipice below me. I crept down, guided by the sound, and presently discovered the nest. It was three feet in diameter, and built of sticks. In it were two young birds, almost fully fledged, and a third which was evidently newly hatched, for it had scarcely any feathers on it at all. It was impossible for me to reach the nest, but I dropped a large stone on the head of one of the big birds, which at the same time killed it, and knocked it out of the nest to a ledge, where I afterwards climbed down and secured it. I went back, and later in the day returned to the spot with a gun, but although I waited long in hiding, the old birds were too cunning to come within shot. I noticed that whenever I was near the nest, and the young birds made their peculiar crying noise of terror, the eagles would appear, but the moment the young were quiet the old birds would disappear. I made a long lasso of string, and dropping it carefully down the face of the cliff, I managed to catch one of the young birds round the neck, and to haul it up successfully. I was, however, not prepared for its strength. When I had it in my hands, it fought with such extraordinary violence with beak and claws that I saw that it would be impossible for me to carry it home. I therefore let it carefully down again into the nest, taking care to keep the string round its neck, and as I thought, securely tethering it to a root above. I hastened back to the camp for a sack, but when I returned, it had contrived to slip out of the noose, and was taking flying lessons from pinnacle to pinnacle far above my reach. For several days the old eagles hung about the spot, until their family were all capable of flying, and then they disappeared. The young gentleman must, I think, have been taken to some very quiet seaside place on the Chilian coast, for his neck must have been extremely stiff, and his nervous system shattered with the adventures he had gone through."

As Zurbriggen was now gradually recovering, I decided to make another start for the summit, and on the morning of 9th January, a week after we had returned, sick and sorry, we set out to make a fresh attempt on Aconcagua. The weather was warmer and the days long, 24th December being the longest day of the year south of the Equator. We started late, as I wished to take it easily, my intention being to go only as far as our old camp under the forked peak. At about four in the afternoon we reached it, and made ourselves comfortable for the night. This was by far the most convenient camp we had in the Horcones Valley. We were well sheltered under a great overhanging boulder, while near at hand a clear spring gave us fresh and pure water, a thing difficult to find in these valleys, where so much of the water comes from strong mineral springs, and often produces dysentery. This time we had brought with us an ample supply of light pine kindling-wood, so that without trouble or delay we could have the luxury of a big fire, that burned up brightly in a few minutes.

Early next morning we started. I was anxious about Zurbriggen, who complained that his shoulder hurt him badly during the night, but he insisted that he would be all right, and that he would not have us delayed on his account. Sleeping on the cold ground seemed to have started the old pain. At about ten we reached our 14,000 foot camp, and found Lanti and Pollinger waiting for us. During our absence they had, according to my instructions, made several journeys to our upper camp with wood, provisions, and blankets. It was therefore possible to look forward to many luxuries that had been absent on our previous attempts. We brought with us from Inca some fresh meat and eggs, also a bottle of port wine. These provisions, together with

AT OUR HIGH CAMP

the kindling-wood I mentioned before, were soon made up into suitable loads for the men, and we started off for our upper camp at about 11 a.m. The day turned out unusually fine, the sun was hot, and there was no wind. We walked slowly and steadily at first, and by this means reached camp at 5 p.m., the journey being accomplished in five hours and a half. The men all seemed in excellent condition, and contented. They were not suffering from the altitude, and were laughing and joking with one another over their pipes until sunset. It is not until one has slept a night or two at this altitude that one begins to feel the weight of depression and hopelessness which I have described before. We all seemed so well that I thought it better not to make an attempt on the mountain next day, but to see what a few days of rest and good food would do for us at this altitude. My hope was that the system would accustom itself to the rarefied air, and if we could only breathe normally with the barometer at $15\frac{1}{2}$ inches, why not at $12\frac{1}{2}$, which is about what the summit should be? I now believe this to have been a mistake on my part; we should have pushed on at once. Every day spent at this height makes one the weaker. The cold, to begin with, is crushing: no matter how many rugs or wraps one has, it is impossible to get really warm. It cannot be the temperature that causes it, but the feeble circulation at this altitude.

Our fresh pine wood gave us a good fire this time, and we cooked a supper of hot soup, eggs, and fresh vegetables. With bread and butter, and port wine, this was not a bad bill of fare, when one considers the difficulties of transport. The meat came from Inca, the bread from the posada at Punta de las Vacas, the vegetables from Mendoza, while the fresh butter was sent all the way from Buenos Aires by rail. All these fresh articles had to be pushed quickly along from camp to camp, care being taken that they were not too long in the hot sun in the valleys. I mention these details of commissariat, for although they may seem trifling to the reader at home, they possess a certain significance for climbers.

We turned into our sleeping-bags after the sun went

down. The sunset had been remarkable, almost menacing in its grandeur: great banks of clouds lay spread beneath us far out to sea, dyed scarlet by the sinking sun. They changed rapidly, assuming curious and fantastic shapes, till finally they shot up all at once like tongues of flame to the sky, while the heavens turned a brilliant purple from their reflected light. As I looked on this sea of fire stretched out beneath me for over one hundred and sixty miles, it seemed at moments like looking down into some infernal region.

Soon after we had turned in we heard the wind moaning fitfully about the tent. The men became restless, and tossed about as they slept, while a strange uneasiness seemed to move them, as when a herd of cattle on the pampas scents an approaching storm. The wind gradually increased, and soon the men's breathing was silenced by the roar of the hurricane, as it shrieked and howled round our little tent, threatening every moment to rend in shreds the canvas which strained and tugged at the guy-ropes. We tightly fastened up the double door, and lay panting and struggling for breath. Thus, hour after hour, the night passed slowly,—how slowly I am afraid to say; it was unspeakably long.

Towards four in the morning the wind abated, and we got a little rest. Poor Zurbriggen suffered agonies from his shoulder, but with the indomitable pluck and tenacity he always shows, he refused to give in, though several times I suggested to him that he had better return and take another week's rest. The morning reading of our minimum thermometer showed 31° of frost—the lowest we had so far experienced. Hot coffee was the only thing we could bring ourselves to take. The storm had entirely ceased, though there was still a cutting ice-cold breeze from the north-west. We strolled about near our tent, trying now and again to get some sleep in the sun, sheltering ourselves under overhanging rocks. The men did not speak much, they mostly sat about in moody silence, seldom smoking. We had great difficulty in keeping warm, even in the sun; coming up we had got our leggings covered with water, which had frozen on them, and the icicles remained all day.

OUR HIGHEST CAMP ON ACONCAGUA (18,700 ft.)

As resting here did not seem at all a success, I made arrangements for a start next morning, should it prove fine. The night passed fairly quickly, in comparison with the night before. Repeating my tactics of our last attempt, we did not hurry over this departure, but before starting waited until the sun had risen sufficiently high in the horizon to strike the mountain side. At nine o'clock I was off, accompanied by Zurbriggen and young Pollinger. The night of the storm, coupled with our inaction of the day before, had evidently put us in bad condition, and for my own part I knew, after the first quarter of an hour, that the attempt would be fruitless. However, I pushed along, hoping against hope that by some chance I might feel better as we went on. I had barely reached 20,000 feet, when I was obliged to throw myself on the ground, overcome by acute pains and nausea. Zurbriggen, on the contrary, seemed to feel much better, so I let him go on ahead that he might prospect for a good route for us to follow at the next attempt, and thus possibly save time. The great question was, where we could get the firmest ground to tread on, and whether the rolling stones could not be avoided.

I remained thus lying on the ground for some time, but as I did not improve I was reluctantly forced to turn back. Seeing that we were evidently in for a long campaign, I sent young Pollinger to meet his brother, who was coming up from our lower camp with supplies, to bid him return to our base camp at Inca for a fresh store of provisions. About noon I crawled back to the camp, and sat waiting there in a helpless and hopeless state, half unconscious. I had not even the energy to light a fire and cook a meal for myself. Sheltered from the wind by a projecting rock, I sat warming myself in the sun. About two o'clock the sun had gone round and I was sitting in the shadow, while the wind changed and blew upon me with full force. So feeble was I, both in brain and body, that I had not the wit nor the energy to move some twenty yards away, though I could thus have escaped again from the wind, and received what little warmth the sunlight afforded.

About four o'clock young Pollinger returned. He seemed

full of vigour, after his walk half-way down to our camp and back, and rescued me from my hapless condition, lighting a fire, giving me some hot soup and brandy, and placing me in as warm a corner as he could find. During this time I had lost all feeling in my right hand, but under a vigorous rubbing the circulation slowly returned to it. Pollinger then took a field-glass, and began examining the mountain, to see what had become of Zurbriggen. After a few minutes, he discovered him coming slowly down the great slope of stones that ran up to the saddle between the two peaks of Aconcagua. He was apparently quite exhausted; he could only take a few steps at a time, and then seemed to stumble forward helplessly. We watched him thus slowly descend for about an hour and a half; first he sat down for four or five minutes, then he slowly plodded onward again. At last he reached a large patch of snow, where, by sliding, he was able to make better time. He did not reach the tent till after sunset, and then he was speechless with thirst and fatigue. When he had left us in the morning, he had not intended going so far, and had not taken with him any of the cold coffee that we had prepared for our climb. We got him to the tent as soon as possible, and he gradually revived, but I remained still in a hopeless condition.

Zurbriggen reported he had reached the saddle between the two peaks, and that the east peak was distinctly the highest point. This we learnt with surprise, for when looking at the mountain from Inca, the west peak seems much the higher of the two. He had taken a different route from that we had followed on our last attempt, bearing away to the east, and climbing behind the great ridge of rocks that form the northern arête of the mountain; he thus avoided the great slope of loose rolling stones that had overcome us so much upon our last attempt. He had found the ground firm, and the slopes of a much easier gradient, and moreover the great ridge of rock had sheltered him considerably from the cutting blasts of the north-west wind.

Bitter experience having taught me that waiting at this altitude for a day, doing nothing, was fatal, I resolved to make another attempt at once. The next morning we started earlier, but again under bad auspices: a tin of condensed milk that we had used with our tea was sour, and made us all very sick. We determined, nevertheless, to continue our attempt, thinking that we might possibly revive on the march. To be made sick by chemical causes, is much worse when one is already fighting against what may be called meteorological sickness, than when one is at a level which permits ordinary health. We struck directly for the small peak on the northern ridge, under which Dr. Güssfeldt had built his last cairn. The day promised well, for there was but little wind, and the sun rose in a cloudless sky. I began to mend slightly, and was even beginning to have hopes of success in the attempt, when just on reaching Güssfeldt's outpost, I tripped and fell. I did not really hurt myself, but the fall seemed completely to shatter me, and in a few moments I was again desperately sick. I rested here for over an hour, but it was no use, and at an altitude of a little under 21,000 feet, we all turned back.

Our two porters had suffered greatly from the cold that morning, so much so, that we had several times been anxious lest we should have a repetition of the accident that had befallen Zurbriggen a few days previously, when he had so nearly had his feet frozen. We reached camp again a little before noon, and after a warm meal—so soon does one recover—I felt so much better that I thought it wise to take a walk up the mountain side to see if I could not by this means get in some way hardened and habituated to the conditions under which we were living. The day, as I have said, was superb,—I think the finest I have ever seen at this altitude,—and I succeeded alone in reaching without difficulty the point where we had turned back that morning; the terrible sense of desolation and depression that had weighed so heavily upon me hitherto seemed to pass away for a few hours, and I was able to appreciate, almost for the first time, the magnificent view from this point on the northern ridge.

I turned back with great reluctance, feeling much better and more cheerful in mind. With renewed hope, therefore, we made arrangements that night for the next day, resolved to do our utmost to push on to the summit. I myself was anxious to make another camp some two thousand feet higher, but the men feared so greatly the effects of sleeping at such an altitude, that with the remembrance of the severe illness of Lochmatter, I dared not risk a repetition of the terrible night we had spent with him before.

On the morning of the 14th the men were out of the tent before daybreak, preparing the morning meal; this time, as I was feeling much better, I tried the experiment of eating a large breakfast of meat and then resting for nearly an hour, so as to give time for digestion. The morning was not cold, and as we had begun our preparations early we succeeded in making a good start at seven. The party consisted of Zurbriggen, young Pollinger, Lanti, and myself; we were all in excellent spirits,—so far as it is possible to be cheerful at 19,000 feet.

Making once more for the old point, Güssfeldt's cairn, we walked as slowly as possible, carefully picking our way, never taking a long step where two short ones would do, and by every means trying to save ourselves needless exertion and fatigue. In about two hours and a half we reached this spot, where we sat down and rested awhile. Up to here the way is steep, the first half being covered with rolling stones; beyond, the route is much easier, the slopes not being nearly so steep, and the ground fairly firm. At our last attempt, on 1st January, we had left some articles in a knapsack on the western side of the ridge, where we had turned back at nearly 22,000 feet. As we proposed this time to follow the eastern side of this north ridge, we should not be able to pick up these articles. I therefore sent young Pollinger on by a different route to get them, telling him to meet us at a point about a thousand feet under the great peak, while Zurbriggen, Lanti, and I took the easier side of the ridge, where we should be sheltered from the fierce wind which had now risen.

Before ten o'clock we were again under way, moving very slowly, carefully choosing our way between the great blocks of stone that covered the mountain on this side. Half an hour after midday we reached the point where we had agreed to meet Pollinger, but as we did not find him there, we sat down and prepared a small meal. After shouting for some time we at last heard his voice in answer. He had made a slight mistake as to the exact spot where he was to meet us, and was about a hundred feet above. We had brought some light kindling-wood and a kettle, and Lanti at once started a fire. Our great difficulty was in getting a light; the wind was blowing with great strength, and it was not until after repeated failures that we succeeded in this delicate operation. Once alight the fire burnt fairly well, and at the end of half an hour, we managed to get some soup. Pollinger had reached us by this time with the knapsack; but the bottle of champagne we had left in it had burst, and though we might have known that this would happen, yet — so much importance can trifles assume—it discouraged us greatly. Up to this moment I had been feeling strong, and indeed certain of success, but during our stay here, my old symptoms of nausea gradually came on. It was one o'clock, and though I had sat down half an hour before with success within my grasp, I now felt as if it were impossible for me to move farther on. Of my disappointment I need not write, but the object of my expedition was to conquer Aconcagua; I therefore sent Zurbriggen on to complete the ascent. He seemed in good health, and was confident that he could reach the top. He had been suffering so much at night from pain in his shoulder, that I felt it would not be right for me to keep him at this high camp much longer, and after the good work he had done for me before, I thought that it was but justice to him that he should have the proud satisfaction of the first ascent.

Three-quarters of an hour after he had left, I saw him four hundred feet above me, going across the face of the big stone slope on the way to the saddle between the two peaks. Then for the first time the bitter feeling came over me that I was being left behind, just beneath the summit of the great mountain I had so long been thinking about, talking about, and working for. Scarcely more than four hundred yards separated me from the goal; but after my long journey and my many attempts I felt that I should never reach it myself.

I got up, and tried once more to go on, but I was only able to advance from two to three steps at a time, and then I had to stop, panting for breath, my struggles alternating with violent fits of nausea. At times I would fall down, and each time had greater difficulty in rising; black specks swam across my sight; I was like one walking in a dream, so dizzy and sick that the whole mountain seemed whirling round with me. The time went on; it was growing late, and I had now got into such a helpless condition that I was no longer able to raise myself, but had to call on Lanti to help me. I had sent young Pollinger back to the camp some hours before, telling him to go as rapidly as possible to Inca and have our horses sent up for us, for I felt sure by that time that Zurbriggen must succeed, and we should therefore all come down and rest for a few days. Lanti was in good condition, and could, I feel sure, have reached the summit. He was one of the strongest men we had with us. For a long time past he had been begging me to turn back, assuring me that our progress was so slow, that even should I keep it up I could not reach the top before sunset. I was right under the great wall of the peak, and not more than a few hundred yards from the great couloir that leads up between the two summits. I do not know the exact height of this spot, but I judge it to be about a thousand feet below the top. Here I gave up the fight and started to go down.

I shall never forget the descent that followed. I was so weak that my legs seemed to fold up under me at every step, and I kept falling forward and cutting myself on the shattered stones that covered the sides of the mountain. I do not know how long I crawled in this miserable plight, steering for a big patch of snow that lay in a sheltered spot, but I should imagine that it was about an hour and a half. On reaching the snow I lay down, and finally rolled down a great portion of the mountain side. As I got lower my strength revived, and the nausea that I had been suffering from so acutely disappeared, leaving me with a splitting headache.

Soon after five o'clock I reached our tent. My headache was now so bad that it was with great difficulty I could see at all.

Zurbriggen arrived at the tent about an hour and a half later. He had succeeded in gaining the summit, and had planted an ice-axe there; but he was so weak and tired that he could scarcely talk, and lay almost stupefied by fatigue. Though naturally and justifiably elated by his triumph, at that moment he did not seem to care what happened to him. At night, in fact, all hope and ambition seemed to depart, after four days spent at this height, and that night we got little sleep, everyone making extraordinary noises during his short snatches of unconsciousness,—struggling, panting, and choking for breath, until at last obliged to wake up, and moisten his throat with a drop of water. Next morning we closed up our camp and returned to the Inca.

Thus was Aconcagua conquered. "Sic vos non vobis mellificatis apes."

CHAPTER VIII

BEATEN BACK BY SNOW AND COLD

VINES and I started early on 19th January with fresh equipment. We left Tomas to come along slowly with a pack animal, while we galloped on ahead, meaning to reach our camp under the forked peak in time to spend the afternoon in taking sphygmographic observations. The rivers were in bad condition owing to the warm weather of the past few days, and when we got to the first ford we found it considerably higher than usual. I succeeded in crossing safely, though several times I felt my horse swimming under me, but Vines was unlucky, for his animal stumbled, then plunged violently, nearly throwing him into the water. However, after a great deal of turning round and tumbling over, he succeeded with skill and extraordinary luck in extricating himself. This is an exciting and painful performance to watch, as it is impossible to render any assistance. As we approached our camp, we saw three guanacos browsing on the hillside. We had no gun with us, but, drawing our revolvers, we galloped after them as hard as we could. They suddenly turned up the almost vertical hillside, but we fired several shots at them, and succeeded in wounding one. We jumped off and rushed after him, but he was able to go faster on three legs than we could on two, so we were obliged to give up the chase, much disappointed, as we had cherished hopes of getting some fresh meat. Zurbriggen galloped up early next morning with the mail that had just arrived, and also a most friendly telegram from Valparaiso, as follows:—

A FRIENDLY TELEGRAM

"The British Colony in Valparaiso congratulates you on the success of your expedition.

(Signed)

KENNETH MATHESON.	GEORGE DUNCAN.
THOMAS WOODSEND.	DANIEL MORRIS.
JOHN NICHOLSON.	JAMES GRACE.
EDWARD COOPER.	ANDREW SCOTT.
E. SANDIFORD.	GARRETT WEIR.
WILLIAM BRETT.	H. WEATHERALL.
THOMAS GIFFORD.	EDGAR HOWE.
E. JOSTE.	ROBERT GILES.
H. SWINGLEHURST.	QUENNELL.
JOSEPH BLANCH.	ROBERT SCOTT.
MAURICE JONES.	A. F. GUILLEMARD.
GEORGE SIMPSON.	RUSSELL YOUNG.
MAX WOLFFSOHN.	ARTHUR EDMUNDSON.
JOHN WOLFFSOHN.	ALFRED BALL."

Zurbriggen rode back to the Inca at once, while Vines and I determined to push on to the next camp, though we were feeling very unwell, the result of an unfortunate culinary effort of mine at dinner the day before. We reached our 14,000 foot camp at about eleven, and found the three porters that I had left to look after this and our upper camp—these were the two Pollingers and Lanti—in a most woeful state of depression after their five days all alone. They reported to me that on the 17th (three days before) the German party from Valparaiso passed our high camp, talking to Pollinger and Lanti, who were there at the time.

I had left instructions that one man should always be at our upper tent, as this would give them a night every third day at that altitude, but as they found it so lonely, they preferred staying up there two at a time. Lanti, who was as a rule a cheerful man, drew a very long face when I talked to him about this upper camp. His constitution, he was sure, had been permanently shattered by his stay up there, and in fact all the men were on the verge of tears. I sent a couple of them up to the camp with some surveying instruments and kindling-wood, and told them they might come down again the same day. They certainly all looked in excellent health. We ourselves rested for the remainder of that day. The porters did not turn up until the next morning, and I was very anxious during the night about them, for I feared young Lochmatter might have been taken ill, as he had been before, and his comrades would certainly not know what to do with him. They came down about nine o'clock next morning, with precisely the news I feared—he had been exceedingly ill during the night. I gave him some brandy, and told him to wrap himself well up and get some sleep in the sun. Lanti said the cold had been terrible during the night. Why they did not come down the same day instead of spending the night there, I failed to understand, for, though it was a great strain at times to get up to this camp, it was always fairly easy to get down, as the slopes are steep, and the rolling stones help rather than hinder one's descent. I succeeded in getting down in fifty minutes on one day, while some of the men have done it in less. They all assured me that the cold had become much greater, and that life up there was now impossible. I discovered afterwards that our minimum thermometer did not register as great a cold as we had had before, so the effect must have been produced on the men owing to the weakening of their constitution under the strain of living at that altitude. There was, unhappily, no doubt about one fact—they seemed to bear the cold worse and worse every day. Sometimes now they would throw down their loads half-way, and come back for a day's rest before completing the journey. At half-past eleven, Vines and I started out for the camp, but I was not feeling by any means well, and after the first hour I began to suffer acutely from breathlessness, and my pace got slower and slower, until we reached the top of the great snow gully. Here I was obliged to give up altogether, and was very sick. Vines seemed in fairly good condition, but he repeatedly complained of weakness in his legs. We lay here for some time, but soon saw that it was no use, and that we should be unable to reach our camp that afternoon. We therefore turned

A SHORT CUT

back. That night we took the utmost pains to prepare a light and nourishing meal. The men insisted that we should eat some onions, for all the natives about here have the greatest faith in the efficacy of onions, as a preventative of this breathlessness and nausea. I had taken them myself before, but had never noticed that they did any particular good. Aconcagua rises so abruptly from the valley to the east of us, that the sun did not strike our little tent until after eight. We tried the experiment that morning of taking two cups of Brand's beef-tea instead of coffee. At eleven we started again, and when we were half-way up the great ice-gully, I suggested to Vines that we might shorten our route by climbing some steep rocks I saw to our right; accordingly we tried them, but soon got into difficulties, for the climbing grew harder and harder, until at last we came to such a bad corner that I was unable to get up until Vines shoved me from behind. Once up, I saw that the short cut had succeeded, and that the great slope of loose stones lay in front. I then leaned over the edge, and prepared to give Vines the same assistance from above that he had given me from below. Unfortunately, a small piece of projecting rock which I had used to pull myself up by, snapped off owing to his greater weight, nearly giving him a nasty fall. I was leaning over the edge watching him come up, and was just about to give him a hand, when I saw him slip. I rapidly clutched at the nearest part of his person to me, namely, his hair, but, no doubt fortunately for him, I missed him. He now found it impossible to scale this place, and was obliged to turn all the way back again and come round by our old route. This annoyed him greatly, and, in consequence, instead of sticking to the slow steady pace we had taken at the beginning of the day, he plunged forward as rapidly as he could walk. The result was that when we met again at the top of the gully, he was suffering from the first really acute attack of breathlessness. He lay down in the sun and rested here for some time, and, fortunately, the breathlessness in his case was not followed by the nausea I always experienced after it, and at the end of about half an hour we were able to continue upwards. The weather had been looking more and more threatening as we had come up that morning, while the wind was blowing a tremendous gale, and great black clouds were collecting in masses on the Chilian side, slowly but surely rolling up the valley. We were evidently in for a storm, and the sun was already obscured by the clouds that surrounded us. I had dressed myself at the start in all the clothes I wore at our high-level camp—as much clothing as I could walk comfortably in. Vines, however, fearing the heat of the day, since for the first 3000 feet the valley is shut in, and we had frequently experienced oppressive heat, was carrying most of his heavier clothes in a large bundle on his back. As it was now very cold and rapidly growing colder, I advised him to put them on, which he did after much pulling, and pushing, and panting. We now started again, but had not gone far before he began to complain bitterly of the heat, also of the inconvenience of wearing so many clothes. They bound his limbs down so, he said, that he was unable to move freely, and therefore soon grew tired. The sun coming out after a few moments decided him to take them all off again. It was now two o'clock in the afternoon, and by a little stream of water trickling down from the rocks Vines made the change, and we ate a few biscuits, and had a drink of water, knowing that this was the last water we should see, the snow never melting above this height. At three o'clock we reached the little plateau of rocks at 17,000 feet, where I had camped on our first attempt, and where I had spent Christmas Day four weeks ago—four weeks which seemed in memory like as many years. Our physical condition was now getting rapidly worse, so we pushed on as quickly as possible. Snow began to fall heavily, and I had great difficulty in keeping my bearings, being obliged several times to resort to my prismatic compass to see if our direction was right. The slopes of this mountain are so vast that it would be easy to get hopelessly lost on them; for there are few landmarks or distinguishing features to show the way. Vines was making the worst noises of

A TRYING CLIMB

panting I had ever heard, and every few moments he had to stop breathing for a second to swallow and moisten his parched throat. During this second he was unable to breathe, and therefore, often had a violent choking fit. As the cold was intense, and I could hear the distant rumbling of thunder, I suggested that we had better go down. He was, however, keen to continue; he had never been to our high camp, and declared he was sure he could easily reach it if I could find it. The snow was now coming down heavily, and we could only see a few feet before us, while the flashes of lightning followed one another rapidly, and the thunder echoed from hill to hill.

I do not know how I succeeded in finding our tent that day. I think it must have been instinct rather than anything else, for certainly there were no landmarks to recognise on these great slopes covered with snow. I myself now began to pant and choke, and as the wind increased in fury every moment, I really thought I should never get my breath again, but must be suffocated. At four o'clock I sighted the rock under which our tent was pitched, and though it was only some twenty yards away I think we must have taken a quarter of an hour to reach it. I only stopped outside long enough to take readings of the barometer and thermometer. The minimum during our absence was 28° of frost, while the temperature at the time was 13° of frost, and I could see the mercury rapidly sinking. There was no possibility of lighting a fire, so we were obliged to crawl into our tent chilled to the bone, and covered with snow. All the water was frozen, so was the wine. It was now necessary for Vines to put on his thick clothes again. He was unable to do this outside on account of the cold, and besides, he would have been covered with snow. He therefore had to do it in the tent. Now, for a man to change his clothes in a tent only 3 ft. 6 in. high, by 4 ft. wide, by 6 ft. long is not an easy matter, even if he has it all to himself. When, however, he has another man in the tent, and a large quantity of provisions and instruments strewn about, it becomes a very delicate problem. It must be remembered, too, that he had to stop constantly to get his breath. At last, however, he did it. We then crawled into our eider-down sleeping-bags with our boots covered with snow, and commenced more preparations for food. We started by lighting half a dozen candles, thinking that the illuminations would at least give the appearance of warmth, for in spite of the care with which we fastened the flap and stopped all the chinks with snow, the temperature was gradually dropping. We lit our spirit-lamp, and with great patience and many matches succeeded in thawing some wine and brandy, which we made into a tepid punch. This revived us greatly, and we next turned our attention to food. Our fresh meat was frozen into a solid block which we could not cut, and if it had not been, there was not sufficient warmth in our spirit-lamp to cook it with, so we were compelled, much against our will, to return to our tinned provisions, and tried some curried rice and chicken, but ate very sparingly of it.

The wind was now rising every minute, and blowing a hurricane outside : we were slightly protected on two sides by the rock under which we had pitched our tent, but the wind would come swerving round in tremendous gusts, while fine snow was driven in quantities against the front of our tent, and came pouring in like so much sand. We were powerless to prevent this snow silting in, and soon it became a serious problem, as it threatened to cover everything. We plugged up with blankets all the holes we could find—then we lit more candles. We got but a poor light, however, for candles did not burn well at this camp, presumably from the want of oxygen in the air. We tried to sleep, but I do not think either of us succeeded in getting much rest. The breathlessness we were suffering from made sleep almost impossible, as we woke up choking. Vines kept a careful diary all the time, and I quote an extract written on the spot :—

"One feels 'puna' in one's sleep at these heights. Fitz-Gerald is now fast asleep and gasping like a grampus beside me. The inside of the tent is sparkling with frost as I write, and the candles will hardly burn, so I must stop writing. I

The Summit of Aconcagua.

am overpowered by our sense of isolation and utter loneliness here."

Thus passed the night. As the dawn came the weather became worse. The wind subsided, but we heard the distant rumble of thunder, and the snow fell fast and silently—we could just hear it as it pattered softly against the sides of the tent.

We decided to stay one night more on the chance of better weather next morning. The difficulty of reaching this place was so great that we were always loth to come down only to come up again a few days later. We were forced to have recourse to our tinned food again. The morning went drearily along, the snow fell, and our hopes with it. About 2 p.m. Joseph Pollinger came up with fresh supplies. He had some dry wood, and he cooked us some hot soup. We remained in the tent so as not to bring in more snow than necessary. I sent him down at 3.30. About 5 p.m. the wind rose again, this time in an appalling fashion. It seemed to shake the very mountain side in its fury, and if our tent had not been secured with fourteen strong guy-ropes we must have been swept away.

The snow now began to drift in an alarming fashion, while the temperature went down rapidly. Our tent was nearly buried. The situation was getting critical, and we wondered whether we should not have to take to the spur to avoid being buried alive. Then I suddenly remembered that our boots and ice-axes were outside. Without them we were lost. Vines volunteered to get them. I opened the flap of the tent, and for a moment we were blinded by the rush of snow hurled in our faces by the wind. He was not gone long, and when he crawled in with the desired articles, I managed to secure the tent. After a long search we found the matches, and I lit the candle and looked around. At first I thought I must have made a mistake and admitted a polar bear, so white and matted with frost did Vines appear. This made our situation well-nigh hopeless, for the atmosphere in our tent was so cold that this snow would not thaw at all, so he entered his sleeping-bag as he was. Everything in the tent was now covered with fine powdery snow, and the temperature still kept sinking. The thermometer registered 16° of frost inside; the wind howled round our tent in fierce onslaughts, at times making us fear that we should soon be buried alive. We hammered at the canvas sides to throw off the snow as much as possible, and thus we sat up through the long dreary night hour after hour, not knowing from one moment to another what would be our fate. As the dawn appeared we were quite exhausted with cold and fatigue after our long vigil. I saw it was imperative that we should get out of this situation at once, as every hour that we spent up there made our strength less, and we needed it all, for the descent in this storm would be a difficult and dangerous task. We therefore put on our boots, and all the clothes we could lay our hands on, and made a break for the open. I had not gone more than a few steps when I fell into a huge drift of soft snow. After considerable difficulty Vines rescued me, but we had not gone far before the same mishap occurred again. The wind cut to the bone, and being thus rolled in the snow was a terrible experience. For about an hour we struggled on in this way; then the wind abated slightly, and the snow stopped. We could now see about us, and though very weak and ill after thirty-six hours' confinement in that little tent, we crawled down to our 14,000 foot camp. Here our men soon made us comfortable with a hot meal, and we were so much refreshed that I suggested to Vines we should walk down that day to the Inca camp, some twenty-two miles over a rough country with two great fords to cross on foot. We set out at once, keeping as near the river-bed as possible, and reached our camp under the forked peak in two hours. We remained here a few minutes for some refreshment, and then continued our way to the Inca. About three in the afternoon we reached the first ford. Fortunately for us the snow was still falling, so there was not as much melted snow and ice-water rushing along as usual. We selected a place where there was a big boulder some ten feet high that we could jump off from and leap half-way across the stream, thus escaping the more rapid water which ran close to the boulder. We

WE TURN BACK

got across fairly well, though of course drenched to the skin. Vines came last, running up the stones at a tremendous pace, evidently with the desire to leap farther than anybody else, and thus perhaps save a wetting, but as he jumped he slipped, and fell headlong into the middle of the stream. We soon had him out again, none the worse for his adventure, but an object of much merriment to the men. I unfortunately sprained my ankle at this jump, so the rest of the journey was painful to me. When at seven o'clock we reached the last ford we found no convenient place to cross: there was indeed one huge boulder from which some of the men leapt over, but it was so high that with my sprained ankle I dared not attempt to do so. I called to the men who got across to go on to the Inca and send back some horses. Vines and I then hunted for an easier passage for more than an hour. Lanti thought he had found one, and got across, but as he was nearly swept away in the attempt, the water being much deeper than he expected, we thought it best not to follow. I finally ended by returning to the great rock that the other two men had leapt from. By sitting upon the edge of it for about half an hour, and watching the ground below, I gradually accustomed myself to the distance, and at last ventured to jump. It was much higher, however, than I had thought, and I landed in a heap at the bottom, hurting my ankle again. I hobbled along towards the camp, but had not gone far before I met the men returning with the horses. I rode on from here and soon met Vines, who had crossed a couple of miles lower down, and we all reached camp half an hour later.

CHAPTER IX

FURTHER ATTEMPTS ON ACONCAGUA

THE strain of the two nights spent in that fearful snow-storm at the 19,000 foot camp had told considerably upon us, and several days elapsed before Vines and I recovered. The weather meanwhile had been hopeless; snow fell even at our base camp at the Inca, while every day tremendous wind-storms raged. If we had not been compelled to come down to recruit our strength, we should still have been unable to do anything on the mountain side. Aconcagua seemed always obscured in mist, but when occasionally we did get a glimpse of it through rifts in the racing storm-clouds, we were discouraged by seeing its whole face covered with fresh white snow, while the tops of all the surrounding peaks showed that the snow-fall above twelve or thirteen thousand feet had been considerable.

On 26th December I received a telegram from a friend in Valparaiso, saying: "National Observatory say no record similar extraordinary January weather. Should improve. Germans in Espinazito to north, abandoned attempt." This was intended to be a consolatory message, and indeed we needed consoling, for the weather did not improve, but grew worse day by day; hail, snow, sleet, and gales of wind following each other in grim succession.

On the 28th another kind telegram came, saying: "Weather definitely improving. From appearance mountain see you have suffered. Every Englishman and Englishwoman, from minister down, hopes you will succeed." The weather, however, continued to be bad in our valleys, though, as it had apparently cleared from the Chilian side, we hoped soon to be able to start again. Our time meanwhile was spent in taking what observations we could round our base camp at Inca. We generally managed to get a few hours of clear weather every night, and continued our astronomical work to determine the longitude. All this time Philip Gosse was busy collecting botanical and zoological specimens, and he had got together in camp a miscellaneous lot of living creatures, which we called the "Zoo." It would perhaps be wrong to include among these captives a favourite staghound "Stella," and her little black mongrel puppies. The leader of the Zoo was certainly a fine horned owl (*Bubo Magellanicus*), which Gosse had procured from a Scandinavian gentleman in Los Andes. There was also a mouse or vole, which increased our population by eleven offspring in one day. In a tin box without a lid there lived four lizards. A fat toad added little to our amusement, for he would never stir. A little black scorpion, a fox, a dove, a water-dipper (*Cinclodes fuscus*), a greenfinch, a Chingolo sparrow with one wing, and two dear little sand-snipes, looking like fluffy partridges, completed Gosse's happy family. The end of this collection was extraordinarily tragic. The mice ate one another until only one was left, and that survivor died of over-feeding. The lizards dried up. The dove broke its wing, and served as dinner for the owl, whose name was "Majordomo." This delightful bird was the most beloved of the whole collection, and the joy of everyone in camp except the puppies, who curled up and howled at his approach. He came to a most distressing end, being struck on the head by a stone, furtively thrown at him by a half-breed. Philip Gosse looked long for that native, with obvious intent, but could never be sufficiently sure of the culprit to take action. The sand-snipes Gosse took into his sleeping-bag at night to keep them warm, but unhappily woke up one morning to find that he had rolled upon them, and that they were quite flat. An exceptionally cold night was fatal to the dipper and the finch. The scorpion died from having been carried in a pill-box in Gosse's pocket, while he was racing Lightbody down the side of a mountain. Last of all the fox died of the bite of a guanaco dog, and the Inca "Zoo" put up its shutters.

Gosse was the richer by several amusing episodes, however, connected with tracking the specimens. I find the following entry in his diary :—

"One of our arrieros, Tomas Sosa by name, told me that at night a fox always visited the camp to pick up any odd scraps of food it found lying about. So the next night I slept in the open shed we called the 'scullery,' and, it being a fine moonlight night, my patience was rewarded by seeing, at about 1 a.m., what looked like a small slinking shadow within a few yards of me. Unfortunately I had my poncho on, and couldn't get my arms free quickly enough to shoot. The fox was very suspicious of me, probably because of the moonlight shining on the barrels of the gun, and he slunk off behind a small knoll. The moment he was out of sight, I arranged the poncho comfortably for shooting, and, getting the gun up to my shoulder, rested it with my elbows on my knees. I had been squatting in this position for what seemed a very long time, and was just beginning to think that Reynard had left for good, when, behind a bush, I saw two round lights watching me. I kept quite still, and presently the two burning eyes drew a little nearer, and soon I could make out the faint outline of the fox's body. After some hesitation he came out from the bushes into the open space before the camp, into the bright moonlight, his shining eyes looking quite uncanny. I waited quite still, hoping that he would come a little nearer, but he seemed to be suspicious that something was wrong with the bundle in the scullery. Thus we waited, watching each other, neither making any movement, except that now and then the fox raised or lowered his head. At last I got tired of waiting for him to come nearer, and, aiming as well as I could at his indistinct outline, I fired and—missed!"

As the weather was improving I began to prepare for another start, and on the morning of 7th February I sent up to our camp under the forked peak four porters and several pack-mules. The last two days had been mild and fine, but we knew that, owing to the immense amount of snow that had fallen on the mountains above 15,000 feet,

THE PASO MALO

A HOT DAY

it would be useless to attempt anything till the great part of this had melted away. We had not been using our animals for some time, and our arriero Tomas had great difficulty in collecting together a sufficient number for us, as they had gradually strayed far up the hillsides in search of better pasturage. Our own Swiss men were quite helpless in their attempts to catch the animals, though they ran and shouted and got very warm and angry over it. The natives gallop after them, and throw their lassos round their necks from a distance as great as forty or fifty feet, with unerring accuracy. It is a curious fact that, even if these men miss their animal with the lasso, the mule, directly he feels the rope hit his body, comes to a dead stop, under the impression that he has been caught. They have a wholesome recollection of the strangling noose, for the man who has thrown the lasso backs his horse suddenly and there is a terrible jerk and strain round the neck of the captured beast.

We finally got our men off that morning, but Vines and I did not start till evening, as we had some work to finish and knew that we two alone should not take more than a few hours to gallop up to the camp at the forked peak, if we had no cargo-mules to drive or bother us.

The day was one of the hottest we had experienced that year at the Inca, the highest reading of the mercury in the shade being 79°. The temperature in our tent was of course considerably more, and we both fell asleep over our work, so it was not till nearly half-past five that we saddled and galloped off towards the Horcones Valley. The sun was low on the horizon, and we dreaded the approaching night, as we did not wish to ford the rivers in the dark, knowing well that after so hot a day the amount of water in the torrents would be considerable, especially as the high mountains were now covered with a thick layer of newly-fallen snow. We reached the first ford in about an hour, for we had by this time made so many trips up and down the valley, that we had worn for ourselves an excellent track, there being only one place that still remained difficult and dangerous to pass. That was the Paso Malo, just beyond the second ford. I succeeded in crossing the first ford without difficulty, though the water washed completely over the back of my horse, and several times he was swimming. Vines was not so fortunate, for he had barely reached the centre of the stream when his animal was swept away. He succeeded with great skill and presence of mind in keeping his seat, and was luckily able to land some fifty yards farther down the bank. After Zurbriggen's accident, I dreaded these crossings very much. From here we pressed on quickly, though the path was not of the best, but we knew that before us was the worst ford of all, and that dangerous defile, the Paso Malo. We reached the ford long after sunset, but there was still a faint twilight, and we got across safely. Here we met our arriero coming down with the pack-mules we had sent up that morning. He had bivouacked at this spot for the night, as he dared not ford the river with his tired animals. We hurried on, hoping to get to the cañon in which the Paso Malo was situated before absolute darkness overtook us. We were unfortunately just too late. It was eight o'clock when we reached the mouth of the defile, and though the stars were shining brightly, it was pitch dark under the shadow of those precipitous rocks. As we were drenched to the skin after the two fords we had crossed, we naturally did not wish to spend the night here, so we dismounted and drove our horses before us, trusting to their wonderful instinct to see the frail path that led across the steep and slippery rocks. Vines's horse passed successfully, but my animal slipped out of the track at the worst place. The track at this point was not more than four inches wide, and here and there we had been compelled literally to hew steps out of the great slabs of smooth rock. Below us out of sight we could hear the roar of the angry torrent of Horcones, as it boiled among the rocks, while directly under this spot was a great basin where the water, falling down from several cascades, formed a seething, foaming pool, and this we had named " The Cauldron." The illustration on the opposite page will convince the reader at a glance that there would be no hope of saving anything that fell in here. The

THE CAULDRON

sides were so precipitous that it would be impossible even to approach it to give aid to anyone who had fallen in. My horse, as I said, slipped at this critical spot, and seemed to us at the moment actually to fall over the edge. We instinctively peered over, expecting to hear the splash as he fell into the torrent; but with an agility and intelligence which seemed well-nigh superhuman, he succeeded in righting himself, and clambered back to the track more like a cat than a horse. He stood trembling like an aspen leaf, evidently realising as well as we did the imminent peril he had been through. We waited for some time to let him recover his nerve. Then, with much patting and soothing, we induced him slowly, step by step, to continue along the path till he was past all danger. It will always be a mystery to me how he succeeded in recovering himself in this marvellous fashion, for after closely examining the spot where he slipped, I came to the conclusion that if a man had fallen as far as he did, he could not possibly have saved himself.

From here our path was easy, winding in and about the moraine that lay in great heaps at the junction of the two valleys. Soon after ten we emerged into the great plain at the head of the valley, and then progressed faster. We galloped with a loose rein among the great stones and boulders covering the river-bed, and reached our camp at eleven. We unsaddled our horses, and drove them some way up the valley, leaving them to collect what little grass grew upon the hillside.

Our camp was so placed that when they attempted to come down the valley to escape to the more open pasturages below we were able to hear their footsteps, but, in order to do this, we had to sleep with one eye open, so to speak. Then, when we caught the clatter of hoofs as they trotted by, we were obliged to jump out of our sleeping-bags—an exceedingly difficult operation, I may mention, as we had them tied tightly round our necks to keep out the currents of air that blew about the floor of our little tent. Once out of the bags, we could circumvent the horses by running down a small, steep path, and thus drive them back to the hillsides.

It was our unhappy lot to be obliged to perform this operation several times during that night, so our night's rest was but a poor one.

We were driven out of our tent at six by the heat, for the fierce rays of the sun were already beating down on the canvas. We collected our luggage, and galloped on to our 14,000 foot camp, which we reached soon after eleven. We found here the men I had left before, namely, Pollinger and Lanti. I despatched them at once to our high-level camp, with a supply of fresh wood and warm clothing. As the whole mountain side was covered with snow, I directed them to take a shovel, to clear the tent thoroughly, and sleep there that night. Vines accompanied them part of the way up, but returned shortly after two. The day remained fine, but towards night the wind rose and blew heavily, and we could see huge clouds of white snow drifting on the slopes of the mountain.

Lanti returned late that night very much exhausted. He reported that our tent was surrounded by deep snow, and that they had had great difficulty in ascending the last thousand feet owing to the drifts. In spite of their fatigue they had shovelled away the snow that surrounded the tent, but Pollinger was so tired that he had not returned with Lanti, but was coming down next day.

On the morning of the 9th the gale showed no signs of abating, and at an early hour great masses of fresh snow were blown down from the crags above in great whirlwinds. The day was bitterly cold, and the prospect far from reassuring. Vines and I set out after breakfast with the intention of reaching our upper camp. We soon turned back, however, as we saw that in such weather the attempt must be fruitless.

Next day we again attempted to push up to the 19,000 foot camp. The wind still raged round the mountain side, but we were tired and restless from our prolonged inaction, and annoyed by our fruitless climb of the day before. I had taken elaborate pains to provide the camp with an ample supply of new provisions. Fresh meat, eggs, and butter we had brought with us in large quantities. I had been most particular during the last few days as to our diet, to see that our meals were taken regularly, and that they were carefully and thoroughly cooked. At these altitudes this is the one thing most essential, and the results amply repaid me for my care, for both Vines and I were in such excellent training that though we did not leave our camp till ten in the morning, we reached the upper camp at three that afternoon, having accomplished the intervening five thousand feet in three and three-quarter hours, exclusive of halts. This was by far the quickest journey we had ever made, and was due to nothing but our precautions and consequent good condition. The sad story of how we lost this training and our systems became run down, is to follow. We had provided ourselves this time with a number of bottles of port wine, with half a dozen eggs shaken up in each. This drink we found very useful, as it both nourished and stimulated us.

As we had a large stock of wood up here we were able to cook an ample and wholesome supper. Cooking, however, at these altitudes, is a problem. Water boils at 180° Fahr., and it required twelve minutes to boil an egg! Still, with patience even tea can be brewed by letting it steep in boiling-water for twenty minutes. Vines took a walk some three hundred feet above us to get a view down the Cañon del Volcan, to see the route by which Güssfeldt and the German Turnverein had approached the mountain. He returned full of enthusiasm, and in excellent health, and I began to think that at last we were going to overcome that terrible illness that had crippled us before. The day was superb, with little or no wind, but as usual in such cases, extremely cold. The sun set that night in an absolutely clear atmosphere, and, though the horizon of the Pacific was one hundred and sixty miles off, we seemed to see innumerable ripples on the water scintillating in the sunshine. The sun looked enormous as it sank in a great seething cauldron of liquid fire. The sky was brilliantly illuminated for a few moments, and then night was on us. The cold was so bitter that, though we wanted to wait longer to see the gradual transformation of the red glow to the dark grey and purple of night, we were obliged to return into our tent.

We slept well that night, and did not wake till eight next morning. The days were getting shorter and shorter, and, at this time, we had not more than ten hours of sunlight at our camp. The wind had risen again with great force, so much so that all hopes of making the ascent that day were gone. This was a great disappointment to me, as I think, had the weather proved fine, we should have been able to reach the summit. As it was, huge clouds of driven snow, fine as sand, nearly suffocated us.

The lighting of the fire that day was a very difficult operation owing to the wind. Just as I succeeded in getting it to burn, and as Vines was stooping over to rearrange some parts of it, his hat was whisked off by a gust, and was driven under the legs of the mercurial barometer. He made a dive for it, but was too late; the next moment it disappeared over the rocks to the east. We rushed around to search for it, but the wind was so strong, that we had scarcely time even to see in which direction it had gone. There was only a little white cloud racing away towards the Mercedario, and we were left speculating whether the hat reached the mountain, or fell into one of the valleys.

We spent that day under the lea of a rock above our tent, taking some observations with the sextant to determine the latitude and true bearing of our camp with regard to Aconcagua. We found this place so sheltered that we determined to move our camp up here, as it had the advantage that we could lie in our tent and see the coast-line of Chile, and watch the sun set over the great expanse of the South Pacific Ocean. Vines, who was full of energy, climbed up that afternoon past the place where Dr. Güssfeldt had erected his last cairn. I remained behind, and superintended the moving of our camp. This took us the whole afternoon, as it is no easy matter to move a tent fastened by so many guy ropes when you cannot drive a single peg into the ground. A rock had to be rolled into position for each rope to be tied to. Vines returned for supper about six, and we turned in before sundown, to avoid

ANOTHER ATTEMPT

the chill night air. The thermometer then showed 26° of frost.

We were favoured with magnificent weather next day the 12th; the wind had completely gone down, and the plains of Chile and the Pacific Ocean beyond were clearer than I had ever seen them before. As Vines complained of being tired in his legs after his climb of the day before, we decided to put off our attempt on the mountain till next day. Lanti and Lochmatter arrived about 11.30 with fresh provisions. They seemed completely broken down with fatigue, though we were at a loss to know why. That is one of the most curious things about these altitudes: one can never tell beforehand how much a man can do. He is frequently so fatigued that he can scarcely walk, and the cause cannot be found; while at other times, when one would expect him to be excessively tired, he will arrive quite fresh. I kept Lanti with us that night, thinking he might be useful next day should one of us break down in the ascent. Lochmatter was sent down to the Inca camp to bring up a complete supply of fresh provisions, as I did not then know how long we should be obliged to remain here. The night was fine, but I was unable to sleep most of the time owing to a racking headache, the cause of which I also could not explain. Vines did not suffer. Lanti slept the whole time so soundly that I really feared the vibration from his snoring would loosen the guy-ropes.

We rose early next morning, and made elaborate preparations for the ascent. It was bitterly cold, and we collected every article of wearing apparel that we could lay our hands upon. Vines's frost-bites when he returned that evening proved he took none too many. At about half-past eight we started, slowly making our way by the old route, namely, steering for Güssfeldt's cairn. The day was fine, and we had every prospect of success. The usual disappointment followed, however, for I soon found I was beginning to lag behind, and before ten o'clock, at an altitude of some 20,000 feet, I was compelled to give in, in a state of complete collapse from violent nausea. The season was already far advanced, and I realised that we could no longer spare the time for these fruitless attempts of mine upon the mountain I therefore begged Vines to continue on and make the ascent, and to leave our maximum and minimum thermometers upon the summit, while I turned my back for the last time upon these slopes — with feelings that I had perhaps better not try to describe.

SERACS OF THE HORCONES GLACIER

CHAPTER X

BY STUART VINES

THE SECOND ASCENT OF ACONCAGUA

"My readers must kindly set their imaginations to work in aid of feeble language; for even the most eloquent language is but a poor substitute for a painter's brush, and a painter's brush lags far behind these grandest aspects of nature. The easiest way of obtaining the impression is to follow in my steps; for in watching a sunset from Mont Blanc one feels that one is passing one of those rare moments of life at which all the surrounding scenery is instantaneously and indelibly photographed on the mental retina by a process which no second-hand operation can ever dimly transfer to others."—LESLIE STEPHEN.

IF the author of "The Playground of Europe" feels the inadequacy of the "second-hand operation" of writing, how much more must I crave the reader's indulgence before I attempt a description of the ascent of Aconcagua.

Unlike many ascents that have been made to peaks above the height of 20,000 feet, Aconcagua was climbed under the most favourable conditions for beholding a view that for extent and magnificence has had no equal. The indulgence of the reader must therefore be in proportion to the difficulty of the task before me.

"I'll rest a minute or two and get over this attack of indigestion; you go slowly on,—I'll join you," FitzGerald said, as we left him. And "slowly on" we reluctantly went up the steep snow, and then sat down to wait for him. He was sitting on a rock about five hundred yards from us: I watched him intently, expecting every moment to see him come after us, but, to my disappointment and dismay, when he did get up, it was only to turn round and descend in the direction of the camp. Then I realised that I should have to make the attack alone with Lanti. Disheartened, I felt that if I looked after him any longer, I should descend and join him. But he had said, "Whatever you do, make the ascent," and I turned once more in the direction of the summit, and took the lead up the steep snow slope.

The illustration opposite p. 91 will give some idea of our surroundings at this point, though our route during the first few thousand feet lay to the left of the picture. The illustration is from a photograph taken at the end of March, from the 19,000 foot camp, at a time when the whole mountain side was white with fresh-fallen snow. Zurbriggen had made the ascent in January, almost without putting his foot on snow. Now, owing to the unprecedentedly bad weather during the last month, the snow lay in large patches over this north-western side. Yet these patches were mere dots on the mighty slopes forming the approach to the great peaks and walls of rock that shut out the summit from our view. The couloir, leading to the last thousand feet, by which Zurbriggen had made the ascent, was straight in front of us, about three thousand feet above. It looked absurdly near. The most direct route would have been to ascend in a bee-line up the great slope of debris to it. This was impossible; it would mean a tramp of hours up a very steep slope, exposed to the whole force of the north-west gales, over ground rendered rotten and unreliable by innumerable years of denudation. Our intention was to follow the route which, in the first place, gave the least abrupt ascent, and, in the second, avoided this rotten debris. To our left was a more or less broken line of cliffs, running down to the north from the summit. We determined to make for the base of these, and follow their line in a south-westerly direction towards the couloir which now lay straight above us. We were carrying two rücksacks, about 17 lbs. in weight, containing amongst other things some Kola biscuits, three flasks of wine, some slabs of chocolate, a couple of onions, extra clothing of all kinds to put on as the day got later and colder, prismatic compasses, a case containing the maximum and minimum thermometers to be left at the top, and, as I imagined, the small camera. Alas! one's memory is not keen at these altitudes. I had made elaborate preparations the night before in order to have everything ready for the start. The camera, carefully packed in two handkerchiefs, I had placed in the corner of the tent at my feet, and could not, it seemed, possibly forget it, and yet now, a thousand feet above the camp, on readjusting the contents of the two rücksacks, I found no camera. My feelings were more bitter than I can describe. We had made such a late start that it was very doubtful whether we should reach the summit even now, and to turn back for the camera was out of the question. I trudged on, feeling much depressed, and at 9.50 reached the base of the cliffs.

I had brought with me an aneroid barometer, made by Carey, that registered as low as 12 inches. I judged it to have always worked pretty consistently, though there was a minus error of nearly an inch at starting. At the camp, before we left, it marked 14.75 inches, and now, after we had been ascending for an hour, the reading showed 14 inches. No doubt it exaggerated the whole day, but for an aneroid at such heights it exaggerated regularly. During the first hour we had not appeared to make very much progress; in fact I was getting anxious about our rate of going, for no one could imagine that we should be able to go faster as we got higher; there was, on the contrary, every reason to fear that the pace would decrease. I made the rests as short as possible, and yet we fell into a bad habit of stopping frequently,—as we said, to admire the view. As usual, the wind became stronger as the morning wore on, and consequently counteracted the benefits we hoped to receive from the warmth of the sun. I had anxiously awaited its warmth for some time, as, in spite of two pairs of thick stockings and boots several sizes too large, shortly after starting I had little or no feeling in my feet. However, by dint of working my toes about in my boots at each step for the next thousand feet, I managed to restore circulation, and was not troubled again in this way during the day. Lanti complained bitterly of the cold, and I was not surprised, as he had not taken the precaution of putting on the extra clothing provided for him. I picked my way over the solid rock at the base of the cliffs, glad to have something firm under my feet, an advantage which cannot be over-estimated, and thus we pushed on for five hundred feet, unwillingly forced, now and then, to take to the debris, and eventually returning to the snow, which was very steep at this point, we zigzaged up it, till at 10.40,—two hours from the camp,—we reached Güssfeldt's point. I had been told there was a stone man marking the spot, but at the time I could not bring myself to believe that the small pinnacle of red stones, so narrow in proportion to its height, had stood since the year 1883: it was only on discussing the matter later with FitzGerald and Zurbriggen that I satisfied myself that the small red pile, in an unsheltered spot, was indeed Güssfeldt's stone man. Instead of taking a straighter path to the summit, we chose the route that offered the least incline, and made as if to arrive on the north-east shoulder of the mountain, our direction being almost due east. Though our pace did not merit the reward of a rest, we were soon forced again to sit down for some time. Nearly three hours had passed since our scanty breakfast at the camp, and I was feeling hungry. We had arranged to eat what we called lunch at a spot where, on all the previous attempts on the mountain, a halt had been called, in order to get food and gain strength for the last two thousand feet. I had been told that we should find some provisions there, and the means for preparing hot food; for all the party, except Lochmatter and myself, had reached the place before, and at different times provisions had been carried up and left there. Though they had failed up to now in heating any food there, I hoped for better luck in our own attempt.

Before leaving the Inca I had prepared for myself a small bottle of a mixture of port wine and egg, as I had often found this a good pick-me-up when in a state of physical exhaustion. Its chief recommendation on this occasion was that it was palatable, and I always had an inclination to take it. Unfortunately this inclination was shared by Lanti. I should not have objected if the sharing process had not extended further than the inclination, but unhappily it did so. Having refreshed himself Lanti sat down, and, as we lay and gazed over the ever-increasing expanse of blue ocean to the west,

LANTI DISCOURAGED

the pick-me-up having loosened his tongue, he gave me his views on the situation. Could this despondent and grumbling creature be the same bright and cheerful Lanti of a few weeks ago, who had ever been ready to carry the heaviest load, and crack a joke after the hardest day? Having felt less the effect of the altitude than the other porters, he had been chosen to accompany me on this attempt. But now all the spirit and ambition seemed to have gone out of him. "Two hundred *lire*, Lanti, if you reach the top with Mr. Vines," were FitzGerald's last words to him, and yet, though to all appearance physically strong enough, he had an honest desire not to continue the ascent. From his own words I diagnosed his case as "Heimweh," for he said to me, "Signor, the mountains of Europe are healthy: these mountains are very unhealthy. Why do we climb these mountains, and why encamp and sleep at these great heights? We who have done so, will find our lives wrecked by it." Seeing that this was leading us to a proposal to descend, I cut him short in his lugubrious meditations by starting on again.

Still we kept on to the east, and I hoped before long to look over into the Vacas Valley, but on Lanti's suggestion we now turned sharp to the south towards the summit. Two days before I had reached this spot by another route. I was now higher than I had ever been before. In half an hour—fifteen minutes past midday—we reached the halting-place. In an arena, surrounded on two sides by an amphitheatre of rocks and aiguilles, and on the southern side by a mighty mass of overhanging cliff, forming, as I thought, the summit of the mountain, lay a couple of rücksacks. The peculiar palisade of pinnacles around formed only protection enough from the wind to make it the draughtiest place in the world. It was therefore not an ideal place to make a fire. The contents of the rücksacks were examined: some tea, a little wood, a heliograph and stand, binoculars, and two self-cooking tins were what we found. While I made a few notes, and examined the aneroid, which read a little over 13 inches, Lanti attempted to make a fire. He struck some forty matches, and, as each fizzled out, there followed a string of expletives in his own Italian patois. We tried every available means to ignite the wood, but I could see it was no good. Hot food, therefore, was out of the question; but worse than that, Lanti shared my egg flip so liberally that we left the empty bottle behind.

After three-quarters of an hour's rest in this very uncomfortable spot, we started off again at one o'clock. De Trafford had planted a heliograph station some sixteen miles away on the other side of the mountain, at the mouth of the Horcones Valley, and I knew, by previous arrangement, that on this day, between three and six, he would be watching, with telescopes directed and instrument aligned on the summit of Aconcagua. I determined, therefore, to take the heliograph with me, and send him the first news of the ascent, should we reach the summit. Horses would be standing by ready saddled, and, at the first message flashed from me, Gosse would gallop the eleven miles to Vacas, and despatch the news by cable to London.

The full weight of the instrument with the stand was 14 lbs. This I made my load, and gave Lanti the rücksack with extra clothing, compasses, etc., and a bottle of sour Chilian wine, which, with some slabs of chocolate, was all we now had to sustain us for the rest of the day,—not a tempting meal for exhausted men. Our rest had been a long one, and we should have been quite willing to make it longer, had not the cold been so intense. Let me call the reader's attention to the photograph opposite p. 91. The halting-place was beneath the wall of the cliff on the extreme left, and we now made our way behind the rocks towards the peak in the centre of the picture. We emerged from behind these rocks beneath this central peak and some three hundred feet below it, our object being now to reach the couloir on the right hand side of the peak, as this was the only route to the summit. No photograph can give any idea of the vastness of things here; what looks like a mere step from one part of the mountain to the other meant hours of toil to us. The actual summit of the mountain lay some distance behind the central peak, and some three or four hundred feet above it. The only peak of the mountain visible is the lower western peak, which lies to the right of the illustration. Now, there were two routes open to us from the point we had reached :—to go straight across the great slope of debris (this appears in the picture as a *snow* slope) to the couloir, or to ascend by the rocks to the foot of the great central peak, cling to it for the sake of the hard ground, and so reach the couloir. No doubt the latter route was the longer. Lanti persuaded me, much against my will, to cut straight across the slope, declaring that this was the course pursued by Zurbriggen. I did not know what I was in for, or I would never have consented. At a quarter to two, over five hours from the camp (the aneroid reading 12.75 inches) we found ourselves half-way to the couloir, in the middle of the slope of debris, and convinced, both of us, that the longer route would have proved shorter in the end. This crossing the mountain side was perhaps the most trying part of the whole ascent. Not a single stone or rock that we trod on afforded any support. Everything, however firm in appearance, gave way beneath us. We could rely on nothing, so that instead of passing straight across the slope, we were forced to keep on ascending, in order to maintain the right level. Every minute either Lanti or myself would slip down five or six feet, bringing with us sand, stones, and rocks, and seemingly the whole mountain side. We were now considerably over 21,000 feet above the sea, and in such a condition that the slightest rebuff damped our spirits, and forced us to stop and rest. Rebuffs were frequent. We were continually thrown sprawling on the rotten surface. Our patience and endurance were tried to the utmost: we seemed to stop every ten yards for rest, and, in fact, spent far more time in resting than advancing; and yet we soon found it impossible to sit, or lie down to rest as inclination dictated. The relaxing of the muscles of the legs on assuming a reclining posture acted disastrously as soon as we resumed the ascent. For the lower limbs seemed first to have lost power, and then, after a step or two, were racked with a dull aching, which I can liken to nothing so much as to what has in a child been called "growing pains." This hardly wore off before it was time for another rest. Experience soon taught us there was only one position for rest and recuperation: to stand with the legs wide apart, the body thrown far forward, the hands grasping the head of the ice-axe, and the forehead resting low on the hands. In this way the circulation returned to the brain, and was maintained in the lower limbs, the diaphragm being free for respiration. After resting in this position, ten or a dozen violent respirations brought the breathing back to its normal state, the legs gradually regained power, and we were able to plod on another ten paces or so, according to the condition of the path. The general symptoms and the mode of relief from our sufferings point—and I make this suggestion in the humblest spirit—to anæmia of the brain, and to a general want of circulation caused thereby. I do not think that Lanti suffered so much physically as I did, but mentally he certainly suffered more. The whole man had entirely changed; his conduct was altogether inexplicable.

It was not until nearly three o'clock that we reached the foot of the final couloir. This great detour from the camp in the morning to this spot, had taken us nearly six and a half hours. And yet I am convinced that it was a better route than directly up the slope, although, perhaps, nearly twice the distance. As surely as a thirsty animal will go miles for water, the climber in these ruined masses will go miles out of his way to avoid loose footing.

We were still from a thousand to fifteen hundred feet from the summit,—it was late, and I felt myself in no good condition. I had neither opportunity nor inclination to collect anything in the way of specimens of rock at these heights. But at the mouth of the couloir I noticed a small piece of black rock lying loose on the surface,[1] and as it was quite unlike any of the rocks around, and I had not seen anything of the kind previously on Aconcagua, I pocketed it.

[1] See Appendix, p. 318, "*R.*"

AT TWENTY-TWO THOUSAND FEET 113

After about three hundred feet the gully widened, and we entered an enormous amphitheatre, the floor of which, filled with masses of broken red rock, sloped up in front of us to the great ridge that joins the eastern and western peaks, continues on beyond them in descent to the Vacas Valley on the one side and the Horcones Valley on the other, and so forms a mighty arc from one base of the mountain to the other.

This ridge will be seen in reverse from the south in the frontispiece, and also in the illustration opposite next page.

To our left rose a huge bastion of rock, which, no doubt, was the summit. To our right, great cone-shaped rocks and aiguilles towered into the clouds. I cannot conceive anything more sublime in its desolate grandeur than this rock-bound wilderness, quarried by what forces one cannot imagine, perched up amongst the highest crags of the great Andine chain, receiving in its lap the red ruins of the towers above. Contrary to the idea given in the illustration opposite p. 91, not a vestige of snow was to be seen within the vast enclosure. We were over 22,000 feet above the sea, and in no mood to cope with the petty annoyances incidental to clambering over the great rough stones and boulders now blocking the way. I sat down in the midst of this lonely scene and looked ahead, wondering how much longer I could last. What was it that would strengthen me for the final effort? Certainly the sour Chilian red wine, which was icy cold, offered no temptation. In my desperation and wretchedness I thought as a stimulant of the onion that I had slipped into the rücksack at the last minute. A raw onion at any time is bad, but sucking and gnawing a raw onion in a biting wind at 22,000 feet is unendurable, and, though I persevered with it, I cannot say that I derived any immediate benefit from the vegetable. However, all things have an end, and after struggling on for another hour amongst the fragments fallen from the heights around, and after innumerable halts, we reached the upper end of the basin.

My excitement as I neared the arête in front gave me

fresh vigour, and even Lanti cheered up a bit. In a few minutes the whole southern aspect from which we had so long been cut off would burst into sight.

At half-past four exactly I stood upon the great arête. I crept to its edge, looked over the southern wall of Aconcagua, and gained my first view of the country to the south. The sight that met my gaze was an astounding one. An immense distance separated us from the glacier below—the difference between 23,000 and 13,000 feet. It was a precipice of gigantic size. As I looked down its dizzy sides, I saw spurs of the mountain flanking the glacier beneath to the left and right, giving the appearance of some huge amphitheatre. The sun was low in the heavens, and did not penetrate into this vast pit, and the great masses of vapour slowly moving about in it far below, gave it the aspect of a giant cauldron, into whose depths the eye failed to penetrate, two miles vertically below. The arête, about five feet wide at this point, ran east to the summit and west to the snow-clad western peak of the mountain, growing ever narrower in that direction, until, where it sloped up to the highest point, its edge became knife-like. Indeed, I felt it was lucky the eastern peak was the highest point of Aconcagua, for this snow peak to the west would probably demand of the climber considerable step-cutting. But time was now everything to us, for it was late, and we did not know how far off the summit might still be. Small clouds had been hovering on the north-west slope all day—the mass of Aconcagua seeming to attract them, and we hurried on, in hopes of reaching our goal before they entirely surrounded the mountain-top and cut off all chance of a view. We turned once more in a north-easterly direction along the arête, over which we had no difficulty in walking, as it was composed of loose stones and a little fresh snow. Was it the excitement of the thought that perhaps a few hundred feet alone separated us from the summit, that gave us fresh vigour and strength? Anyhow I felt stronger. There seemed more air to breathe after we had left the basin surrounded by rocks where we had been, to a great extent, sheltered from the wind, and con-

Aranxquez from the Gardenlis. Telepholt View.

sequently the pace improved.¹ The arête soon became precipitous and very crumbly, and I perceived an easier route by leaving it and turning more to the north. My excitement now became intense; a cliff in front barred the way and shut out the view ahead. I scrambled up the cliff, and, once level with the edge, beheld Zurbriggen's stone man, and the ice-axe planted in its centre not twenty yards from me. A few steps more, and Lanti and I stood on the summit of Aconcagua.

It was two minutes past five; the thermometer showed 7° Fahr., the aneroid had reached the limit of its markings and stood still at 12 inches. In silence I turned and grasped Lanti's hand, our feeling of triumph too great for words. The summit was attained—our labours were at an end. Over the abyss beneath me and down the Horcones Valley I looked eagerly for the flash of those who were patiently watching the summit. But to my great disappointment nothing could be seen, for a thin curtain of cloud hid the mouth of the valley from view.

We were on a square plateau, measuring 75 paces each way, sloping at an angle of 7° down towards the south-east, and entirely free from snow. On its northern side I found Zurbriggen had built a most substantial pyramid out of the loose stones lying on the summit. Lanti produced the bottle of wine, but it was not to our taste, and we poured its contents as a libation over Zurbriggen's stone man: and then, no longer forced to stand and rest, flung ourselves down at the foot of it. I set about writing a hasty record of the ascent. There was no time to lose. The clouds were slowly moving up the north and north-western slopes. I wrote Lanti's name on my card, and the date, etc., and had just finished when a gust of wind snatched it from my numbed fingers, and I was forced to begin over again. On the second card I wrote:—

"*Made the ascent with Lanti Nicola, miner, of Macugnaga, Italy. FitzGerald Expedition, England.*"

¹ See Freshfield's *Caucasus*, pp. 168, 169.

And then the following note on a piece of paper:—

"*Eight hours and twenty-three minutes from a camp on the north-western slope of the mountain at* 19,000 *feet. Saturday,* 13*th February* 1897. *I am leaving here my ice-axe and maximum and minimum thermometers in a box. I have brought up a heliograph, but cannot use it owing to cloud.*"

I then took the thermometer-box, set the instruments, put my card and the piece of paper inside, and wedged them in the rocks at the foot of the stone man, and beside it placed the empty bottle. Having cut my name in large bold letters down the shaft of my ice-axe, I substituted it for FitzGerald's, which Zurbriggen had left. All this was done as quickly as possible, but with the thermometer at 7° Fahr., and with one's fingers numb and clumsy, it took some time. I got up and looked around; clouds were already hovering beneath the western peaks, and the sun was getting very low in the heavens.

My eyes were suddenly drawn to the south. Flash! Flash! Flash! The dots of the Morse code! A thin white light but quite distinct! They had then seen me, as the cloud shifted, with their powerful telescopes, and were trying to attract my attention! Lanti and I were hard at work at once, only too glad to have something to keep us warm, for we had got chilled to the bone while sitting by the stone man. In a few minutes our heliograph was set up to answer the signal. The aligning of the instrument was no easy task in 25° of frost, with the wind whirling great clouds of snow up from the arête and the western peak into our faces. It was the more difficult as the sun was at an awkward angle, being very low in the sky, and de Trafford's signalling-station was to the south-east. Only with great difficulty, therefore, could a shadow-spot be got with the single mirror, so that the time I had given to the first aligning was useless and I had to begin work all over again with the double mirror. As soon as this was adjusted and the instrument aligned I began to flash,—but, another disappointment!—I was too late. The clouds had already risen from the valley again and come between us and those below. I had now been on the summit three-quarters of an hour, and Lanti was very anxious to begin the descent; he felt the cold intensely, and had no sympathy with the heliograph. However, I was determined to wait as long as possible, and as near as I could judge, I kept my instrument in alignment. I knew that de Trafford had two powerful telescopes directed on the summit, and thought at the time that he had seen us on the top and had begun signalling in consequence. This afterwards proved not to be the case. There was a tremendous wind blowing down the Cuevas Valley from the west, which, though their heliograph was weighted with stones, shook the instrument and made the flashing I had seen. I waited patiently by my instrument for five minutes, and then came to the conclusion that, as the clouds showed no sign of lifting even for a moment, I would make other use of my time.

CHAPTER XI

BY STUART VINES

TWENTY-THREE THOUSAND FEET ABOVE THE SEA

THE marvellous panorama that lay around and beneath me demanded some study for its comprehension. Northwards over the cloudless expanse, my eye wandered down the great slopes of the mountain, over glaciers and snowfields beyond, down the Penitente Valley, by which Güssfeldt had made his attack, to where the great snow mass of the Mercedario, towering above all the surrounding heights, barred the way.

In height but a few hundred feet lower than Aconcagua, and outstripping, in the vastness of its proportions, all other mountains in this region of the Andes, the Mercedario, like many another peak in these parts, has a reputation for inaccessibility far beyond its deserts. Seen from the summit of Aconcagua, its ascent, from the climber's point of view, seemed to offer no special difficulty. The precipitous parts —if they exist at all—must lie at its base, which, in the denuded state of these ranges, is highly improbable. It appeared to me as one gigantic snow-slope, slanting up from the south-east at an angle of not more than 20° to the summit. There was nothing in its shape to lead me to think its volcanic activity any more recent than that of Aconcagua, and probably its northern side consists of similar debris-covered slopes. In the enormous distance to which I could see beyond, numerous other giants reared their mighty heads—many of them in the shape of perfect pyramids having a distinctly volcanic appearance.

Over Argentine territory range beyond range stretched

AN UNPRECEDENTED VIEW 119

away; coloured slopes of red, brown, and yellow, and peaks and crags capped with fresh-fallen snow. I had hoped to look from the summit right down upon the pampas of Argentina. In this I was disappointed, for, though I gazed intently over the range, far beyond the Uspallata Plain, a sea of mountains some sixty miles in width, and averaging a height of quite 13,000 feet, made such a view impossible from the summit of Aconcagua. It was only far to the north that a break in the Cordilleras gave a glimpse of the distant plains.

Away over the surging mass of white cloud that lay on the glacier at my feet, rose the southern frontier chain, Torlosa and the Twins, on either side of the Cumbre Pass, like colossal sentinels guarding the great highway between the two Republics; the lofty glaciers lying between the rugged crags of Juncal; the ice-peaks of Navarro and Pollera, the Leones and the Cerro del Plomo, that overhangs the city of Santiago, and some sixty miles farther on the magnificent white summit of Tupungato. And here my attention was arrested for the time: in every detail I scrutinised the outlines of that great dome. Aconcagua now at our feet, the next attack would be on Tupungato, another mountain with an evil reputation; described by the natives as a volcano attracting all the storms of the heavens. But my investigations in this direction were cut off by the rising clouds, and I turned my eyes elsewhere.

No lens or pen can depict the view on the Chilian side. I looked down the great arête, past the western peak of the mountain to right and left, over ranges that dwindled in height as they neared the coast, to where, a hundred miles away, the blue expanse of the Pacific glittered in the evening sun. Far down to the south, and fifty leagues away to the north, stretched the vast blue line. The sun lay low on the horizon, and the whole surface of the ocean between the point of vision and the sun was suffused with a blood-red glow. The shimmering of the light on the water could be distinctly seen. So near did it all seem that I could not realise the immense distance that separated me from it.

There lay the Bell of Quillota and the Cerro del Roble. And were not those the heights of Placilla which on one side look down upon the harbour and the town of Valparaiso, and on the other on that field of carnage where but a few years ago Körner dealt the deathblow to the power of Balmaceda? The valleys filled with cloud had all the appearance of arms of the sea clasping the maritime ranges in their embrace. The sea-girt Cerros rose like huge island rocks from these phantom waters.[1]

And now I turned to the mountain itself, its satellites, and the valleys running from it.

Within ten miles, surrounding the base of Aconcagua to the east and west, lay the heads of the Vacas and Horcones Valleys—wide, bleak wastes of grey stones, bounded by black crags or red and brown slopes, and ending in glaciers encircled by peaks of ice and snow. Very similar was the Penitente Valley to the north, though the glaciers were far more extensive. There in the dim distance beneath me stood the bold outlines of the Almacenes that but a few days before we had seen from the Horcones Valley, towering so high above us. Could those small rocks down there be indeed the same great coloured cliffs that overhung our valley camp? Could that be the great barrier that after many a cold night kept back the warmth of the sun till so late in the day? Far away and small they all looked now.

From this platform, raised above the culminating ridge, the nature and shape of Aconcagua were very clearly revealed. On the one side I beheld the mountain falling sheer down to

---

[1] Charles Darwin, in vol. iii. chap. xiv. p. 311 of *The Voyage of the Beagle*, mentions a similar effect produced by cloud in August 1834, when looking over the same country from the ridge of Chilecaugnen.

"These basins and plains, together with the transverse flat valleys, which connect them with the coast, I have little doubt, are the bottoms of ancient inlets and deep bays, such as at the present day intersect every part of Tierra del Fuego, and the west coast of Patagonia. Chile must formerly have resembled the latter country, in the configuration of its land and water. This resemblance was occasionally seen with great force, when a level fog-bank covered, as with a mantle, all the lower parts of the country: the white vapour curling into the ravines, beautifully represented little coves and bays: and here and there a solitary hillock peeping up, showed that it had formerly stood there as an islet."

ON THE HORCONES GLACIER

the southern glacier, and on the other gently sloping towards the wide snowfields to the north at an average angle of 25°. Some two thousand yards to the south-west along that narrow edge and fully two hundred feet lower than the point on which I stood was the western peak of the mountain. Everything beneath bore witness to the tremendous denudation that had been going on for countless ages. All the forces of nature had been brought to bear on this mountain giant. Visible signs lay around me of the power of the weather and rapid changes of temperature to destroy. Aconcagua with all its cherished secrets and its mystery lay bare before me, confessing itself as nothing more than a colossal ruin, for not a single vestige of the ancient crater of this extinct volcano remains. Foot by foot the relentless forces of nature have reduced the mountain to its present proportions. As the fog banks in the valleys near the sea so graphically illustrated to one's mind the prehistoric state of Chile, so the innumerable traces of ruin and decay around me, the crumbling rocks, and the disappearance of the crater, told of an Aconcagua of the past, whose gigantic base filled the glacier-beds around, whose sides rose towering to the heavens several thousand feet higher than the Aconcagua of to-day, the reckless vehemence of whose volcanic force was the beginning of its own destruction; of an Aconcagua of ages yet unborn, split, broken, and powdered by frost and heat, pouring itself over valleys and plains in sediment and shingle, a mere shapeless mass, whose height will no longer distress the mountaineer; an Aconcagua, whom the agencies of destruction, more vigorous here than elsewhere in the mighty chain, will have forced to abdicate, no longer monarch of the Andes.

It is true that while passing through the great basin filled with red stones, I had imagined for a moment that I was indeed in the crater of Aconcagua, but its shape, the direction of its slope, and the insignificance of its size as beheld from the summit, when compared with the vast proportions of the mountain, dispelled at once all such ideas.[1]

[1] Many stories are rife in Chile of eruptions seen during the present century. Admiral FitzRoy, in the *Voyage of the Beagle*, talks frequently of the volcano

We had now been considerably more than an hour on the summit, and while making these different observations, I divided the time between adjusting the shadow-spot of the heliograph and stamping and dancing about to keep from being frozen as I stood. I may here mention that I did not feel the damaging effects of altitude so severely on the summit. So soon as we ceased ascending, the trouble seemed to leave me. Lanti had long ago had quite enough of summit and view, and said he could stand the cold no longer, begging me to descend at once. In desperation I turned to the instrument, and through the thin veil of cloud very slowly and clearly sent the following message: "Vines, Lanti on summit. Cold wind. Few clouds. Grand view," on the chance of something being seen by those below.

of Aconcagua (vol. iii. chap. xiv. p. 308), and Darwin, in his *Geological Observations* (pp. 388, 481, 591), mentions Aconcagua, amongst others, as being a *dormant* volcano. Dr. Güssfeldt says, in his *Journey in the Andes* :—

"Conjectures are at variance with one another in nothing else so completely as in the question whether Aconcagua is of volcanic or non-volcanic origin. I myself inclined to the latter opinion, but without being able to bring forward completely convincing reasons for it. But the fondness of speaking of particularly striking mountains as 'volcanoes,' which is so prevalent in South America, made me all the more distrustful, as I myself possessed no geological knowledge, and distrust always goes hand in hand with the lack of specific knowledge. I can at least assert with assurance that through the *shape* of the mountain the assumption of its volcanic origin is certainly *not* proved. In Chile, on the contrary, especially in the middle provinces that lie nearest to it, people were always inclined to call Aconcagua 'el volcan.' To judge by the specimens of stones brought home by me, which have no doubt been affected by decay, the mountain seems to have built itself up by volcanic activity. In all probability, therefore, the popular belief had hit upon the truth, although neither written documents which have been handed down, nor yet the appearance of the mountain at the present day can establish a volcanic activity. Is it not possible that in this there lies an indication that oral tradition, inherited from generation to generation, reaches back to those times when Aconcagua was still an active volcano?"

No doubt the stories of its activity as a volcano, emanating from Chile, have been the result of mistaking the snow-clouds swept up by the terrific gales from its north-west slopes for clouds of volcanic steam. Aconcagua, by Professor Bonney's estimation, must have retired from active volcanics some fifty thousand years ago, or some period of time with which history cannot cope.

The specimen of rock which I picked up lying loose on the summit, has been pronounced by Professor Bonney to be a rather decomposed hornblende andesite, with numerous crystals (rather small) of plagioclase felspar. Another small piece from the summit plateau was an andesite, possibly with slight traces of fulgurite.

THE SUMMIT LEFT

I looked at the time. It was twenty minutes past six! In less than half an hour the sun would have set. Yet still I hesitated to leave a spot that overlooked the two greatest States of a mighty continent, affording a view over nigh 80,000 square miles of mountain, sea, and land; to peaks to north and south fully two hundred miles beyond Mercedario and Tupungato, unknown to me by name, but that rose out of the endless Andes, to right and left, at the lowest estimate five hundred miles apart—

> "Where Andes, giant of the Western Star,
> With meteor standard to the winds unfurled,
> Looks from his throne of clouds o'er half the world."

But I was alone. Lanti had begun the descent, and was already wending his way down the rocky bed of the pseudo crater. With many regrets I took one last look round and followed him.

Though to the climber it often means the most dangerous and difficult part of his work, to the reader the descent must always come as an anti-climax. I will therefore be brief.

Lanti leading, we passed the arête on our left, and made our way with all possible speed direct down the great basin to the couloir by which we had ascended.

The eighty minutes spent on the summit had been to me all too short, though no doubt from the point of view of prudence they had been far too long. To reach a peak of such a height a little over an hour and a half before sunset and to remain there for so long a time was, no doubt, somewhat rash. It meant that we should be entirely dependent on the moon to find our way; and should it be overcast, we were in no condition for further exploration in the dark.

Down we stumbled over the red rocks, racing with the falling light of day, the muscles much relieved for the time by the new sensation of descending. But on reaching the couloir we had to check the pace, for it had told on us very considerably.

I had been stumbling wearily down the snow that filled

the couloir for what seemed to me like ages, with hat and helmet bound close about my ears, and eyes fixed on Lanti's heels in front, when, on emerging from the couloir on to the great slope, I raised my goggles for the first time since we had left the summit, and looked around. It was fortunate for me that I did so, for in my tired condition I might have so plodded on to my journey's end without seeing what I can only describe as the most sublime and gorgeous colouring I have ever beheld.

The sun, a great ball of blood-red fire in a cloudless sky, was dipping into the waters of the Pacific. Rapidly it sank, and disappeared from view. Yet, as if still struggling for supremacy with the fast-approaching night, an after-glow of surpassing beauty spread over land and sea in a series of magnificent changes of colour. The mighty expanse of water from north to south, together with the sky above it, was suffused with a fiery red glow. While the red in the sky remained, the waters, through a variety of intermediate shades of colouring, turned slowly to purple and then to blue. And yet we were not in darkness, for with the sun's departure the risen moon declared itself with wondrous brightness, penetrating the thin atmosphere and flooding everything with its colder light.

The effect produced by such a combination of brilliant moonlight and glorious sunset was beautiful beyond words. For during half an hour that wonderful glow rested on the horizon of the Pacific—a great red line of subdued fire suspended in mid-air, the darkness that had fallen like a pall on sea and land beneath severing its connection with the earth.

Nothing could be conceived easier in theory than the descent down the great slope from the couloir to the camp. But for men in our exhausted condition, it seemed a never-ending labour. The two hours taken over the descent seemed more like six, as with heavy, weary steps we floundered down the steep snow or broken stones, from time to time attempting to glissade in our anxiety to reach the camp by the quickest means. Too exhausted to support ourselves with our axes, and with the snow in bad condition, we had to give this up.

And now a word or two about my companion, the man who shared with me the honours of the day.

A big-boned man, slightly above medium height, spare almost to emaciation, Lanti Nicola always seemed trained down to the finest point of condition. We had many times to admire his excellent qualities as a porter, and this day's experience gave me additional proof of his splendid powers of endurance. Of the two I was by far the most done up. He was more inured to the conditions of things than I was, having taken part in all the earlier attacks on the mountain, and being by now an old hand at battling with the atmospheric difficulties on Aconcagua, whereas, compared with the other members of the expedition, I was a raw recruit, this being practically my first attempt. Again and again I begged a rest, grumbling and disappointed that I seemed to derive no benefit from the ever-increasing pressure. On the contrary, the breathlessness and weariness continued to the end, as I continually threw myself forward on my ice-axe gasping, as in the ascent, until I gained relief.

The way seemed never ending, but our direction was good, for the moonlight helped us, and soon we heard the voices of the Pollingers, sent from the camp by FitzGerald to meet us and bring us in. It was long after eight, however, before we reached the 19,000 foot camp. After this I have vague recollections of seeing FitzGerald in a huge bundle of clothing outside the tent, grasping his hand, and hearing something about congratulations and hot whisky. Later, of being bundled into the tent, of finding that I could not get my hat or helmet to budge, as they seemed to form a solid, frozen mass with my beard as foundation; of making feeble and pathetic efforts to do what is an athletic feat for a man in prime condition on the seashore, viz. to pull my sleeping-bag up my body and round my shoulders; of hearing something about Lanti going on to the lower camp with the two Pollingers, and wondering how he could possibly do it, and above all, of someone bringing me a hot drink. Hot food had always been looked upon as an uncertain quantity at this camp. But the trouble and difficulty they must have had to boil water in 20° of frost at nine at night, and make this hot toddy, never entered my head at the time, though the toddy did so immediately, and with it my recollections ceased.

CHAPTER XII

A TRIP TO CHILE

THE day that Vines made the ascent was very cold. I sat in the sun, near our camp, watching their movements. After passing Güssfeldt's last cairn they disappeared behind the northern arête of the mountain, and not until after midday did I catch sight of them again, when I saw them skirting along to the westward by the base of the final peak. I watched them with the telescope as they slowly and painfully made their way over the rough and broken ground. They seemed excessively fatigued, for I noticed that they went with great effort, and paused every few moments, leaning on their ice-axes, and at times they would slip and fall. They kept steadily on, however, and at last reached the couloir that leads to the saddle. They seemed an interminable time here, and I was even beginning to fear that they would break down, when finally they quickened their pace and I saw them stand on the saddle. They then walked up towards the summit, and disappeared from view. A few hours later I saw them coming down. By this time the sun had set, and the night was intensely cold. I piled on the fire all the wood I could find, and made as big a blaze as possible, yet I was compelled to stamp up and down to keep warm.

At about 7 o'clock the moon rose, and the great white snow-slopes sparkled and scintillated under its bright light, while seawards, to the west, a ruddy glow illuminated the heavens, marking the place where the sun had set. The wind had dropped, and all was still—still with that intense quiet that is so oppressive at night, when one is surrounded by these gigantic cliffs and peaks that seem to threaten those who invade their solitude. Range after range spread out between me and the ocean, brilliant in the moonlight, giving the feeling that one was standing on some extinct planet, for there was not a trace of vegetation, nothing but the bright white lights and shadows, like the scene one sees through a powerful telescope of the mountains of the moon. Life seemed a thing impossible in such surroundings, and as the air grew colder and colder, I wrapped myself up in my blankets and shuddered with an unreasoning fear that perhaps even the very atmosphere might die out and leave us frozen stiff in this frozen land.

I was brought back to the realities of life by hearing Vines shouting to me. He was now nearly at the camp, and after a few minutes more he arrived broken with fatigue, parched with thirst, and covered from head to foot with ice and snow, his beard and moustache being like one huge icicle, so coated were they. I gave him a hot drink that I had prepared, and got him into one of our sleeping-bags in the tent. His nose was badly frost-bitten, and he was pretty well chilled to the bone. Lanti said that he would prefer to descend to our lower camp, so after I had supplied him with some hot refreshment I let him go down with Pollinger.

Next morning Vines's beard was still covered with ice. Even in the tent we could not thaw it out. We collected together some of our effects and came down to the lower camp, for I was feeling very ill after so many days passed at 19,000 feet. I had slept in all fifteen nights there, and it had told heavily on my constitution. As the mountain had now been climbed by Zurbriggen, and by Vines with Lanti, I decided to go over into Chile for a week to rest and if possible get strong again after the fatigues we had endured at these high altitudes.

We soon reached our 14,000 foot camp, and after a good meal we started down on foot for the Inca. I had sent a man on the day before to send up our horses to take us down. The animals, however, had not arrived, but we had not gone far before we met them, and Vines and I then galloped down as fast as we could. All went well till we reached the first ford.

WE CROSS TO CHILE

There was a huge quantity of water rolling down, as the day was hot. I crossed first, but unfortunately my animal fell into a hole at almost the first step. I was lucky enough to be able to keep my seat and regain the bank. My second attempt was more successful, and I got across without accident. Vines drove his horse across, and descended the river-bank to a great boulder, from the top of which he was able to jump half-way across the stream. He arrived safely, with only a wetting. We soon reached our base camp at Inca, where we met Lightbody, who had left the Transandine Railway to join us in our work. Vines was suffering acutely from his frost-bitten nose, which was much swollen. I left Lightbody in charge of our camps, and on the evening of 19th February Vines and I started for Chile. We left the Inca at about 5 p.m. and reached Cuevas for dinner. At about 10 p.m., after the moon had risen, we started out to cross the Cumbre Pass. The people at Cuevas assured us that we should be attacked and killed on the Pass, but we did not listen to them. During the whole of our work, extending over seven months and more, in these regions, we were molested on only two occasions. The people are, as a rule, peaceable, and the upper valleys uninhabited. I have not heard of any combined system of highway robbery on these passes during the summer months.

The night was a perfect one, and we greatly enjoyed our solitary ride. We reached Portillo in Chile early in the morning, but only stopped here a short time to rest ourselves and the horses, and then pushed on to Salto del Soldado, the terminus of the Chilian part of the Transandine Railway.

From here we went on by rail to Los Andes, where we remained for a few days. For two nights I was very ill, suffering from fever and nausea brought on, no doubt, by my prolonged stays at our high-level camp, and seeming to have ruined my digestive organs completely for the time. From Los Andes we went to Santiago, remaining there for a day only, as it was very hot; we then went down to Limache, where we stayed for a couple of days, going on afterwards to Valparaiso. But as my stay in Chile did not seem to be doing me any good I decided to return to the Inca next day. I was taken violently ill that night in Valparaiso with a high fever, and the doctor thought at first that I was about to have typhoid: I recovered, however, in a few days. Before returning to the mountains we were anxious to make some arrangements to test if it would not be possible to heliograph direct from our 19,000 foot camp to Valparaiso, as from the camp we could see the coast-line very distinctly. Mr. Dinnigan, of the West Coast Cable, very kindly offered to set up a heliograph upon the heights just above Valparaiso, and keep it aligned on the mountain side, where our camp was situated, during certain hours of fixed days that we should arrange by telegraph from Vacas. I returned from Valparaiso to Los Andes better in health than I had been for some time, thanks to the kindness and hospitality of Mr. Ball. At Los Andes we picked up the horses we had left there, and started by road for Juncal. During our stay the animals had got completely out of training. Habituated as they were to pick up a scant livelihood from the withered and dry snow-grass upon the Andes, the unaccustomed rich green forage of Chile had proved too great a temptation for them, and they were so fat when we arrived that it was with difficulty that we could make the girths meet round them. We had not gone very far before we saw that it would be impossible for us to reach Vacas with them that night, and we decided to leave them at Salto del Soldado and hire other animals to go on with; we could then send our arriero over from Argentina to fetch them when we returned. As we were riding along the road from Los Andes to Salto we met a Chilian gaucho, who followed us in a rather suspicious manner. As our horses were so much out of condition, whilst he was well mounted, we were powerless to get away from him. He stopped at a small posada, where he apparently met several of his friends, for we afterwards saw him come on reinforced by three companions. We pushed on as quickly as possible, for the road was lonely. The man had previously made one or two attempts to enter into conversa-

tion with us, trying to run his animal up alongside as near as possible, but we had succeeded so far in keeping him off. Fortunately for us several parties mounted on horseback passed us on the road, and therefore these men did not succeed in getting us alone; had they been able to do so, I feel convinced that they would have attacked us. We were the more suspicious as I had just drawn £50 in gold from the bank in Chile, and I was afraid that in some manner these men had learned the fact. When we arrived at Salto we succeeded in getting a coach that took us up to Juncal, and next morning we hired mules and crossed the Cumbre, reaching our camp at Inca soon after midday. Here I met Lightbody and Gosse, who had been working together since we had left. Lightbody had run a series of levels from the rails of the Vacas station to the mouth of the Horcones Valley, and had also completed a triangulation that we had begun at Inca. Gosse had spent his time in collecting and in managing the camp for Lightbody. I quote a couple of amusing extracts from his diary:—

"*4th March.*—Besides the cattle which are driven over the pass from Argentina into Chile, there is one other kind of live-stock, which I have seen exported. I was skinning birds in camp at Inca to-day, when I heard a loud squeaking going on. On looking round I saw down the road towards Vacas a man approaching on a mule and leading another mule by a rope. The second animal was loaded with two large wicker crates, and at each step the mule took a loud squeak was audible. At first I took this noise to be caused by the wicker itself, or by the harness, but when the noisy little cavalcade drew near, I found that the crates were filled with small green parrakeets, which gave a squeak of terror every time the mule took a step."

"While all the others were in Chile, one Sunday afternoon I received a note from a lady, who said that she and her husband were staying at Inca, and would so much like to try to convert my 'foreign guides.' I asked the porters if any of them would care to go, but I am sorry to say that only one candidate came forward, in the person of Lanti, who did not understand a word of English, and scarcely any Spanish. He started off, however, and about an hour afterwards he returned with a knowing look in his eye; a few moments later all the porters began to come to me, one after the other, to say that they would so like to go and hear the English missionaries. It looked well indeed for the missionaries, that they should have managed (speaking only in English, as I afterwards heard) to convert so stout a Catholic as Lanti in so short a time. I had given leave to three of the others to go, when my suspicions were aroused by Lanti coming and asking permission to go again. This I refused, and when the other three returned to camp, I made inquiries. I found that the missionaries conducted their services in the bar of the inn, and that, after service, each man in the congregation was asked what he would take. This latter part of the ceremony was apparently the only one Lanti had understood."

Next day Vines went up to the high-level camp to see if it would not be possible to set up the heliograph communication which we had arranged for in Chile. Lightbody and I remained behind and went over the trigonometrical work of the survey round Inca. A few days later we went up to the 14,000 foot camp to meet Vines, and to see what success he had had with the heliograph. As we started late in the afternoon, it was not until long after dark that we reached the upper camp, where we found that Vines had just come down from the 19,000 foot camp. He reported a great amount of snow and intense cold. Moreover, he had been unable to set up communication.

CHAPTER XIII

BY STUART VINES

THE FIRST ASCENT OF THE CATEDRAL

ON the 16th of March I descended to the 14,000 foot camp from the high camp on Aconcagua, where I had been attempting for some days to make heliographic communication with Mr. Dinnigan, late instructor of signalling in the Royal Engineers, who had a station some ninety-seven miles away on the heights of Placilla above Valparaiso, and was on the lookout during certain prearranged hours of the day, and of the night as well, because I hoped with such a clear atmosphere and a bright moon to be able to get lunagraphic communication also. Indeed I had obtained a "shadow-spot" without the slightest difficulty; but sad to relate, our old enemy, the weather, spoilt all my chances of success, though I remained there several nights alone. Soon after I reached the valley camp I was joined by FitzGerald and Lightbody, who had come up from Inca to fix the longitude of the place. The news from Tupungato and the south was of such a dismal nature that all thought of penetrating that part of the country was abandoned for the time being, and they had come to spend some days at the head of the Horcones Valley fixing positions. I had spent a very lonely time during the week, so I gave them a hearty welcome. Unfortunately, as I did not take the precaution that night of turning in first I had reason to regret that I was not still alone. The three of us shared the Whymper tent: two other small tents were used by the porters. FitzGerald had thrown himself down on one side, and Lightbody's most elaborate couch of sheepskins, ponchos, and sleeping-bags, encased in a

Robert's valise, had been carefully and neatly spread on the other. I humbly and thankfully crept into the narrow space —about two inches wide—they had so considerately left for me. FitzGerald is a restless sleeper and his elbows are sharp. Lightbody has a habit of sleeping heavily in more senses than one. How well they slept, how sharp Fitz-Gerald's elbows were, how unmovable Lightbody's bedstead, I shall ever remember. The next night I resigned the place of honour, and hacking up a bed in the debris with my ice-axe, took a sleeping-bag and Robert's valise and slept outside. But a circummeridian observation of Jupiter at ten o'clock in 16° of frost and a biting wind before turning-in, and a small gale all night, made me wish once more that FitzGerald and Lightbody had never come up from Inca.

As the greater heights were for the present out of the question, FitzGerald suggested that I should take the brothers Pollinger and make the ascent of the Catedral, a mountain on the western side and at the head of the Horcones Valley, overlooking the glacier basin. It stood in a very conspicuous position overlooking the Cuevas Valley and the Chilian Andes to the west. Moreover, its summit was not more than seven miles from the summit of Aconcagua. My purpose was to take bearings of certain positions as a help to those surveying below, get some photographs of the summit of Aconcagua and the peaks to the north-west, and more especially to collect geological specimens in order to see how they compared with those from Aconcagua. The summit was not then reckoned at much more than 5000 feet above us, being about on a level with the high camp on Aconcagua; so that an unusually early start was not necessary. The night in the open with a biting wind had not refreshed me, and I had vowed to sleep inside the tent in future, however restless the other occupants might be. We were off at half-past six, and as we made our way across the valley to the huge moraine heaps guarding the snout of the Horcones Glacier we made a careful examination of the mountain. The northern and eastern sides of the Catedral, which rises from

THE FIRST SLOPES

the glacier, were rocky and precipitous, and probably the rocks were in as brittle and ruined a condition as those on Aconcagua. The southern side consisted of a great *névé* or snow-slope through which rocks here and there appeared. Pollinger made out what he thought to be one or two crevasses higher up. The easiest route was on the left hand side of the *névé* on the south-west side of the mountain, where the snow-slope seemed to lead towards the summit. This would mean a long and tedious walk, followed by a wearisome tramp for hours up the snow; we therefore made for the point where the southern snow-slope and the eastern rock face seemed to rise from a platform above the Horcones Glacier. We crossed the glacier stream and ascended the moraine. Some yellow patches on this side of the valley had long attracted my attention, and I turned to the left, somewhat out of our direct route, in order to examine them closely, and obtain some specimens. I found I had to cross a deep gully and scramble some distance up another before reaching these patches, and the detour took me far longer than I had intended. I did not, however, consider the time wasted. The yellow patches were evidently composed of sulphur with some iron in it, from its strong smell and the red tint here and there. We now resumed our former direction, and, scrambling up for some little way, came to a plateau or basin where there had been snow or water. Indeed all the ground was covered with more or less fine earth both in the basin and on the slopes near it, produced, no doubt, by the action of the wind and melting of the snow; for the ripples on the ground had all the appearance of soil that had been carefully prepared by the harrow to receive seed, though somewhat stony in places.

Every step was now taking us higher and farther away from the mighty mass of Aconcagua, and what the view to the south lacked in beauty and softness, it made up in impressive grandeur. We had been living for so many weeks under the crags of Aconcagua, that we had no chance of gaining a more general impression of the details of its formation and its vast proportions. Leaving the plateau we crossed the great mass of debris leading up to the eastern precipice of the mountain. Great boulders of brown rock lay on all sides, hornblende andesite, like the summit of Aconcagua, blackened on one side by exposure. Numerous loose stones, with vein-like cracks filled with what I thought at the time to be crystals, arrested my attention. The specimen I took with me was examined at a later date, and my "crystals" proved to be merely some white mineral. The delay caused by this cursory collection of specimens by no means pleased the Pollingers, who were giving all their attention to the question of the route to be taken, for we had passed the precincts, and were beneath the walls and buttresses of the Cathedral itself.

It was nine o'clock, and we had only ascended some 2000 feet above the camp, being at a height of close upon 16,000 feet. To compare with specimens collected from a similar height on the opposite rocks of Aconcagua, I chipped a piece from the solid rock wall of the mountain.[1] The crumbling state of the edifice on this side made us decide at once to ascend by the snow route, so skirting the edge of the rock wall, we made our way round to the southern side of the mountain, and began the ascent of the great snow-slope. The way was very steep and we laboured up the deep snow, Joseph Pollinger, who was leading, rather forcing the pace as a reminder to me that there was to be no more geologising until we reached the summit. An hour's fatiguing tramp, bearing gradually away from the rock wall, and westwards, brought us to a wall of ice twenty feet in height, beyond which were signs of crevasses, and we put on the rope. We reached the top of the ice wall at ten o'clock and halted for breakfast.

We rested here for twenty minutes, and glad we were to do so, for the way had been steep and the going had been very hard over the deep and powdery snow. There was no doubt about the wisdom of choosing the Catedral for ascent. It was the only peak that gave an uninterrupted view of the northern and western sides of Aconcagua from base to

---

[1] See Appendix, p. 322 (1) and (3).

summit. But even now I wished the odd seven miles between the summits of the two mountains were nearer fourteen. For the vast mass seemed still to hang right over us, and I could not yet form a clear idea of its proportions. I looked into the valley beneath, and realised as never before how unearthly in its dreariness and desolation the last and highest reach of the Horcones Valley is,—walled in on one side by the rugged rocks of the Dedos, cliffs and crags dotted with yellow patches, and on the other by the ruined battlements of Aconcagua built by successive flows of lava, high perched amongst which, at a height where one would never have expected to see it, were masses of white gypsum. The numerous white pieces, I might almost say boulders, of this deposit which we had so often ridden amongst in the valley directly beneath bore witness to the composition of the white masses above. Everything, as far as the weather was concerned, was as it should be, and I looked forward to another fine view, to getting some excellent photographs of the summit of Aconcagua, and perhaps to be able to make out Zurbriggen's stone man with the aid of the glasses. I could see the surveying party far below. They were watching us, and no doubt wondering at our slow progress, and why we were not already near the summit. The younger Pollinger here broke in upon my meditations by declaring that if an hour's rest was to be the only outcome of the splendid pace he had set us during the last hour, we had much better have come slowly. He was right, so seeing that it would not do to remain longer, we started on again. At eleven we saw the summit to the north. Here a discussion arose, for our surest way of reaching it would be to turn to the left until we reached the western side of the mountain, and then wind up northwards by the snow-slope to the summit. There were several reasons against taking this route. We had been tramping for two hours over snow, and the detour mentioned would necessitate a similar tramp for two or three hours more. This would have been all very well had we not wasted so much time, but a cold wind had sprung up, there were already signs of the weather not holding out. I feared the clouds that had a habit of collecting round Aconcagua in the afternoon would spoil all chances of a view of the summit. Lastly, a shorter route lay due north of where we were, the only drawback to which was that it went up a steep rock face which would offer considerable difficulty. Above this wall of rock the way was more or less easy, between rocks, ice and snow, to a cornice, leading to the summit. The longer route would not get us to the summit much before three, and as the Pollingers thought the rock wall could be negotiated, we decided on the shorter one. We stopped, therefore, to examine this route. Some *nieve penitente*, or ice-needles (so called by reason of their similarity to crowds of white-robed penitents), led up in steep gradation to a snow platform, about four feet wide, from which the cliffs rose up. Joseph pointed out a spot about fifty feet up where a ledge covered with deep snow ran almost diagonally across its face. If we could only reach the right-hand end of this ledge we could traverse the face of the rock to the extreme left where a chimney or gully would take us direct to the snow arête above. The opinions upon the subject of whether or not this route would be feasible were somewhat conflicting. The ledge was no doubt deceptive in appearance, for it had a large mass of snow clinging to it, giving the impression that it was a broad and easy path. Louis Pollinger urged, on the one hand, that this would probably afford an insecure foothold; his brother, however, maintained that the only difficulty to be encountered would be found in the first fifty feet which it was necessary to climb in order to reach the ledge; after that, he averred, it would be all plain sailing. I was rather inclined to take Joseph's point of view, so I threw in my casting-vote, and elected to try these rocks. Joseph led the way, and scrambled with considerable difficulty up the first twenty feet or so. The wall was exceedingly steep, and it was with great difficulty that he managed to proceed at all, as the rocks were in a very crumbly condition, and did not afford a very secure hold for hand or foot. I followed him, and I must confess I did not like our position. It seemed to me that we were risking too much to avoid a detour which had only the fault of being long. However, as Joseph thought it could be done, and as I knew that he was a first-rate guide, I followed him without much hesitation. The ledges on which we had to cling were extremely narrow and filled with snow and ice, while the wind now blew with terrific force, numbing and freezing our finger-tips, so that at times I had no sensation whatever in them. Joseph Pollinger is a lightly-built man, and can climb like a cat. I found many places that he had been able to go over safely were very much more difficult for me, weighing as I did nearly thirteen stone. The rocks crumbled, the footholds broke away, but at last I stood beside Joseph. With numbed and frozen fingers I could only just manage to cling to this place, while Joseph slowly made his way to a spot some ten feet below the ledge, whence he called down that he was afraid the traverse did not look as easy as was expected, but that he was "ganz sicher" for the moment. He was now about twenty feet above me, a little to the right, and the rope between us was tight. As I was some distance from the snow below, Louis was obliged to follow, and we were—all three of us—on this rocky face. One by one we took up higher positions, and Joseph after considerable struggling succeeded in reaching the ledge itself. I called out to him to discover what it was like, but it was some time before he made up his mind. He seemed to take ages scraping the snow off the ledge, while we with numb fingers patiently clung on below, the wall being so steep that it took all our strength to keep our precarious footholds. Joseph finally reported that the ledge was all right for a short distance, but that beyond there was a point impossible to negotiate; at the same time he said that the rocks on which he was standing were so dreadfully rotten that he could not hold on where he was very much longer, and that we must descend at once to the snow plateau, as he felt his handhold slowly crumbling away from under his fingers. He said he would not move until we were safe off the face of the rock. The situation was critical. In order to go down I was forced to unrope myself, and having done this Louis Pollinger came up to where I was, so that he might render his brother assistance, I meanwhile cautiously scrambling down to the snow platform beneath. As I was thus engaged several showers of small stones came from above, and I heard the exhortations of the two men begging me to be as quick as possible. I looked up and saw Joseph about to descend. He had put his ice-axe on the ledge, and was peering round to find the safest way to descend, while Louis and I shouted suggestions to him. The rocks by which he had ascended for some ten feet beneath him were very rotten and almost perpendicular, and it seemed impossible that he could come down by this route. Louis tried to ascend to his brother's assistance, but nothing would bear his heavier weight. The next moment Joseph appeared to have found a secure handhold, some way to one side, when suddenly the rocks to which he clung gave way and he fell forwards. I was foolishly standing immediately beneath him, and a shower of stones was the first warning I got of the impending catastrophe. I threw myself back on the snow-slope only just in time, for the next instant, with a terrible cry and amid an avalanche of rotten rock and debris, Joseph crashed down on to the very spot where I had been standing. A moment later I saw him on his hands and knees deep imbedded in the snow.

We were at his side directly, yet for more than a minute he remained as he had fallen, refusing to move or take the slightest notice of our anxious questions, an awful look of horror on his face. He was perfectly dazed by the shock. Collecting his thoughts, he rolled over on his side and began to gasp and groan, and then he seemed to lose consciousness. I applied my flask to his lips, but it was fully ten minutes before we could get a word from him. The information we at last got was of the worst. He lay and muttered, "My back, my back!" In order to get some better idea of his condition, I persuaded him to try and stand up. A groan of anguish was the only answer, and he described himself as "ganz gebrochen." Gently at first, and then more vigorously,

AN ACCIDENT

we examined, probed, and rubbed him. At length to our great joy, he made no objection to the somewhat rough handling we resorted to, and we found that, though he was terribly stunned and shaken by the fall, no bones were broken. The soft snow had not only broken his fall, but saved him from pitching forward down the slope on to the ice-needles beneath, where he must have been cut to pieces. Yet his escape with so little injury was nothing less than miraculous: he fell with his head not six inches from one of the sharpest pinnacles of ice—a lurch forward and his brains would have been dashed out. We laid him down on the snow, and began to discuss what it was now best to do. We could not leave him where he was, and continue the ascent; we could only wait till he recovered a little and then try to get him safely down. At the mention of the word "descend," Joseph roused himself: a liberal pull at the flask, and he said he could stand up if we gave him a hand. In fact in ten minutes he said he was ready to continue the ascent, but begged us to go very slowly. We were delighted to see this change, and though we did not think for one moment there was any chance of getting him to the top, his words proved conclusively that no bones were broken. The short cut had been a failure, and now there was nothing for it but a long and weary tramp westwards over the snow; in fact I do not think one of us thought we should ever reach our goal. We were all disheartened, and Joseph groaned at every step. Suddenly Louis called my attention to a break in the cliffs, which so far had been hidden from our view. If we could ascend by it, it would lead us almost directly towards the summit. On examination we found some step-cutting would be required. The question was whether we could get Joseph up or not. He had brightened at the very first sight of this new route, and remarked with more enthusiasm than accuracy that he was feeling quite well. We roped again, and slowly and carefully ascended.

In half an hour we were on the snow above the rocks. A great cornice overhung the north-east side of the mountain overlooking the Horcones Glacier, and continued along the arête to the summit. This curious formation of snow is made by the wind perpetually blowing and drifting, till gradually a great mass of overhanging ice forms itself on the leeward side of the ridge, frequently, as in this case, actually overhanging the precipice. These cornices form one of the greatest dangers that Alpine climbers have to contend with. It was only a few weeks before we started for South America that Dr. Max Günther and his two guides, Roman Imboden and Peter Ruppen, perished by a fall through a cornice on the eastern arête of the Lyskamm. They were on the eve of making an expedition to the Himalayas when they were thus unfortunately killed. Before that there had been many accidents from these treacherous overhanging ledges of snow. If you go too near the edge, on the one hand, the whole mass of snow may break away and precipitate you to the valley beneath; while, on the other hand, if you get too far away from the crest you are sometimes in danger of falling down the slope on the other side. Louis led us along as near the edge as he dared.

His brother now becoming disheartened by the distance the summit still appeared away, began again to complain of his injuries; in fact, a few steps more, and he sat down begging us to go on—he would wait for us. This was no place to leave an injured man, and after a little wine and rest we persuaded him to make yet another effort. Crawling along the edge of that cornice with the third man on the rope a cripple was no pleasant task, and whenever we could get a chance we turned away from it down the steep slope on our left. There was the usual disappointment accompanying the ascent of a new peak, for the actual summit was a great deal farther off than we supposed, and again and again Joseph rested and doubted. However, Louis and I persuaded, and Joseph persevered, and at one o'clock we all three stood upon the summit of the Catedral.

The wind was intensely cold, and there was by no means an ideal light for photography. I made Joseph more or less comfortable in a sheltered spot, while Louis busied himself with the construction of a stone man. The actual summit

THE CUERNO

THE SUMMIT REACHED 143

was free of snow, and consisted of brittle rock of dark grey and brown colour, precipitous on the side overhanging the Horcones Glacier to the north-east, and on all other sides falling away in great snow-slopes. The summit rock is hornblende-andesite.[1]

Aconcagua hid its head in cloud, so I busied myself taking other views and bearings. To the north I looked down upon the snow mountains that encircled the Horcones Glacier, most conspicuous amongst which was the Cuerno, a mountain which from certain points of view has a resemblance to the Matterhorn. From the Catedral I had my first look into the valley which runs parallel with the Horcones to the west—the final stretch of that enormous valley formed by the Mendoza River, with its mouth at Boca del Rio, some twenty miles south of the town of Mendoza. A tributary valley, even more bare and desolate, if that were possible, than the Horcones, ran from it to the western snow-slope of the Catedral. The particular view that I climbed this peak to obtain, however, namely, the summit of Aconcagua, was still cut off from me by cloud; so I sat down with Louis on the rocks at the northern edge of the summit, to make a few notes and wait in hopes of a clearer view. Once more to-day I was to be reminded of the dilapidated state of the Andes. While quietly sitting by Louis I stretched out my arm for a piece of rock of peculiar shape. In a moment—as it had done with Joseph an hour or two before—the whole ground gave way beneath me. What had seemed hard rock a minute ago was nothing but crumbling rubbish. In another minute I should have been sliding down with a shower of debris, and have gone over the precipice on to the Horcones Glacier, had not Louis, with wonderful quickness, seized me by the arm and held me up.

After nearly an hour on the top, Aconcagua was still enveloped in cloud. I waited a little longer, and at length got a fairly good view of the summit, with clouds below. At three o'clock we began the descent. Joseph was stiff and cold, but said he felt better as soon as the descent began.

[1] See Appendix, p. 323 (2).

He suffered great inconvenience from having no ice-axe, as he had placed his on the ledge above him just before he had fallen. In the first place, we should want it badly for the descent, and moreover, having left one on the top of Aconcagua, and three having been broken at one time and another, we could not afford to lose this one. I therefore proposed we should descend to the cliffs above the scene of his accident in order to see whether we could secure it. We could not see it from above, but we knew it must be there as it had not fallen with him. Joseph, being the lightest, would have been the best man to let down, but his condition made that impossible, so it was decided to let me down. It was a question whether the rope would be long enough to reach to the ledge, moreover the others had to be very careful how they placed themselves, owing to the crumbling condition of the rocks, which we now fully recognised as an ever-present source of danger. They lowered me with about forty or fifty feet of rope by the very chimney we had proposed to ascend. I reached the western extremity of the ledge, walked along it for a couple of yards, until a buttress of rock barred the way, held on while they changed the position of the rope above, and on receiving the word "ganz sicher," let go my hold, dangled round the obstacle, and perceived the ice-axe almost within my reach. I shouted up for more rope, but word came back that there was little more to give. It was therefore hopeless to attempt to get hold of the axe and bring it up with me, so the only thing left to do was to dislodge it, in hope of being able to find it on the descent. As it was a little beneath me, I tried throwing and kicking down stones, but without success; so, with a shout of warning, I stretched as far as I could, gave a kick with my toe, and the dislodged axe fell clattering amongst the *nieve penitente* below. I scrambled back with the aid of the rope, and thankfully reached the Pollingers without mishap.

It was now nearly four. The descent was slow, as we had repeatedly to wait for Joseph, but otherwise it was without incident. We reached the camp at half-past six—

Joseph very sore and tired. We rubbed him all over with spirits of camphor, and got him into a sleeping-bag. He passed a wretched night, and in the morning his back was terribly stiff, and he spent a painful day being conveyed down to Inca on mule-back.

CHAPTER XIV

WORK IN THE HORCONES VALLEY

LIGHTBODY and I spent the day that Vines was ascending the Catedral in finding the true meridian at our 14,000 foot camp, and in triangulating the altitude of the surrounding peaks. When he returned we decided to leave on foot next day for our base camp. The days were getting very short, and we feared that winter would soon be upon us; it was therefore necessary that we should make our attempt upon Tupungato as soon as possible. Vines's painful experiences at the 19,000 foot camp a few days before indicated plainly that any ascent made now would be far more difficult than it would have been earlier in the season. Nothing is more fatal to success than the long nights one has to spend at high altitudes at this season of the year; proper rest is not to be had inside one's tent, and the monotony of the long sleepless hours, coupled with the intense cold, produces deep depression.

At daylight next morning, we started down, wishing to reach our base camp as early as possible, to make immediate arrangements for the Tupungato trip. We followed the old route by the riverside that we had taken when travelling on foot down the valley. Between this camp and that under the forked peak the river winds among old moraine beds, cutting for itself a passage two or three hundred feet deep in places. The slopes are composed of great rolling stones, and as we were walking along the base of these by the river edge we nearly had a bad accident. I was in front, picking my way carefully so as not to dislodge any of the lower stones of the slope, and thus start an avalanche, and we were all keeping our eyes on the upper slopes for fear lest some rock from the top should roll down on us. The torrent was continually eating away at the base of these slopes, and avalanches of stone fell repeatedly in the course of the day. By a clumsy slip I disturbed a large, loose pile of stones; they started rolling; the stones above them commenced to come down, and in a few seconds the whole slope was moving under my feet, while, to make matters worse, big rocks started from the top of the slope and came bounding down towards us. We were obliged to jump and run as quickly as possible over this moving mass to reach the solid ground a dozen yards in front. It was very difficult to keep our balance, stepping as we did upon these rolling stones, for to put a foot between two of the stones would have meant breaking an ankle. We were fortunate enough to reach a place of safety without anything more serious than a sprained ankle on my part. Luckily none of the big stones from the top of the slope had struck us, although we had some close shaves. We were obliged to concentrate our attention at the last upon skipping over these moving stones, and had not a moment's time to look about us and see where the falling rocks were coming. My ankle was very painful, and retarded our progress considerably. When we reached the ford below the Paso Malo I was unable to jump from the top of the high rock as we had done before, consequently I got thoroughly wet whilst crossing the ford, besides being nearly carried away by the force of the water. We reached the Inca camp late that night in a bedraggled and sorry condition. Zurbriggen was there, and was horrified on hearing of the accident on the Catedral. He took it very much to heart that he had not been present, and said to Vines—" If you do go out without me—you see! You *do* get killed."

On the next day we began to prepare for the attack on Tupungato, on which expedition I finally decided to send Vines and Zurbriggen, and to remain myself in the Horcones Valley. My reasons for this were twofold. In the first place I was exceedingly anxious to complete the traverse of the Horcones Valley, and to make complete measurements to determine the height of Aconcagua. Lightbody had now finished the levels up to the mouth of the valley, and I wished the further triangulations to be as nearly perfect as it was possible to make them. If I accompanied Vines on this trip to Tupungato, winter might have set in by the time we returned, and that which I considered the most important part of our work would be unfinished. Secondly, after my failures upon Aconcagua I came to the conclusion that I should only be a drag upon the party, and perhaps ultimately spoil their chance of success. Vines was in excellent health, but the trip to Chile had not improved mine; I had a fearfully bad bronchial cough, and was spitting blood, so I was not really in a fit condition for camping at high altitudes. It was of course a great disappointment to me, but in work of this kind one must sink all personal considerations if one wishes to be successful. I therefore despatched Vines and Zurbriggen next day, telling them to get an arriero at Vacas, as I would keep our man José with me and go up the Horcones Valley with Lightbody. I sent word down to Gosse, who was then shooting with Lochmatter in the Vacas Valley, to come up and join me in my work. There were still some photographs to be taken from our high-level camp at 19,000 feet, and as Lightbody had never been up there and was anxious to see the place, I sent him up with two of our porters, asking him to take a round of photographs, to pack up our luggage there, and to bring everything down and meet me in the valley below.

Next day I started up the Horcones Valley alone with José, and slowly pushed up the traverse survey station by station. After a day's work alone in camp, feeling the need of some company beyond that of José, who was rather gloomy and morose, I rode back to our base camp and collected Lightbody's dog Stella and her three puppies. The puppies I put into a canvas sack, while the mother meekly trotted on behind. It was a real relief to have them in camp, as the loneliness of these barren valleys has a most depressing effect upon anybody who has no human companion to converse with, especially when the nights are so long.

JOSÉ'S VIEWS ON CAMPING

Gosse came up upon 26th March and joined me. He at once took charge of the camping arrangements, as it was necessary for my work to move our camp every day a few miles farther up the valley. I had found that José was incapable of striking a tent and re-pitching it in one day. To his way of thinking, so weighty a job as this should take two or three days, as follows—first, one should have a day to strike the tent; next, a day to ride down to Inca and celebrate the occasion by numerous drinks; and then another day on which to return and re-pitch it, with perhaps a friend to help him. However, I found this method inconvenient, as it compelled me to sleep in the open two days out of three. My work here was of a more or less monotonous character; I will therefore only quote one day from my diary, in order to give the reader a general idea of what I was doing.

"On 27th March I arose before dawn, and having told Gosse that we would have our camp moved from the lake where it now stood to some suitable spot just beyond the Paso Malo, I set out with Lochmatter and my theodolite to continue the traverse of the valley. Our work that day was rendered both difficult and painful owing to the fact that we were obliged to cross the torrent of the Horcones many times. Our horses were busy transferring our camp, so we were obliged to go on foot, and the repeated fording of the ice-cold river necessitated our getting wet to our waists. I then had to stand for hours by my instrument, taking rounds of angles, while the cold wind that was blowing seemed to go through me.

"At five o'clock I was obliged to give up: the sun had set behind the hills some time since, and it was too bitterly cold to continue. Just as I was finishing, José came down, driving a mule before him. He seemed in a very excited frame of mind, and told me volubly a long story in Spanish. All that I could make out was that one of the pack-mules carrying the provisions had got caught by the current in the second ford, and thrown over and over, and that the packs had been lost. I was extremely annoyed at this accident, for it seemed to me, as the water was very low, that it must have been owing to gross negligence on the part of the arriero. I left my theodolite where I was working, ready for the next day, and hurried up to the camp. When I arrived I found my worst fears realised. There was no tent pitched and no luggage, only two wet blankets lying on the ground. Gosse told me that as José was driving the mule up the steep part of the Paso Malo the animal slipped on the edge and fell, its hindquarters going over the precipice while it held on by its fore feet. José's thoughts were entirely turned towards saving the mule, and in his anxiety to do so he cut the rope that bound the pack on the animal's back. The mule was saved by this manœuvre, but all the luggage was lost. Among the things that had gone into the river, and that I regretted most, was my Paradox gun."

Gosse and I prepared to sleep out during the night, wrapped in our ponchos; but we had not remained thus very long before José arrived with some horses and mules, bringing up the rest of the encampment. We got out our big tent and put it up in the night, a very difficult operation, as it was pitch dark, there being no moon at this time. We had to feel for all the guy-ropes, and succeeded in putting everything up crooked, tripping over the ropes, pinching our fingers, and losing our tempers. We then found that all our sleeping-bags had been carried away with the luggage, and we were obliged to lie down without any covering. The puppy dogs came up in a sack as usual, and they whined and howled most of the night, owing to the cold. We had no blankets for them, and were obliged to let them sleep between us, covered by our coats.

The next day I spent in continuing our traverse, and on the following day Lightbody returned from the 19,000 foot camp, giving me a most lugubrious account of his sufferings there. The snow, he told me, was falling again, and he had given orders to the porters to bring down everything, as it would be impossible to do any more work at those altitudes that year. Already he had had several frost-bites, and he did not dare to run the risk of being snowed up for a long time at one of those inhospitable camps.

LIGHTBODY'S SUFFERINGS

Lightbody gave me the following account of his work. He left me upon 23rd March, and continued up to the 14,000 foot camp, where he spent the night. Next day, with two porters he climbed up to our high-level camp. He told me that his sufferings had been intense on this climb, and that towards the end of the time the cold and the altitude had had an almost deadly effect upon him. The first night that he spent up there a tremendous gale arose, which loosened the guy-ropes of the tent, and they had hard work to fasten them again. The men with him seemed to have suffered as they had never done before, and he told me that many times during that night he felt as though he must die. All ambition ceased in him, his one idea being centred in an intense desire to get down. This was the first occasion upon which he had gone to the camp, and it was indeed trying for him to have done so just as winter was coming on, and even the men with him, who had been there so often, had suffered more from breathlessness than on any of their previous experiences. He told me that during the next day the cold was so intense that the men sat down, and absolutely cried, great tears rolling down their faces, simply because of the cold, which they were powerless to resist. In spite of all these difficulties, however, he succeeded in taking some photographs. Knowing this camp, and the feelings that one experienced while at these altitudes, I appreciated what a plucky performance this was. Nobody can conceive, unless he has tried to work under similar conditions, the feeling of utter lassitude that overtakes one. I have heard people complain of the same sort of feelings from acute sea-sickness. Having suffered badly from that malady myself I can say that a man could go about and cheerfully do his work while suffering from the worst attack of sea-sickness far more easily than he could take his pocket-handkerchief out to blow his nose at an altitude of 19,000 feet.

The following morning, unable to bear the strain any longer, Lightbody reluctantly gave orders to the men to strike the camp, and bring everything down. He then returned to the 14,000 foot camp, and remained there for some days, taking a series of photographs upon the glacier. He and the men were still suffering from the effects of those two nights spent at 19,000 feet a week before, and their frost-bitten fingers bore ample testimony to the torture and anxiety they must have been through. Lightbody now joined me in my traverse work, and together we were able to push on much more rapidly. We soon finished the valley up to the junction or fork, and again moved our camp to a spot some two miles below the foot of the Dedos, in plain view of the top of Aconcagua.

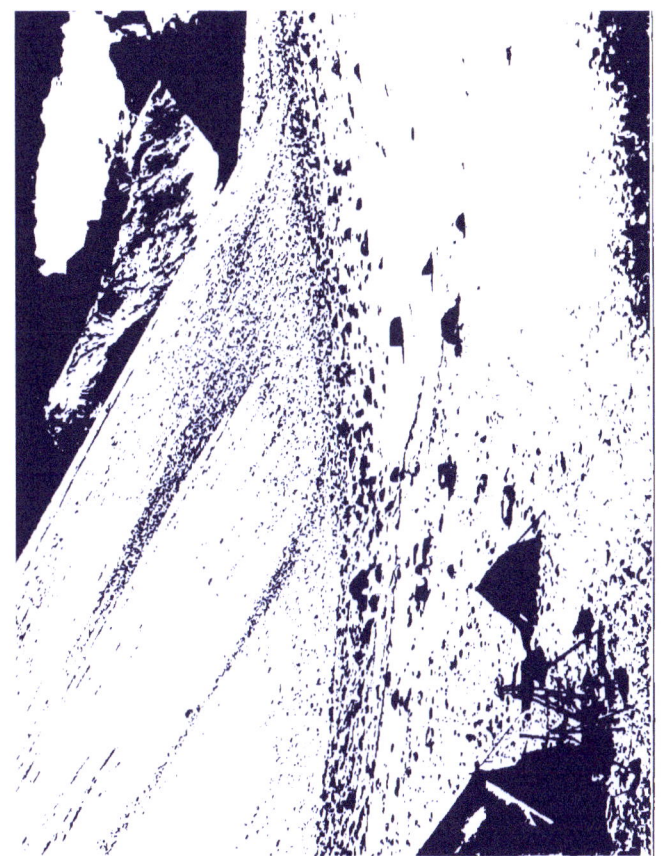

K. 3. CAMP, HORCONES VALLEY (11 821 feet)

CHAPTER XV

BY STUART VINES

HEADING FOR TUPUNGATO

PANNIERS stocked with provisions and equipment for an attack on Tupungato had long been lying at Vacas. But as far as the weather was concerned it seemed probable that they would remain undisturbed for some time to come. Almost the last week in March had come before the boisterous gales and unsettled weather gave way once more to clear skies and bright sunshine.

I galloped down to Vacas on the evening of 24th March, Zurbriggen had gone down the night before, and Lanti had been sent for from the Vacas Valley, where he was in camp with Gosse.

At the posada there was a scene of unusual animation. The change in the weather had brought a crowd of travellers from Mendoza, eager to seize this opportunity of getting over into Chile. With their arrival the Villa Longa Express Company had sprung into life, the patio was crowded with arrieros, the corral with mules and horses.

Inside the crowded comedor I espied Gosse and Zurbriggen, both busily engaged in worrying a very tough steak, as if their lives depended on it. I sat down and joined in the struggle, and of course the conversation turned on the weather. Fiorini, our host, gave out that the change foretold an unusually fine autumn, and shepherds and arrieros agreed with him, but they were equally unanimous in assuring us that Tupungato had a private climate of its own, and that we need not think for one moment Tupungato was about to shake off the storm clouds that surrounded it because of clear skies elsewhere.

Reports of a similar kind had reached me from Mendoza. While Zurbriggen was having his injured shoulder cured there, he had listened with a smile to these stories of the stormy and inaccessible mountain. Amongst other doleful presages, odds had been freely offered against any of us ever making the ascent. Thereupon the tough old Alpinist had promptly made a "book," and now there seemed every possibility of several fresh entries being made in it. In fact, a most unusual interest was taken in our movements, and many were the suggestions and warnings offered. One aged gaucho, with a twinkle in his eye, opined that what we were after was gold. He then held the company's attention by telling us that not far from the top of Tupungato was a lake of great depth,— the extinct crater, I mentally decided,—around whose shores were immense caves; and that somewhere thereabouts lay a vast quantity of gold, though whether it was on the shores or in the caves, or at the bottom of the lake itself, I could not make out. Only one man had ever climbed to it, and on returning for the means of securing his wealth, had been murdered. His murderers, it seems, had then made an expedition to the mountain, lost their way, and with poetic justice perished in the snow. He added that he himself was the only man who knew the secret road to this untold treasure; but I did not understand why he was still a humble shepherd at Vacas, instead of a millionaire in Buenos Aires. It was necessary, however, to leave these fascinating legends to make transport arrangements for the morrow.

Fiorini, the inn-keeper, had supplied us with four mules under the charge of an arriero, who rejoiced in the auspicious name of Fortunato—a man, he informed us, who knew more of the Tupungato Valley and its difficulties than any other muleteer. He also gave him a character for punctuality and promptness which he did not in the least deserve, though he has since perforce become acquainted with these virtues.

We calculated on a three days' journey with pack-mules to the base of Tupungato. It lay some thirty-five miles to the south as the crow flies, but the roughness of the valleys and the tortuous windings to avoid obstacles would no doubt nearly double the distance. Zurbriggen had already penetrated some way up the valley, and his tale of swollen rivers and unfordable torrents was not precisely encouraging. For every reason, therefore, it was necessary to start early on the morrow. Fortunato declared that every arrangement in his power had been made. So—influenced by Fiorini's glowing testimony to his punctuality—we told him to be ready to start at six, and retired to rest. Gosse and I found beds prepared for us in one of the mud-floored hovels, dignified by the name of bedrooms. The young hunter had enjoyed great sport up the Vacas Valley, which, according to his account, swarmed with guanaco, condors, and foxes, and, until we fell asleep, he regaled me with amusing stories of the chase.

At daybreak Zurbriggen, Lanti, and I stood in the patio surrounded by panniers, rücksacks, and bundles of tents, but no Fortunato and no mules. It would take us half an hour to catch the mules, but Fortunato, with his lasso, could perform the same feat in five minutes, if so minded. So Zurbriggen went in search of him. He found him taking a tender farewell of his wife, broke in upon the affecting scene, and bustled him back to the corral.

As soon as we had the mules in the patio and commenced to pack, Fortunato was again found wanting. For he asked me in a dazed sort of way if the señor really meant to go up the Tupungato Valley. On my replying in the affirmative, he said that in that case the mules would all want reshoeing. If the señor would confine himself to civilised routes, well and good — but, *caramba!* in the Tupungato Valley! And the man turned with a shrug of his shoulders and a look of disgust on his face. Only half-shod as they were, he protested, they would go lame in a few hours over the rough ground and sharp rocks. We reserved our remarks for the evening, when he would be far away from the posada, and would find it less easy to throw up the task. On examining the animals, we found that there were only a dozen shoes among the four, and some of them hung on loosely by a nail or two. In the Andes mules and horses require frequent shoeing; for they are shod cold, and the shoes soon get cast when they are off the high roads.

Zurbriggen took in the situation at once, and went in search of Fiorini, who, after much delay, obtained seven pairs of new shoes, with rough appliances for shoeing. He assured us that these were all there were in Vacas. But, he added, "You'll be all right, I have a lot of horses grazing about six miles up the valley. You will be sure to pick up some of their cast shoes, or if you don't, you may catch some of these animals and pull off from them any shoes you want."

Owing to these delays, we did not get off till past nine o'clock. The passengers for Chile started at the same time, and we all galloped up the road together. A detachment of the Argentine Military Police, who were in search of one of the numerous delinquents escaping from one Republic to the other, accompanied us, and gave an imposing appearance to the cavalcade. A mile along the high road and we came to the junction of the Cuevas and Tupungato valleys. Our ways divided, and after many farewells and good wishes, we left them and plunged through the ford across the Rio Mendoza. From the plateau on the opposite bank we had one of the finest effects of Cordilleran scenery. At the far end of the great pass road, overhanging the Cumbre Pass, some twenty miles westwards, rises the imposing pyramid of Torlosa, its black rocks and hanging glacier very clear and beautiful in the morning light.[1]

The traveller over the pass road turns westward at this point, and this giant of the Andes, over 19,000 feet in height, bursts into view with startling magnificence. This first close acquaintance with one of the great heights impresses every spectator; he plies his arriero, or guide, with questions, and invariably swallows the information that this is indeed a spur of the mighty Aconcagua.

---

[1] This view of Torlosa is seen in the illustration opposite p. 291, though since the light is behind, the effect of the contrast of black and white is lost. The illustration opposite p. 301, taken with a telephoto-lens, is, however, more successful.

Tupungato thirty miles away. Telephoto view.

ROUGH PATHS

The sight of the great white dome of Tupungato, seemingly so near to us—

> "Whose sun-bright summit mingles with the sky,"

gave the lie to the stories of chronic storm and cloud; the clear sky and the wide flat valley before us, like an easy causeway to its very base, made us eager and full of hope, and we told Fortunato to put the pack-mules to their best pace—it would be time to slacken when we reached the torrents and defiles that loomed so large in his imagination.

We forced our way through the resisting thorn bushes, so luxuriant that some might always be called trees, and now and again we galloped over green pastures where horses were grazing.

We had ridden but a few miles by this easy route when suddenly our way on this side of the valley was blocked and we were compelled to ford the Rio Tupungato. Fortunato showed us the place to cross, which, though it did not look at all inviting, afforded a firm gravel foothold, and we were soon on the other side. It was pleasant to cross over dry-shod, but thoughts of the keen frosts on the heights which were evidently keeping back the unmelted snows, mingled with our pleasure at escaping a wetting

The heights gradually converged, our path became confined to the river-bank, and we recognised that Fortunato's description of the route as rough was no exaggeration. Great masses of fallen rock, descending from the cliffs above to the water's edge, lay right across our path. The stones, on an average twice the size of a man's head, hard and unworn by the forces of nature, presented a surface of sharp jagged edges, and this giant's causeway was tilted to an angle of 40°. We dismounted, watched the loads, and coaxed the beasts forward. Boulders soon blocked the way, and it was interesting to watch the pack-mules as they manœuvred their panniers past obstacles to right and left, and wriggled in and out among the rocks. A worse place for beasts of burden cannot be conceived. The crevices between the sharp stones continually entrapped their feet, and bleeding fetlocks were the result.

It was nearly two by the time we had passed over this difficult ground, and on reaching a little green spot at the water's edge, we unloaded and bathed the animals' legs in the river.

The valley now widened out again, and, ascending to the top of a mass of loose shingle that filled it from side to side, we beheld a great flat plain spread beneath us, its surface covered with grey pebbles, over which the river ran riot. No doubt it had once formed the bed of a lake, which silting and denudation had filled and drained. Far away to right and left the hills rose from the flat plain in brown, red, and purple slopes, bare and bleak enough, but soft in comparison with the barren wastes in tbe Horcones Valley, their monotony relieved by the green banks of long grass that waved at their base. Here and there, where the slopes were broken by some mountain torrent, a giant talus would force itself far into the centre of the plain, thickly covered with yareta, the ubiquitous thorn bush of the Añdes, whose root is indispensable for firewood to the shepherd and pioneer.

We made our way across the flats to pasturage on the left hand side of the valley, and halted an hour before sunset, for men and animals were weary with their struggles amongst the rocks, and Fortunato wanted to give his mules time to feed on the good pasturage hereabouts before reaching the scantily covered slopes above.

We still had much to do. One by one the animals' feet were overhauled. The rough stones had played havoc with the hoofs, and half our reserve stock of shoes was called into requisition. Zurbriggen's knowledge of farriery piqued Fortunato into using his utmost skill, and further dilapidations in this direction appeared unlikely. We pitched no tent, but slept among the long grass.

I must now introduce to the reader another member of the party. Fortunato had with him a magnificent specimen of the guanaco hound, answering, as the advertisements say, to the name of Paramillo. Paramillo was very shy at first, and

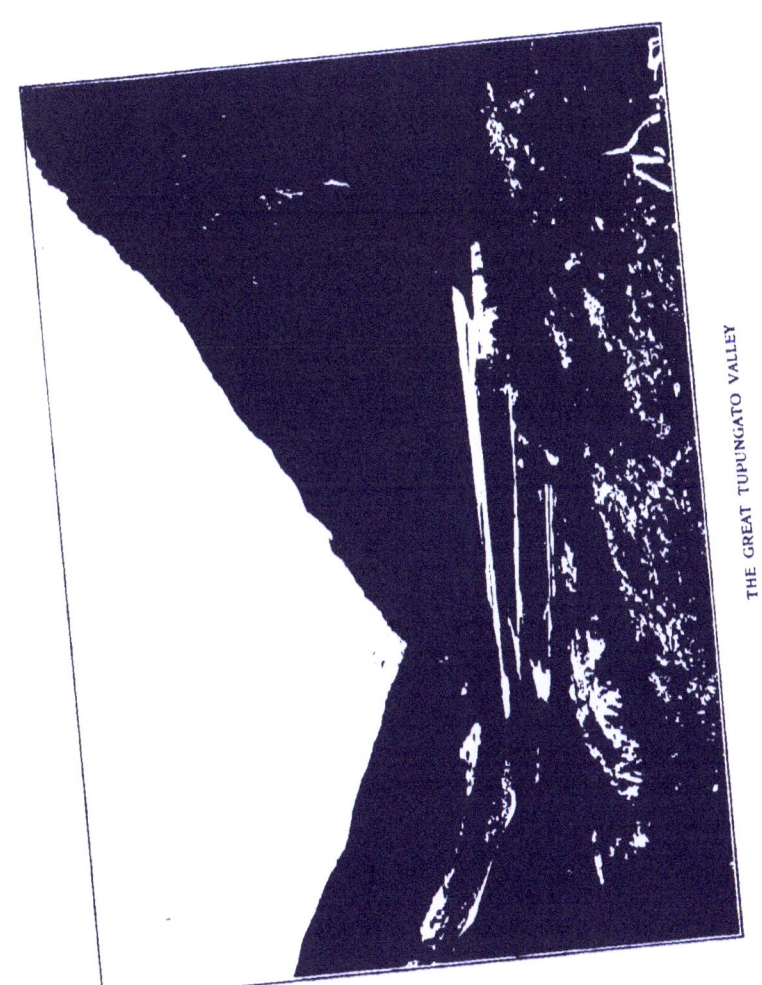

THE GREAT TUPUNGATO VALLEY

by no means ready to make friends with gringos, whom he looked upon with distrust. Although quite a young dog, he had already gained a reputation as a mighty hunter. Numerous trophies at Vacas testified to his prowess: the young guanaco bleating in the patio, the numerous fox-skins on the walls, all had the same history: "Paramillo caught that in the Vacas Valley," or, "Paramillo brought that home one day last winter." As he gradually made up his mind that we were hunters too, and that we had common interests in life, he laid aside some of his exclusiveness. Zurbriggen and I vied with each other in heartily coveting this splendid beast. He stood about two-thirds the height of a Scotch deer hound, similar in build, length of hair and shape of head, though somewhat thicker set, and in colour a tawny yellow. The illustration opposite p. 167 shows Fortunato holding him in front of our camp.

We were off again at daybreak, after some difficulty in catching the animals, who were loth to leave the luxuriant herbage.

We had lost sight of Tupungato, as the valley turned away from it to the right, running due west to the water-parting, and Zurbriggen, pointing ahead, said, "Fix your eyes on the right hand slope of the valley in front: in a few minutes you will see the twin brother of the Weisshorn." And sure enough, as we slowly neared the turn in the valley, over the brow of the hill in front, a white peak, a saddle, and then a magnificent giant of ice and snow burst into view. This, Fortunato informed us, was the mountain of Pollera, so called owing to its resemblance to the short, hooped petticoat women wear hereabouts. There certainly was some resemblance in its outlines to the shape of a lady's skirt, as the white folds fell from its topmost pinnacle and spread out at its feet.

We ascended the valley on its southern side over one talus after another, where the thorn bushes grew in great profusion. As Tupungato had hidden its head, and the valley ran west, I did not see exactly the route to take. But Fortunato pointed out a narrow gorge on the left side of the valley, which he told us would take us south and eventually to Tupungato. The path, he said, was far from easy, and he warned us to be extremely careful, for he had known of many animals, driven up to be pastured in the valleys beyond, being lost in this defile. I have a shrewd suspicion that Fortunato's knowledge of this route points to his connection with the smuggling trade. There are, I believe, passes over the frontier chain on either side of Tupungato which a man bent on avoiding the customs may negotiate in good weather.

To enter by the narrow gorge was impossible, and our only course was to ascend the valley side for some thousand feet and make our way far above the river-bed. At Fortunato's suggestion, we all dismounted, girths were tightened, loads reset and adjusted, and the most valuable packs placed on the strongest mules. Their shoes were overhauled once more, and the work of the previous evening proved good.

We soon found Fortunato had not over-estimated the risks to be encountered. Our route lay across a steep slope, with the torrent from three hundred to one thousand feet below us, according as we ascended and made our way over the buttresses of rock jutting from the slope, or descended to crawl beneath them.

Where these buttresses occurred, *quebradas*, or ravines, seemed to run out from the torrent bed, cutting a circular abyss in the mountain side, round which we had to creep, the only footing being bare and slippery rock, often at the same angle as the mountain slope itself. I was riding a nice little mare, an animal of some blood compared with the usual run of mountain ponies, in fact, quite a smart little hack. I did not trust her over these slippery places, however, and dismounted, though Fortunato begged us all to remain in the saddle, saying that a mountain horse only falls when not ridden. This may or may not be so, but my animal was not of the true mountain breed. The best horses and the steadiest in an emergency were, we found, the most slovenly and evil-looking. The true mountain steed has a careless and indifferent way of treading in dangerous places, as if wandering peacefully along a country lane.

A DIFFICULT QUEBRADA

The other horses were wonderfully sure-footed, and Fortunato and his pony showed a recklessness which seemed little short of madness. With the pack-mules it was different. They had barely room to tread on the slippery rock, which sloped down to the gorge on the right, and rose in precipices on the left. The panniers, which kept catching on the rough surface of the rock, threatened every minute to push them off their legs into the abyss below. It was exciting to watch a mule laden with one's most precious belongings wriggling round these uncomfortable places. We were powerless to do anything more than shout from behind or give a lead in front. It was impossible to unload them all where two men could not stand abreast; moreover, they were in the midst of it before we could get at them.

An hour of hard and anxious work and our difficulties were nearly at an end, when a quebrada, larger and deeper than those yet encountered, lay right across our path. We could not get round the head of this ravine, and our easiest course was to descend into it and climb out by the opposite side. Fortunato led the way in his reckless fashion, and was at the bottom in a moment, where he stood talking to the animals as they carefully stumbled, slid, and slipped almost on their haunches after him.

The ascent on the other side presented no difficulty to within a few yards of the top. But the previous hard work began to tell on some of the animals. The mountain pony will go anywhere if sufficiently urged: the mule discriminates. He is a wonderfully clever climber up to a certain point, but there is a limit to his pluck. He cannot be forced to do what he personally considers impossible. We tried every means, and eventually, by forcing the horses up first, got the mules to follow; but the last of the caravan, when within a few feet of the top, fell back on its haunches. I was behind, but the way being too narrow for me to get at its head, I shouted to Fortunato, who seized the halter and tried to get it up. Our efforts were unsuccessful; a jerk of its head, and Fortunato's grip was shaken off. Then with a plunge or two it rolled over on its side, fortunately by this movement unhooking the packs, which I was just able to seize and keep from following the mule, as it went bounding and rolling down the steep incline. Then on the verge of the precipice the poor beast made a desperate struggle to regain a footing, while anxious faces watched him from above. With a tremendous plunge, however, he fell backwards and disappeared from view. I sent Lanti down to secure the harness, and shoot the animal if not already dead. Mingled cries of exhortation reached us from below, and soon, to our surprise, Lanti appeared leading the mule. It was a sorry-looking beast by this time, cut and bruised in every part of its body; but it seemed to have sustained no serious injury, and, lightly loaded, continued to work for the rest of the day.

At last the gorge widened and we could descend to a more comfortable road in the valley, where we were glad to find more long grass. All were in need of rest; we unloaded, as usual, watered the beasts and let them feed for an hour.

On resuming our way we found the river-bed flanked, now on one side, now on another, and often on both sides, by sloping terraces of gravel. In attempting to describe these, I cannot do better than quote Darwin, who, though speaking of the valleys at a somewhat lower altitude, gives a graphic account which represents equally well the valleys we ascended from here to Tupungato :—

> All the main valleys on both flanks of the Chilian Cordillera have formerly had, or still have, their bottoms filled up to a considerable thickness by a mass of rudely stratified shingle. In central Chile the greater part of this mass has been removed by the torrents; cliff-bounded fringes, more or less continuous, being left at corresponding heights on both sides of the valleys. These fringes, or, as they may be called, terraces, have a smooth surface, and, as the valleys rise, they gently rise with them . . . From their uniformity, they give a remarkable character to the scenery of these grand, wild, broken valleys. In width the fringes vary very much, sometimes being only broad enough for the roads, and sometimes expanding into narrow plains . . . Higher up the valleys, the terraces have frequently been removed on one or the other side, and sometimes on both sides; but in this latter case they reappear after a short interval, on the line which they would have held had they been unbroken. Where the solid rock has been reached, it has been cut into deep and narrow gorges.[1]

[1] *Geological Observations*, p. 290, 291.

Darwin remarks that these terraces afford great facilities for the construction of roads. This we observed at once, and being in the river-bed, determined to gain the smooth surface above at the first opportunity. But how to scale the "cliff-bounded fringes"?

Using our spurs freely, we were able to force the horses up the slope to the terrace above. But the mules were very obstinate. Half-way up they swung round and jumped back into the valley. A strong black mule was put to the task, while we stood below and urged it on. Driven by our shoutings and the sting of Fortunato's lasso, it careered up the debris at the foot of the cliff. Then came some yards of hard and slippery stone; there was a futile struggle, and it swung round and fell backward nearly on the top of us. We were just able to spring out of the way in time. A third trial was made, and at last we managed to get him up. The mule which had been the hero of the last fall was then put to it, Zurbriggen leading him by the halter, with the same chorus of shouting and whip-cracking below. Man and mule reached the rocks, but in the tug-of-war which ensued, Zurbriggen came off worst, for the mule dragged him right down to the bottom. Too much time was being thus wasted, so we unloaded, and Lanti and I joined in. As usual, the mule gave a jerk at the top, and down we all came in a heap. At last we got a rope and dragged him up in this way. In such a case as this the horse is so much better than the pack-mule in the Andes; for the horses, though with a struggle, all managed to carry their riders to the top at the first attempt. We were soon able to take the line of the river-bed again, for the valley became wider as we ascended, opening out once more in a great flat plain, from which the mountains rose abruptly. After riding on for an hour and a half, we found that this valley also ran west to the frontier, and, for the second time, we turned up a valley to our left. Here we saw guanaco at frequent intervals. Paramillo became more alert than ever, for throughout the day he had trotted on ahead of the caravan, taking for granted that our object was hunting and not climbing mountains; now and then he would stop and gaze earnestly up at the heights to right or left. There was hardly a spot on either side of the valley that he did not carefully examine all the way from our camp in the morning to Tupungato; and very careful examination is needed, as anybody who has stalked deer in the Highlands will easily believe, for guanaco, even in great herds, are difficult to see, especially when at a great height. So we worked our way, choosing the best route, now on one side of the river, now on the other, often forced to wade in the river-bed itself. At last we found ourselves about a hundred feet above it on an old guanaco track. This was doubtless good enough for the guanaco, but another story for laden mules and horses. I rode on ahead, and, having passed the difficulty, came down again into the river-bed, where I halted and awaited the caravan. Our course next lay along the bed of the stream, which again widened out, and, to our astonishment, we saw, far in the distance, a great bank of green grass leading down to the water's edge—an ideal spot for a night's camp after a hard day. It was getting dark, and we made all haste to reach this pleasant resting-place. But the banks were steep, and springs above had rendered the grass at the river's edge far too wet and sodden for camping, so we determined to ascend the bank and see what we could find above. This move was disastrous; the whole place was a swamp; the mules began to plunge violently, and Fortunato had his work cut out for him to get them down again. Two mules fell and had to be unloaded as they lay. I was fortunate in striking a drier route. Looking back, I saw Fortunato and his pony frantically struggling in a bog. The animal—only a young one, but as clever on its feet as a monkey—recovered itself for a moment, and then fell sideways down the bank. Fortunato was equal to the occasion. As soon as he felt his horse falling, he threw himself down the bank clear of the horse, and it was well he did so, for the animal did not recover itself till it had turned completely over several times. Fortunato had fallen head foremost into the bog, and had to be dragged out by Lanti.

The party reached the terrace above quite worn out, and

some of its members far from dry or clean. We looked around once more for a camping-ground. Instead of the usual arid waste, we were surprised to see that the springs had created a small oasis—two small ponds at the foot of the hills surrounded by coarse grass.

CHAPTER XVI

BY STUART VINES

THE FIRST ATTACK ON TUPUNGATO

AS we approached the camping-ground in the dusk of the long and trying day I have described, we saw that a little tragedy of animal life was about to be enacted. On the water were a few ducks, and at the far side, creeping down between the rocks, we spied a very large dog-fox intent on supping. Our approach was unnoticed both by the hunter and prey. But where was Paramillo? There was no need to ask. He had taken in the whole situation long before, and was intent on stalking the stalker. The ducks, now scared, rose and flew away. Alarmed at this, Reynard looked up, caught sight of Paramillo, and in a moment turned and made straight up the mountain side with a good sixty yards' start, the dog in full pursuit. We watched for a minute, thinking that Reynard was running to earth and the chase would soon be over, but there was fine sport coming. The path up the steep mountain side suited Paramillo excellently, for he gained at every yard; so the fox changed its course, and sweeping round, began to descend. Fortunato loosened his bolas and handled them affectionately.

It was a splendid contest of speed. They swept down the mountain side at a tremendous pace, and no sooner had they reached the valley some two hundred yards from us than Fortunato clapped spurs to his horse and galloped full tilt over the rocks after them, swinging his bolas and shouting at the top of his voice to the hound. A jingle of spurs, and the whole field was swinging recklessly down the wide terrace towards the river. For weary riders and tired steeds, over

The Base Camp, Tupungato.

ground strewn with rocks and boulders, and deeply scarred by quebradas—down one side and up the other—the pace was certainly trying. We heeded nothing, only too glad to break the monotony of the long day in such glorious fashion. After half a mile or so, I found myself tearing down a dry torrent bed with Fortunato in front, the rest of the field nowhere, Paramillo within thirty yards of the fox and still gaining. We lost sight of them for a moment, and then suddenly the arriero, without drawing rein, slipped from his saddle and disappeared from view. I galloped up and jumped off. In the hollow beneath me the fox had turned to bay. But for the fact that Fortunato was dancing round with bolas ready, waiting for an opportunity to use them, there was little to choose between the combatants, for the fox was far bigger than his fellow of the shires. It was going to be a splendid fight. After the first rush they fell over and over, snarling and snapping. Nothing could have been more clever than the guanaco hound's tactics. He threw the fox off and stood waiting for an opening. Fortunato saw his chance and rushed forward to brain the animal with his bolas. But an ugly snap at his wrist made him draw back, and the hound, rushing in, got the fox by the throat. Dog and master had played this scene before and understood each other perfectly. Again the beasts separated, and we tried to interfere, but again Paramillo seized the throat, this time in so firm a grasp that for ten minutes no persuasion could make him let go. When the contest was at an end we examined the hound for wounds, and found that he had come off without a single scratch.

In triumph we carried Reynard back to the ponds and green grass. In size he was, as I have said, far larger than the English fox, and tawny rather than red in colour. Zurbriggen did the skinning while we prepared supper. This episode sealed the bond of friendship between the dog and ourselves. Paramillo no longer regarded the gringos with suspicion; he received our congratulations with delight, became a favourite with us all, and enlivened many an hour in camp by his playful ways and great intelligence.

We had made a considerable ascent since the morning, and it was now both dark and cold. There was plenty of yareta, no longer indeed a tree or even a bush, but a crawling humble weed, hardly a foot high, and all root. For purposes of firewood this was a distinct advantage, and its blaze enabled us to sleep again in the open. Soon we were snoring in a circle round the fire, while Paramillo, still useful in the night hours, curled himself round his master's feet and protected them from the frost.

Next day, Saturday, 27th March, a somewhat late start was made. The animals when disturbed at their morning meal showed more reluctance to move than ever. While they were being laden I took a look round. High above us a mighty glacier peeped over the eastern slope of the valley, its ice and snow sparkling in the early sunshine—a delightful spectacle after the bleak rocks on which our eyes had rested so long. I saw in it a great resemblance to the glacier of the Weisshorn, as seen from Randa. No doubt it was an offshoot of the La Plata group, which should lie not far to the east of it. Every man saddled his own beast, for saddles need careful adjusting when numerous sheepskins, ponchos, and cloths, part of one's bedclothes, act as a foundation. It is this custom of "packing" beneath the saddle that gives the mounted arriero in the Andes an appearance of such great height. Except the clothes on the rider's back, everything he carries goes under the saddle.

As we started we looked eagerly ahead, knowing that we must be nearing the precincts of the giant with whom we had come to do battle.

Still for many hours the mountain remained hidden. Soon after midday we ascended the valley side, and looking ahead I beheld a memorable scene. The valley spread itself out and divided, and Tupungato, from base to summit, rose before us. An immense distance still separated us from its white height. The huge mass threw out spurs and ridges, topped with dark pinnacles of rock. A spur of gigantic proportions ran out some six miles northwards, towering high above the heights around, yet itself several thousand feet lower than the dome.

Beneath us a wide plain marked the confluence of the valleys, and everywhere lay perfect and wonderful examples of Darwin's sloping terraces, their bare gravel surfaces dotted alternately, and at regular intervals of about a yard, with low stumps of yareta and tufts of coarse grass. We rejected the southern valley and chose the one to the right, leading directly to the mountain. Ahead of us this valley was again divided by one of the off-shoots of Tupungato pinnacled by aiguilles, the left branch pointing to the dome, the right in the direction of Pollera.

Having ascended a gentle gradient all the way from Vacas, we had attained a height of 10,000 feet. We saw no valley that would conduct our mules to 14,000 feet, as the Horcones Valley did in the case of Aconcagua, for where the ridge of rocks divided the valley, the ascent became suddenly more abrupt and vegetation entirely ceased. The ramparts of Tupungato were evidently much more formidable than those of Aconcagua.

This introduced serious obstacles. Our base camp would have to be made at a low altitude: the way was inaccessible for further mule transport after that point, everything would have to be carried on men's backs to a far greater height, and our porterage was extremely limited.

It was still early in the day, and we determined to push on as far as possible, hoping that we might take camp and mules up higher. We ascended to our left by a steep route, where there was pasturage, but no means of obtaining water, for the torrent was in a cleft far beneath us. We looked on ahead up a steep and narrow gorge. Would it be possible to take animals up it? Another fifteen hundred feet would make all the difference. Anyhow a retreat was necessary, for water and pasturage we must have at our base of operations. So we returned and made our camp in the valley beneath, and in the afternoon I set off with Zurbriggen to make a reconnaissance. Above the gorge the valley side was too steep for mule traffic; the torrent bed would be dangerous from ice in the morning and from the rush of water later in the day, while the other side was formed of a confused mass of sharp broken stones for the greater part of the way. Baffled, we retraced our steps to the camp, supped, and discussed the situation. Zurbriggen, not to be put off by obstacles of this kind, and sanguine of success, proposed to me to give up all idea of a night on the mountain and make the ascent in one journey from the base camp. I replied it would be the longest day's climb I had ever attempted, but that I was ready, if he thought it possible—so little at the time did we appreciate the immense distance that separated us from the mountain. Eventually, our ideas moderated, and we decided to spend Sunday, the 28th, as high up as possible, and try to reach the summit on Monday.

Lanti and Pollinger started off early next morning on horses, with the strongest mule laden with the barest necessities for a night on the mountain, while Zurbriggen and I made our way down to the stream in order to soak our boots thoroughly before starting; a very necessary precaution where the dryness of the climate so affects the leather that the nails become loose and are easily wrenched out by the rough ground.

As we hurried after Lanti and Fortunato, by a somewhat different route than that of the day before, we began to realise heights and distances better, and again discussed the matter of transport. Our experiences on Aconcagua had taught us that one of the surest obstacles to success in climbing to great heights was anything approaching to inertia caused by fatigue, and we had always been careful to take a day's rest before attempting an ascent. Now we saw ourselves forced to carry heavy loads some four thousand feet if we hoped to make a bivouac at about 14,000 feet, and to lose a day might be fatal so late in the season. There was but one thing to do—the mule must somehow be got up another two or three thousand feet.

We found the caravan waiting for us above the gorge, Fortunato about to unload and return. We explained to him the situation and our intentions, and after a good look at the route he said he would do his best, but asked us to take all responsibility of accidents to the animals.

We reached the torrent bed without mishap. Progress was very slow; we three kept pushing the mule from behind, while Fortunato gave a lead by manfully riding, or rather scrambling ahead on horseback. He refused to dismount, saying that where he could go his horse could carry him. The beast kept his feet in wonderful fashion in ice and water; far better in fact than I did, for stepping on an ice-covered boulder, I struck the inside of my left knee against a rock. I suffered acute pain for the moment, and then thought no more about it.

Thus we reached a height of 12,000 feet, and Fortunato said he could go no farther. Indeed it looked as if he were right; the water poured over the rocks ahead, and for the moment I did not see how we ourselves were to get out of this *cul-de-sac*. Zurbriggen descended a short distance and found a way out of the gorge on what appeared like moraine above. This was a great discovery; the going on the moraine was comparatively easy, and we were able to ascend another five hundred feet. There was no doubt about this being the animal's limit; so, unloading, we sent Fortunato back, and spreading out the baggage, made yet another selection, reducing its weight still further by leaving behind the Mummery tent and Robert's valises. Lanti carried the sleeping-bags and provisions; Zurbriggen and I the extra clothing, photographic and other instruments.

I shall not easily forget that fifteen hundred feet up the steep moraine, which seemed to fill the head of the valley. I was suffering agonies, for when half-way up a sharp pain had followed the blow on my left knee. By loosening putties, knee-straps, and garters I gained some little relief, but for the last five hundred feet I was almost dead lame.

At three o'clock we reached the summit of the moraine and the end of the valley. We were in a kind of basin about 14,000 feet above the sea, filled with moraine heaps and the remnants of a glacier, shut in on all but the north-east side, by which we had made our approach. On two sides of us black cliffs towered high above; on the south an enormous ladder of *nieve penitente*, rising some two thousand feet, showed the obvious route to the summit. The encircling heights afforded good shelter from storm and wind, and we threw down our packs. It was a wild and desolate spot, the only outlook being down the valley towards our base camp, where we saw Fortunato still struggling in the torrent bed. He had probably found the descent as bad as the ascent, or he would have reached the camp before this.

We scooped out a sleeping-ground with our axes beneath the shelter of a boulder, with a wall of ice on one side, and the torrent on the other, but having neither food nor sleeping-bags for three men in case of emergencies, we sent Lanti back to the valley camp, with orders to come up as early as possible in the morning to relieve us with our loads on the ascent.

My knee being still very painful, I feared I should be unable to start on the morrow. Loosening everything in order to secure free circulation, I kept descending to the torrent, and applying cold compresses until late in the night. I imagined I had bruised a vein. At last I took a block of ice and placed it on the painful part inside my stocking, and turned in. This proved a painful but excellent remedy.

Lanti's voice from below roused us early next day. He appeared fresh and well, and said he was going to the top with us. A sample of the weather in the shape of racing grey clouds appeared above the aiguilles to the north-west, and our hearts sank. We made straight for the *nieve penitente* wall to the south. The wearisome monotony of ascending between these pinnacles of ice which rose in steps never less than two feet in height,[1] for nearly three hours, was most trying, especially for me, for I did not dare to make full use of my left leg. We were more weary than we had bargained for when we reached the top of the ladder, and for the first time a feeling of disappointment and doubt took hold of us.

[1] The illustration opposite p. 174, from a photograph taken half-way up these needles at 15,000 feet, gives a good view of similar smaller ladders of *nieve penitente*, with Pollera and Navarro in the background. Our route lay to the left of the illustration.

Before us a snow plateau stretched to the base of the huge northern spur. This enormous mass rose 1500 feet above the plateau, and by a gentle gradient, ascended to the dome. Beneath us the ridges were topped by a succession of savage aiguilles.

"Look? What's that?" we exclaimed simultaneously. What was that dark mass to the north that for the moment blotted out all other thoughts? It was Aconcagua, startling in its magnitude at sixty miles away, overwhelming in its solitude and isolation. If this is what we see from the lower slopes of Tupungato, what magnificence of view is yet to come! We pushed on over the snowfield to the base of the spur.

The distance, however, utterly deceived us, as indeed did all heights and distances on Tupungato, and an hour passed before we arrived, depressed and weary, at its base. We struck the ridge many miles from the summit, almost at its lowest point, and sat down to rest. Lanti now looked up at the crumbling slopes of the spur above us, and said he could go no farther. The announcement coming from so strong a man, depressed us still more, and foreboding failure, Zurbriggen and I took what we most needed from his pack and continued the ascent without him. Two hours of weary toiling up the rotten surface of the slope brought us to the summit of the spur. In an instant our field of vision was doubled. All Chile lay before us, but the enormous width of the spur prevented us from seeing the extent of the valleys immediately beneath it. The increasing grandeur of the scene had the effect of rousing our ambition, and we turned upwards once more towards the dome.

It was half-past one, we were a little over 18,000 feet, and for two more hours we tramped up the never-ending gentle slope; the dome came nearer and nearer, but we never seemed to reach it. How sadly had we underestimated the distance to be traversed!

And now came the *coup de grâce* to our hopes of success. Clouds that had been rolling up all day from the west gathered round the dome, burst in storm, and rolled down its sides towards us. The sturdy Lanti, starting from the lower camp at 10,000 feet, had broken down after ascending some 6000 feet. We had reached a height of 19,000 feet, having started at 14,000, and were both thoroughly tired out. We sat down under the scanty shelter of a boulder, and decided to retreat,[1] realising better the great difficulty of the task before us, and bearing in mind the scantiness of our porterage, equipment, and provisions, the lateness of the season, and the necessity of a return to Vacas before another attempt could be made. All we could do was to leave a record of our ascent thus far. So I placed a card in a bottle at the foot of the boulder, announcing that Zurbriggen and I had been driven back from this ridge by storm on the 29th of March 1897.

[1] The surface of this spur, or satellite, of Tupungato is composed of debris, with here and there boulders of moderate size rising from it. It is from one thousand to two thousand yards in width, and slopes towards the dome at a gradient of about one in six. Not a sign of snow or ice is to be seen upon its surface, though its south-east side near the dome is similar to the south-east face of Aconcagua, sheer rock and ice fall from base to summit. No mountain side could be more exposed to the fury of the wind, and, as in the case of the north-west slopes of Aconcagua, the nature of its surface is no doubt due to its being swept clean by the terrific force of the wind.

NIEVE PENITENTE ON TUPUNGATO

CHAPTER XVII

BY STUART VINES

MORE ATTEMPTS ON TUPUNGATO

WE turned our backs on the summit and retraced our steps, and such relief did the descent of this gentle slope afford us that we halted and debated whether we could not yet make the ascent, so near did the base of the dome appear. But we had misjudged distances the whole day, there was a storm—no doubt the chronic storm spoken of by our friends at Vacas—raging round the summit, and we turned to descend to the snow plateau.

The *nieve penitente* ladder was not reached till five, and the monotony of the steps, like unending pyramids, exhausted us. In comparison, after a long rest at the night bivouac, where we found Lanti, the descent to the main camp seemed child's play.

As we neared the camp, feeling thoroughly disheartened, Paramillo came bounding up the hill, greeting us in his own boisterous fashion. We tried to explain to him that we were returning defeated, but he heeded not,—we had returned from that stupid mountaineering, and had evidently now come down to hunt guanaco with him.

The next morning everything was packed inside the tent, the guy-ropes and poles slackened to let it collapse, and half convinced that the Argentine stories of chronic storms on Tupungato were something more than a superstitious exaggeration, we started for Vacas. More tents and provisions would be required, and, above all, more porters. We had hardly started before Paramillo spied a large herd of guanaco moving along at a great height above us, and tried to lure us on to hunting. It was a long time before we ourselves could see them, as the slopes they were crossing were almost identically the same colour as the skins of the moving herd. Paramillo looked appealingly at us, received a word of encouragement from Fortunato, and made straight up the mountain side to head them off and drive them down to us. Should we join in the chase? It would take us considerably out of our way, and after all, were we after guanaco or Tupungato? It could not be both. So calling Paramillo in, we hurried on to Vacas.

I had changed my horse and was now riding an animal we called the White-eyed Kaffir, from a white patch that surrounded one eye—certainly the ugliest quadruped I had ever set eyes on, but perfect in slippery places, so I took Fortunato's advice and did not dismount when we came to the scene of our previous troubles. When we came to the quebrada where the mule had fallen, Fortunato treated us to an exhibition of the qualities of his pony. Galloping up to it, his horse hesitated on the very edge; down came his huge spurs upon its sides, and man and beast toppled over the cliff together. I hastened up and saw the game little beast sometimes sliding on its haunches, sometimes jumping down the steeper places where the rocks appeared, now swinging to one side, now to another to avoid obstacles, but keeping up the same break-neck pace the whole two hundred feet to the torrent bed below. Zurbriggen was filled with admiration, and promptly made overtures for the purchase of the animal. He was impatient to conclude the bargain on the spot, saying that was just the horse for him, and though he had to wait, as it was Fiorini's property, he bought it as soon as he reached Vacas. The price, I believe, was forty dollars—not quite £3.

The weather changed again, and at sunset we could see Tupungato clear and peaceful once more, after the storm that had raged around it all day. So Zurbriggen and I left the pack-mules, now unladen, early in the morning, hurried on, and reached the mouth of the Tupungato Valley at noon on the second day. I proceeded at once to Inca to find

VILLA SIEJA'S FAREWELL

FitzGerald and make arrangements for another attack at once.

It was not until the 2nd April that I could again start for Vacas. On the way I overtook a horseman magnificently apparelled in a flowing black poncho lined and faced with red, a wide sombrero, and the usual gigantic spurs. It was no other than old Villa Sieja, a shepherd and arriero who had always taken a most fatherly interest in our movements. But why this holiday attire? After the first greetings—he was a most courtly old gentleman—I told him I was going to Tupungato, and asked him where he was off to in this royal fashion. He muttered the word "Tupungato" several times in a sad voice, and then said, "To-day, señor, I leave the mountains for the plains of Mendoza. It is my habit always to do so on the 1st of April, when winter begins. I am a day late. I am going for a hard-earned holiday with my friends. My two sons left yesterday. In the course of a week all these valleys may be blocked with snow. One never can tell after the 1st of April. So the señor is going to Tupungato? Has he not seen the numerous little crosses on the pass road?"

I tried to get him to take a more cheerful view of the situation, but at Vacas he bade me a solemn farewell with "courtly foreign grace," saying he was sorry not to see "el Jefe del Expedicion" to warn him of coming disaster, and departed with the remark that it was a matter of great grief to him that such a fine young señor should be doomed to so early and terrible a death.

Long before daybreak on Saturday, 3rd April, Zurbriggen packed off Fortunato and the caravan of pack animals. We had now with us Joseph Pollinger and Lochmatter, besides Lanti; also extra mules, all picked animals, laden with three weeks' provisions. Every man was mounted in order to save as much time as possible, as I hoped, by forcing the pace, to be able to reach our Tupungato camp in two days.

An English physician in Valparaiso, Dr. Cannon, had been very anxious that we should try a herb used for relieving both men and animals at high altitudes in Bolivia and Peru. In consequence of a letter from Dr. Cannon to FitzGerald,[1] I had written to our friend Mr. Ball, in Valparaiso, and he had most kindly put himself to a great deal of trouble in procuring me some of the herb.

The directions were :

> FOR MEN.—A cup of tea made from the herb with boiling-water in the morning, or to be smelt frequently while ascending; even at times chewing the dry herb.
>
> FOR ANIMALS.—A bunch tied to the bit, so that the mule inhales its strong odour while ascending.

During this journey and attack on Tupungato, I gave *chacha coma* a trial. I considered that if there were any merit in the herb, it would be well to get the whole party used to it, by making a brew two or three times a day from the time we left Vacas. It has the appearance of a dried-up bramble, bright yellow in colour, and with a yellow-white flower

---

[1] 323 BLANCO, VALPARAISO,
10th March 1897.

DEAR SIR,—As one who, although a stranger to you, takes an interest in your explorations, I venture to give you a hint which may be of use in your future mountain ascents.

Some years since a man came into contact with me as a physician, and he had just come from the higher Andes of Bolivia where he was surveying. He told me that a plant called by the natives "Chacha Coma" was found there growing near the snowline, and that it was a most wonderful remedy for "puna" or shortness of breathing caused by rarefied air, both for men and animals such as mules. He said that by smelling the plant, or tying a bunch under the nostrils of the mules, the breathing immediately became easy. He promised to send me a sack, in order to try it medicinally in asthma, etc., but the sack never turned up.

This was some twelve years since. Last Saturday the same gentleman came in again to see me, and reminded me of my promise to send the plant, saying that he had not returned to this district afterwards.

I said, "Why, that is the very thing for Mr. FitzGerald, since the great difficulty in scaling great altitudes seems to be the difficult breathing."

He promised at some future time to send the herb, which may be most useful medicinally.

I do not know the man's name but he lives in Huasco, is a civil engineer, and is now in the city here awaiting instructions about some railway to Huanillos salt deposits. He is to be found at Messrs. Vaughan & Co., merchants here, Calle Blanco, and I have no doubt will provide you with the plant and give you all information, so as to make a trial in your coming explorations. I have no doubt that "Excelsior" is your motto, and that perhaps you will even have a try at Mount Everest later on.

Wishing you success.—I am, your obedient servant,

DR. RICHARD CANNON.

A BOLIVIAN HERB 179

somewhat resembling edelweiss. Sticks and leaves were put each morning into a saucepan, boiling-water poured on, and the whole left to soak a minute or two. Sugar was used according to taste. Then, calling up the porters, I served half a cup all round. Each one would drink, thank me, and say it was very good. But they never asked for more, and I feel sure there was far more politeness than sincerity in their gratitude. Doctors say that a great many patients amongst the working-classes of England think nothing of a remedy unless it has either a striking colour, a nasty taste, or a strong smell. If the last two qualities are proof of a medicine's value, then *chacha coma* must be an excellent remedy, for it possesses a distinctly nasty taste and has a very strong pungent smell.

During this second journey up the Tupungato Valley, as we had two extra porters to help us, I made a point of having all the animals unloaded over the bad places. No doubt considerable delay was caused by this, but we made up for it on the good ground, and reached the Tupungato camp late on the afternoon of Sunday the 4th.

Soon after we had reached the camp an extraordinary incident occurred. The porters were busy getting the tent up, and Zurbriggen and I were sitting at the camp-fire drinking the tea of the *yerba maté*, which we invariably indulged in at our lower camps, when I noticed a whirlwind on the top of the high terrace bank opposite. Though we felt no wind at all where we were, columns of dust quite fifty feet in height were moving along the top of the bank, blades of grass, small sticks from the yareta, and even large stones being whirled along. Soon we noticed that the roaring noise accompanying the phenomenon was increasing, that the columns increased in size, and that there were now three of them. And here my observations ceased, for I suddenly felt as if I had been hit violently over the head, was knocked backwards and fell to the ground, with what seemed to me half the camp-fire in my face. My gourd of boiling maté went all over my face, and I was insensible for a minute or so—it was lucky the boiling-point was low. When I looked round I found that

Zurbriggen was also sprawling on the ground. The porters, arranging the Barrow tent twenty yards away, felt nothing, and the tent was uninjured. It took some time to get things together. The fire had been completely blown from its grate of stones, our store of thornwood was scattered over the hillside. Plates, mugs, and wooden boxes had sailed away up the hill behind us to a distance of a hundred yards. I much regretted that I had not been a spectator of the whole incident. Something had hit me hard between the eyes, and I had a big swelling on the back of my head, where I think I must have struck a boulder behind me. I vowed as I rubbed my sores that in future I would not sit and criticise when the wind became frolicsome, but take proper precautions.

As I had been riding now for two days, I determined to do some hard walking, so started up the steep grass slope at the back of the camp with the intention of trying to get a view of the sky low down to the north-west where all the storms originated. I tried my powers to the utmost, both legs and lungs, and after two hours reached the camp in the dark. Fortunato had prepared *pochero* for supper, an inevitable dish that one can never escape in this part of the world, consisting of boiled beef, potatoes, onions, and sometimes cabbage, served in more civilised parts in a soup plate with much gravy.

And now for our plan of action. I urged strongly the advisability of making a night bivouac some three thousand feet higher than on the first attack, in order to lessen the distance of the final ascent. But Zurbriggen pointed out that now we had Lochmatter and Joseph this would hardly be necessary. They would be able to take all the burden of the packs off our shoulders; moreover, he had been making a careful examination of the slopes of the great spur, and had discovered a shorter route that would enable us to avoid the loose surface and take us from the snow plateau almost straight on to the dome. We therefore decided to sleep once more at the old 14,000 foot bivouac.

We were disturbed in unceremonious fashion from our

slumbers next morning by Paramillo bursting through the fastenings of the tent, and dancing a species of sword-dance on the top of us. It was useless to protest, as we were prisoners in our sleeping-bags. There was no necessity for an early start, so, after a substantial breakfast and the usual ordeal of *chacha coma*, the porters started up at ten. Two strong mules were laden with provisions and sleeping-bags for five men for two days. Zurbriggen and I started at noon and reached the limit for mules soon after two. On our way up the steep moraine we met Lanti returning with a sad face and a tale of woe. He had had the misfortune to break a bottle of wine. We did not spare him in our remarks on the subject, and he calmly sat down on the debris and wept bitterly, where we left him. Zurbriggen seemed much moved by this little incident, and said this was another peculiar instance of the effects of the altitude. "Here is Lanti Nicola, the stoutest-hearted man I ever knew, a terrible fellow in the Valley of Macugnaga. For when the report goes round that Lanti is on the war-path all the inhabitants shut themselves in their houses and bar the doors. And now he breaks a bottle of wine and it breaks his heart, and he cries like a child." The thermometer dropped rapidly at the bivouac as soon as the sun left us, and the water froze on the cups and spoons while Zurbriggen was washing them. However, we had the luxury of a tent, and passed a good night.

It was perfect weather, but intensely cold when we started a few minutes after 6 a.m. to make our second attempt on Tupungato. We reached the snow plateau at 8.45 and halted for breakfast, to which I alone did justice. The guides were content with a sip or two of wine and a few raisins. Now Zurbriggen showed us his new route. Instead of crossing the snow plateau as before to the foot of the great spur, we turned to the south, and ascended the spur, close to where it joined the dome, up the rocks, using the rope—a much more interesting route than by the crumbling side of the ridge. The weather still continued bright, though the cold, in spite of the sun and the good pace we were making, was still very bitter. A rest was taken on the top of the rocks. We sat down with our faces to the east, and it was a wonderful sight which disclosed itself to our view. We had ascended high enough to look over the single range to the east, and the endless pampas of Argentina lay beneath us. It was astonishing to me to find ourselves so close to the eastern limit of the Cordilleras. I saw also for the first time the continuation of the main Tupungato Valley, from the point where we had left it to form a camp on the 27th. It ran round to the south-eastern side of Tupungato. And there this great valley that we had ascended for over forty miles terminated—not in glacier, as I fully expected, but in a lake, the water of which looked muddy brown, like the waters of the Nile. Could this be the lake of gold of which our friend at Vacas had told us such glowing stories?

Double gloves and helmets were now a necessity, and yet we were still in comparative shelter. What, then, would be the temperature on the top of the great exposed ridge? At 11.30, after cutting steps for some little distance,[1] we found ourselves on the summit of the spur, with the dome rising up on our left, seemingly close to us. All eyes were at once directed to north and west. What was our fate going to be? A few fleecy clouds were coming from the Pacific. That Tupungato was going to indulge in his usual afternoon storm we felt certain, but we were in good time, and ought to be up and down again long before that occurred. We were not deceived in our forebodings as regards the temperature, and we emptied the rücksacks for all the extra clothing available. We were making our way southward to the dome, and the wind struck the right side of our faces with such bitter force that we could no longer look ahead. Besides this, we were on debris again, with the inevitable result that we began to feel the exhaustion caused by an altitude of over 19,000 feet, and soon found a long rest necessary. Zurbriggen gazed anxiously to the north-west, and asked me if I didn't think it better to take some photographs, as he was not quite easy about the pace at which those clouds seemed to be approaching.

[1] Right hand side of illustration opposite p. 186.

It was too cold to remain long. We were huddled together on the leeward side of a rock, round which the wind whistled mercilessly. It was now midday, and from this time on everything went badly with us. The wind became more violent, the cold increased, the storm-clouds drew nearer and nearer, a sullen persistency about them foretelling mischief. Juncal and the Leones were already wrapped in storm. Worse than this, Zurbriggen began to be very sick. He had no doubt been feeling ill for some time, but had said nothing about it. His voice was full of chagrin as he confessed his condition to me. He could not understand it. He had never felt like this before. He tried a little port wine, and said he could get on if we went a little slower. He looked very bad, however, and groaned at every step. Certainly he was in no condition to continue the ascent. But nothing would make him turn back, though he was suffering intense pain, and the effort of will he exercised in continuing was truly heroic.

Another mishap also occurred. We missed Lochmatter! But looking back we saw him shuffling up the gentle sloping debris so slowly that he seemed almost motionless. We shouted to ask what was the matter. He answered feebly, and as if ashamed to confess it: "Nothing's the matter: it's my legs, I can't make it out; they won't work any more." It was a ridiculous situation. Here was a strong and powerful young fellow, with a splendid physique, carrying but the lightest of loads, saying that nothing was the matter but that his legs had given out. I had had experience of this paralysis of the lower limbs on Aconcagua, and recognised the necessity of sending him back. We told him to continue down the gentle slope of the ridge for a couple of hundred yards, and signal to us if power had returned at all to his legs. He said he was sure they would be all right as soon as he began to descend. The signal was given, and as Joseph was still strong and Zurbriggen said he felt a trifle better, we continued to struggle with the elements. But the clouds had reached their old playground, the dome, and I began to realise that the peak might be again snatched from us by storm. But as we were now ascending the dome itself, we imagined we were at a height of 21,000 feet, and therefore could not be far from our goal. We sought shelter every ten minutes, finding it impossible for any length of time to beat up against the wind, which forced us out of our course like boats without keels going to leeward. Zurbriggen grew worse, and at two o'clock, on coming to an overhanging rock, we made a protracted halt. It was at anyrate an intense relief to get out of the wind, and we determined to wait for half an hour and see if there was any chance of the storm abating. After a bit I crept up above our sheltering rock to see if any improvement had taken place, and saw at once it was hopeless to wait. The whole sky looked threatening, and as a matter of fact, if the sky had cleared, I do not think we could have reached the summit. Indeed I doubt if under any circumstances it would be possible to reach the summit from our bivouac at 14,000 feet,—certainly not at this time of year. We told one another we were but six hundred feet from the summit, but it is a common error in the Andes to imagine one is but a few hundred feet from the top when one is really three times that distance from it. I came down and joined the other two, almost perished with cold. Zurbriggen's condition was alarming, the storm reached far below us, enveloping the great spur and the air was thick with clouds. It would have been madness to proceed or even to delay. This was to be our last attempt, for the season was now over, and with bitter feelings I followed Zurbriggen and Joseph down to the spur. For Zurbriggen's sake, we went very slowly for a long time, and he gradually got better as we descended. At five o'clock we found Lanti preparing some hot brandy and water at the night bivouac, and certainly Zurbriggen needed something of the kind. He lay down and said he could not go a step farther, but the stimulant revived him, and after I had described the luxuries of a night at the base camp in sufficiently glowing terms, he consented to continue the descent.

Paramillo's joy at our return was unbounded, but Fortunato

greeted us with the remark that he knew we could never succeed, and went on to preach the philosophy of the school of the courtly Villa Sieja, telling us that we should be snowed up and never get back to Vacas if we did not start soon.

I felt more convinced than ever that the great distance to be traversed, the effects of the altitude, and the shortness of the days, made it impossible to ascend the mountain from so low a level as 14,000 feet at this season of the year. Yet everyone seemed too dispirited to accept the suggestion that I had at heart; namely, that we should carry our night bivouac some three thousand feet higher up the mountain and make yet another attempt; so we turned in with the order for a return to Vacas the next day uncancelled.

I never saw men drink so much tea as we all did the next morning. One brew after another was made and finished: our thirst seemed unquenchable. After an effort to slake it had been made, however, I propounded my plans: "Now, Mattias, we will rest here to-day, make a bivouac below the spur at 17,000 feet, and you and I and Joseph will sleep there to-morrow night. From there we will make the ascent the day after, and return triumphantly with the top of Tupungato to Vacas on the 10th."

Zurbriggen pointed out the great risk we ran from frost-bite in sleeping up at those heights so late in the season, with the nights so long and the days so short, but after some discussion it was decided to wait and see what the weather would be. We were all thankful to lie about and rest. We watched the storm-clouds moving about the summit of Tupungato all the morning, and could see that the wind had not yet abated.

I wished very much to use this day of rest in exploring the main valley and the Rio Tupungato to its source, and examining the shores of the "lake of gold." So after the midday meal I set off on horseback with Zurbriggen and a camera. We had a very fine view up a side valley of the whole south-eastern face of Tupungato,[1] examined the summit of the dome, and adhered to our opinion that the highest point

[1] Illustration opposite p. 186.

was at its northern extremity. This was from a distance of some nine or ten miles. Then after some two hours of feats of horsemanship amongst snow and ice, we found we could ride no farther, and as we wished to reserve our legs for Tupungato, we retraced our steps without getting as far as the lake.

The 8th April was a fine morning, with no wind. Preparations were immediately made for restocking a new bivouac at 17,000 feet,—some three thousand feet higher than the old one,—and the three porters were sent off at eight o'clock. Zurbriggen and I reached the summit of the *nieve penitente*, made our way across the snow plateau, and about four in the afternoon reached the foot of the great spur, where, some little distance on the rocks above us, we espied the porters still busily pitching the tent. Lanti and Lochmatter had carried the heaviest loads, and were now sent back to the base camp, with instructions to come up and meet us on the following day. Lochmatter had proved, many a time, that 19,000 feet was the greatest altitude he could attain, while Lanti had tired on the first attempt, and had not the slightest ambition to make the ascent. As Joseph Pollinger had been fit and well, so far, we determined to keep him with us. The little tent was pitched lengthways against some cliffs forming part of the spur, the opening to the north. The whole sky was dull and overcast, but the clouds were high. It was, however, comparatively warm, and altogether I did not like the look of things at all. So when Zurbriggen proposed that the descending porters had better come up at midday and take everything down, whether we were successful or not, I demurred. However, they were all so strongly against making further attempts should this one fail, that I reserved my persuasions for a more favourable time, and contented myself with the order that the tent should not be moved on any account. Our quarters were not what could be called spacious for three by no means small men—$3\frac{1}{2} \times 4 \times 6$ feet for three men would be overcrowding even in a London slum. The tent was the lightest we had, with separate flooring of macintosh sheeting, and supported only by ice-axes at each

TUPUNGATO FROM THE EAST

A TERRIBLE NIGHT

end and numerous ropes. During the evening I took care to keep the conversation from turning to the all-important subject of the weather, for the stillness and warmth of the air foreboded no good, and I avoided a discouraging topic. Joseph ensconced himself near the rocks, Zurbriggen in the middle, and I on the outside. Our overcrowded state gave warmth if it did not give comfort. The ground beneath us was intensely cold, and indeed this was not to be wondered at, for we subsequently discovered the porters had pitched the tent on debris-covered glacier.

I had slept about three hours when I was suddenly awakened by a tremendous roaring sound, which seemed to come from far above us to the south. To describe it I cannot do better than quote my remarks written on the spot:—"THURSDAY, 8th April 1897. Zurbriggen, Pollinger, and self bivouacked in small tent, 17,000 feet, base of great spur, on rocks close to ice. Calm and warm outside when we fell asleep at 8 p.m. Awful noise from above me to south woke me. It must be thunder. I listened intently. No, it is wind—but there is no wind. Around the tent it is motionless. Roaring above continues, increases, becomes deafening. Zurbriggen and Pollinger start up. Both declare it is thunder, but come round to my opinion that it is an awful storm raging round the dome of Tupungato—for that is its direction. All hopes of an ascent on the morrow are therefore at an end. Tent in dangerous position right beneath rocks. A pitch-dark night, the cold intense, can't decamp, impossible to find our way down. Our only alternative to remaining to move on to the snowfield. The noise increases, the storm is evidently growing in strength and approaching. Lying and listening—sleep out of the question, the roar is awful—like Niagara—impossible to hear one another speak. The storm is upon us—grasp the ice-axes to keep the tent from being wrecked. Sleeping-bags no protection. The icy wind penetrating everything cuts us through and through; glacier beneath. Sound of falling stones above—may be crushed any moment. But how can we move? Past midnight, storm furious—for three hours we lie huddled, fearing that some rock from above will crush the tent. The guy-ropes give way—complete wreck. The wind fallen a little at dawn—all exhausted fall asleep. Awoke at 6.30. No one spoke. Wind outside tells its own tale—madness to go higher. No human being can live on that great exposed ridge with hurricane at zero—crawl out—a hopeless dawn. Thermometer at 5°. Sit in silence, knowing we must retreat."

We all three recognised the inevitable, but no one liked to put it into words. This was the end of Tupungato for us. We sat in silence. However, we were miserably cold, and at eight o'clock made a stir in order to get something hot to drink. Pollinger suggested we should finish up everything and pull down the tent and decamp. We were too tired and too disheartened to move. I had no suggestions to make. There was no need to start early, so we eked out a miserable morning. But a thought struck me. A small flask of old liqueur whisky had been brought up for emergencies. Why not finish this too? I set about preparing it hot, with sugar, and gradually we threw off our depression. Zurbriggen and Pollinger sat up and had a hot argument about Alpine accidents, their causes, and how they should have been avoided, and when the question of retreat arose, I broke it to them that I intended, even now, to make another attempt, and proposed to leave the tent standing. I put it to them that after this tremendous storm we were sure to have a spell of fine weather. My keenness made me eloquent, the toddy made them indulgent, so that at noon we left everything as it was, and started down. Once more we had to confess our failure to the ever-energetic Paramillo.

Fortunato preferred the open, and always slept on the leeward side of our tent. We had given him a sleeping-bag the night before, and, with Paramillo curled round his feet, he had fallen asleep, muttering, "mucho lindo." The weather was nightmare enough to us all day, yet I dreamed that night that someone kept shouting, "Mucho malo tiempo! O malo, malo tiempo!" Then I awoke. It was dawn, and the voice was that of Fortunato outside. The words so exasperated me that my legs itched to kick him,—if the weather was still bad, he needn't advertise the fact,—but to a man in a sleeping-bag kicking is out of the question, so I contented myself with shouting to him that discussion must be confined only to *good* weather.

He was right, the weather was "mucho malo." Yet it might improve, so we rested a day—a day during which I wandered about ostensibly geologising, but really watching the weather in general, and the top of Tupungato in particular from every point of view. *Chacha coma* was served plentifully that day, and we had onions with all our meals. But all the herbs in the world won't change the weather, and it was with great anxiety that we looked out of the tent on the morrow.

Sunday, 11th April, was a glorious day. Cold it certainly was, but that was a good sign. Lanti and Lochmatter started early to provision the bivouac, and after the necessary soaking of our boots in the torrent Zurbriggen and I started at ten, and reached the high bivouac at four. It was a bright cold evening, and we were hopeful. Lanti and Lochmatter descended, while Zurbriggen, Pollinger, and I once more squeezed ourselves into the tiny tent for the night.

CHAPTER XVIII

BY STUART VINES

TUPUNGATO ASCENDED

OUR fourth attempt on Tupungato was made on 12th April. The night had been bitterly cold, and none of us slept very well. The small Mummery tent, in which I was packed with Zurbriggen and Joseph Pollinger, was now pitched in a safer position, where there was no danger of rocks from above falling on us, yet the ground underneath was still so near the ice that it chilled us to the bone as soon as we lay down. During the night the thermometer sank to 24° below freezing, but fortunately there was no wind — a great improvement on the zero with a hurricane of four nights before. Remembering our experience of frost-bite on Aconcagua in the early morning, we decided to risk nothing by climbing before sunrise. We had two alternatives before us, either to crawl out of our tent and start in the night-hours before sunrise, thereby spoiling a good night's rest, greatly needed, if not an absolute necessity for a day's work at such high altitudes, with the additional hardship of the cold of the early morning, and the risk this involved; or, on the other hand, to start, after taking something hot, at daybreak, and reach a height of 21,000 feet at one or two o'clock, the warmest time of the day, fortified by a good night's rest for that terrible last thousand feet, with the disadvantage, and risk, no doubt, of a descent after sunset, exhausted by the ascent. It was the cold and the wind we dreaded, especially so late in the season, and the cold was far less after sunset than before sunrise; therefore I think we pursued the least risky course, and the one most likely to lead to success, in starting late. It was half-past six before we crawled out of the tent, and there was no guessing what sort of weather was in store for us, as the western horizon, which always gave the best indication, was completely shut out from our view by the great wall of the spur under which we were encamped. We set to work to boil water for the coffee with the windproof kettle and spirit-stove; but again we had an example of the unwillingness of methylated spirits to burn quickly, for the water took an unconscionable time to boil. I ate some food, but the guides refused to do more than drink coffee. At seven we made a start. It was still intensely cold, and Zurbriggen and I set out in our ponchos—garments far better adapted for riding than for climbing. In selecting the route, our chief thought was how best to avoid the broken and crumbling surface over which we had already toiled.

This was now our third ascent of the spur. The first had been made by the broken slope on the northern side, which we had found very fatiguing, and the second by the rocks nearer to the actual dome of Tupungato, where the rope had been needed. Zurbriggen led us now by fairly firm ground half-way between the two previous lines of ascent, I came next, and Joseph Pollinger brought up the rear. This order was maintained during the greater part of the day. I knew well enough that this would be our last attack on the mountain—it was now or never. The season was already so far advanced that the rigours of winter were beginning to be felt, and the danger of frost-bite at these high altitudes had determined us, whatever might be the result of the fourth attempt, to leave Tupungato, and return to Vacas as soon as possible.

Nothing of any importance happened until we reached the top of the spur. Although we had chosen a fresh line of ascent, the soil underfoot was still much the same as before. There was the same dreary slipping on the rotten ground, the same relief when the ground was firm. As we ascended, the necessity for halts became gradually more frequent. It was at half-past nine, when we were some fifteen hundred feet above our camping-ground, that we reached the summit of the ridge, about 18,500 feet above sea-level. After ascending another five hundred feet, thinking it better to take a long rest before going farther, we sat down under a boulder and tried to make a meal.

Now I must discontinue the ascent for a moment in order to discuss this meal. My reasons for doing so are that I cannot lay too much stress on the question of nourishment taken on such an exhausting climb at so great an altitude. Nine days before we had purchased bread at Vacas as a pleasant change from the eternal biscuit. In the dry air this had gradually become harder and harder, so that it now resembled nothing so much as a piece of pumice, and one's mouth became quite sore in eating it. Still, I preferred it to biscuit. Before starting from the base camp two days before, I had packed some of this bread. Happily we had been able to secure really tender beef from Fiorini, and I had had a piece of fillet carefully grilled over the camp-fire. Unlike the rest of the men, I found food necessary and most beneficial at these great altitudes, and on this bread eleven days old and the fillet I made a hearty meal at over 19,000 feet. I have every reason to be thankful I did so. The guides, however, remained true to their conviction that food had better be avoided while climbing, and contented themselves with a sip or two of wine. They attempted the ascent of Tupungato without a morsel of solid food! I quite agree that they were right not to take food if they felt an absolute distaste for it, but I have a suspicion that their reluctance to do so was the result of their experience in Switzerland at lower altitudes, and that they decided not to eat before considering whether they could do so or not. It seems to me all a matter of digestion: if a man at these heights cannot digest, let him take no food, but if he is fortunate enough to be able to digest, even if he has no particular inclination towards food, let him take it by all means, provided there is no actual repugnance. Anyhow, I am sure I could not have got to the top of Tupungato without

THE QUESTION OF FOOD

it. On Aconcagua we felt no inclination to eat, but then, it being impossible at these great heights to get warm food, there was nothing at all to tempt the fastidious palate of a man in a more or less exhausted condition. Now I had hit upon something tempting, though cold, and I shall ever feel grateful for this really excellent meat supplied us by Fiorini: it was the only tender beef (we only once touched mutton) that I came across during our whole seven months in the mountains. There was certainly one great obstacle against our obtaining such cold nourishment in the Cordilleras. The great herds of long-horned cattle that arrive at Vacas or Inca—the latter some 9000 feet above sea-level—are very different animals from the sleek beasts that were driven to Mendoza some weeks previously fresh from the rich pasture grounds of the pampas. The fat, tender animal from the pampas is shod with iron, and driven up some 10,000 feet. Naturally it arrives at these heights, after its tramp of 150 miles, no doubt an excellent specimen of training and muscular development, but hardly in first-rate killing condition. A few weeks' grazing in the pastures of Chile should intervene before the butcher's knife. There is a great difference at Vacas between "road" beef and "railway" beef. But the cattle that come by train to Vacas are only a portion of the vast herds that pass over to Chile in the summer months, though neither can be recommended for tenderness or flavour. I was lucky on this occasion in obtaining meat that one's teeth could penetrate. A tender piece of fillet of beef, grilled over the camp-fire, whether hot or cold, must be always tempting to the appetite, and there is no question of its keeping fresh in such a climate.

When we reached the summit of the ridge, we were able to take stock of the weather. It was a perfect day, without a cloud in the sky. Even the hilltops on the Pacific coast were entirely free from haze. Nothing could have been more encouraging, for it was from that quarter that all the storms that had hitherto assailed us had come. The wind was as before in the north-west, and still very cold; but it was as nothing compared with the hurricane from which we had suffered on the second attempt. These signs cheered us greatly, and we started again at ten o'clock, feeling more hopeful of success than ever before. Zurbriggen now proposed a new route. Instead of turning towards the south and ascending the gentle slope of the ridge to the dome—as we had done on the two former occasions—he pointed out that we should gain relief from the wearisome monotony of tramping up the debris-covered surface of the spur, by making our way to the ridge of rocks on the western or Santiago side, leading towards the summit, where we should have a firm foothold. As we marched on in that direction, I noticed that many of the stones in my path were covered with a white deposit. In some cases it nearly enveloped them in a thin layer, but elsewhere, it lay over them in lumps, and I even found pieces of this superficial deposit lying loose.[1] It seemed to be a white mineral of some kind. Many of the stones on the surface of the spur were hollowed out in the centre, and cup-shaped. Professor Bonney, after hearing my description of them, has suggested that they were probably volcanic bombs thrown from the prehistoric crater of Tupungato, twisted into this peculiar cup-like shape by their flight through the air and sudden cooling. Unfortunately, I could not find a specimen small enough to carry away with me.

There are many difficulties in the way of collecting geological specimens en route for the summit of a high mountain. When ascending, the specimens lie naturally closer to the eye, and invite collection; but it is scarcely possible to gather them, for on the way up, and at such an altitude, one's pack must be kept as light as possible. When coming down, on the other hand, the specimens are not so noticeable, being farther from the eye; one is frequently driven down by storm, and has no chance of looking about. It is also generally late, and too dark to discriminate and collect.

At half-past ten we reached the rocks on the western side of the spur, and began to climb them. Up to this time I had worn my poncho—it was a fairly long one, fashioned to cover the knees when riding, but so inconvenient for

[1] See Appendix, p. 327 (IX. and XII.).

A NEW VOLCANO

walking that I could not take it with me up the rocks, though I knew how intensely cold it would be on the summit, and as I hoped to get there early enough to remain a considerable time, I had looked forward to having it with me. The scramble up the rocks was most interesting; these did not present any great difficulty, and we were able to dispense with the rope. In spite of the fact that the ascent was more abrupt than by the former route, and required more exertion, none of us seemed at this time to be much affected, though we were considerably more than 19,000 feet above the sea. I always look back upon this part of our ascent of Tupungato with particular pleasure. It was before our troubles began, and while we still happily imagined that we should reach the summit about two o'clock. The rocks we were climbing formed a narrow ridge, like a balustrade between the spur and the dome of the mountain, rising about eighty to a hundred feet from it on one hand, and descending in sheer precipice some four thousand feet to the valley on the Chilian side. As we ascended, the view was superb, for we looked right over the edge of the rocks into the valley beneath us, and far away to the west. At our feet, as it seemed, was spread out a wide plain intersected by rivers; beyond was a great range of hills running north and south, which could hardly have been less than 12,000 feet high. This immense line of cliffs, about twenty miles from Tupungato, diminished in height towards the north, but not very far from this extremity was a sight that instantly arrested our attention. It was nothing less than a volcano in full eruption. The discovery took my breath away, for I had always understood there was no volcano in these regions, dormant or active, except the lofty San José due south of Tupungato. We halted and looked at the volcano long and intently. The clearness of the atmosphere at this time in the morning—it wanted yet half an hour to noon— enabled us to observe its features with accuracy. The whole structure of the crater was peculiar. There was no cone, and the opening was not in the summit alone, but an enormous V-shaped aperture, tapering towards the bottom, seemed to run from the top of the cliffs to their very base. In the distance it had the appearance of an immense grey talus turned upside down. From the top of this opening there poured forth vast volumes of dark brown steam, which floated away through the air for a dozen miles towards the south-east. A curious circumstance of the early morning now came back to my mind. When ascending the slope of the great spur from the east, and entirely cut off from the view to the west, we had, all three, been conscious of a strong smell of burning. As Zurbriggen was directly in front of me, and my nose was not far from his boots, I imagined that the strong smell was of burnt leather, from his having put them too near the fire at the base camp the night before. I now realised that this sulphurous smell had not been caused by burnt leather, but that the wind must have been more from the west earlier in the day, and so have brought the fumes of the distant volcano towards us. Zurbriggen was as much struck as myself by the remarkable sight, and declared that, though in the jet of steam it bore resemblance to the numerous volcanoes he had seen in New Zealand, its shape and structure were entirely different. I proposed photographing it at once, and taking bearings, which would probably have involved a delay of more than half an hour. Zurbriggen pointed out, however, that we could not be more than two hours from the summit, and that as the day was clear and settled, we should get an even finer view of it from above. We all felt in good condition, and not in need of a rest; so we pressed on, and I contented myself for the moment with making a very rough sketch of the volcano in my notebook. Two hours had been spent in coming up these rocks, and at 12.30 we left them for a wide couloir filled with snow, which we imagined would shortly bring us to the summit. We cut a few steps in the snow here and there, and sometimes returned to the rocks, where they afforded an easier route. In this way we ascended for an hour, with frequent halts, and were now at an altitude of 20,000 feet.

We had felt comparatively little fatigue while moving over

The Water-parting between Chile & Argentina from Inpungate.

POLLINGER BREAKS DOWN

easier ground and at a lower level. But at so great a height every increase in altitude tells at once, and exhaustion now began to come quickly upon us. My legs moved heavily, and I made the sides of the couloir re-echo with my heavy breathing. No one spoke a word. Zurbriggen strode on in front of me, and frequently looked impatiently ahead, evidently expecting to see the summit of the mountain loom up every moment over the brow of the slope we were ascending. We had had ample opportunity of examining the nature of this slope from different points of view to the north, and we were convinced that the highest point lay on this, the northern side of Tupungato. Two days before, when I had taken photographs of the mountain from a point nine miles away in the valley, whence we could see the several peaks rising above the circle of the dome, Zurbriggen and I had fully discussed the matter and concluded that, unless the mountain stretched away a great distance to the south, the northern peak must be the highest. The moment was at hand when we should know whether our conjecture was right. As we marched on, I looked time after time at Zurbriggen, and admired the steady pace he was keeping, wondering whether the heaviness of my legs would increase, and how long I should be able to follow him. Joseph Pollinger was behind me, and I fancied he must be watching my efforts with feelings in which admiration had a very small part. He was an excellent guide, and, although I did not know how he had done on Aconcagua, as he was never with me on that mountain, he had always lasted out well on Tupungato. Suddenly, about half-past one, we all three paused by common consent. One of us had stopped abruptly, and the others stopped too, without a word being uttered. Zurbriggen and I turned round and looked at Pollinger, who was lying flat on his face and groaning. He was suffering violent pains in the abdomen, and he declared between his gasps that he felt very sick and ill, and could not go another step higher. We were anxious to take him with us, so I tried to persuade him that he would be all right after a short rest, and proposed that Zurbriggen and I should divide his pack between us, so as to make things as easy as possible for him. But, as he still insisted that he felt far too ill to go on, and seemed to have a great desire to descend as soon as possible, we gave up trying to persuade him. "Let me get down lower! For God's sake let me descend! I shall die if I stop here!" was his only answer to us. Yes, he was right. The only remedy for his illness was to descend with all speed to a lower altitude; he would be well if only he could get down a thousand feet or more. I then discussed the matter with Zurbriggen, and determined on the route he should take. If he descended by the couloir, and walked along the whole length of the spur until he came above the camp, and then turned to the right and descended to it, he would be able to gain shelter without risk. He would find Lanti there, and could wait for us, or go down still farther, as he felt inclined. We had always found descending such an efficient remedy for the sickness, that we felt confident he would be all right again at 18,000 feet. I divided his pack with Zurbriggen, and we decided to leave everything that we should not absolutely need, including a rücksack, behind. Pollinger said he felt much better already, and would wait a little longer and rest where he was. As we could watch him for a considerable distance, we continued the ascent, telling him to signal if he did not feel all right. Then we went on our way, and looking back from time to time, we were thankful to find that he made encouraging signals, and that his pace increased until we lost sight of him on the distant declivity of the mountain.

I was now feeling in no very good condition myself, as the difficulty of getting enough oxygen out of the rarefied atmosphere became every moment greater. My breathing grew at every step more and more laboured. The sides of the couloir which we were still traversing seemed like prison walls to my lungs. It would be a stretch of imagination to suppose for one moment that there was less air in such a place. But I had suffered far more from breathlessness in the couloirs and enclosed places on Aconcagua, and instinctively felt that my breathlessness at this moment was due to the same causes. The air seemed "flat" to my thirsty lungs, where it was not stirred and freshened by the wind. It is interesting to note what Mr. Freshfield says on this subject of the "stagnation of the air" in his account of the Ascent of Mount Elbruz.[1] "The gale which nearly defeated us saved us from mountain-sickness. I have compared the accounts of many mountain travellers, and it seems apparent that those who suffer from 'rarity of the air' do so mostly on still days and in hollows rather than on ridges. From De Saussure's time 'the stagnation of the air' has been complained of. I have myself been on Mont Blanc three times, and once only, the day being perfectly still, did I suffer in any degree from nausea and headache. On that occasion I had been living at 6000 feet for some weeks previously, and was in exceptionally good training. Two years later I came straight out from England and felt no inconvenience of any kind, although the pace from the Cabane Vallot to the top was hurried." This is particularly interesting as it coincides exactly with my own experiences when we reached the great arête of Aconcagua, and still more with those I am about to relate.

Gradually we began to emerge from the couloir, and, looking ahead, beheld at last what we had so long desired to see. It was the northernmost peak on the dome of Tupungato, which, according to all our calculations, ought to be the very highest point on the mountain, and this peak was the one we had selected when looking from below. It was nearly two o'clock, the hour at which we had calculated to reach the summit. We felt confident that in half an hour we should be rewarded for three weeks of struggle and hardship, and should have hours before us to look upon one of the finest views ever beheld by man, for the sky was absolutely cloudless. Slowly, and with short steps we tramped on, our eyes turned towards the summit, when suddenly, without a moment's warning, Zurbriggen sat down on the ground and exclaimed, "I am finished—I go no farther!" Fearing that the strain had been too much for his heart, I was greatly alarmed, but when I asked what was the matter he only pointed in the direction of the peak, and declared that he could go no farther.

[1] *The Exploration of the Caucasus*, vol. ii. p. 168.

I saw in a moment the cause of his collapse. Looming up beyond the nearest peak, which we had expected to be the highest, was another peak far to the south, and certainly higher by a good two hundred feet. "That point," said Zurbriggen, pointing a dismal finger at it, "is an hour away from where we are, and I cannot do it." In the greatest anxiety I asked him to tell me his symptoms. It appeared, however, that there was nothing more the matter than exhaustion, and the effects of sudden disappointment. "It's my legs!" he answered. "They will not carry me a step farther." I tried to persuade him that the southern peak was scarcely half an hour away from us, though I knew only too well that he had probably underestimated the distance, although in the clear air it looked only a few steps. He was not to be persuaded, however, that the distance was less than he knew it to be. I thought it possible, nevertheless, that after a rest and some stimulant he might be able to resume the ascent. Half a bottle of wine had been reserved for the summit, but I now gave it to him, and said, "Look here, Mattias, if you sit down behind this rock sheltered from the wind and take twenty minutes' rest, and promise me to drink the whole of this wine, I am convinced you will reach the summit. I will take your rücksack, the camera, and things, and go on a bit to see how the land lies." Leaving him behind me, I turned my steps with bitter feelings once more towards the summit. For nearly a month we had tried together to conquer this hoary-headed giant; we had made four separate attempts and had suffered severe privations and many disappointments; and now, when success lay almost within our grasp, I felt that I was likely to reach the summit alone, and I seemed to have no heart left in me for the task.

Zurbriggen's exhaustion was not hard to account for. He had led the way all day, and had tired himself out by doing so; for the labour of the leader of a party up these slopes is very much greater than that of any of his companions. At these altitudes every step must be made with the view of expending as little exertion as possible. Those who follow have not the trouble of selecting the footholds, and can mark where the man in front has slipped, and profit by his experience. Moreover, his foot by slipping makes in the loose ground a firm place for the next man to step in; so that the man behind gains as much as the leader loses. After I had gone thirty or forty yards, I hesitated, and then stopped. It was painful for me to go on without Zurbriggen, and I almost decided to wait for him. But on looking back I saw that he seemed to be doing better, and was now seated under the shelter of the rock, solacing himself with a pipe. After all, I reflected, I could do no good by waiting for him, and probably he would make a greater effort if I left him and pushed on. So I resumed my way alone and strode out as vigorously as I could.

I was now well free of the stifling couloir, and there was a cold wind blowing which seemed to refresh me, while with each step that brought me nearer to my goal, I gained new energy, and my excitement rose. Between the northern peak—the cause of our first disappointment—and the higher point which I was now making for, there was a wide bed of black volcanic scoria, across which I moved at a pace which fairly astonished me. Amidst the general gray, pink, and brown colour of the mountain surface, and the patches of white snow which lay here and there, this black volcanic bed stood out in marked and peculiar contrast, looking for all the world as if it had been brought there in cart-loads to fill up the depression. Having crossed it, I came to the base of a ridge leading to the peak. I even increased my speed—I know my legs ached and that my breathing was laboured, but I did not heed the suffering and it did not prevent me from rushing on at what seemed at this height a mad pace. The steep slope of the ridge made no difference. I stopped for rest and breath as often as before, but between the halts the pace was maintained. It was shortly after three o'clock when I reached the summit of this peak.

Alas, another disappointment was in store. As I set my foot at last upon the highest point and looked eagerly around, a most unwelcome sight presented itself. Far away on the southern edge of the mountain-top, which until now I had never seen, another peak rose up, and seemed to challenge supremacy with that on which I stood. Between me and it was a wide depression. I brought my Abney level to bear upon it, and my fears were realised. I was not yet on the top of Tupungato: the new peak was considerably higher than the one I had surmounted. I felt that it would probably take me an hour to reach it, but I believed myself quite equal to the new task. I looked back. Zurbriggen was still sitting on the very spot where I had left him, and I had small expectation that he would ever reach the summit of the mountain. This was very disheartening, but there was nothing for it, and without halt or rest I set out for the third peak.

In front of me to the left lay a great field of snow, and to the right a rock arête. Either might be selected as the route, but I did not know the condition of the snow, and considered that the safer way lay by the rocks. With more haste than prudence I scrambled down them, elated by the view which every moment widened out before my gaze, for I was crossing the western side of the dome, and each step increased my first sight of the outlook to the south. I reached the end of the rock arête, and, without resting, hurried across the bed of the depression and began at once the ascent of the opposite slope. I had at least four hundred feet to climb, but I kept up the same pace until at last I gained the top.

It was 3.45, nearly two hours later than the time at which we had expected to be upon the summit. I had surmounted the third of those baffling peaks, but were my labours really at an end, or was fresh and fatal disappointment in store? It was almost with a sinking heart that I looked around. But one desperately anxious glance told me enough. No other and loftier peak rose before me. Everything was beneath my feet, and at last I stood on the highest point of Tupungato.

CHAPTER XIX

BY STUART VINES

THE SUMMIT AND THE DESCENT

I WAS on the summit of Tupungato at last, and all my efforts and disappointments were more than repaid. I stood on a great mound, in shape like a pyramid with a blunted top some two yards wide, rising several hundred feet above the general surface of the dome. Its whole surface was entirely free from snow and covered with loose rocks and debris, though this debris, from the appearance of things, was a mere superficial deposit, close beneath which lay a solid rock foundation. I picked up the highest piece of rock, the veritable tip of the mountain, which lay loose on the ground and was an excellent example of the stones that lay around. As this, however, was far too large for me to carry down, I flung it to the earth, when it broke in half and disclosed a hollow inside, in which was a quantity of a substance like glue or gum, transparent, hard and brittle, probably fused matter and glass. The half I brought away with me proved, on examination,[1] to be a very fine specimen of andesite, riddled with fulgurites, or tubes melted out by lightning. Having thus examined my foothold and secured the fallen monster's head, I threw down the rücksack, and without the loss of a moment set to work to commemorate the ascent by a stone man—a cairn that would be a sufficient memorial of the FitzGerald Expedition to future climbers of Tupungato. But though they were interesting and valuable from a geological point of view, the stones on the summit did not lend themselves well to the

---

[1] See Appendix, p. 330 (II.).

construction of a stone man. The larger and heavier ones were frozen to the ground, and most of them, resembling pumice in structure, were much too light and brittle for the substantial edifice I wished to erect, for was I not standing on the very spot where the storm-fiends of the Andes gathered daily for their wildest orgies? I had, therefore, to descend ten or twenty feet every now and then to bring up more durable material. It was hard work, but I went at it with an energy that surprised me, and, though panting for breath, I was not seriously distressed. I felt fit and well, and was satisfied I was doing an immense amount of work. After some considerable time spent at high altitudes, one becomes so accustomed to working slowly and deliberately that the fact that one is doing little at the cost of much labour does not strike one very forcibly. It was only by comparison, therefore, that I felt I was working quickly, for the excitement and the glorious circumstances of the situation kept me going. Secondly, there was no longer any necessity for me to husband my strength. The highest point had been reached: I could now let myself go. The disproportion between the labour and its results only became evident to me afterwards when I calculated and summed up the outcome of my labours on the summit of Tupungato. The exertion of gathering and piling up the heaviest stones I could find kept me warm, which was very necessary, for there was a strong wind blowing, and the thermometer registered 19° of frost.

I had scarcely been working for more than ten minutes when I heard a shout, and looking up saw Zurbriggen on the northern peak I had just left. As I afterwards learnt, he had felt so much revived by the rest and the wine I made him drink, that not long after I had disappeared from view on the peak he pulled himself together and decided to follow me, thinking I had already reached the summit. He got there only to find himself again disappointed, but seeing me already on the last peak, and engaged in the work I have spoken of, he promptly followed. I waved my arms in answer to his shout, and went on with my task. As he began the descent towards me, I had hopes that it would ease and rest him for the ascent of the final few hundred feet. Not many minutes after I saw him he was descending the snow slope at a great pace. It was a shorter and quicker route than the rock arête that I had followed, and in a very short space of time he was within fifty feet of me. I ran down to meet him, and grasped his hands. Now that we stood on the summit together, I felt that at last Tupungato had really been ascended. As soon as he had breath enough to speak, he turned to me with a smile, and said, "Now I'm off to Mendoza to settle my book, and make those men pay for doubting the FitzGerald Expedition." And for some time after, I caught him muttering the words, "ten to one, indeed! ... doubt Zurbriggen ... Mendoza ..." and chuckling to himself. He was quite his old self again. The wine, the rest, and the pipe had worked wonders, otherwise the fresh disappointment that awaited him on surmounting the second peak must have made him give up the attempt. He helped me to put the finishing touches to the cairn, which, when completed, was a solid and substantial erection, about four feet high, that might even bid defiance for many years to Tupungato's furious storms.

It was now half-past four, and no time was to be lost. I wrote on one side of my card, "*FitzGerald Expedition*"; and on the other :—

"*Stuart Vines, with Mattias Zurbriggen, Swiss guide, made the ascent of this mountain on* 12*th April* 1897, *after three attempts, being stopped by storms.*"

Also the following words upon a leaf of my notebook :—

"*Joseph Pollinger came with us from our bivouac, about* 17,000 *feet, below ridge on north side of mountain, but turned back sick about* 1000 *feet from the summit. Temp.* 13° *Fahr. Zurbriggen and I reached the summit at* 3.45."

My card and the piece of paper I enclosed in a wine bottle, which Zurbriggen placed at the base of the cairn and carefully covered over with stones.

In spite of all the bad weather we had suffered from throughout our work—and indeed the weather experienced during this summer was described by the Meteorological Office in Santiago as without a record—we had no cause to complain on the days of the two chief ascents. The circumstances were very similar. Both summits were reached about an hour and a half before sunset. But the 12th of April even surpassed the 13th of February, the day of my ascent of Aconcagua; for now in the whole expanse of sky around, over ocean and land, I could not discern a single cloud. Only in the direction of the Pacific a haze hung over the mountains, and to my great disappointment, I could gain no further view of the volcano seen earlier in the day. I accounted for this by supposing that the haze which hid it from sight was probably caused by the smoke of the volcano itself, the wind having shifted and dropped, so that the vapours now hung in a cloudy form around the mountain. This haze was not due, I thought, to the weather, for in all other directions the view was magnificently clear. In the brilliant air the spectacle that lay before us was one of extraordinery extent and grandeur. Range beyond range of mountains stretched away towards the great plain of Santiago, forty miles to the west. Far away, beyond the hills that almost seemed to lie at our feet, stretched the great waters of the Pacific, a tract of blue ocean sparkling to the horizon, and clearly visible, although the distance from Tupungato to the sea-coast is not less than 130 miles. The view from the top of Tupungato is in many ways even finer than that obtained from Aconcagua. The expanse of ocean visible towards the west is less vast, but there is ample compensation in the outlook over the great unending plains on the eastern side. The pampas of Argentina stretched almost without a break from our very feet to the South Atlantic Ocean. The position of Tupungato could be very clearly defined: it forms part of the great frontier barrier between Chile and Argentina, which is also the waterparting of all the rivers to the Pacific and Atlantic. I could see those glittering rivers winding like ribbons through the

POLLERA FROM THE TUPUNGATO VALLEY

A MAGNIFICENT VIEW

pampas, spreading fertility around them, and scattering plenty through the land—a sight which contrasted strikingly with the turbulent and unending array of rugged peaks and ridges that surrounded me on every side but this. Though Aconcagua lies in Argentina, yet the view from its summit towards the west over Chile is far more interesting than that to the east. From the summit of Tupungato the conditions are reversed—Aconcagua seems to belong to the Chilians, Tupungato to the Argentines; and in order to gain a really perfect idea of the Cordilleras of the Andes at this latitude, one ascent does not complete the picture without the other.

The Andes seem to rise up from Santiago in ever-ascending gradation, until at last they culminate in the immense mass of Tupungato; beyond, they fall abruptly away; mountains disappear; and a country almost fen-like in its monotonous flatness succeeds. Our nearest neighbour on the Argentine side was the pyramid of the Cerro de la Plata, not more than twenty miles to the north-east. It seems to rise from a mass of high mountains surrounding it on every side and merging imperceptibly into it, so that it possesses no well-marked or definite base of its own. Its height has been estimated at 19,200 feet. The chain on which I stood, the frontier boundary between these two great States, ran southward towards the Peuquenes or Portillo Pass, trampled each year by the iron-shod feet of many thousand head of cattle passing from the rich pastures of the pampas to supply the mining settlements on the coast of northern Chile, and on to the volcano of San José, reckoned at some 19,500 feet, and Maipo, the scene of Güssfeldt's triumphs in 1883. On the Chilian side scores of dark rocks reared their heads, a sinister array of precipitous impossibilities from which any climber would turn away in despair. And to the north the same great barrier ran: at my feet the great mountain-spur on which we had suffered so many hardships and disappointments from wind and weather; beyond, a snow arête leading up to the steep walls of ice and rock that support the virgin cone of Pollera, in shape not unlike the Weisshorn, so well known to Zermatt climbers; and, towering above the Pollera, the pyramid of Navarro. Then in one great curve sweeping westward to the lofty glacier perched high between the two peaks of Juncal, and thence northward again, the clear-cut features of this immense ridge ran to the Cumbre Pass.

Looking along this distinct and sharp-edged chain to north and south, it was hard to understand how any frontier question between the Republics could come about. But indeed it is not here that the boundary dispute arises. It is the exploration of the rich country to the south, the Patagonia of former years, where the mountains are lower and the natural features less clearly defined, that has raised the great question which now divides Chile and Argentina, and leads them at times to the brink of war. The danger of a conflict, however, is not so great as it sometimes seems to those who hear the resolute language indulged in by both sides, for it is a singular fact that with the advent of spring each year there comes a spirit of peace and goodwill between the two States, spreading its benign influence abroad as long as summer lasts and the passes over the Andes lie open. With autumn, and the closing of the passes by the heavy snows of early winter, the war spirit is born. Argentina sends up troops to Mendoza, Chile mobilises her national guard. On each side the militant party is bold and reckless, and remarkably outspoken in language, so long as fighting is impossible and they cannot get at each other. But as I looked down on this great line of division between two unfriendly States, I wondered how long this game of bluff would continue, and whether a few years hence the white bones of men would not be mingled with those of the cattle lying strewn along the passes of the Andes, in silent witness to the perils of those great mountain ways.

The subject of Aconcagua as seen from Tupungato deters my pen. In our many struggles up its flanks, we had often gazed with ever-increasing wonder on the mighty contours that rose above our heads. I remember the first occasion we beheld it we all stood gazing at it in silence until one of the porters broke the spell by ejaculating, "What's that?" That

THE SURFACE OF THE DOME

Aconcagua was a high mountain we well knew. We had all suffered from its height. But when near at hand it was quite impossible to realise the vastness of its proportions. Not so from where I now stood on a pinnacle sixty miles away. I had long known it was over four thousand feet higher than any mountain within thirty miles of it, but it looked ten thousand feet higher, as it reared its immense head and shoulders from amongst its neighbours, like some huge rock towering out of the waves of the sea. It stood before me without rival. Even the great crags of Juncal did not challenge it, though they were almost thirty miles nearer. Facing us was the wall of that enormous precipice. Dark and sinister it looked, for this southern face of almost perpendicular ice and rock seldom sees the sun. Behind Aconcagua, but almost forty miles farther and too far off for comparison, I could see the white slopes of Mercedario. Then I turned my eyes upon Tupungato itself and surveyed the surface of the dome, an undulating plateau at my feet covering an immense area. It is comparatively free from snow, except on the eastern side, where enormous snowfields fall over the precipice and sink down almost to the great moraine-filled valley beneath.[1] On the plateau comparatively little solid rock appears above the surface, the same denuding agencies having been at work as on Aconcagua. Three peaks—or rather three huge debris-covered mounds—present themselves, one on the northern side, one to the east, and the highest to the south. I traversed the plateau from end to end, and, as on Aconcagua, discovered no traces whatever of a crater, though the nature of the rocks and the general shape of the summit tend to make one believe that its volcanic origin is of more recent date than that of Aconcagua. The peak on which I stood was as a mere excrescence on the enormous circle of the dome, whose sides, bellying at the top and falling sheer below, cut off all view of the valleys lying beneath the base of the mountain. This prevented me from seeing the nature of the southern and south-western face. Sixty-two years before, Charles Darwin beheld this side of Tupungato, when cross-

[1] See illustration opposite p. 186.

ing the Portillo Pass on 22nd March 1835, and he says of it :—

"We had a fine view of a mass of mountain called Tupungato, the whole clothed with unbroken snow. From one peak my arriero said he had once seen smoke proceeding; and I thought I could distinguish the form of a large crater. In the maps Tupungato figures as a single mountain; this Chileno method of giving one name to a tract of mountains is a fruitful source of error. In the region of snow there was a blue patch which no doubt was glacier, a phenomenon that has been said not to occur in these mountains."[1]

It is extremely unlikely that there would be anything approaching a crater half-way down the southern slopes of the mountain. I presume, therefore, that Darwin thought he could discern the outlines of a crater in the three peaks rising above the dome, or perhaps in the rock arête by which I had reached the summit.[2] As to the arriero's remark, it only shows that the mule-drivers of the Cordillera played with the truth sixty-two years ago as badly as they do to-day. It is a peculiar fact that right above the spot where Darwin made this observation, but behind him to the south, there is a great hanging glacier, which cloud must have prevented him from seeing.

I took the compass bearings of the principal surrounding heights, and then setting the little camera on the cairn, I took two views of Aconcagua, one of La Plata, and one of the eastern peak of Tupungato and the pampas. I would gladly have taken more, but we had now been more than an hour on the summit, and Zurbriggen, not without cause, became very impatient to go. It was nearly five o'clock, the sun was getting very low over the Pacific, and in less than an hour it would set. It was tempting Providence to remain.

During these seventy minutes on the summit I had worked as I never worked in my life. The cairn, the record, the bearings, the photographic views, the examination of the

---

[1] *Voyage of the Beagle*, vol. iii. chap. xvii. p. 397.
[2] See illustration opposite p. 218.

THE HARDSHIPS OF PIONEERS

dome, formed my tale of work, and yet I had not half seen all there was to see. Why had I not time to wander at leisure over that great summit; select specimens from every one of the peaks; examine more carefully its contours, and try to form an opinion as to the reasons of the total obliteration of the ancient crater? This must be left to others. I hope to hear of the ascent of Tupungato by some geologist in the next few years. Let him start early in the season, and, apart from the altitude, all he will have to fear is the wind-storms. It has often been remarked in mountaineering, since the first ascent of Mont Blanc, that the pioneers make far too much of the hardships they endured, and the difficulties of their ascents. It seems to me that those who come after do an injustice to those who have gone before. What one man has done, another can do, or feels confident that he can, and this confidence is itself a great factor of success at high altitudes. Dangers and difficulties seen and experienced for the first time always seem, nay, are more terrible than after they have been overcome and described. Mr. Leslie Stephen said of his first ascent of the Rothhorn, "The next traveller who makes the ascent will probably charge me with exaggeration. It is, I know, very difficult to avoid giving just cause for that charge. I must therefore apologise beforehand, and only beg my anticipated critic to remember two things: one, that on the first ascent a mountain, in obedience to some mysterious law, always is more difficult than at any succeeding ascent; secondly, that nothing can be less like a mountain at one time than the same mountain at another."[1]

Zurbriggen was right; it would be worse than foolish to wait a moment longer. We had no camp awaiting us at 19,000 feet as on Aconcagua, and the distance to our 17,000 foot bivouac was considerably greater than that which separated the camp on Aconcagua from the summit. At the high bivouac there was little food and no methylated spirits, so we planned to reach the base camp in the valley that night by pushing on in the moonlight, on which we could

[1] *The Playground of Europe*, chap. iv. p. 110.

rely for the greater part of the descent. With much reluctance I shut up the camera, and put it in my pocket. As it was, I had given too much attention to my photographs and too little heed to surrounding conditions. To manipulate the camera properly gloves were out of the question, and photographing on Tupungato with 19° of frost and half a gale blowing is dangerous work—as I was quickly reminded by finding that two of my fingers were frost-bitten and lifeless. I showed them to Zurbriggen, who seized them in his powerful grasp and instantly started down, forcing me to follow. Down the slope of the peak and across the hard snow of the eastern slope we made our way hand in hand, Zurbriggen crunching my lifeless fingers in the most merciless manner as we went. He was saving time as well as my fingers, for I was loth to leave the spot so hurriedly, and tried vainly to snatch a specimen or two with the other hand. The edge of the dome, eight hundred feet from the summit, commanded a magnificent view over the mountains and valleys near, and I insisted on taking two more photographs,[1] Zurbriggen waiting with impatience, and demanding after this delay that we should press on with all possible speed. We plunged down the couloir by which we had ascended, but the ground unfortunately was very rotten, and we had not gone many yards when the pace and the tired state we were in began to tell, and Zurbriggen, putting his foot on a loose piece of rock, slipped and came down on his back with great violence. Before leaving the summit of Tupungato he had hastily packed away the monster's head—the topmost rock—in the inside pocket at the back of his coat. It was on this that he fell, and the top of Tupungato, as if in revenge for being thus carried from its home, bit him badly in the back. A volley of oaths rang over the mountain, and Zurbriggen lay on his back writhing. Under ordinary circumstances it would be absurd to suppose two able-bodied men could not descend this couloir with care in safety, but, now the excitement of the summit was over, we suddenly realised how tired and feeble we were, and the rotten state of the ground

[1] See illustration opposite p. 197.

became a real danger to us, for we stepped heavily, and our foothold on the stony surface was uncertain. Zurbriggen lay where he had fallen for some time groaning, but I, in my turn, preached the necessity of pressing on unless we were to spend another uncomfortable night at the 17,000 foot bivouac, and he pulled himself together once more. Straight down by the slopes of snow from the dome, we at length reached the great spur, which, with its gentle descent, afforded much relief to our weary limbs. Night was closing in, and we determined to push on to the bivouac by the route with which we were best acquainted—*i.e.* to descend the spur for its full length and then turn sharply down the slope on the right to the great snowfields which lie at its base. Owing to the gathering darkness I was unable to collect any specimens. At six o'clock we reached the point where the descent to the snowfields began. At last we must bid farewell to the great horizon line of the Pacific, into which the sun was dipping, and we stood in silence gazing westward, our faces suffused by the light of its last rays. It seemed impossible to tear ourselves away, but suddenly Zurbriggen turned to me and asked where I intended to sleep. It was quite enough—visions of comfort in the camp below, and dreary reminiscences of the lofty bivouac where we must stop unless we made haste, determined us to hurry on, so leaving the sunset behind us, we turned our backs on the west and dived down the long slope eastward.

I shall never forget the weary struggle down that steep declivity of broken stones and crumbling rock. The light had faded, and whether one hurried or went slowly it was impossible to avoid falls. Our arms were too tired for us to support ourselves by our axes, and soon we began to realise that we should never reach the main valley and its sheltering camp that night, even if it were possible to find the way by moonlight. I stumbled along, trying to remember what provisions for supper had been left at the bivouac. It was all that we had now to look forward to. Suddenly my attention was arrested by the magnificent spectacle of the afterglow following the sunset, as it hung in the eastern sky over the pampas. A line of fire, as it seemed, was spread across the heavens, slowly changing to colder tints. The rainbow of shifting colours that hung thus in the far-distant east in the twilight, was even more wonderful than the sunset we had seen from Aconcagua. The effect was extraordinary, for, the eye being unaided by any sight of foreground leading up to it, this fiery streak seemed assuredly some startling meteoric phenomenon. All objects at a great distance seen from a high mountain have, to the inexperienced eye, especially at first sight, the appearance of being lifted up too high. The observer looks down for the horizon,—and lo! it is high above. The higher one goes the greater is the illusion. This lasts only for a time, for the eye is led by the ground beneath, the slope of the mountain, the ranges and valleys between, up to the distant blue line, and the horizon humbles itself and resumes its proper place. Now here there was nothing to lead the eye or to teach it that this band of fire across the dark arc of heaven had any connection with the earth. I shall never forget its grandeur. The colours turned pale and faded out, night came on, but the moon shone brightly in the sky, and bathed the wide expanse of stony peaks and aiguilles beneath us in its sombre light.

At eight o'clock we heard a voice calling from below, a distant shout and then another. We soon recognised it as the voice of Lanti, and he came up to meet us and reported that he and Lochmatter had been at the bivouac since midday, and that Pollinger had arrived about three in the afternoon, seeming fairly well and strong. It seems that after we left him he had taken the descent very easily, and each step downwards had relieved his pains and given him fresh life, so that after two hours' rest and some food he had descended with Lochmatter to the valley camp. As soon as we reached the bivouac, Lanti tried to get us some supper, but nothing would induce the self-cooking tin lamps to work or the methylated spirits to burn, and we went supperless to bed. Thus ended one of the most eventful days of our work in the Andes, and of my life.

AT THE BASE CAMP

Next morning, as soon as the sun appeared above the Plata range, we were moving about and warming our aching limbs. We had been too tired to sleep much, although, after so many hours spent above 19,000 feet, we no longer suffered from the altitude at 17,000 feet. It was a glorious day, and we did not leave the scene of so many hardships until ten. The descent to the base camp was long and wearisome; it was one o'clock before we stumbled in at last, feeling quite exhausted. The sun was hot, and even Paramillo was too much overcome by heat and sleep to come out and meet us with his usual boisterous greeting, which at last we really deserved. A substantial meal was prepared; we drank the one flask of wine that had been left, and made merry, resting in the sun until evening, Joseph Pollinger was sent out to the high camp once more to bring in the rücksacks, rope, ponchos, etc., that we had been obliged to leave behind us on the great spur. In the morning we had seen these articles marking our course of yesterday, and I wished if possible to recover them. I knew FitzGerald wanted me to return to Inca and join him in the high valleys at the base of Aconcagua, as soon as the ascent of Tupungato had been made. I therefore discussed with Fortunato the possibility of making the journey to Vacas on the morrow. His opinion was that two horsemen unhampered by a baggage train might accomplish the journey, if the animals gave no trouble over the difficult passes, and did not lose their shoes or go lame on the rough ground. It would be necessary, however, to start before daybreak and ride till after sunset. I anticipated no trouble with the horses, which had so far proved themselves equal to anything, so I resolved to make the journey next day, cost what it would. That night we caught the best of the horses and hobbled them in readiness near the camp, and I gave orders that, as soon as the porters had brought down the tent on Tupungato, the caravan should follow us with all speed to Vacas. We turned in at an early hour, and the camp was soon wrapped in profound sleep.

At 3.30 next morning Fortunato aroused us. It was pitch dark, and the cold was intense, but we soon had a blazing fire of yareta. I was determined to start with the very first light of day. We were taking no tents or sleeping-bags, and did not relish the idea of being caught by night at this season of the year, even at the comparatively low altitude we should reach by that time. We crouched round the crackling fire, impatiently waiting for the light, with our horses standing by ready saddled; but at 5.30, although it was not yet dawn, we could delay no longer, and started in the dark, giving our horses their heads, and letting them find the way for us. As the first streak of sunrise struck the white top of Tupungato far above us, I looked up at the old giant. All that had passed might have been a terrible dream. I could scarcely realise that after all those weeks the ascent was over at last, and the topmost rock of Tupungato safe in my rücksack en route for examination in London. Now the winter snows might descend, tempests might rage, thermometers fall their lowest—we were no longer the slaves of the weather. Feelings of regret crowded in with those of elation and contentment. During our hard and long struggle I had become familiar with the magnificent panorama seen from our bivouac on the spur, and had learned to appreciate it the more each time I beheld it. Of the view from the summit I had seen enough to make me long to gaze upon it for hours, instead of minutes.

The angle of my horse's back, as he descended into a deep quebrada, called my attention to the route along which we were feeling our way. Three ponchos over thick clothing afforded little protection from the biting wind which came up the valley, and we both suffered intensely from the cold. It was very tantalising to watch the warm sunlight high above us on the sides of the valley, and we looked eagerly ahead for the spot where we should come under the influence of its rays as the shadow-line slowly descended. We turned corner after corner, only to dive again for another half-hour into some icy passage between high walls of rock. Not till three hours and a half had elapsed did we come into the sunlight, which brought us intense relief and enjoyment for at least an hour. But we had soon had enough of it, for by ten o'clock

IN THE TUPUNGATO VALLEY

the heat was overpowering. We reached the main valley at noon, and an hour later dismounted to water our horses. We had ridden nearly eight hours without drawing rein. As we lay resting in the sun, a magnificent spectacle was before our eyes. The great white peak of Pollera towered into the clear air high above us, and it was hard to believe that this was indeed the same summit which only a few days ago we had seen beneath our feet, when looking down upon it from the crest of Tupungato, some 12,000 feet nearer the sky. Verily, man is never satisfied. The same thought was in both our minds—regret that we could not add Pollera to our list of triumphs. Zurbriggen thought the peak would afford by far the most difficult climb of any mountain he had seen in the Andes, that it would take a week of very hard work, even if we were fortunate in hitting on the best route, for a camp would have to be formed if possible a few thousand feet up its slopes. We fell to discussing the routes up the different sides of the mountain, until the time for rest expired and we had to saddle our horses and resume our way. It was half-past six when we reached the junction of the Rio Tupungato with the Rio Mendoza, and crossed the ford to the great pass road. Our game little animals then broke into a gallop, and they kept it up steadily all the way to Vacas, where we arrived at seven o'clock. We had been nearly fourteen hours in the saddle, and had covered upwards of fifty miles. Rocks, boulders, and dried-up torrents formed our way, and we had traversed difficult and precipitous passes.

Outside the huts at Vacas was the usual crowd of peons, shepherds, and cattle drovers with their dogs and their huge clanking spurs—all gazing, as was their wont, at the distant Tupungato, its white slopes still lit up by the afterglow. This evening, we soon learned, the mountain had a special and piquant interest for them. The mountain drover is a born gambler. Often when two caravans have met on one of the passes across the Andes, their leaders have fraternised, and spent the night with cards, until the loser has gambled away all his ready cash, then his poncho, his big spurs inlaid with silver, his clothing, and last of all his packs and mules.

Thus in the morning the two caravans have become one, and go off in the train of the winner, while the loser, sad and denuded, departs alone. Our attempt on Tupungato was a welcome sensation to those eager spirits. The odds had been heavily laid against our success, and there was betting even against our return; our sudden reappearance at Vacas caused, therefore, some excitement, and a good deal of money promptly changed hands. Fiorini insisted on uncorking some special champagne for us, and as we were very thirsty, we drank. Our lucky star was still in the ascendant, for we were alive next morning.

Fiorini having sent an arriero early next day to FitzGerald with the news of our ascent, we rested that day at Vacas, and anxiously awaited the arrival of the caravan, men, and baggage left behind. It came late in the evening. Joseph Pollinger had spent a night at the 17,000 foot bivouac, and had succeeded in picking up all that had been left, up to 19,000 feet. The volcano, he said, he had seen in great activity, vast volumes of smoke rolling up towards the western slopes of Tupungato.

Next morning we were annoyed to find that the arriero had returned without going farther than Inca, so that FitzGerald was still without news of us. I resolved at once to push on myself, leaving Zurbriggen behind at Vacas, and bring the report of our success that day. I had left FitzGerald at Inca on the 1st of April, and it was now the 16th. It was arranged that should he hear nothing from us in two weeks' time, he should send down to inquire, but I knew he could ill afford to do this, as he needed all the men available to carry the heavy instruments he was using in the high valleys. In an hour and a half I reached Inca, where I hired a fresh horse from a troop that was being driven over to Chile. I was to pay a dollar if I brought it back the same night, and two dollars if I kept it until the next day. Not a ruinous price, I thought, until I had ridden on a few miles, and found that neither whip nor spur would get more than a sluggish jog out of the animal. I had got far enough to sight the lake in the Horcones Valley, when I spied two

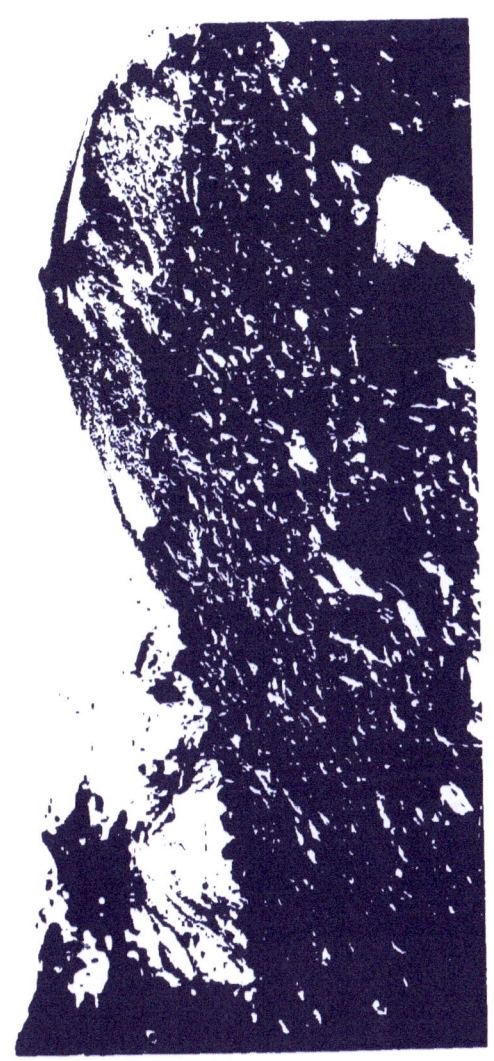

View from the summit of Tepanyeche — Aconcagua in the distance.

MEETING WITH FITZGERALD

horsemen coming towards me. Their costumes were not those of arrieros, or of our own porters. They had the appearance of travellers crossing the Andes, who had turned up the Horcones Valley by mistake, and they seemed to be looking for something. As soon as they saw me they came in my direction at full gallop, and drew up in front of me. Their town clothes were covered with mud and dust, and they were the most weary-looking men I had seen since our recent struggles on Tupungato. They seemed also to have great difficulty in settling certain differences of opinion between themselves and their mules. With much gesticulation they addressed me at a great pace in Spanish, and I was just preparing to explain to them their mistake, and direct them the best way to reach the main valley once more, when I caught the word "Tupungato." What had those men to do with Tupungato? Suddenly it dawned upon me that they had penetrated up this valley to interview me. I addressed them in French, and sure enough, one of them explained that they were correspondents of *La Union* of Santiago, specially commissioned to seek me out and get the first account of my ascent; that they were staying at Inca, and, having heard that I was up the Horcones Valley, had come to look for me. They had endured great sufferings, they said, and were glad it was now possible to return to civilisation. Then they began to put a series of questions to me. But as I considered FitzGerald had the right to the first news, I pointed out that it was very late in the day, and that they had better return to Inca at once, as it was extremely risky to be caught in this valley by night.

Later I saw four horsemen coming towards me, and soon made out FitzGerald, Lightbody, Gosse, and Mr. Ball of Valparaiso, who had heard the news of the ascent of Tupungato and had ridden up to tell FitzGerald. They were coming down to Inca for Easter. We were all very ready for a rest, and as we were in great spirits we celebrated the occasion by a stampede at full gallop all the way to Inca in the brilliant moonlight.

CHAPTER XX

THE LAST OF ACONCAGUA

AFTER Vines had joined us we continued with the survey traverse and levelling of the Horcones Valley. The whole of our party, consisting of Lightbody, Vines, Gosse, and myself, together with our porters and arrieros, were now collected together in one great camp in the open plain of the valley, just below our old tent under the forked peak. From here we had a splendid view of the topmost peak of Aconcagua lying due south from us. We had measured the height from many stations, but as a method of checking our work, and of making doubly sure that we had made no mistakes, we very carefully measured a base-line on this level plain, and made a fresh and independent triangulation of the mountain. This occupied us for many days, as our base-line from here was, owing to the formation of the country, necessarily a small one. We therefore took very elaborate pains to get our measurements absolutely correct. The altitude angles were measured with three theodolites, and checked with the sextant, these altitudes being repeated again and again at various times in the day, so as to minimise any errors that might possibly creep in owing to refraction. The angles and altitudes, when worked out, corresponded exactly with our previous heights, so we were at length satisfied that the measurements were as correct as it lay within our power to make them. We then turned our attention to continuing our traverse to the head of the Horcones Valley. Meanwhile Lightbody made a series of plane-table sketches from all our trigonometrical points, which we plotted out, to get the detail of this valley as perfect as possible.

TRIANGULATION

On 24th April, at an early hour in the morning, Vines and I started up to the head of the valley for the last time, in order to reach our 14,000 foot camp, and finish our work.

The days were getting much shorter now, and everything gave us the impression of approaching winter—dull, leaden skies, and bitterly cold nights. We had set ourselves the task of finishing our triangulation at the head of the Horcones Glacier. As we rode up the valley we found the streams a mass of hard ice, and the rocks all glazed and slippery with icicles. I had sent on a couple of men with our instruments before sunrise, to avoid delay, and by about 11 a.m. we reached our old camp. The ground here was covered with snow, and a cold biting wind from the north-west made our work very trying. We at once set ourselves to carry out the measurements we required on the glacier, and continued thus employed until 4 p.m. ; then, as it was getting late, we decided to make the last trigonometrical station at the head of the valley on a great pile of loose stones that lay on the glacier. The sun was now setting, and the Catedral had already cast its long shadow across us. During the last of our observations at this point we got our finger-tips severely touched by frost, for the screws upon our instruments were so cold that our skin peeled off as we touched them. It was impossible, we found, to adjust them properly with our gloves on. At about 5 p.m. I turned homewards, and it was with a feeling of great reluctance that I looked for the last time at this vast amphitheatre of ice and snow that had been the scene of so much of our labour. Many a day had I gazed out on it from our high camp with a feeling of utter hopelessness and bitter disappointment. Then all the forces of nature seemed to have combined to hold me back in my work ; even the elements themselves threatened at times to overwhelm our little camp, while many a weary day was wasted in waiting to see if it were not possible to overcome the fearful nausea that disabled me. Many a time had I crossed this glacier on my way to our upper camp, full of health, vigour, hope, and ambition ; then, alas, how many times had I passed down, walking in the same tracks, disheartened, dejected, weary, hopeless—my work still undone, while I was mentally and physically broken by cold and suffering, and failure stared me in the face—to return once more to an attack that at the time seemed well-nigh in vain. Just as we were leaving, the sun set, lighting up the scene with a fiery glow. I turned once more to look on this great glacier surrounded with snowy peaks, before taking leave of it for ever. Though we were now in the shade of evening, the sun having disappeared behind the neighbouring hills, the great battlements of Aconcagua still rose up on our right, bathed in sunlight, the shadows gradually creeping up its sides, till at last darkness like a cloak enveloped the peak, and only the summit remained tinged with red. Recollecting the lateness of the hour, and the long rough track that lay before us, we hurried towards the spot where we had left our horses, and mounting, we pressed on as fast as the dangerous way allowed. It was soon night and the stars gradually came out. Suddenly, before we had gone more than a mile, the light seemed to come back, as if the sun were rising again, and once more the great crags of Aconcagua rose above us, bathed in a ruddy brightness which seemed to invest them with even more than their wonted mystery and grandeur. This strange afterglow was caused, no doubt, by the reflection of the sun's rays, now invisible to us, from the surface of the Pacific Ocean to the clouds. It lasted but a few moments, and disappeared as suddenly as it came, leaving us in utter darkness, our eyes still dazzled by its radiance. The night was cold, and we pressed onward, reckless of consequences, trusting to the instinct and intelligence of our horses to find the way safely through the defiles. It was nearly midnight when we reached our camp.

The next morning, our work at the head of the valley being completed, and the mountain being measured, it only remained for us to make the exploration of the south face. Vines and I rode up the eastern branch of the Horcones Valley, to make a general reconnaissance, and to see how we could best place our trigonometrical stations. This was the first time we had penetrated into this valley, and we were

UNDER THE SOUTHERN PRECIPICE OF ACONCAGUA, LOOKING SOUTH

A HURRICANE

much struck by the magnificence of the scenery there. The approach to the great dizzy precipice of Aconcagua, some 10,000 feet in height, was an experience never to be forgotten. We were unable to get very far that day; in fact our intention, as I have said before, was only to get a general idea of how to approach the valley. A great glacier flows down, filling the whole of it, but this glacier is covered with masses of stone and moraine, and we were able to ride our horses over it. There are few places that an Andine pony will not climb to. At some points we had to dismount and lead our animals, as the coating of snow and sand over the ice was so thin that the horses' feet broke through, and they slipped about desperately. We had several narrow shaves, but fortunately no serious fall, and we returned late that evening and rejoined Lightbody, full of enthusiasm at the remarkable views and scenes that had greeted us.

Early next morning we carried our theodolite up and commenced the survey. We pushed along with it until about two o'clock in the afternoon, when we had reached a path halfway up the valley, and at such a height that we could see right on towards the end of it. The wind had been terrific that day, and we had had great trouble in steadying our instrument sufficiently to take accurate observations. We left the theodolite built round with a pier of stones, intending to return next day and take a few more heights of the surrounding country. Our next business was to secure some photographs of this marvellous scene. Vines and two men put up the camera at the top of a small moraine heap, holding the legs tightly against the blasts of wind. When we were all ready to take the photograph, and I was about to take the cap off, a fearsome hurricane of wind swept down the valley. It blew Vines and the men off their feet, and we all of us went rolling over and over, the camera getting considerably battered up. I mention this scene particularly to give the reader some idea of the force of the wind in these valleys. When three men steadying themselves as firmly as possible are unable to hold up a light camera weighing about ten pounds, it is easy to imagine that photography and surveying under these circumstances present a difficult problem. Later on we made another attempt to take a photograph, and this time we were more successful, as we built a stone pier on which to steady the instrument. This done, we sent the men back to camp, while Vines and I determined to ride on to the head of the valley. We worked our way over to the east side, and soon got into a small, narrow, flat plateau that lay between the mountain slopes and the glaciers, covered with smooth, hard sand. On this we were able to gallop along at a good pace, and we soon approached the base of the great rocky foundation of Aconcagua. The illustrations of this valley were not taken by us at that time, as unfortunately the photographs we took that day proved a failure. Lightbody, in the following spring, penetrated again into this inhospitable region, and took the illustrations which appear in this chapter.

This precipice, over two miles high, comes down at an extremely abrupt angle, the great overhanging glaciers which cover the face of the mountain splitting and turning in fantastic shapes, by reason of the excessive declivity of the slopes on which they lie. The valley forms a small amphitheatre at this spot, which is quite hidden from view from any point in the Horcones Valley. The whole scene that lay before us was new. Vines, of course, had seen it from the summit, but then a view from the base, looking up the great precipices, is as a rule even more impressive and imposing than the same seen from above. It is then that one realises most completely the colossal proportions of these immense crags and precipices. The day was getting late, and already the long shadows slanting across the valley warned us of the setting sun. So thrilled and entranced were we at the prospect that lay before us, however, that we were unable to wrench ourselves away, and we stood there, watching the sun slowly sinking, the lights receding, and the dark shadows slowly enveloping this great basin. A slight mist arose from the ice and floated about, its biting cold breath occasionally sweeping across us and chilling us to

GREAT PRECIPICE ON ACONCAGUA

A WONDERFUL SUNSET

the bone. It was then that we remembered, for the first time, how far we were from camp, and the thought compelled us reluctantly to turn our steps homeward. It was entirely through the sagacity of our clever ponies that we covered the first few miles safely, for I am sure that neither Vines nor myself paid any heed to the route we were taking. We were both of us twisted round in our saddles, eager to get the last glimpse of this stupendous amphitheatre that had been so long hidden from the gaze of man. We wondered if the Incas had ever penetrated into these recesses, and if so, what their feelings had been on first gazing upon this unique sight. Had they taken it as a matter of course, and let it pass unnoticed by them, or had they also been awed by the majesty and the overwhelming mass of the mountains? Had they been reduced, as we were, to speaking almost in whispers lest they should break the sacred stillness of these mysterious precincts? As the sun set we again saw that marvellous afterglow we had seen two nights before, but this time we looked from the other side of the mountain, and the effect was still more striking and magnificent, for it tinged the great white glaciers on the face of Aconcagua with wonderful pink and purple hues. The whole mountain shone out, and seemed to raise its head miles and miles higher than before: it seemed gradually to tower almost out of sight. Then some clouds blew up towards the peak, and it disappeared, hidden by the black night that was upon us—its evening cloak of clouds.

We now had to give serious attention to the problem of getting home. The way across the glacier was steep and slippery, and several times we lost our way. When finally we arrived in camp it was about ten o'clock at night, and Lightbody and the men were already organising a search party to go out and look for us. We arranged to go back next morning to this same valley as early as possible, to take more photographs, and finish the detailed survey. We woke up on the following day, however, only to find the ground covered with white snow, and a dull, leaden sky above. As I feared this might possibly mean a break-up of the weather, and the advent of the true winter snow, I thought it advisable to strike our tent and push down. We accordingly did so at once, loading up our tents and equipment upon all the animals then with us. When we reached that part of the valley just above the Paso Malo, and the ford in which Zurbriggen had been so nearly drowned, we decided to pitch a small camp, leaving most of our things, as from here we could equally well explore the east head of the valley; and besides, we were much lower and nearer to the Inca, in case of heavy snows. The passage of the Paso Malo was very difficult on this side. The path we had built up upon the face of the sheer smooth stone had to a great extent been worn away by the repeated passage of mules up and down the valley, coming to and from our camps. Some time before, I had given strict orders that nobody should ride across this pass, and that no valuable luggage should be taken on the mules, but carried across by hand. I had always lived in dread that somebody would lose his life on this most dangerous place, for if once anyone fell or slipped down some six or seven feet there would be no hope of recovering him; he would roll down the whole way, and be for ever lost in the river. On this occasion we unloaded all our mules, and carried the luggage carefully across. We then drove the animals down slowly one by one, and watched them as they traversed this perilous spot. Vines, who had come down in front, had mended it to the best of his ability, but it was impossible to do very much, as there was really no place to build up from,—always upon the slope of the smooth and slippery rock. Nothing is more painful than to stand and watch animals crossing a dangerous gulf like this, and to be unable to give them any assistance. They had to be driven straight at it, and allowed to take their time, and we had to trust to their marvellous instinct and intelligence to guide them safely over. The horses all passed safely, for these intelligent animals pause before the dangerous points, and look at them carefully, even stooping down and sniffing at the ground, as if to determine its solidity by that means. The mules, however, came out badly. They would not pay any attention, and came shuffling across the worst places

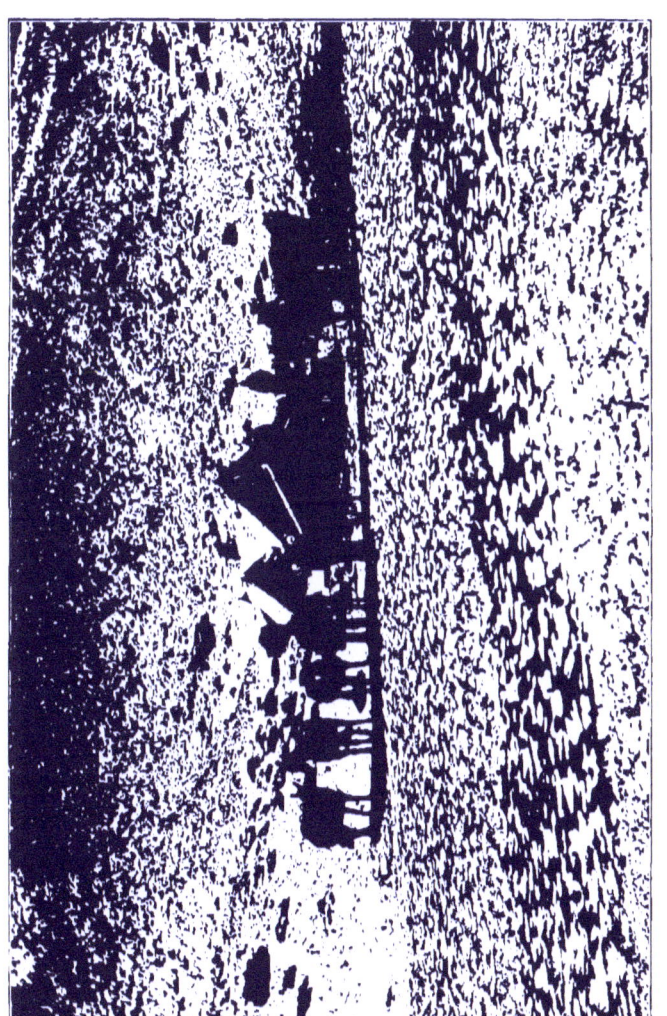

STRIKING CAMP IN HORCONES VALLEY

with the same confidence and negligence they would have shown had they been walking down the high road. Three of them slipped and fell at the worst places, only just managing to recover themselves in time. One we felt quite sure was lost, but he managed in some miraculous way to slide along and recover himself, and crawl back to the path again, looking merely tired and bored the while.

When we reached Inca, the weather slightly mended. I determined to send Vines over to Chile, to see if he could possibly reach the volcano he had seen smoking from the top of Tupungato. He knew that it could be got at by ascending one of the valleys which start from near Santiago. The question was, however, which valley? The survey of these valleys is exceedingly rough, and they are by no means clearly marked, the positions of the high peaks being naturally the first points that a mountain survey starts from. I have no doubt that the Commission de Limites will bring out a much more correct and detailed map of the country, as they have been through most of these valleys by now. I sent Zurbriggen with Vines in case he should have any climbing to do, while I decided to remain with Lightbody, and to see what more could be done in the Horcones Valley. I told Vines to take José, and as many mules and horses as he wanted for his luggage, and he was to send José back as soon as he reached the railway at Salto del Soldado.

In the following chapter Vines will tell the story of this journey.

CHAPTER XXI

BY STUART VINES

A LOST VOLCANO

THE volcano seen by myself and Zurbriggen from the great spur during the ascent of Tupungato was regarded by FitzGerald as an important discovery of volcanic activity in the vicinity of the city of Santiago, and he therefore desired that Zurbriggen and I should cross over to Chile, make our way to Santiago, and there get information about the valleys to the east, and make transport arrangements. We started from Inca at 2 p.m. on Sunday, 2nd May, crossed the Cumbre and reached Portillo at seven o'clock the same night, where our friend Louis gave us a hearty welcome. The next morning we reached the Transandine Station of the West Coast Cable Co., at Rio Blanco. Here Mr. Tuffield, Manager of the "West Coast," has a charming little bungalow by the roadside, at the junction of the Rio Blanco and Rio Aconcagua. The valley of the Rio Blanco, with its luxuriant vegetation, is particularly beautiful to anyone descending from the arid wastes above. About three miles down the valley is the terminus of the narrow-gauge railway that is intended some day to join hands with the line from Mendoza to Vacas. On this day there was no train. We therefore called on Mr. Tuffield to ask him to telephone down for an engine and trolly to come up and take us to Santa Rosa de los Andes. He was away, but his wife immediately telephoned to him, and all arrangements were made. This was not the first time nor the last that we had reason to be grateful to Mr. Tuffield for his great kindness and hospitality to us. Between Juncal and Santa Rosa there is not a single place of any kind where travellers over the Andes can obtain food or shelter, and people of all stations in life, from the Ministers of foreign countries down to the Irishman who has slipped away from some ocean tramp and escaped to the hills, have one reason and another for calling at Tuffield's house. Some receive valuable information, and some food. No one is turned away from that hospitable door. The first words that came over the telephone in answer to my inquiries were, "My wife will ask you to lunch," but they were needless: Mrs. Tuffield had already done so. My reply was, "I lunch only on the condition that you dine with me to-night in Santa Rosa, and that you order the dinner." Tuffield accepted my conditions, and I accepted his wife's hospitality at Rio Blanco. I had no sooner sat down than my hostess asked me whether I had heard about the duel. I had not. What duel? And then her daughter took up the conversation and told me the story. As far as I remember it was as follows:—General A., a retired officer of the Chilian army, a deputy and a duellist of great fame, though a man of considerable age, had a quarrel with Major B., an officer who had distinguished himself in the Civil War of 1890, owing to some aspersion cast by General A. on the officers of the National Guard. General A. set his heart on fighting, evaded the laws, shut himself up in his estancia in the country and practised shooting. He would speak to no one, and for days the only words he was heard to utter were—"I will shoot him dead; I will kill him!"

A duel was arranged, but could not take place in Chile, so again evading the police, the principals made their way by road to Santa Rosa and on to Salto del Soldado with the intention of fighting on Argentine soil. "Oh, yes," said Miss Tuffield, "it was very exciting. It was in the middle of the night, two nights ago. Two carriages drew up at the door, and we had never seen real carriages up here before. The people wanted food and drink; they said they were famished. They were going over to Argentina. What for? Oh, never mind—important political business. We couldn't understand. We gave them food. One party came in, and the other remained outside. They wouldn't speak to one another; and then mother said, 'I believe it's a duel,' and told Enrico, he's our *mozo* you know, to saddle Santano, our swiftest horse, and follow them. They had disturbed the whole house, and everybody was up, but in ten minutes they were off again in the dark, Enrico after them.

"And at the door next morning—ten coaches! All the people from Chile! And everybody talked at once. Soldiers banged at the door, woke us up again, and asked if anyone had passed in the night. Suddenly everybody was silent. Somebody was galloping down the road from Juncal. Yes, it was Enrico, swaying from side to side in the saddle, swinging his spurs, and shouting, '*Un medico! un medico! por l'amor de Dios un medico!*' Oh! he looked terrible. He could hardly see out of his eyes for dust, and when he got to the gate they helped him out of the saddle and Santano fell down as if he were dead. Poor Santano! He has not eaten anything since, and drinks, drinks, drinks—I'm afraid he'll die! Enrico! Just think! From the Cumbre in two hours! The duel was fought at six; he was here at eight, and it takes passengers seven hours at least from the Cumbre to Rio Blanco." "What news did Enrico bring of the duel?—did he see it?" "Oh no, they were clever: it was very early in the morning. No sooner were they on the other side at the top of the pass in Argentina than they got behind some rocks and fought quite quietly. Everybody says the General reserved his fire and wouldn't shoot. Then Major B. raised his arm and shot into the air. And then the General shot straight at him, hit him in the head and he fell down as if dead. They found Enrico coming up the pass after them and shouted, 'Get a doctor for heaven's sake.' He knew nothing, only that Major B. was dying and General A. was unhurt.'

"More people came from Chile, more newspaper men, and a doctor, but we sent for another. And then hours—hours after, the two coaches came galloping down from Juncal, they stopped at the door, and the doctors rushed out, and that bad General came in. He was quite mad: he walked up and down the room and said, 'I knew I'd kill him, kill him, kill him,' and rushed from one reporter to another, and told them what they were to say and what they were not to say, and then we heard the whole story. Everybody was very excited, and they all came in, and were very hungry and very thirsty, and they thought it was a restaurant, and wanted to pay mother for what they had. The doctors said Major B. could only live a few hours; he was shot in the head, and the bullet had gone right round his skull under the skin. They would not let him get out of the cab and come in: we wanted to take care of him. They took him in that jolting cab twenty miles to Santa Rosa. Oh, he's terribly bad!"

Such was the interesting account given me by Mr. Tuffield's daughter of this extraordinary duel. I am here glad to be able to add that I saw Major B. some months later, thoroughly recovered from his extraordinary and desperate wound, at a review of cadets at the Escuela Militar in Santiago.

But the telephone rang us up, and Tuffield's cheery voice shouted, "Your engine was sent up half an hour ago." So we got on to our horses and galloped down to Salto del Soldado. It was a most amusing and interesting ride, down the thirty miles of railway to Santa Rosa on the little engine, with two seats behind like the back seats in a gig. The stationmaster at Salto told us we had too much luggage to take down on the steam trolly. He was quite right—we had. Tents and mule panniers were scattered all over it. Some were hung on at the side, some were in the coal-box; in fact the driver and stoker could hardly move, and Zurbriggen and I had to hang on anyhow. Our drivers were Englishmen, and they took us down the steep inclines and round the sharp corners in true sporting style. Every now and then a donkey or calf would stand across the line, and only just move away in time as the brake was clapped on with full force.

Arrieros seem to use the line as a highway for their cattle, and horsemen in wide sombreros and short, coloured ponchos would come dashing down the line towards us—their horses swerving cleverly to one side not a second too soon, as we dashed past with a wild whistle. And so shouting and whistling and applying the brake, we arrived at los Andes without any more serious mishap than having run over a couple of barn-door hens. Tuffield met us at the station,—this was my first return to civilisation for several months,—and we spent a jolly evening. And then it began to rain, while snow fell in the mountains, and we were prisoners at the Hotel Commercio for several days. Santa Rosa is an extremely picturesque place in dry weather, but commend me to any other spot when it is wet. The water comes through the roofs, and the streets are knee-deep in mud. At last on the 6th I started to Santiago, and here we continued to wait for the weather to clear up. After interviewing numerous people, military and civil, I came to the conclusion that our best course of action was to go down to a country town called San José de Maipu, some thirty-five miles south of Santiago.

On Sunday morning, 9th May, I started down by a small private railway which ran south to a place called Puente Alto. It was a clear, bright morning after the rain—I have seldom seen the atmosphere appear so thin and clear. The fresh snow that had fallen on the heights overhanging Santiago made the scene one of dazzling brilliancy. The magnificent range of the Cerro del Plomo with its glaciers and precipitous crags, thirty-five miles to the north-east of the town, was particularly striking. John Hicks, an English mechanic, accompanied me as interpreter. He had lived for years in this neighbourhood, and yet he showed a remarkable ignorance of the mountains which he beheld with his eyes every day of his life. We went to an inn kept by an extraordinary gentleman by the name of Gussmann, perfectly Spanish in his origin in spite of his name. I inquired of everyone about the large mountain to the south-east, and nobody knew its name: one man called it the Cerro del Colorado. I took bearings, and felt certain that it was Tupungato. I was astonished to find I could not obtain a horse—in this country where everybody is on horseback. They promised me horses, but when it came to the point, I found there were none. Every man in the place was drunk, and why? It was Sunday, and it was the season of the year when *chicha* was being drunk. I have heard some people describe *chicha* as a species of champagne. They could not have had the same sort that I drank—a muddy yellow-looking liquid, in appearance like orange juice, in taste somewhat like cider, though made from the juice of the grape: and, as far as I could see from the results around me, extremely intoxicating. To one who had not spent Sunday in a town in the plains of Chile, the scene around was of an extraordinary nature. In order to reach Gussmann's tavern from the railway station, we had to make our way from one end of the village to the other. Crowds of picturesque wild-looking fellows, with enormous jingling spurs were lolling round the *bodegas*, from which proceeded loud shouts of merriment. Soon we came upon more exciting scenes. A crowd was standing at a safe distance watching three horsemen, who, though evidently in the last stage of intoxication, were still able to keep in the saddle. The game seemed to be for the horsemen to ride at anybody on foot, and if this person ran for protection into the houses, to gallop full-tilt after him. The hunted pedestrians seemed to enter into the spirit of this rough horse-play with as much zest as their pursuers. A horseman would dash towards a narrow doorway of some house, duck his head and disappear. There would be a crash, and the sound of a general break-up inside, and the man would appear again generally backing his horse out, where the room was too small to turn. It was interesting to watch their perfect control over their horses in spite of their condition. The spur seemed to play an important part in the guiding of the animal, and these picturesque-looking ruffians swayed about from side to side in the saddle, but they never fell. Hicks turned to me and said, "I am afraid, sir, they have been having a little more than usual to-day." Then he made some excuses about it being some particular saint's day; but he added, "For God's sake, humour them whatever they do." And I soon found that he had to practise what he preached. He seemed to have many acquaintances amongst the crowd, and was forced to submit himself to many endearing embraces before we reached Gussmann's. Except that I had to shake hands with three or four of the more pressing of these revellers, I was in no way molested. Gussmann was also in a lively state of intoxication. I came to the conclusion that as nobody was fit to attend to business, it was better to return to Santiago. There was no train back for some time, but the stationmaster and his wife, who were both decidedly tipsy, offered chicha and sundry amusements to while away the time.

Mr. Kennedy, the British Minister, took me that day to see the Minister of Foreign Affairs, in Santiago, Señor Morla Vicuña, and I had a very interesting chat about the great boundary question between Argentina and Chile. He showed me a map of the south, and, pointing to a large space on it, covering three degrees of latitude, where there was neither mark nor name, he said, "When Mr. FitzGerald has finished with Aconcagua, tell him to go down south and explore this piece here, and we will call it *Tierra del FitzGeraldo.*

I learnt that it was no good going down to Puente Alto on Monday, as the inhabitants would require that day to get over their Sunday's revellings; so that it was not till Tuesday, the 11th, that I started again, got a coach with four horses abreast, and arrived at two in the afternoon at San José de Maipu. There we found a very decent inn kept by a Frenchman. He had been there many years, and I understood "knew all about the mountains." I mentioned Tupungato, and he said, "Oh, yes! Tupungato. My son knows it quite well. He has ascended it many times with ladies from my hotel." After that I sought no more information from our host. The next day we started at daybreak on horseback to find out the lie of the country, and determine on the best route to take. We had not been riding two hours when Zurbriggen complained of feeling ill, and we were forced to return. He was suffering from an attack of dysentery, and I had to send for the doctor. On the 13th I remained with him, hoping that he would be able to start the next day. But he was no better; so on the 14th, taking two arrieros and a couple of mules, I started alone for the Yeso Valley, which leads to the Portillo Pass. It was an extremely picturesque ride along this road southwards; the inhabitants, amongst whom were a great many half-castes living in huts made solely out of the branches of trees. These dwellings seemed to me suitable enough for summer, and though I noticed that their owners were busily engaged in patching them with green branches for the approaching winter, they promised to afford but a very poor protection against the snow which often falls in this valley. We made our way as far as possible up the Yeso Valley, and camped at an altitude of some 6000 feet. I had much trouble with my two men to make them move quickly. It was a warm night, so I did not put up the tent, and we made ourselves comfortable round a fire. At least, it would have been comfortable but for the fact that in the middle of the night I must have moved in my sleep too close to the burning embers. I found them getting extremely warm, and then I was nearly suffocated. I woke up to find the lower end of my eider-down sleeping-bag one mass of charred feathers.

Early the next morning I determined to start up the mountain side to some height above, to see if I could recognise any of the views of the country that I had seen from the top of Tupungato. I hoped to get bearings of that mountain, and perhaps even see something of the volcano, which I was fully convinced must now be within ten or fifteen miles north of the Yeso Valley. I set apart sufficient food, some instruments and ponchos, and a complete change of clothing, saying that I would return to the camping-ground at midday. I arranged that one arriero, Rodriguez, should take the pack-mules, and go on in advance ten miles up the Yeso Valley to the foot of the Portillo Pass, to a spot well known to me and to the other arriero, Tomas. Tomas was to accompany me fifteen hundred feet up the mountain side, and then return and wait for me at the camping-ground. All seemed nicely arranged, and I started at 6 a.m. on horseback up the lower slopes. The snowline after the recent bad weather was extremely low, coming down to within two thousand feet of our camp; so, repeating my instructions, I sent Tomas back, and proceeded on foot. For five hours I tramped through the heavy snow, often above my knees, and in places badly drifted, but could gain no satisfactory view of the country. It was heavy dull weather, and I could see no distant peaks. So I aimed for some high tableland, going many times out of my way to traverse wind-swept patches where the snow was less deep. The weather showed no signs of clearing, and after an uncomfortable scramble up a couloir filled with snow and rotten rocks, I reached a peak which seemed to be the highest point for many miles. The Yeso Valley beneath me was clear, and I could see a fine hanging glacier above the point where that valley turned westwards to the Portillo Pass. In the direction of Tupungato I could see nothing, and cloud lay between me and the north. My aneroid, which I had had adjusted at the Meteorological Office in Santiago, read 20.65 inches, on the top. It was later than I had intended, and so I turned to descend. I found the gully filled with hardened snow, and was enabled to glissade some two thousand feet at a splendid pace, and at two o'clock I reached the valley, drenched to the skin, and terribly hungry. Tomas was waiting with the horses, and I asked him for the bundle I had left behind, containing the change of clothes, ponchos, and food. In my tired and hungry condition, his answer impressed me considerably. "Señor, Rodriguez has taken them : I did not tell him, and he started before I returned from accompanying the señor up the mountain. If the señor had arrived two hours ago, we could have caught Rodriguez up in a short time, but now I fear he has a good ten miles start of us." I mentally consigned Rodriguez to the infernal regions, and crawled, dripping, into the saddle. My animal was a sluggish brute, I had no spurs, and Tomas's ideas of hurrying were meagre. After a mile or two Tomas pointed out to me that there was a low road and a high road. The *camino bajo* was a mere bridle track by the bed of the river, which led into the Laguna Seca or Laguna de los Peuquenes of the Yeso Valley at 7000 feet. The camino alto, he informed me, was broad and good in summer, but was impassable now, being entirely blocked by snow-drifts. Therefore, Rodriguez would have taken the camino bajo. We decided to do so too. We reached the Laguna Seca at three o'clock, and proceeded up it for some time, but no signs could we find of Rodriguez. It was now exactly twelve hours since I had tasted food, except for a few slabs of chocolate which I had taken in my pack.

The valley beyond the lake was covered with deep snow. It was bitterly cold, and there were no rocks under which to shelter from the wind. Telling Tomas to follow me, I returned once more down the Laguna Seca. Then Tomas informed me that there were some huts used by the cattle drivers in summer at this lower end, and he was certain we should find Rodriguez there. The reader can imagine with what excitement we approached these huts. We shouted; Tomas said he must be asleep, but I could see no mules. We came up to them—they were empty. It was now eleven o'clock at night. "Will the señor come to the foot of the camino alto. We may see tracks in the snow." The floor of the hut was wet mud and the ground around marshy. I therefore consented. Tomas was right. In the snow where the camino alto turned into the Laguna Seca were tracks of mules and horses, which Tomas assured me belonged to Rodriguez' caravan, for he dismounted, struck a match, and examined the footmarks. "See," he said, "this mule has no shoe on its off foreleg, and this mule has only one shoe. I know they're our mules. See, señor, two mules and a horse," as he examined them carefully. "And you see they run back over the pass. Rodriguez has returned this way to find us." It was pitch dark—for two hours we tumbled among the snow-drifts in the pass. It seemed unending work following these tracks, and at 1 a.m. I told Tomas I would go no farther. I cleared away the snow under some rocks, and with the saddle, a worn-out sheepskin, and my poncho for covering, spent a miserable five hours waiting for the dawn. At noon the following day, we found Rodriguez encamped on the same spot where we had rested two nights before. His excuses were futile. There was no doubt about it; the depth of the snow in the valleys beyond Laguna Seca and the look of the weather had made his heart fail, and, in dread of being snowed up, he had returned. In spite of Tomas's entreaties on his behalf I gave him the thrashing he deserved, and made him get us something to eat as quickly as possible, for I was half-frozen and almost dead with hunger.

After a substantial meal I felt inclined for sleep, but I could not afford to lose another day, so slept in the saddle, and arrived at the western foot of the Portillo Pass in the evening. I climbed to a neighbouring height and examined the country round. All the valleys were blocked with snow, and the air was thick with cloud. The pass was impossible, and Tupungato, which is not more than ten miles from this spot, was entirely hidden from view. I could not see a mile around me. Even in the very brightest weather I doubt whether it would be possible to penetrate up these valleys—which looked to me like one huge drift. We turned and floundered back to the Laguna Seca, where we spent the night, and the next day returned to San José de Maipu. Zurbriggen was still feeling weak and ill. Torrents of rain had been falling for hours, and there seemed no chance of the weather clearing. It was out of the question to work in the valleys at higher altitudes. The little town itself was white with snow, and I determined to return to Santiago. There I found a message from FitzGerald, who had also fled to Mendoza owing to bad weather, telling me to join him as soon as I could get over the Cumbre Pass.

In a few hours I left Santiago for Santa Rosa, where, after much discussion at the railway station, the stationmaster decided to let the train start. He told me I should find the pass road not improved during the three weeks I had been away in the south. He added, "You will also find the prices of transport have gone up considerably." ' And who are all those military-looking men?" I asked. "The Argentine Boundary Commission, returning for the winter, after their work on this side of the frontier," was his reply.

THE COMMISSION DE LIMITES 239

"They have been waiting for ten days to get over. I have not let a train go up for a fortnight." At Salto we all crowded into a coach, and galloped off for Juncal. The stationmaster was quite right, the prices were extortionate. At Rio Blanco, Tuffield came out and stopped the coach, and would not dream of letting me pass without refreshment. He said, "Surely you are not going up on the roof again? I thought you had returned to civilisation. It is a terribly early winter, and Rio Blanco is no place to be in such weather. You won't be able to go much more than another five or six miles in that coach; then they will probably have mules for you, but I doubt if you will be able to get farther than Juncal." I told him I could walk. I said these officers of the Boundary Commission have hired riding mules over to Cuevas. "Then," said Tuffield, "they won't get their money's worth. It is a common trick of the arrieros at this time of the year to make you pay for mules for miles of road where it is impossible to use them." At Juncal my friends did not like the look of things, so stopped for the night, but Zurbriggen and I ascended to Portillo. The next day the caravan arrived with the Boundary Commission, ten other passengers, some dozen arrieros and not fewer than fifty mules. They were determined to force a way over to Cuevas and catch the weekly train at Vacas. Zurbriggen, Louis, and I watched them for some time winding up the snow; now one arriero taking the lead, now another. "They're doing very well," said Louis, "but they can't possibly get past the drifts below the second casucha some two miles further on: they will be forced to do the worst part of the pass on foot in spite of all the animals they have."

Three hours later I started alone on foot, as Zurbriggen had to go back to Juncal for some of our baggage that had been mislaid. Only for a short time could I use the tracks of those who had gone before, for there above me was the long winding caravan, making no further progress. Had they lost the way, or was the snow at last too deep? I made straight for the top of the pass by a short cut, and when above them I looked back upon an extraordinary scene.

The mules were wandering in the snow, most of them unladen, the packs were lying everywhere, and arrieros and passengers were grouped together, while forcible adjectives in Spanish came to me over the snow. Some difference had arisen between the Chileno mule-drivers and the Argentine passengers. Two men rushed to a mule, began pulling the packs off and throwing them in the snow. Several of the blue-coated commissioners interfered, angry at seeing their valuable instruments so roughly handled. I heard on one side, " You contracted to take us over on muleback to Cuevas, and you Chilian rascals shall do it," and the blue-coated men drew their revolvers, and threatened to shoot. " Neither we nor the mules will go a step farther; the snow is too deep. Shoot if you like—we are not afraid of Argentine bullets," and though unarmed, the arrieros laughed at them. Then the voices became more subdued, and a move was made to the casucha hard by. I did not envy them a night in that narrow hovel. The wind got up, it began to snow, and I proceeded on my way; got to the top of the pass, and glissaded down almost the whole way to Cuevas, where I got a bony beast, without a saddle, and floundered through the drifts to Inca, arriving at five o'clock that evening. So ended my vain hunt for a volcano. I accomplished nothing, and the tale has no importance; but perhaps this little glimpse of travelling in out-of-the-way Chile may be good for half an hour's interest.

SNOW PEAKS ON THE BOUNDARY

CHAPTER XXII

THE HORCONES VALLEY IN WINTER

THE day after Vines left for Chile was a perfect one; the sun was warm, and Lightbody and I agreed that we should have another week or so before the winter snows came in earnest. We therefore arranged to go back up the Horcones Valley, do a little photography, and run our traverse up some of the side valleys. Vines's arriero, Fortunato, who alone was with us now, as José had gone with Vines and Zurbriggen to Chile, begged us not to go up this valley, saying we should be snowed up and all lose our lives. I told him he would have to go, and I had no more time to listen to his nonsense.

The next day Gosse started with a number of pack-mules, two porters, and the reluctant Fortunato. As we had still important work to finish, Lightbody and I did not start till late in the evening, and the dark had long fallen before we reached the tent. I pause at this moment before recounting the evil fortune that overtook us and finally destroyed all hope of further work, for I am reminded of a plan adopted by Mark Twain in one of his recent books. It had often annoyed him, he says, in reading other people's books, to come across descriptions of the weather every few pages; they interrupted the continuity of the narrative, they withdrew one's attention from the characters, and those people who had to read about weather anyhow, feeling that the world is already full of it, and that it might at least be kept out of books, threw down the volume in disgust. Yet he realised that weather affected human plans—how warmly I can support him there!—and that it could not be left out of any book that pretended to deal with life as it is. Besides, he was conscious that he could write about weather as well as any man. He therefore conceived the idea of making a sort of weather appendix to his novel; he described states of weather and atmospheric effects, thunderstorms for the crisis of peoples' souls, sunsets to accompany pathetic deaths, glowing noon-tides to go along with picnics, moon-rises for the love scenes, and slight showers to get the comedy characters under one umbrella. In the body of the book not so much as a snowflake of winter nor a beam of summer sunshine was permitted to appear. Then, as the entranced reader hurried through the tale, when he felt himself parched, so to speak, for want of weather, he could turn up the appendix and select any sample that seemed good to him, taking the circumstances of the story and his own private tastes into consideration.

Perhaps I am unwise to quote this humane system, for readers of my record may wish heartily that I had followed it myself. In self-defence I may be allowed to say that I defy any writer, no matter how gifted, to confine the weather on and around Aconcagua to an appendix. Such a plan would simply have this result: the appendix would be the book, and everything else would sink insignificantly out of sight. Perhaps after all this might have been the wiser plan in attacking the subject; to have started out fairly to make a compendium, a dictionary, an encyclopædia of weather in the Andes, and allowed our work, meagre beside the ceaseless toiling of the elements to produce new kinds and worse kinds of weather, to leak out by the way.

As it was, a tremendous storm arose on the very night that we reached that tent at the fork of the Horcones Valley. Keen and ready for some difficult but interesting work, with our porters, mules, instruments, cameras, and the rest in particularly fit condition, we had to lie and listen to the gale, amidst whose violence I could detect the persistent, stealthy, and most unwelcome arrival of the snow. As soon as the light came in the morning and we looked outside, we saw the whole country-side covered with it. It seemed as if the

A RETREAT

words of Fortunato were coming true, and that we were to be snowed up.

I am not, and never shall be, any friend to snow. There are times when I would have said that I hated rain more than anything, and other times when I could have declared that wind was the most unbearable form of weather. After all it is only wind that bullies you; no other weather ever does that. But on mature reflection I think I hate snow most. There is a low, surreptitiousness about snow, which revolts a mind of even average straightforwardness. You never know how much you are to have of it. An hour, an afternoon, or a week; in the neighbourhood of Aconcagua towards the middle of May, it is wiser to count upon the week.

I thought it prudent to move down at once. We had a great deal of luggage at this camp,—far more than we could possibly load on our animals,—so I picked out a few of the more important things, and told Fortunato to take them down to Inca as best he could, saying that we should follow on foot. This I did early in the morning, as I did not want the horses and mules to get blocked by the way. Lightbody, Gosse, and myself started out at about two o'clock. We had waited till then, hoping that perhaps the weather would moderate, for if it had, we might still have been able to do some work. As the snow still continued to fall in immense quantities, I realised that it was wiser not to stay another night, and to risk being snowed in. The wind was blowing heavily, and the cold intense. We suffered keenly in the descent; the tracks of the animals were completely covered up, so we had to make our own tracks the whole way. Towards the end, as we were nearing Inca, we were almost overcome with the fatigue of ploughing through the new snow, and the difficulty we had in breathing—surrounded as we were by eddies of the fine drifting snow which filled our nostrils—was extreme. Still we reached Inca safely, just as it got dark, to find that José had returned over the Cumbre Pass, with the mules that Vines and Zurbriggen had taken with them. It had been a most difficult task coming down from Cuevas, but fortunately he had got through. We were greatly relieved, for we had feared that he might be cut off on the Chilian side, and that we should never see our animals again on this side of the water-parting. The snow continued to fall all that night, and next day it was deep all over the country.

I need hardly write here of the disappointment we felt. All hope of our work cut off; the season at an end; five animals in the camp who could no longer find any food for themselves; only three days' supply of maize in hand; that miserable Fortunato clamouring to be allowed to leave for Vacas; and, worst of all, or so it seemed to me at the time, a large number of most valuable instruments, notebooks, undeveloped plates, and general impedimenta, which I was under no circumstances prepared to abandon, shut up and buried in incalculable snows at the high-level camp. First it was necessary to deal with Fortunato—the Jonah of this expedition, as I shall ever maintain. He implored, he wept; gusty southern sobs rent his bosom beneath the soiled tatters of his arriero's poncho. "If I stay another day," he gulped out, "I may not get down to Vacas again this winter. I think the snowfall is going to be tremendous, and I do not think that anybody in the Cordilleras will be able to move for the next fortnight." Undismayed by the vision of the inhabitants of the Cordilleras rooted to the spot and becoming snow men where they stood, we yet found the opinion far from cheering. But we had to let him go, and take with him some of our animals, keeping with us five only; and we begged him, if possible, to send up further supplies of maize, of which I had a cart-load at Vacas.

The outlook, however, was undoubtedly growing very serious. It seemed impossible for supplies to be brought upon the animal's backs, since they would not be able to make the journey heavily laden through the heavy snow. Dr. Cotton, our host at the inn, suggested that the best course would be to build a sledge; accordingly we went to work, and spent all that day manufacturing a weird vehicle out of timbers that were being used for the construction of a new wing to the building. We built, Dr. Cotton assisting us, a strong but heavy sledge, and got it out next evening; all our five horses and mules were attached to it, and we started off in great style to put it to a practical test. Soon, however, we found that the runners were not high enough, and that it was unable to ride over the top of the soft snow, being "towed under," like a boat made fast behind a steamer with too short a painter. We then made another attempt, and young Lochmatter volunteered his services, declaring he was accustomed to make sleighs in Switzerland—in fact I gathered he was a sleigh-maker by profession. This was fortunate, as our ideas on the subject were rather crude. He soon made a splendid sledge for us, raising the body two and a half feet above the runners. That evening Fortunato, unable apparently to quit the scene of his sufferings, came up from Vacas with some telegrams. He said that the road was in a fearful condition, that he had only just managed to get through, and that it would be impossible to bring up maize on the animals' backs. He was again overwhelmed with fear of being snowed up, but we induced him to stop until next morning. Paramillo, his dog, a creature of great heart, and in every way a finer character than his master, was with him. I am constrained to record, though I would willingly consign the fact to the appendix, that the snow had been falling all these days, and already the inn was nearly buried.

On the Friday morning, the 7th of May, the situation was about as critical as it could be. We had no more maize to give our beasts. The mules wandered about outside the inn, sometimes forcing their way in at the doors and eating the very bedclothes off the bed when they got the chance. They consumed, that morning, two wicker-chairs and a large quantity of the roof of one of the rooms, which was composed of bamboo overlaid with mud. This could not be allowed to go on—for one thing, the furniture of the inn would not last long. That member of the expedition who was generally charged with commissariat duty, and prided himself on his powers of gauging the rate of consumption of victuals per man, per mule, per anything in fact, went into the matter with his accustomed practicality, and reported to me, with due solemnity, that, setting aside the crockery and the *batterie de cuisine*, which, though he might be wrong, he ventured to believe would have a fatal effect upon any animal so careless as to eat it; and taking into consideration merely the bedding, mats, curtains, and woodwork of the inn, we could not hope to keep the pack-mules at their kicking weight if this outfit was expected to last them more than eight, or, at the outside, nine days. At which point, it was borne in upon us, that if the mules wrecked the inn and ate the roof, we should be left to the mercy of the elements, with no protection save a dinner-service and an old frying-pan or two.

It was absolutely necessary to make a move without delay. We arranged, therefore, to start for Vacas upon the new sledge, and put all the five animals to it. José upon his horse, and Fortunato upon his, rode as postillions on either side, while we urged our animals from behind, and Paramillo danced ahead, barking and rolling over in the fine snow, very happy. The sleigh went fairly well, though we had one or two close shaves in some heavy drifts; but if we did not actually upset the thing, we succeeded in spilling ourselves out of it many times. As we approached Vacas we found the snow getting lighter and lighter, till, about two miles from the railway station there was none left, and we were obliged to drag the sleigh across the hard, stony ground. Late in the evening we reached the posada at Vacas. I need hardly remark that it snowed again that night, and next morning. As there was nothing whatever to be done, I suggested to Lightbody that we should take the train down to Mendoza, and say good-bye to the many friends who had been so kind to us, and helped us so much in our work. Since we had it in our minds to return by way of Chile, we should not see them again, and such a visit seemed a more agreeable means of filling in this disheartening time than any other. Accordingly we took the down train that morning, leaving Gosse and Dr. Cotton to return to

Inca, whither they were to convoy some maize for the feeding of the horses. Lightbody and I spent several days in Mendoza, the telegraph daily depressing us with the intelligence that the weather still continued doubtful. As soon as we heard that a slight thaw had set in we returned to Vacas, and there, where he had been for several days, I found José in a shockingly drunken condition. With the weather as it was, I think it would have been difficult to convince a person of slender intellectual resources that he could have been more profitably employed. We got hold of him, balanced him more or less upon his mule, and drove him up to Inca before us.

The next few days Lightbody was ill, and unable to get about, while it became evident that the weather had completely broken up. There was no blinking the fact that winter was really upon us, and that if I wished ever to get back the things I had left up the Horcones Valley, it would be necessary to press up at once, irrespective of whole dictionaries of weather, as every storm increased our difficulties, while the sun was now too low in its declination to melt the ice and snow that blocked these valleys. Next day I despatched José, all the porters and some mules with pack-saddles, at an early hour in the morning. Soon afterwards Gosse started, and I left at 11.30. A gale of wind was blowing, and it was hard to find one's way between the drifts. The tracks of the men who had gone before were, of course, completely obliterated; in a word, all the obstacles we had encountered on our way down were present, in a rather more paralysing form. I pushed along as quickly as possible to catch up with my party, but I was unable to go very fast, as great detours had perpetually to be made to avoid banks of snow.

Alone, with no other soul in sight, with no sound save of the wind, horrid in my ears, though homely enough, I do not doubt, to the great mountains whose one playmate, whose born companion it is, I rode upon my way. No climber willingly attempts his work in such circumstances; the task would be, of course, absurd; the finest weather, the picked heart of the season, is wanted for undertakings of any moment among peaks of magnitude. Yet it often happens that, owing to variations in the season, miscalculations of its character and development, the most cautious explorer finds himself face to face with weather the very antithesis of what he would desire. It must be remembered that the "plant" of an expedition like mine is composed of instruments which, apart from their initial cost, become indescribably dear to one in the course of one's work. This may sound incomprehensible to the reader; I can only say that the theodolite or camera with which one has achieved the most cherished results, over which long days or nights have been spent, in connection with which one's best and most delicate capacities may have been strained to the utmost, which one has rescued, preserved, and restored amidst hair-breadth escapes and moving accidents by flood and field—risking, it may often be, one's own safety and that of one's horse in the effort—these things become beyond expression precious. The notebook, faithfully carried in an inner recess of the coat and drawn out at evening time, when the sense of physical exhaustion has been numbing and the inclination to rest, to *laisser aller*, the only live feeling in one's mind; drawn out and filled with painful, stiff, and conscientious memoranda (not untinged by irony and the rough sarcasm of a man at hand-grips with life and death)—things like this are more than one can bear to leave. I write, I am aware, in extenuation of, almost in apology for, the account that is to follow. Many might blame me, as the leader of such an undertaking, for my action in this matter. I am even inclined to blame myself now, as I look back upon it, for risking life to such a point for such an end. But that day I had no scruple. I did not act hastily, and I acted in the only way that seemed possible at the time. A man who any day may meet with some moment which might easily be his last but one, does not view risk and danger with the same eyes as the man who holds this book, leaning back in an arm-chair at his club or hearth. The occupant of the arm-chair may have ten times the pluck of the man who is mountaineering, but he would not choose so hardy a course — simply because the danger comes more sharply home to him by reason of its contrast with his security. At no time is the mountaineer one-hundredth part as comfortable or as safe. So his habitual discomfort and insecurity make his danger less dangerous and his risk less acute. I do not wish to suggest that my reflections took this turn on this particular occasion: far from it. Being alone, I was more disposed to recognise some of the compensations of a poor climber's life. It is a privilege, no matter what distress it brings with it, to see the scenes that I saw upon that ride. Here was Nature looking and acting in the "grand manner," among fitting surroundings, duly costumed, with marvellous *mise en scène*. The difference between a Greek heroic drama—such a tragedy as "Œdipus the King," played two thousand years ago when Athens was in her prime under the blue Hellenic skies to an audience among whom Pericles and Phidias might be spectators, the walls of the theatre of Dionysus yet erect to encircle it—and a twopenny-halfpenny farce in some playhouse of the Strand, with scratch company, scratch jokes, and every parody of life vulgarised — this difference is not more marked than the unlikeness between that moment of epic winter in the Andes and a snowstorm on Primrose Hill.

Nothing can surpass the grandeur of these vast ranges, thus clad in their winter dress. White, cold, a veritable valley of desolation, the long, gray shadows proclaiming the winter sun, though the hour was but little after midday. The feeling of solitude about the place was indescribably poignant and seizing. I had passed and repassed the same spot earlier in the season, but then, though there was in reality the same solitude, everything spoke of life. Now it was the cold of death—the white mantle of annihilation—something that the brain cannot compass, but that strikes and overwhelms one with despair.

I rode on up the valley through the deep drifts, the falling snow, driven by the wind, nearly blinding me the while. The sky was of a leaden hue; small fleecy clouds raced across from peak to peak, torn in shreds, as it seemed, by the jagged rocks that flanked us on either side. My horse was numb and stupid with cold, covered from head to foot with matted snow, a creature divorced from his element, stunned by the incompassable nature of his surroundings. In the deeper drifts we at times rolled over and over in the light, powdery stuff till it seemed as if we must be suffocated.

All the time I could see no traces of Gosse and the mules. Here and there where the wind had not reached to blur the record of their passage, I saw fresh footprints of my pioneers, so I kept on, sometimes riding, sometimes on foot. At the bend of the valley, near the little lake of Inca, I saw, about a mile away, some black spots moving on the white ground, and was glad to know that, so far, no ill had come to them. The wind went down slightly, and I was able to make better progress. Still the drifts got deeper and deeper, and it was with difficulty that I managed to force my terrified horse along. In another hour I was up to them. They were crossing a great plateau of deep snow, and our animals sank so far that at times we were left standing on the thin crust which was just strong enough to hold us up, while the beasts floundered below us, their backs just on a level with the surface.

At last I came up with Gosse. He told me a doleful tale of their difficulties, and how they had nearly lost one animal in a drift. We were getting to the point where we used to ford the river in the summer. In those days we dreaded these fords as most dangerous places. Now there was practically no water at all; only the slenderest little stream trickled under the ice, whilst the snow covered it, so that we could ride across without difficulty. The snow grew deeper and deeper as we advanced, and there were places where we thought that we really must give up, that we could not drag or force the animals through. Moreover, the horses were getting unmanageably frightened; they had nearly lost themselves several times in these vast drifts of fine powdered snow. They would plunge about on these banks till the stuff, entering their nostrils and mouths, almost choked them. To make things worse, it came on to snow again. We pushed along, fearing the darkness would be upon us before we got through the worst places, which we knew were to come. At the old first ford, instead of following the path that we usually took, we found it better to stick to the river-bed—that one place of all others we had so carefully avoided during the summer. We had several nasty falls here, the animals keeping their feet with difficulty upon the great boulders glazed with ice, and covered with their deceptive mantle. The day got darker and darker, while the snow fell more and more heavily. The air was so thick with flakes, that it was with difficulty that we could see each other and keep the caravan together. Soon the river-bed was so bad, that we were obliged to take to the steep bank, and work our way diagonally up a precipitous hillside. I got off and tried to lead my animal, but this I soon found to be too dangerous. The snow was too deep for me to move quickly : in fact, it was up to my waist, and when my horse plunged, his legs seemed to be whirling all over me. After receiving two nasty kicks, I tried the plan of driving him from behind ; but this, too, I found to be impossible, for the poor frightened beast refused to move when he no longer saw me. I was therefore reluctantly compelled to mount again, and to urge him slowly forward while he fumbled and blundered along. Several times I thought he would have rolled down the whole slope, or started an avalanche, so recklessly did he plunge. The mules behaved much better. It should be remembered that the animals were necessary to us to bring our heavy luggage down from our camp, otherwise I think we should have done better on foot, for it was more a case of winter Alpine climbing, and hard climbing at that, than of riding ; besides it was unspeakably cold to sit thus helplessly in the saddle, and watch the horse fight for his life, and incidentally for one's own life too. This valley was superb, covered and muffled in its great blanket, the river-bed full of huge masses of tortured ice, which in places formed great caverns, with innumerable icicles hanging from the roofs. There was an unearthly sentiment of mystery in these white masses ; the place looked far greater and larger, and the mountains higher ;

and, as the wind swept down in blasts, carrying before it the sharp and cutting granules of ice, it seemed as if existence must be impossible in such a place, so unhuman, so immeasurable was the loneliness of it all. As I looked around at our little troop, the men and horses seemed only just alive under the influence of it. Nobody spoke, and at times one of us would come to a stop, and remain perfectly still for minutes, paralysed by the overwhelming cold and odds that we were fighting against.

When we reached the top of this great slope, we found a tract that was fairly free of snow, as the wind had swept it almost clean; but we had to pay the penalty in wind and driven ice. The horses would turn again and again, unable to face this cutting blast, which came like a flail, and stung like a whip of wire. They would stand with their backs to it, trembling all over; pitifully willing and gentle, yet obviously so unnerved that they knew not what they were doing. Their long shaggy coats were by this time matted with snow and icicles, while all of us were covered and plastered with snow frozen on to us from head to foot, as we had been rolled over and over many times in the drifts. Still the camp was above us, and there were those instruments and notebooks and photographic plates that we could not dare, could not bear to forego. And we knew this was our unique opportunity. Never again should we return, never again face, with its memory upon us, the experience that we were now winning through. For winter, the first of winter, but as bitter as her heart, was upon us, and we knew that in another week this valley would be blocked so hopelessly that it would be impossible to penetrate into the recesses of it, till the spring sun had melted the snows. Doggedly, inflexibly, we forced our way on, and gradually neared the second ford. Only the *second* ford and this more than a mile from our tent! And now the only obstacle we still lacked arose and joined this sombre-souled little band—darkness! Darkness—and we had yet the Paso Malo to cross. Should it prove as bad as to our gloomy presage seemed inevitable, there would be nothing for it but to bivouac for the night in the open, on

this side of the Pass; and strange though it may seem, this prospect, though far from agreeable, was powerless to enhance our depression. Even the length of the night—and nights were desperately long now—over fourteen hours—combined with the impossibility of lighting a fire, could not plunge us in a lower depth of despondency. We cheered up somewhat at the ford, which gave us no trouble, for, as I have said before, there was no water in the river—all was frozen. Better still, the snow had ceased to fall, and the clouds had rolled away; cheerful little stars were shining when we reached the old place where we had had so many narrow escapes, and, to our surprise, owing to the immense amount of snow that was packed over it, we were able to get across more easily than ever before. My watch showed seven o'clock when we reached our tents — how thankful, how exhausted, I dare not say. The men had been upon the march for nearly ten hours to do that which took us only an hour and three-quarters in summer.

The tents were, of course, completely buried, but we scratched away some of the snow in a sheltered spot, to let the horses and mules stand for the night. The mules had taken the journey much more philosophically than the horses, and, shall I say, than ourselves? Nothing seems to shake the nerves of a mule. Even in the most dangerous places he remains as blasé and as slipshod as when cantering over the plains. He realises none of his responsibilities, presenting thereby an example to the human mind which it might safely follow, for he does his work much better than if he carried a full equipment of nerve-cells and was loaded with a complete and complicated and ever-present sense of just what is at stake. He is always ready, at the most critical places, to fall with the same cheerful *sang froid* with which he would stumble and roll you over on the highroad. There is some sort of legendary belief in which the English tourist is carefully inoculated, to the effect that mules are absolutely sure-footed, and pass along the crumbling verges of precipices as though suspended by an invisible string from paradise. To the man who has travelled in the Andes and lost his best camera or even his breakfast through the reckless shuffling of a mule among loose boulders, this faith is no longer tenable. As a matter of fact, my experience is that horses are the more trustworthy animals.

The reader may recall that we had two tents pitched at this camp; I told the men to make themselves as comfortable as they could in the large Whymper tent, while Gosse and I crawled into our small mountain tent. It was bitterly cold, and we had unavoidably brought in large masses of snow with us; besides, the tent was already half-full of snow that had silted in through the doorway, and we were obliged to spend some time in clearing out a fresh space to lie down in, and in rescuing our blankets and sleeping-bags from under the mass that lay upon them. Still, a faint glow of satisfaction warmed us. We had done what we set out to do; we had reached our tent; the precious belongings were within our grasp.

I had lit a couple of lanterns, and was turning my attention to certain elementary cooking operations, when a cry from Gosse startled me. "Shut the door! shut the door!" he cried excitedly, "don't let him get out!" This puzzled me for a little, as, to begin with, there was no door to shut, and, in the second place, I was not conscious of there being anybody in the tent but ourselves. I turned to Gosse, wondering if the cold had slightly deranged his mind, and I saw him make a sudden dive across me, and apparently try and secure some imaginary body. I was now quite convinced of his insanity, when he relieved my mind by saying, "Don't you see there is a live mouse in the tent?" Then I understood that the collector's instinct, which takes precedence of all others in a naturalist, had now thoroughly got hold of him. He upset a tin of ground coffee, and also two tins of food which I had opened. Fortunately the food tins were frozen hard; even had they not been, I do not think that a little trifle like this would have checked him in his wild scramble round and round the tent. I was soon fired by his enthusiasm, and in a few minutes we were plunging from side to side, while our little covering, only 3 feet 6 inches high, swayed in a most alarming fashion, and I could hear the guy-ropes outside, taut and stiff with their mass of icicles, cracking one by one. We were happily soon able to secure the animal under a heap of blankets. Gosse seized him eagerly, and bottled him, while I turned my attention to the rearranging of the interior, now sadly wrecked. I lighted a small spirit-stove, and, at the end of an hour, had succeeded in warming some water. It was not hot enough to make tea or coffee, so we decided to add a little whisky and condensed milk to it, and sup off that, with some dry biscuits. Gosse had the tin of condensed milk, which he had been heating over the stove to thaw it, and he began to pour spoonfuls of the thick white fluid into the warm water. As he got towards the bottom of the pot he suddenly exclaimed, "Why, here is another mouse! Poor little beast! It must have slipped into the tin while feeding." He extracted it, dripping with thick milk, from the pot by the tail, and eagerly bottled this specimen also. My own mind was dwelling on the fact that this was the last tin of milk we had up here, and besides, it would take another hour to heat more water. We were, therefore, obliged, to consume this beverage, though I must say I judged from the flavour that the mouse had died some weeks before. As we were sitting by the lighted candle, smoking our pipes, and preparing to go to sleep, we observed that the large basin of whisky, milk, and water between us was gradually beginning to freeze. We watched the small crystals of ice forming all over it, first a thin skin, then by degrees a thicker and harder coat. We did not drink any more, and next morning, when we awoke, it was frozen into a solid block. We suffered considerably from the cold that night, as may be imagined, and in the morning we were still just as thickly matted and encrusted with ice and snow, while the icicles upon my beard and hair had not thawed. I sent the men at once to get the theodolite we had left a few miles up the valley, towards the south face of Aconcagua; their path, luckily, was not difficult, for the wind had swept the valley almost entirely free of snow. They returned a few hours later with the instrument. It had been fine in the morning, the sun having shone for half an hour, but presently great banks of clouds approached from the north-west, and the wind began to moan fitfully, while now and again would come a slight flurry of snow. I decided it would be best to make for our camp on the Inca as soon as possible, for a long, protracted snowstorm here would have cut us off hopelessly from our friends below, and our camp was not provisioned for more than four weeks at the outside.

What I most feared was to be caught between the two camps in one of these terrific blizzards, when the blinding particles fly so thick and fast that it is impossible to breathe. This frequently happens to those crossing the ranges in winter, though all along the Pass there are shelter-houses, sometimes only a mile apart, or even less; yet parties are caught out between two such refuges, are overcome, and die in a few minutes.

By ten o'clock we had struck our camp, and packed everything on the animals. Going down seemed almost worse than coming up, for on this day the wind was flying more in eddies, and the way in a more dangerous condition, though, on the whole, it was not so cold, and we had the advantage of having the wind behind us. We progressed slowly, keeping to the route by which we had come up, yet, owing to the blinding storm, our tracks might have been searched for in vain, and the valley looked as lonely and as untrodden as on the day before. Gosse and I rode part of the way, but Gosse's horse got into a highly nervous condition, and he had several very dangerous falls, owing to the wild plunging of the beast. Several times I thought José's animal was going to lie down and give up, but he managed to get it along. I had taken great precautions against frost-bite, having seen to the gloves and the clothes of the men before starting, and impressed on all the party the necessity of stopping at once, if frozen, and having the affected part rubbed with snow. Owing to these precautions being rigorously enforced, we were fortunate enough to escape all injury, and we arrived late that evening in triumph at the Inca, bearing down all the articles we had gone up to rescue. Man, horse, and mule came back in safety, and lived to fight again another day; but I shall always remember the cold, the suffering, and the hardships of the two days and that night spent in the Horcones, and I am still uneasy sometimes at the thought that I risked the lives of men to bring back these inanimate companions and the records of our work.

CHAPTER XXIII

THE POSADA AT INCA

THE day after our return was the 24th of May, the Queen's birthday, and Her Majesty's health has seldom been drunk amid more dreary surroundings. Snow was still falling all round us, the mountain sides were riddled and streaked with the tracks of fresh avalanches, and the valleys were rapidly being blocked by deep drifts. I was reluctantly forced to recognise that our work that season was now at an end, and that beyond taking a series of photographs of the mountains clad in their winter garment, we must look upon our labours in these valleys as finished.

I spent the day in making arrangements to send all my Swiss and Italian men home, so that they should not miss the climbing season. I also had to take steps to get the masses of luggage containing our equipment, specimens, etc., down to the plains. Our base camp was now nearly obliterated by the mass of snow that had fallen, and we had been obliged to take refuge with Dr. Cotton in the little posada at Inca. We had sufficient maize for our animals for a short time, but the horses were looking poorly, and they could not be induced to touch this maize, though the mules throve upon it.

That evening the wind rose, and great drifts and banks of snow filled the courtyard at the Inca inn. The wind howled during the night, and it seemed as if we should be snowed up for good and all, so fast did these great drifts accumulate, blocking up the doors and piling themselves upon the roof. The provisions at the inn were not very plentiful, and generally the outlook was black. In spite of the cold and dismal surroundings, however, we managed to make merry,

DEPARTURE OF THE GUIDES 259

and toasted Her Majesty in the last bottles of wine that were left at the Inca.

The next morning, day broke over a wild and dreary scene of driving snow. We might have been in some small outpost in the Ural mountains, from the desolate and lonely aspect of the scene that day. I sent Pollinger down to Vacas, with orders to come back with José, three horses and a mule, and all the fodder that they could carry. The snow continued to fall, and again drifted in the evening, till the rafters of the ceiling began to bend and crack from the weight. Next morning we tried to shovel some of it away, but the effort was vain, for fresh snow drifted upon us so quickly that we could make very little impression. The storm was now at its height, a veritable blizzard. Pollinger returned with the horses alone, without fodder. He reported that the drifts were so deep in the valley that it would be hopeless to try to get the horses through with any loads on their backs; besides, José was, as usual, hopelessly drunk at Vacas. I sent all the men down towards evening with two horses, as the storm abated slightly. A little cream-coloured mare we had was too weak and fatigued to accomplish the journey, so we had to keep her at Inca. The men were to return to their own country under the charge of Zurbriggen.

We were now left alone, with nothing but native labour to rely upon. On the morning of 30th May the storm broke, the sun came out, it grew warmer, and the snow thawed in places during the day. The little mare was very ill during the morning, and died in the afternoon of rapid pneumonia. We did everything we could to save her, but her case was hopeless. José came up at last with more men, but no hay fodder, and that morning we decided to make an expedition to our base camp to clear away the snow which now completely covered it. The journey took us two and a half hours, though the distance was not more than half a mile. The snow was so deep that we sank in up to our armpits the whole way, and were obliged to push a passage with the weight of our bodies. We took it by turns to lead, and were all much exhausted when we reached the camp. Although I had a very large bell-tent set up here, which would accommodate as many as twenty people, and numbers of other tents, packing-boxes, panniers, etc., covered with large tarpaulins, we were unable to see anything at all; in fact the only sign of the existence of our camp was a slight mound of snow, and about four inches of the centre pole of the big tent sticking up through it.

We spent the whole day, with spades and shovels, digging out a passage round our luggage, and we brought a few things back to the inn that evening, but the digging had left time for almost nothing else.

The next few days passed in bringing up such portions of our luggage as we were able to move through the heavy snow, and piling them in an empty room at the inn. We also brought all the firewood we had collected at the camp, for the firewood at the inn had completely run out, and now that there were some four or five feet of snow spread over the whole countryside, there was no possiblity of collecting the dead sticks and under-bush that, as a rule, furnished the posada with fuel. Our communication with Vacas was cut off for the time, and it was impossible to bring much upon the backs of the animals through the heavy drifts in the valley. We had already been reduced to pulling up the floor boards and burning them to cook our meals.

The iron-grey pony that I had myself ridden during the whole of my work in the Andes was taken ill at this time; he refused his food, and finally died. We could not induce him to touch the maize; and though we tried him with everything we could think of, including condensed milk and cabin biscuits, he would have none of them. Losing this animal was a great blow to me, as I had become much attached to him; he had carried me faithfully through many a dangerous passage, and had saved me from many an accident in the cold fords of the Horcones torrent.

One of those days a poor German tramp came over on his way to Chile. He seemed very ill and weak, and was absolutely unequipped for a winter passage of the mountains. We did all we could for him, each of us supplying him with

DIGGING OUT OUR BASE CAMP NEAR INCA

various portions of clothing and equipment, and he left us on the evening of 31st May. We urged him very strongly not to attempt the crossing, but he seemed absolutely bent upon it. Next morning I met a peon who had slept that night at the casucha next the inn. I asked him if he had seen this German, and he mentioned in a casual way that he had seen a man dying by the roadside as he came along, about a mile from the inn. He had left this unfortunate fellow-creature insensible, without a thought of offering him assistance. I was greatly shocked at this news, especially as I only heard it some twelve hours after the event. Vines was furious with the man, and for a moment entertained a passionate thought of executing rude justice on the spot. I dissuaded him, however, from this intention, and suggested that the best thing for us to do would be to set out and see if we could not find the German. The peon shrugged his shoulders in true Chileno fashion and said, "Of what use is it? The man is dead by now, and the next snowstorm will cover him." We went out and searched for a long time, but found no trace of the man, but afterwards we heard that he had passed the night in one of the casuchas. He had evidently been able to drag himself that far.

The weather now began to cloud up and assume a threatening aspect once more, and that night the snow commenced to fall again. Next day Vines rode down to Vacas to see what could be done about the removal of our luggage, and to send off some telegrams, amongst them one of congratulation in reply to a message announcing the birth of the son of dear friends at home. He returned the day after in a violent snowstorm, reporting that it was raining at Vacas, but that as he came up the valley, and before he reached the Penitentes, the rain changed to snow. Some peons came up with him, and we entered into negotiations with them for the transport of our luggage to Chile. We had offered this contract to our man José some days before, but he had failed to get anyone to do anything for us. When we came to settle with these new peons, José seemed excessively dissatisfied, and retired to the kitchen in a most discontented frame of mind. He sat up a great part of the night talking to the men, and we felt that there was trouble brewing. We were never able to find out exactly what was the true story—whether José had threatened them if they carried the luggage, or in what way he had managed to turn them against us. At anyrate, on the following morning they all came in to look at our luggage. They lifted it up, said it was too heavy, and then filed out of the room one by one, leaving us alone. We rushed after them; we offered them more money, asked them what they wanted, but it was useless—they would not carry it under any condition. Our anger and chagrin knew no bounds. Here we were caught, we did not know for how many weeks, absolutely at the mercy of these natives, for without them we certainly could not move our belongings. The snow might fall again, and we had missed the favourable opportunity given by the thaw of the last few days, when we knew that the track over the pass was fairly good. It was already clouding for another storm, and in any case it would take us many days before we could find other men. I sent for José and told him roundly that it was all his fault, and that we knew he had intimidated the men. His demeanour was exceedingly bold and aggressive; he did not attempt to deny the charge, and, moreover, did not take off his hat on entering the room—a great mark of disrespect for a Chilian arriero. I told him in few but forcible words exactly what we thought of him; but as he did not seem in a frame of mind to receive these remarks respectfully, Lightbody, who had had years of experience in dealing with this most difficult class of men, seized him and prepared to hustle him out of the door. Instantly he drew his knife, but next moment he dropped it; Lightbody, perfectly ready for this move, had gripped his wrist with lightning rapidity, and given it such a twist that the man screamed with pain. In a second he was thrown to the ground, and without more ado Lightbody carried him to the door and gave him a gentle but firm drop-kick, which sent him flying some fifteen feet out into the snow. All this took place far more rapidly than I can narrate it. José had come into the room, addressed us, and left us in this elegant fashion, all in about ten seconds of time. There was nothing more to be done; the man was Chileno, and everyone knows that a Chileno never forgives a blow; that he would have a knife into one of us if possible for the morning's work, was certain. It was for us now to be exceedingly cautious how we went about at night or in lonely spots, for this man would most assuredly lie in wait for one of us. It had always been our rule to be armed in these districts, so we decided that, if the man attacked us, he should be allowed no mercy.

Next day Dr. Cotton and Lightbody went down to Vacas to see what they could do about getting more peons to take our luggage. They returned next morning with some fresh men, and we considered ourselves fortunate. This time we had José in, and explained to him beforehand that he would show a due regard for his own welfare by not tampering with our new porters.

On the same afternoon, Vines, Lightbody, and I set out to take photographs at the head of the Horcones Valley, some three miles distant; also to take some views of the surrounding country in its winter covering. This occupied us the whole afternoon; and though we were desperately tired when we returned, we were amply repaid by the beauty of the scenery. The day was clear, the sun shining brightly and nearly dazzling us with its reflection from the newly-fallen snow. The mountains looked most awe-inspiring with their great mantle of white, while Aconcagua, with its colossal crags and precipices, came out very sharply upon its south side, looking even more majestic than usual, with its huge load crumbling and breaking away in many avalanches.

That evening the Argentine post for Chile arrived, having succeeded in forcing its way up the valley. They had some thirty bags of mail, which they had packed on mules, and to make a path they had driven up a great herd of these animals in front, unloaded, so as to cut a passage. When we met them, they were attempting to get on to Cuevas, or perhaps to the casuchas in the Paramillos, that night.

But on hearing from us of the great drifts through which we had had to force our way, they turned back to the Inca for the night. The rooms of the inn were now in a terribly wet and cold condition. We had more or less cleared the roofs, but still the snow had melted on them and soaked its way through the mud ceilings, and the water was dripping in everywhere, compelling us to shift our beds from side to side, and to cover ourselves with macintosh sheets to avoid getting wet through. The common-room had a tin roof, which was fairly water-tight in places; besides, there was a small stove in this room, a luxury not contained in any other of the apartments. Gosse had been suffering for some days past from a bad cough and sore throat, so we moved a bed for him into this room, hoping that the extra dryness and warmth would cure him.

On the morning of the 7th, José set out early with three horses and two mules for Cuevas, taking our luggage. I sent Lightbody to take charge of it to Chile, while I thought it better to remain for another day or two and see the rest of our luggage moved down to Vacas. Cotton volunteered to accompany Lightbody, as he wanted to get out of the mountains for the winter, and Vines decided to go as far as Cuevas with them, and help in case José proved troublesome. Vines' tale of this trip to Cuevas will be found in the next chapter.

They left upon a dull and dreary morning. It was not actually snowing, but the sky had that dull, grey, leaden hue which in the Andes invariably foretells the advent of a heavy storm. I spent the day in clearing the snow off the top of the room in which I had put Gosse's bed. In the evening he seemed much worse, high fever declaring itself, and I made him go to bed. Soon the fever reached such an alarming point that I feared pneumonia. The room was fearfully damp; but that I could not help, as the firewood ran out, and I was reduced to burning the floor and the woodwork of the building, cutting out those beams in the roof which I thought could be spared without a catastrophe. I sat up all that night, watching by his bedside, and keeping a roaring fire in the little stove. All the woollen garments I could find I crowded on him and about his bed. The wind howled terribly, and the snow began to fall fast in the early morning. My fear was that Vines would be caught at Cuevas, and be unable to rejoin me, and that I should thus be left all alone with Gosse, which would be a terrible position for me, if he got worse. I should have nobody to send for assistance, and the winter snows had cut us off to such an extent that we were compelled to rely upon ourselves for everything that we needed. These thoughts were not cheering for me as I spent that lonely night watching for the symptoms that I so much dreaded. Fortunately he was slightly better in the morning, but I was still very anxious, and in the afternoon of the next day he was again worse. Just as dusk was setting in, and I had given up all hopes of seeing Vines for perhaps weeks to come, I heard someone rap outside the door, and, when I opened, to my delight I saw Vines. It had been snowing steadily all day, but with great pluck he had managed to rejoin me. Our luggage, he said, was safely in Cuevas with Cotton and Lightbody, and would be carried over on the first opportunity. José had apparently not covered himself with glory, but I had cautioned everybody the day before to keep a very close eye on him, to see that he played none of his old tricks.

That night José got very drunk in the kitchen, and was making himself unpleasant to the peons at the inn, and threatening everybody. The comedor communicated with the kitchen by a little door about three feet from the ground, large enough to pass the plates through. To reach the interior of the kitchen it was necessary to go outside and walk round the whole building. I stuck my head through this door, and told José that he must leave the kitchen and go to the casucha, as I could not have him in that condition disturbing us. At first he did not pay the slightest attention to me; and finally, losing all patience with the drunken brute, as I could not get round by the door—the snow having completely blocked it—I crawled through this window and jumped down into the kitchen, some four feet below. José now thought it was about time to be moving, especially as Vines, who was close behind me, came leaping through, head first, and arrived in a heap on the floor; so he took to his heels, and went to the casucha. Vines, who had rather hurt himself in his wild leap through this small window,—a form of entrance which must have resembled the method by which Harlequin enters the stage in a pantomime,—was not satisfied with the flight of José, and did not rest until he had turned out several of the postmen who were also the worse for liquor. The kitchen having thus been thoroughly cleared, we returned by the same route by which we had come, in as elegant and dignified fashion as possible, always with regard to the risk of being attacked in rear at the moment we were crawling through, which would have been embarrassing, to say the least.

MULES ON THE CUMBRE PASS IN SUMMER

CHAPTER XXIV

BY STUART VINES

THE PASS IN WINTER

BY 7th June it seemed at length possible to make a final start with our baggage for the Cumbre Pass and Chile. Snow had not fallen for some days, and we thought it would be better to make a move as far as Cuevas, where we heard peons were waiting to convey the mail-bags over the Pass. These men would be quite willing to let the post wait if they could get more lucrative employment with us. It was a dull, gusty morning. We sent José on in advance, with three mules and two horses heavily laden with the thirteen panniers for Chile. The man was still in disgrace, smarting under the thrashing Lightbody had given him. His movements had therefore to be watched, for we could not trust him long out of our sight with the valuable baggage he was in charge of. Lightbody, Cotton, and I started at noon on foot, with two men from Inca, Alfredo and Acosta, as extra porters.

But now that, after so many delays, we were really able to extricate ourselves from our wintry surroundings, another trouble arose. Owing, no doubt, to the complete climatic change that had taken place in the last ten days, the heavy snows, melted by the sun, turned the Inca, usually so dry and dusty, into a streaming slough of slush: the water poured through the roof of the inn and down the walls: our bedding and clothing were damp and clammy. Philip Gosse had developed what we thought at the time was only a slight cold and sore throat, but FitzGerald thought it advisable to stay behind with him and follow us to Cuevas on the morrow.

This was the first occasion on which we had reason to employ native porters, and I was much struck with the footgear worn. Their light home-made alpagatas of untanned hide were bound round with any old rags or cloths they might have handy; over this they fastened a sheepskin, shaped so as to be brought up and secured round the ankle. As we trudged along to Cuevas I compared the tracks made by Lightbody, in boots, and Acosta—who carried a heavy load—in these foot bandages. There was no doubt that the peon scored very considerably in the snow. Whereas the hard crust on the surface frequently gave way under the boots, the sheepskin bandages passed quietly over, hardly leaving a track behind them. But the greatest advantage arising from this footgear lies in the fact that its looseness and warmth allow a free circulation, and make frost-bite almost an impossibility.

During the last few days of sorting and packing we had found many things we wanted to get rid of, and the peons and porters had been glad to purchase different articles from us. But what they most set their hearts on were our putties. Nothing of the kind had been seen in the country before, and they valued them highly, offering us as much as two dollars a pair. This admiration did not extend to the numerous pairs of climbing boots we had to dispose of, and one man, whom FitzGerald presented with a very good pair, asked for putties instead.

When we reached the wide, flat part of the valley beyond the Paramillos del Inca, we found the traces of the last caravan of mules making the journey not yet obliterated by the storms that had closed the route. They had evidently ploughed through at the time of a heavy thaw succeeded by a very severe frost, and the subsequent snows had been swept off the hard and lumpy track thus formed. It was toilsome work; we crossed the flats, and reached the foot of the hills beyond, passed the graveyard with its numerous crosses festooned with icicles, found a path that admitted of single file still open on the road round the Paramillos, and, at half-past four, came to the deserted and half-buried Customs House; but who would carry anything beyond the bare neces-

A BURIED STATION

sities of life over such a route at such a season? There was a depression in the smuggling trade, and the customs officials had wisely fled to more comfortable quarters at Vacas.

At five we reached Cuevas, or that part of it that peeped above the snow. The Rio Mendoza Valley, barred by the heights of the Cumbre Pass, twines towards the north just beyond Cuevas, and this northern reach acts as a funnel for the great north-west winds, which sweep the snow from the mountain sides and heap it up at this corner of the valley on the luckless head of the little mountain station.

There was little to indicate that the place was inhabited, but deep lanes, cut through the enormous drifts to the doors and windows, showed that many hands had been at work quite lately. Inside, there was no lack of life and population: three men, whom I judged by clothes ill-fitted to surrounding circumstances to be benighted passengers, were carrying on a hot argument with a couple of peons, whose "patrons" they evidently were; a *capitas* and his band of peons, with an enormous accumulation of post-bags, were waiting for a favourable opportunity to cross the Pass; and an unhappy-looking bar-keeper, with numerous bottles of poison of various colours and strengths ranged in rows on shelves behind him, completed the list of inhabitants of Cuevas at this time, though I was informed that the casucha and some sheds near were full of imprisoned postmen and their mules.

The bar-keeper seemed to be having a lazy time, and was not flourishing, as no one seemed inclined for the time being to commit suicide. The fact was that during the last few days there had been a gradual rise in the price of everything at Cuevas, especially in the price of drinks, and the peons fought shy of paying a dollar for a dram of spirits. Being ignorant of the reasons for the prevailing abstemiousness and the consequent gloom, we gave an impetus to trade by ordering a brazier of charcoal and several bottles of beer. We learnt later that the former was a shilling an hour, and the latter four to five shillings a bottle.

Lightbody immediately began to treat with the capitas for the conveyance of our panniers over the Pass. He had not the slightest hesitation in leaving the post-bags and taking on our job, informing us that if the snow held up on the morrow the crossing would be possible, for although it was very deep on the Chile side, the peons would be able to plunge down through it somehow, and that the wind had swept a great part of it away on the Cuevas side, and the ascent to the Cumbre would not be as bad as was imagined.

The carrying trade and postal service over the Pass in winter is arranged on these lines:—A capitas, generally a man with a little capital to back him in his enterprise, gets together a band of porters at some mountain station, wherever the mule service is interrupted for the time being. He undertakes to find them in board and lodging as long as they are under him—the lodging being a matter of no importance, as the men sleep in the casuchas—and pay them so much a load for what they carry.

The post arrives at Vacas, the capitas examines it, and forms an idea of what it will cost him to take it up to and over the Pass. He then treats with the postal officials, and draws up a contract to deliver the mails at the station on the other side wherever the mule traffic may be resumed.

No time is stated in the contract, and he takes all the risks of delay by weather. In good weather probably he will treat for ten dollars a load, and give his men six or seven dollars. Should any private baggage turn up, he dumps the post-bags on the spot and makes a new bargain, generally for anything up to twenty-five dollars a load, according to the condition of the passes and the impatience of the owner. His porters will probably get two-thirds the amount he bargains for per load.

As we sat and warmed ourselves over the brazier, the peons came up one by one and picked out their loads. We were disappointed to see that there were only five men in the band besides the capitas. This, we thought, would mean the delay and trouble of two journeys. But our anxiety was soon set at rest on this point.

The panniers were chiefly filled with clothes, books, papers, and photographic results, and had been packed carefully in order to distribute the weight as evenly as possible. They were of the regulation size, a foot deep, two and a half feet long, a foot and a half wide—wicker-work covered with Willesden canvas. One of the peons came up and laid two stakes on the table, took one of the panniers, lifted it up and down several times to estimate its weight, and laid it on the two stakes. Then, to our astonishment, he took up a second and laid it beside the first, bound all together, attached hide shoulder-straps, then got another peon to hoist it on his back, and when all was fixed to his liking, walked up and down the room by way of preliminary canter. Was it possible these men would attempt to cross the Pass in its present condition with a load which, in size and weight, a railway porter at home would hardly care to carry a few yards?

Our own porters, Alfredo and Acosta, volunteered for the service as we were short of men, and we told them they could arrange with the capitas about their loads and payment. I noticed that they only took one pannier each, and asked them why they, who were of a more powerful build than most of the peons, were afraid to carry two panniers, and how much the capitas was paying them for it. They said that he was paying ten dollars a load or five dollars a pannier. Alfredo explained that he had lived on horseback all his life and was not used to such heavy portering, and that he was quite content to carry one pannier over for five dollars. Acosta said he had done a good deal of portering in his time, and had carried the mails for many years, but he had always avoided carrying loads beyond a certain weight. He said, "I am fifty years old now, señor, and I am still a strong and active man. If you notice, these porters are all young men. Probably not one of them will live to my age. Sometimes they begin this work at twenty, sometimes at forty. Anyhow, señor, they only last a few years at it. It kills them in the end." They all looked strong men, except one, who seemed in no way fitted for such work.

As Lightbody was successful in treating with a really responsible capitas who could, without doubt, fulfil his obligations—a man who knew the Pass well and would not dump our baggage on the snow and fly at the sight of the first storm, there was no necessity for two of us to cross over with it, and I felt it would be better to return to Inca and cross with FitzGerald and Gosse.

The wind of the previous day had entirely dropped, and heavy snow was falling when we began to stir at an early hour on the Tuesday, 8th June. I consulted with porters and arrieros, and found out that a large caravan belonging to the postal service had been at Cuevas some days, and was about to start for Vacas; that with the *madrinas*, or "bell mares," and my own troop of six animals, it would not be difficult to force a passage to Inca, as there was no wind, if an early start was made. I knew it would be foolish to depend on the words "about to start" where the South American arriero was concerned, and determined to set out independently. If my horse could not carry me, I could make my way on foot, for it was barely twelve miles. I therefore told José to bring round the White-eyed Kaffir—an expert in facing weather of this kind. It was half-past eight before the animal was ready, and then everything had changed for the worse. The snow had increased in volume, and a tremendous wind had risen. Never in my life have I seen such darkness in daytime as was caused by this snowstorm. I crawled out of the door of the hut, and found the Kaffir patiently standing up to his withers in a drift that had formed around him in the last few minutes. The wind was from the west, and it was impossible to turn my head in that direction, for the snow blinded me at once. The storm was so violent, however, that I felt sure it could not last. I left the horse standing, and with great difficulty made my way to some outlying sheds where the arrieros had quarters. These lay to windward; so I put my head under my poncho and struggled blindly forward, almost suffocated by the driving snow. It took me ten minutes to cover the 200 yards to the sheds. Here I found about twenty mules, besides my own animals, which had been ready packed before the storm began. The poor beasts were almost buried already. I entered some low buildings—a large shed, used for storing fodder for the winter, but empty, as no provision had been made this year, owing to the snow falling earlier than had been expected. Half a dozen arrieros crouched round a fire. I began at once to discuss the situation; two of the men had crossed the Cumbre during the last spell of fine weather, with three transport agents, who wanted to catch the weekly train from Vacas to Mendoza, and were under contract to get them to Vacas by the following night. They declared that their "patrons" were grumbling at the high prices charged for food at Cuevas, and did not object to starting, as they did not know the risk they were running, and thought that having crossed the Pass, the worst was over, and all would be plain sailing; that, if the señor could persuade the postmen to start, their train of twenty mules might plough through the drifts until the storm abated. So I turned to the postmen. They had a woeful tale to tell. In the first place they would lose the chance of carrying the next posts up from Vacas if they delayed any longer, and were naturally eager to start. But there were far more potent reasons for getting away from Cuevas at once. They had only brought enough fodder for their animals to last three days, and they had now been five days there; there was not a grain of corn at Inca, and their animals would all die if they did not reach Vacas in two days. Moreover, their own provisions had run out, and it was ruinous to buy from the passengers' quarters. They said there was safety in numbers, that we could, at least, reach the casucha on the far side of the Paramillos de las Cuevas, and that they would risk it, and set out at half-past nine. If the transport agents and the señor would start, and all would follow close on one another's heels, there would be no great danger. So far as the animals were concerned, I had much the same reasons for starting at once, for the little maize I could bring up with the other loads was nearly exhausted. When I made my way back to the passengers' quarters, Lightbody and Cotton declared it would be madness to start in such a storm, but as I found the transport agents bent on following the post, I determined to risk everything for the sake of the mules and horses.

We started at 9.45 in the most blinding snowstorm I have ever experienced. It was hardly possible at times to see the tail of the animal in front, though following close on its footsteps. By the custom-house the road runs through a narrow gorge. This had been long blocked by gigantic drifts, and a path made far up the valley side amongst the rocks. To look after anyone but oneself was out of the question. I do not know if the others fared as badly as my immediate neighbours; I could not see far enough to discover—I could only hear the continuous execrations hurled at the luckless animals in the long thin line in front and behind me. However, the caravan reached the flat ground by the river-bed on the lower side of this defile, where I found José and my beasts all safe. If the storm continued I did not see how the animals could get much farther, and the transport agents with their tight town boots were quite incapable of going on foot. It was all very well for me, with climbing boots, putties, and gabardine. The going was easier on the flat where the caravan followed the river-bed. This they could not do for long, as we reached the dreaded Paramillos. The word means, "little moraines." It is a kind of smaller pass caused by an accumulation of moraine-like heaps, which had at one time blocked the valley. The river had cut a deep gorge through the barrier, on one side of which ran the road. The entire work of progress was left to the animals themselves. They chose the way by the road now obliterated by drifts; the bell-mares went first, and with consummate skill slowly forced their way down the narrow path, steering round the drifts, or, when this was not possible, plunging through them up to their necks. For some time the leading mare seldom hesitated, and a shout from the arrieros far in the rear of the train was enough to make the plucky beast forge ahead again. But after a while halts became frequent, and the arrieros seemed to go mad, in their wild hysterical way, as they cursed and swore at their patient animals. Then worse things happened: one mule fell after another, and, rolling over, slid down the steep snow slope two hundred feet to the river-bed. When they reached the bottom they made no attempt to move, but lay almost buried in the snow, as if dead, for the poor brutes had fallen more from exhaustion than anything else. In a short time most of the arrieros were down by the river-bed, for half a dozen horses and mules had fallen, a horse and mule of mine amongst them. For some little time their efforts to get the mules to take any more interest in affairs—and they did not use the gentlest means—were of no avail; but after struggling waist-deep in the snow they got them all on their feet, and we reached the casucha at the foot of the Paramillos at noon.

Before us a vast flat field of snow stretched to within a few miles of Inca, where the ancient glaciers of the Horcones Valley had thrown a second barrier of detritus across the valley. Snow filled this wide expanse to a great depth: the graveyard with its crosses was nowhere to be seen; almost every landmark was obliterated. The only means of crossing this plain, therefore, was by wading down the river. There were about a dozen animals in front of me as I passed the casucha. I watched them wind down to the river-bed, and I had nothing to do but follow in their track. No one seemed to be coming along after me, so I took it for granted that arrieros and agents had given up the struggle, and were staying at the casucha, regardless of the fact that their animals were wandering on. I pushed forward for some time without looking back, determined to proceed by the river until I reached the second Paramillo, where it became deep and rapid, and then leaving the animals to their fate, force my way through the snow to Inca. My only alternative was to remain at the casucha for the night, but I was far too well acquainted with the habits of the arrieros to relish the idea of becoming the tenth inhabitant of such quarters for eighteen hours.

Fortunately the river flowed wide and shallow through the plain, and the going was not difficult. Walls of snow rose up on either side to a height of four feet. The mules seemed quite content to wade, but it was otherwise with the horses. The Kaffir tried repeatedly to break into the wall on either side, and seized every opportunity of escaping from the river. At length there was a block. A bend in the river brought us to some rapids where the water was deep and the bed rocky. The beasts plunged about in the snow for some time, and we were delayed some fifteen minutes. I had not looked back for half an hour, in fact since leaving the casucha. I now heard voices behind me, and peering through the blinding snow, recognised the three agents. They seemed in a pretty bad way, and explained to me that nothing would induce them to stay with the arrieros at the casucha, for those gentlemen had somehow procured spirits at Cuevas, probably from smuggled stores, had ensconced themselves in the casucha and set to work to drink, and as most were drunk already, the agents considered it preferable to follow me—they relied on me to bring them safely through to Inca. Now this was what I had particularly wished to avoid: the responsibility for three men quite unused to cold and snow and heights, their boots and clothes utterly unfitted for such work, who had started in the belief that they would not have to put their feet to the ground and could ride comfortably all the way. There was no reason, moreover, to believe that the storm would abate, for it had been steadily increasing in violence all day. One of my companions spoke French, and I explained the situation to him; —that probably it would be impossible to wade as we were doing for another two miles, and that then the river entered a gorge; that the animals would be quite unable to force a way through the snow on the Paramillos del Inca, to say nothing of the drifts; that it would need two or three men to beat down the snow and give them a lead. If they were capable of going on foot, well and good; if not, there was but one course to pursue—to return to the casucha. They said they could not possibly turn round and face the storm; they had perfect faith in the señor; and they would follow him to Inca. I told them I would not take any such responsibility, and that they had much better turn back. My advice was unheeded, and so we continued down the river for a little time. Two of the men grumbled at every little difficulty, and soon one began to complain of his legs feeling numb. This was enough warning for me. I told them they

A DIFFICULT JOURNEY

could go on alone, but that I was going back to the casucha, and that if they cared to follow me they could.

For an hour we beat up stream again, against the blinding snow, with our ponchos over our heads, forcing our beasts along with the spur. At last shouts ahead proclaimed that the arrieros had finished their refreshment, and were continuing the journey; also that they were well refreshed. It is no good talking to a drunken South American mule-driver, so, though José was as drunk as the rest, I said nothing. It was not exactly the time and place to give him the thrashing he deserved. It was now one o'clock, and we all hurried down stream, putting our wretched animals to their best speed. The Kaffir swerved aside from time to time into the snow, objecting more and more to the water. It was impossible, however, to break through the snow for more than a few yards, and I spurred the poor beast back into the icy torrent. At about two we reached the Paramillos del Inca, and further progress by the river was at an end. The arrieros tried to make the animals lead the way from the river-bed up the steep bank, which was breast-high in snow, as they had done earlier in the day. The bell-mares, however, seemed to have entirely lost their bearings, and consequently the whole troop began to wander, some up the river, some down, and in fact in every direction but the right one. Then José went ahead, and tried to force a passage with his horse, but after a few yards the animal could not go a step further. There seemed no way round the enormous drift between us and the road over the Paramillos. It was clear that the only way to make further progress was to dismount and beat down a way on foot. It was now 2.30; we were still two miles from Inca, and the storm was as bad as ever. I dismounted, and taking the lead, beat a way in the direction of where the road should be. With great difficulty I reached the top of the Paramillos. I did not know whether the whole caravan was following me or not; my eyes were blinded at once, if I turned to look back. A few mules, and then the arrieros followed close on my footsteps. The latter had at last recognised the necessity of dismounting and going on foot. The agents alone were mounted. As the pack-animals plunged about in the drifts, they loosened their loads, and the halts were interminable. Fortunately the loads were very light. I tried to get the postmen to relieve me for a short time in the heavy work of taking the lead, but soon gave this up. I could not quite make out if they were unable or unwilling to do the hard work, so I determined to do it for them only so far as necessary ; viz., to the spot where the Paramillos ceased and the descent into the plain commenced. I pushed on for some time, and hearing no voices behind me, looked back, and could only make out some mules following close on my heels. I stood still and shouted, but getting no reply, made an attempt to retrace my steps. To my dismay I found that only three mules were following, and that after a short distance our tracks were entirely obliterated. However, I had reached the end of the Paramillos, and no doubt, as I had been bearing too much in a bee-line for Inca, the arrieros had turned by an easier route, or had found signs of the road and followed it. I had the choice of turning to the left, and trying to find the road, which leads by a circuitous route to Inca, or of continuing on in the direction I was taking, which would save more than half the distance, but would necessitate fording the Rio Mendoza. I determined to pursue the latter course, and soon found myself on the edge of the cliff overhanging the river. Skirting along it for some distance, I at length broke through the huge cornice overhanging its edge, and slid down the snow, that had drifted on to the face of the cliff, into the water. It was deeper than I had expected, for I plunged in nearly up to my neck. I reached the opposite bank, but could not find anything to pull myself up with. Repeatedly I fell with great masses of snow back into the icy water, but at last by swimming down a few yards I secured a firm foothold. I landed about three hundred yards from Inca, but my troubles were by no means over. The snow, deeper here than I had so far encountered on level ground, covered the thorn bushes ; there was no vestige of a path ; it was growing very dark ; I was wet through and as cold as ice, and every miuute I fell over the hidden bushes, burying myself in thorns and snow, a most unpleasant combination of evils. In fact these last three hundred yards took me exactly half an hour to accomplish. Even when I had reached the Inca buildings there seemed little chance of gaining entrance, so deep were the snow-drifts. I wandered round for a few minutes, until I found a shutter which I tried to open. A voice came from within; it was FitzGerald's, "Go round to the east side, and I'll let you in by the window. The old door's blocked up with snow. We haven't been out all day. Gosse has a beastly bad throat and fever. Don't bring in too much snow and cold air. What made you tempt Providence for twelve miles on such a day as this?"

So ended one of the worst fights I have ever had with the snow. I was inside the house before six. The last two miles had taken three hours, though it was not fatigue that had delayed me, for I was strong and well at the end of it. I naturally felt much anxiety for my three fellow-travellers, the horses and mules I had left to the tender care of José, and even for the drunken crew of arrieros. However, at seven we heard their mule-shouts on the far side of the river, and they arrived shortly after eight. The transport agents were in the most wretched condition. Two of them had to be lifted from their horses. They could neither walk nor stand. One could do nothing but lie on the floor in front of the fire and groan. A tremendously stiff grog, however, brought them back to comparative life again, and they were convalescent the next morning. Of the six animals José had charge of from Cuevas, only four could be accounted for the next day. The black horse and a mule were missing. I was not sorry in the end that they were lost, for they were the means of saving one life, if not two, a few days later; for two wretched individuals who were wanted by the police in Chile, and had crossed the Cumbre in hasty flight, appeared at Inca late one night riding the lost animals. They had reached the foot of the Paramillos de las Cuevas, when one of them entirely broke down with fatigue, and refused to go a step further.

The other man, at his wits' end, wandered hopelessly off in search of aid. He had not gone far when he saw our two animals knee-deep in snow on the southern bank of the river. As the beasts would not cross to him, he had to wade over and fetch them. The poor beasts had spent two days and nights in the snow, and could not possibly have obtained a morsel of food; for though mules are extremely clever in scratching up the snow to a certain depth and nibbling the grass and yareta beneath, the snow at this time was far too deep for food to be obtained in such a manner. He took them back to his friend, who in a few minutes would have gone to swell the number of crosses at the foot of the Paramillos, got him on to the horse and arrived at Inca some six hours later. They were both frost-bitten, one of them very badly, but we looked after them for a day or two, and eventually got them down to Vacas and Mendoza.

The saddest part of the story is that we were in such a state of famine at Inca that we had not a bit of hay to give the two starved beasts. I tried them with broken biscuit and maize, but they would touch neither. They died of starvation, therefore, before our eyes, fortunately the only victims of an experience that seemed at one time likely to have a vastly more tragic ending.

CHAPTER XXV

LIGHTBODY'S CROSSING OF THE ANDES

BEFORE going further I must say something of Lightbody's adventures on the Cumbre Pass, when Vines left him there on 8th June with that part of the luggage that was to be taken over to Chile. It must be remembered that the packages Lightbody had contained the whole of the results of our expedition, and were of course of the utmost value to us, as they represented our seven months' work. To get these extremely precious articles across the Cumbre in midwinter was a heavy responsibility.

When Vines left him in the morning it was snowing hard, and a bitter north-west gale was blowing from the Cumbre. All that day he was unable to move, for no living man could face the terrible blizzard that swept down from the pass he wished to ascend, carrying with it masses of fine snow as hard and as cutting as splinters of flint. Several times that evening he ventured out from the posada where they had taken refuge, but found it impossible to struggle more than a few yards from the door before he was driven back blinded and half-choked by the blizzard. In the evening a few travellers arrived, who had crossed the pass with the gale behind them. They had been nine hours on the way, coming on foot from Portillo, and they were in a pitiable state, nearly dead from cold and fatigue. Several of them had actually been carried a considerable distance towards the end of the journey, for they had completely lost the use of their feet. Even the peons, their guides and porters, who had helped to carry them, declared that the weather had been fearful, and that at times they thought they should be unable to get through. However, as their passengers were very weak and ill they dared not stop in the casuchas lest these poor people should die on their hands, and never pay them. Lightbody and Dr. Cotton did what they could to help them, but all that night they suffered greatly, and their groans testified eloquently to the privations they had endured. One of them had his feet badly frost-bitten, though at the time they did not know how badly. It was many days afterwards—the very day before Vines and I started for Las Cuevas—that one of these unfortunate men came down on muleback to the Inca, his feet bandaged up. He told a terrible tale of his sufferings during the time he had spent alone in the little posada at Cuevas, with not a soul to talk to, and no medical aid at hand. His feet had been seriously frost-bitten and he had suffered greatly; when he arrived he was in an almost fainting condition, from the pain and agony caused by his having to ride with his feet still terribly swollen and inflamed.

Next day, during a lull in the storm, Lightbody attempted some photography, but the work was carried on under great difficulties, with what he thought at the time would be little success. As a matter of fact, however, these photographs came out very well.

As he was taking some of his views his camera was blown over, and the ground glass in it smashed to splinters, after which he was reduced to photographing with a small fragment of the glass, holding it up at the back of the camera. That he should have got such good results under these difficulties seems marvellous, and tells of the patience and care with which he worked.

In Lightbody's diary, written up day by day on the spot, which is before me as I write, he seems to have been overcome by depression. These prolonged snowstorms, when one is living in the cold, damp comedor of an Andine posada, have a wearing effect on the mind; the ceaseless fall of snow, the short days, the grey skies, the uncertainty of the supply of provisions, all combine to bring on great and abnormal depression.

Towards evening the weather looked more promising,

and he resolved to make a start next day and attempt to cross: so early on the morning of the 10th, the porters began to carry the luggage over the pass. The weight these men bear at a time is somewhat extraordinary, for even to a strong man without a load the crossing of the Cumbre in winter is dangerous and toilsome enough. When one takes into consideration, therefore, that these men took two of our mule panniers apiece—making the load for each amount to from 100 to 120 lbs.—it seems indeed marvellous that they do not more frequently die by the road when overtaken by storms. Most of these porters are half Spanish, half Indian, and have spent most of their lives upon this task. Many of them are killed every year at the work, and it was only last winter I heard with deep regret that one of the peons, Sebastian by name, who had served us most faithfully, had been overwhelmed by an avalanche. He was leaving one of the casuchas on the Chilian side of the Cumbre, when he and several passengers were hurled to their death. They had been obliged to wait a long time in this casucha owing to the inclemency of the weather, but on account of the lack of provisions they were at last compelled to make an effort to escape, and perished on the way. Some of these men die on the pass from sheer fatigue; others are starved in lonely and inhospitable casuchas, while many are overwhelmed by the sudden blizzards, or carried away, like Sebastian, by the great avalanches that sweep the mountain sides. These men are of a hardy race, a very different type to the ordinary muleteer, who never sets foot on the ground unless he is forced to do so. Some of them are honest and straightforward, but I fear the majority can only be described as the land pirates of the snow. Whenever they can, they extort their wages in advance before starting with the traveller's luggage. Then, on arriving at a lonely place where there is no help, they throw down their burdens and refuse to carry them farther, or to lead their passengers either forward or back unless they are paid on the spot some exorbitant sum. This game continues until they have stripped the unfortunate traveller of all he possesses. Lightbody, of course, was not ignorant of these practices. He had lived many years in South America and knew the natives well: besides the peons were aware it would be a mistake to try any tricks upon us. They knew we were all well armed, and that we should not hesitate to use our weapons if necessary. Before starting they made an earnest appeal to Lightbody for an advance of their wages, but we had long ago made it an inflexible rule upon the expedition that no money should be paid to any native for services rendered until their work was actually accomplished. These petitions were therefore in vain, and the march began with the best possible assurance of their fidelity.

The hour at which they started was 6.15 in the morning. The sun had not yet risen, but it was a bright and starlight night, and though the cold was intense, there was little or no wind. For the first part of the journey they walked in the track that the travellers of the previous day had made. These tracks are called by the peons of the country a "beueey." They walked steadily and continuously until the summit of the pass was reached, taking less than two hours, which even in summer would be considered quick going; but of course, owing to the terrible gales of the last few days, this side of the water-parting had been swept clear of snow. When they reached the top of the pass, as they were some distance ahead, they waited for the porters to come up with the luggage, for naturally they did not wish to let these men out of their sight. In about an hour the porters arrived, and the march was continued down the side to Portillo, the peons being kept in front. Here and there the track led directly under cliffs and bluffs where avalanches had fallen and buried the track made by the travellers of the day before. Great masses of newly-fallen snow hung on the slopes above their heads, and instinctively they hurried on, for the peril was great. At any moment fresh avalanches might fall from those upper slopes and sweep them away. There was an immense amount of snow on this side of the pass, and the track along which the party was now struggling towards Portillo was little more than a ridge of ice, slippery, narrow,

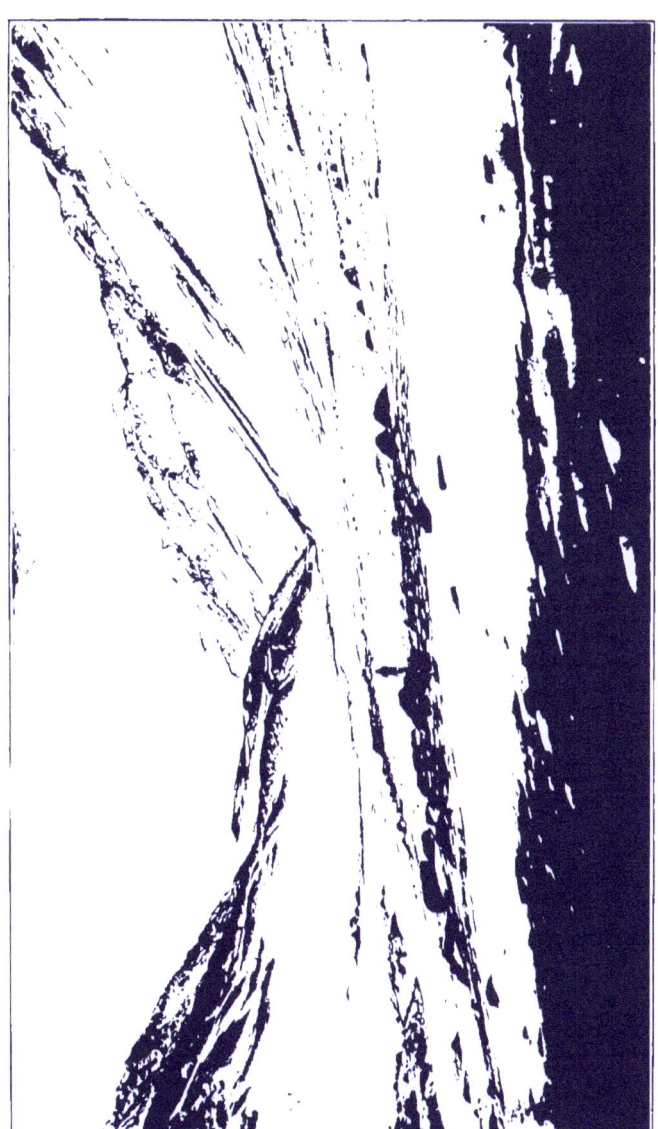

A WINTER SCENE NEAR CUEVAS

and sloping sharply downwards on both sides into fields of soft snow. This had been made by the travellers on the previous day. The sun had softened the snow, and a beaten track formed which had frozen during the night, producing a hard and narrow path of ice. It was like walking along the top of a wall; any incautious step would precipitate a man on one side or the other into huge drifts of powdery snow, where he would sink almost out of sight. These falls are extremely trying, and the struggles one has to make to get back to the track again are most fatiguing. Nevertheless, in spite of these difficulties, they reached Portillo in less than six hours, of which quite an hour had been spent on the top of the Cumbre waiting for the porters. Considering the condition of the snow, and the immense loads the men were carrying, this was remarkably quick time. At Portillo they found comfortable quarters and good food, and the landlord did his best for them.

Next day, in bright and clear weather, Lightbody went back along the road he had already traversed, and took a series of photographs of the Inca lake and the surrounding country. The little party lingered at this lonely inn on the plains of Portillo, thinking that Vines, Gosse, and I would overtake them, and that we might then all continue the journey together. They little knew at that time what anxious nights we were passing at the Inca, on account of Gosse's illness. They waited a few days, and then resolved to proceed, rightly thinking it would be better for them to get the luggage safely down to some civilised spot on the Chilian side.

Lightbody recounts in his notes that, while staying at Portillo, they had an opportunity of studying more closely the characters of their guides. On their arrival at partial civilisation they had thought it right to advance a small part of the money due for work done. The reception of this instalment had the usual consequence. All the wine and beer that Portillo afforded was bought and consumed, directly they had something in their pockets, and in a short time they displayed an unwonted largeness of manner and freedom of discourse. An old man, the father of the company, favoured them with a full flow of conversation. He was, he said, fifty-four years of age, an antiquity of which he seemed to be proud, but in spite of his years, which were great for a man following his profession, this patriarch had done even more than his fair share of the work. He brought over the two heaviest panniers, piling on top of them his own effects. The total weight which he had thus carried across the icy ridge of the Cumbre amounted to over one hundred and thirty pounds. This venerable quinquagenarian told them many tales of adventure in the snowy passes, and boasted of the great loads he had sometimes borne, naturally making much of his own endurance and fidelity. He had often, he said, started in storm and tempest to cross the Cumbre while completely intoxicated, but he had always sobered down on the journey, and never gone astray. Never had he lost the goods entrusted to his care, but had always faithfully turned up and completed his contract. Finally, he produced a cow-horn, on which he proceeded to perform for the entertainment of his hearers, and the noise he produced on this instrument was certainly extraordinary. The notes, although by no means harmonious in themselves, carried far away in those still, rocky gorges and defiles, and reverberated from cliff to cliff in not unpleasing echoes.

In speaking of these porters, I may mention that the weight of each pannier carried was between fifty and sixty pounds, and the charge paid for each, over the complete journey of nearly ten miles was about a sovereign.

Next morning the party started at 8.30, and arrived at Juncal after an hour's good walking. The journey was downhill, and some of the steepest slopes were descended in a curious manner, which the natives taught them. It was not glissading,—the snow had too recently fallen and was too soft for that,—and it could scarcely be called toboganning, unless of a very unusual kind. The way the natives conduct the descent is as follows. Each traveller is provided with a large and stout apron made of sheepskin, which is fastened on behind, the wool next to his body. He then sits down

THE INCA LAKE AND PORTILLO

upon it, gathers his legs together, and pushes himself off. Protected thus against the roughness of the snow, he descends rapidly, guiding himself with a pointed staff, and steering in and out among the great and dangerous boulders studding the mountain side. This way of sliding down the snow-slopes is speedy and not unpleasing, but it is impossible to take the luggage down in one's lap, and it therefore suffers a great deal before the bottom is reached. The men content themselves with rolling the panniers over from the top of the slope, and, in their downward course, they strike against projecting rocks, or occasionally land in a deep drift, from which they have to be rescued. Finally, when they are gathered together, it is plain they have not been improved in strength or shape by the rough usage they have undergone.

At Juncal Lightbody and Dr. Cotton parted from their aged porter and his companions, and found themselves again in the land of mules. They secured some animals both for riding and for carrying the luggage, and continued to Los Andes, a distance of some thirty miles, without further adventure.

The snow soon disappeared, and they were at last able to gallop along the dusty road that leads to Salto del Saldado, where an immense ridge or dyke of rock runs across the valley, dividing it into two. Through a narrow cleft or gorge in this barrier the river forces its way. Lightbody dwells with enthusiasm on the engineering of the Transandine Railway at this point, and, indeed, a remarkable feat in engineering enterprise has been accomplished here. Several short tunnels have been constructed, and the railway, emerging from one of them, crosses a short iron span bridge at a great altitude over the river, and enters the opposite tunnel on a curve. In summer the journey from Salto upwards can, of course, be made in coaches, and in fact the whole pass could be crossed in a carriage, but in winter the passage is invariably performed on foot, after the manner just described. Although for a strong man in good training it offers no difficulties or serious hardships in fine weather, yet, if he is overtaken by storm, he is lucky indeed if he escapes with his life.

They got through the Customs without difficulty as, by the courtesy of the Chilian Government, instructions had been forwarded to let them pass unmolested. As a matter of fact these functionaries happened to be engaged upon the important business of the evening meal, and did not even accost or challenge them.

In the evening they reached Los Andes in safety, and there Mr. Tuffield of the West Coast Cable Co. was able to give them information concerning us. It was not of a pleasant nature, for they learned that Vines and I were still at Inca, snowed in, unable to move, with Gosse dangerously ill.

CHAPTER XXVI

WE LEAVE THE ANDES

THE day that Vines returned, namely, 9th June, José took his revenge—he bolted with our horses to Vacas. I saw him four hundred yards away, galloping as hard as he could, and driving the horses before him. I called on him to stop, but he paid no attention, so I fired a few shots with my revolver against a rock some distance from him, thinking the noise might frighten him into returning; but he kept on at full speed. I should have been considered, in that country, as quite justified in shooting him if I had wished to, for in wild regions a man can commit no greater crime than that of horse-stealing. Murder is looked upon as a gentleman's act in comparison: etiquette says you may kill a man, but you must not take his horse.

In the evening the refugees from Chile that Vines has spoken of arrived with our horse and mule. Gosse was slightly better, but we were still obliged to sit up all night and keep the fire burning.

The day of the 11th I again spent in clearing the snow off the roof and cutting a way through to the doors, but another great snowstorm was evidently coming up. The man in charge of the Inca inn came up from Vacas that evening, and reported that José was in a terrible fright. He swore to everybody that I fired my revolver so close to him that he heard the bullet whistling by his ear. He also said he was ill and unfit for work. That, of course, was simply the result of drink—he had been drunk ever since arriving at Vacas, and evidently intended to remain so for the winter.

Next day the refugees from Chile continued their journey.

I gave them a letter to the proprietor of the posada at Vacas, begging him to look after our horses, and requesting him not to serve José with more drink, as I wished him to be sober two days later, when I was going to take Gosse down, and if possible get him to Mendoza. He was better now, but too weak to cross the Cumbre in winter, and as an old friend of Lightbody's, Mr. Norton, had very kindly offered him the hospitality of his estancia near Mendoza, I had decided to send him down there till he got better. He might then join us by train at Buenos Aires, when we came round the Magellan Straits, which we intended to do a few weeks later.

That night all our mules escaped, and next day Vines, who had contracted a bad cold on his journey from Cuevas to Inca, was completely laid up. Fifteen cargo mules came up from Vacas to take down some of our heavy luggage which we intended to send by rail home to England. The path was fairly clear, and I got off a lot of our more valuable instruments, etc., telling the men to come up again next day for another load, and at the same time to bring some saddle mules.

On the morning of 16th June they came up with twenty animals. It was snowing again, but I got Gosse out, and clothed him in all the blankets I could lay hands on, putting him thus wrapped up on his horse. He resembled a huge bundle, so thickly was he swathed, and he was only just able to keep his balance on the saddle. I promised Vines that I would force my way up the next morning, no matter what the weather was, as he was still ill in bed, though not dangerously so. At nine o'clock we set off. It was a risk, of course, but if I had missed this opportunity of taking Gosse down I should have had to wait another week, for the Transandine train in the winter only comes up once a week, and Vacas was far too damp a place, and the rooms far too cold for Gosse to remain in with safety.

The journey to Vacas was an exceedingly difficult one, and took much longer than we had anticipated. The highroad was completely blocked with huge drifts of snow, and

The Inca Valley in Winter

JOSÉ'S THREATS

we had to fight out new passages for ourselves, mostly by the river-bed. Consequently we reached Vacas only just in time for me to get Gosse into the train that was then starting for Mendoza. I found José at the station, but when he saw me he disappeared quickly round a corner and hid himself. I did not see anything of him during the day, but towards evening he came in a very intoxicated condition to the comedor of the inn, and insolently demanded money. I told him that if he presented himself sober at Inca his wages would be paid him. However, his aspect was very threatening, and I was just getting up to clear him out of the room, when he left hurriedly, telling me to have a care. I did not pay much attention to him, in fact I did not see him again that day, but the proprietor of the inn warned me that he was threatening my life in the kitchen, telling everyone who came in that he would have my blood before I left the country. They told me he spent the evening drinking and sharpening a large knife in an ominous fashion. On retiring to rest, I therefore took the precaution of piling a few objects in front of my door, so that should anyone try to force an entrance in the night I might at least be awakened. The room was terribly damp, there being several inches of water on the mud floor. The night passed without incident. Next morning I saddled my horse, and was about to start up to the Inca, when the proprietor of the posada rushed out and begged me not to go up that day, because José had started a couple of hours before with many friends, and taking two bottles of liquor. I thanked him for his warning, and started as quickly as possible. I was afraid José might reach the Inca before me, and give trouble to Vines, who was unwell. I therefore galloped along as quickly as I could, the roads above Vacas being fairly clear of snow. It was not until I had nearly reached the Penitentes Mountain that the huge drifts blocked up the fair-way. I had not gone very far when, on passing a sharp bend in the road, I came face to face with José. He was not more than twenty yards ahead of me, and had pulled up his horse right across the road. He did not move, but stood there glaring at me. Being rather uncertain as to what might be the possible outcome of this encounter, I cleared for action. What more especially interested me was the question whether he had a gun. It is a favourite habit of the Chilenos to buy American carbines, and then saw off the end of the long barrel, reducing them to a species of large pistol or revolver. These weapons are very deadly at close quarters, and as they can be hidden under the poncho, one never quite knows what is going to happen.

I dismounted from my horse, and slowly approached, covering him with my revolver. From the position in which he was sitting I judged it was impossible that he could have a gun trained on me, so I advanced boldly till I came up to him. He was muttering and murmuring something that I could not make out. I then grasped the fact that he was far too intoxicated to do anything. I kicked his foot out of the stirrup and gave him a sharp pull, whereupon he rolled helplessly on to the snow. The cold seemed slightly to sober him, and he attempted to rise. I then noticed that he had his knife in his hand. I rolled him over and over on the snow a few times, and left him there. It began to snow again, and I drove his horse a little distance along the road to Vacas, and left it, as I thought that it would be good for him to have to walk home. I am sure that a walk such as that is about as great a punishment as one can inflict upon a Chileno, and I knew that if he arrived on foot at Vacas he would at once be made the laughing-stock of all the peons and arrieros of the country.

I had a bad time in getting to Inca from there. The gale was in my face, and a blizzard blew with great violence. Again and again I was forced to turn my horse's head round, and stand back to the wind, covering my head with my blanket so as to be able to breathe at all, so fierce were the blasts and so fine and plentiful the driven snow. I finally reached my destination as dusk set in. Some half an hour after my arrival the post came up, and a number of extra fellows with it. They were an evil-looking lot, the characteristic type of the Chileno gaucho. One of them carried a gun. These men I had seen hanging round Vacas, and I understood that they were friends of José. José was not with them, but I gathered that they must have met him on the road. We dined that night with a gun loaded with buckshot and a five hundred express rifle on the table beside us, not to speak of our revolvers. The men got very drunk, but did not make any attempt to molest us. We took several precautions, however, on retiring to rest that night, barricading ourselves against possible attack. The rooms in the inn adapted themselves to this sort of thing. Once the door was firmly fastened, one would be fairly safe, unless of course someone made a hole in the mud roof above one's head, a process which can be performed without the slightest difficulty. Travellers who wish to take extra precaution in this country should adopt the method of sleeping under their bed instead of on it, for then they do not offer such a good mark from the ceiling.

Vines was much better now, so next day we made arrangements to start. We had a peon with us, by name Alfredo, who had been in the employ of Dr. Cotton all the summer at the inn. He had promised to carry our small bundle of clothes, and a friend of his was going to look after the animals. We had decided to ride up to Cuevas, and then to send them back to Vacas, where I had already made arrangements for their disposal. As the mail was going up that day, and the letter-carriers had an extra herd of mules to drive in front to clear the way, we anticipated no difficulty in reaching Cuevas. Early in the morning we started, giving José's friends as wide a berth as possible. The snow of the day before had ceased, but the morning was by no means fine. There was a cutting wind blowing, and low clouds rested across the valleys from hillside to hillside. We pressed along as fast as possible, knowing that at any moment we might be enveloped in a blizzard of snow. As far as possible we followed the river, and had fearful trouble in getting through some of the drifts, having to make repeated detours; at times, indeed, it really seemed as if it would be impossible for us to force our way through.

About three o'clock in the afternoon we reached the little graveyard just on this side of the Paramillos de las Cuevas. Here we stopped for some moments under the shelter of the casucha to stretch our legs. The men were getting nicely drunk by this time. They had brought a large amount of spirits with them, and this they passed round freely. José's friends also began to assume a threatening attitude. We told our men to stick close to us, but in this country it is really impossible to know which side a peon will take in a fight. We kept our eyes, with extreme vigilance, upon the gentleman with the gun, and insisted on riding behind everyone, a natural precaution in these cases. We also thought it prudent not to pause and let the mail men get ahead, as we saw that José's friends had made up their minds to stick close by us. There was just a possibility, we thought, in case of a fight, that the *correos* and peons might side with us. I noticed, however, that these partisans of José had been passing round free drinks, and in this country that means a great bond of friendship. Just as we started out again, in single file, Vines, who was immediately behind me, called out to me to look round. I did so, and perceived José himself coming up on his horse, not a hundred yards away. We continued on our journey without taking any notice of him, until he had approached within about twenty yards' distance. Then we faced round, as if to go and meet him; upon which he pulled up; we proceeded, and in this manner we kept him at bay till we reached the Paramillos. The snow was then so deep, and moving was so heavy, that we could no longer pursue these tactics, and José came up with us. He seemed fairly sober now, and glared at us from under his big, black, shaggy eyebrows. We got along, however, without any open hostilities until we reached the inn at Cuevas. The last bit of the journey, from the Paramillos onwards, had been desperately difficult, and several times I thought that we should have to give up, and sleep in one of the casuchas until the next day—a prospect by no means pleasing, as these huts are kept in the vilest and dirtiest condition imaginable. It was after dark when we arrived and put up at the little inn.

The cold was extreme, and there were no fires, so we prowled up and down in the comedor, or common-room, trying to keep warm. The food given us was practically untouchable, and the bottle of red, sour native wine that we purchased made us feel sick.

We were thus pacing up and down, smoking our pipes and trying to keep up our fast-ebbing spirits, when José burst into the room, followed by his five companions. There was a long narrow table running down the centre of the room, and Vines and I remained on one side, whilst we informed the men that they would be acting wisely if they remained on the other side.

José assumed a truculent air, and began to demand a large sum of money, far in excess of the wages due to him. I suggested mildly that if he did not keep silent we should be forced to clear him out of the room again in something after the same manner that Lightbody had followed. This cooled him for the moment, and I then worked out, upon a sheet of paper, the exact sum that was owing to him, and handed it to him in the presence of his friends. Further, I proceeded to give him my exact opinion of his conduct, which did not take very long. His friends seemed rather fired at this, and they all looked so threatening that we sharply ordered them out of the room. At the same moment Vines vaulted swiftly across the table into their midst, when they literally tumbled over each other in their efforts to get out of the door. Having disposed of these people in this manner we turned in, telling our men that they might sleep in the inn, as we gathered that José and his friends, being drunk, had assumed rather a menacing attitude towards them.

Next morning we started early. The little inn was built in the shape of half a courtyard, and so much snow had fallen that we were able to walk quietly straight over the roof. We got away unmolested with our men, but had not proceeded more than a quarter of a mile when we saw some men start up from the inn and follow us. As Vines and I were, however, walking at a fairly brisk pace they soon gave up, and turned back. We gradually passed the men carrying the mail, who had started earlier than ourselves. They had shocking loads — some of them amounting to as much as 120 lbs., and it was terrible to see how they suffered under these crushing weights. Their faces were almost green with cold and pain, and they were obliged to rest every few feet.

Our passage up to the top of the Cumbre was not difficult, for the wind had kept the slopes more or less clear of snow, and the day was fine. By rapid walking we were able to reach the top of the pass in less than two hours from leaving Cuevas, and as the rise is some 2500 feet this was by no means bad going. It was on the other side that our trouble commenced, where we found the snow lying very deep.

The route to be followed could be traced by great poles driven into the ground, the tops of which stuck out above the drifts, whilst here and there could be seen a lonely dome-shaped casucha or refuge hut. We suffered considerably from thirst on this descent. The sun came out and shone brightly, and as we had on a great amount of clothing, in the expectation of perhaps encountering very cold weather, we felt the heat very much.

The worst bit to cross was on the plains just before reaching Portillo. The snow was above our waists, and we had slowly to force our way foot by foot. When we reached the little inn we were nearly exhausted, and although we had intended to continue our way down to Juncal that night, we decided to wait until next morning. Louis, the host of the establishment, entertained us right hospitably. He gave us a most excellent supper, the best meal that we had tasted for many a long month. We sent Alfredo on to order a special train for us next day from Salto del Soldado, to carry us on our way to Los Andes, and also to have horses sent up for us, so that we could ride down the long valley. Vines was still rather weak after his illness, and I did not like to tire him more than was necessary.

Early next morning we started down. We had not gone far before we both became very ill, and were obliged to turn back to the hotel. A wind was blowing with great violence, and snow was falling heavily at the time. We waited a few hours, and then succeeded in getting down to Juncal at about ten o'clock in the morning. As we had ordered our special train for nine o'clock that morning, and we were still fifteen miles from Salto, we were beginning to get anxious lest they should think that the weather had detained us, and that we should therefore be forced to remain for the night at Salto, where there was neither food nor lodging. We found no animals for us at Juncal, and the proprietor of the inn evidently wished to detain us there for several days. However, we at once started down on foot, and fortunately after about an hour's walk we met the horses being driven up. Our friend Alfredo had doubtless met many of his friends on his descent the day before, and had forgotten about the animals until the next morning. About three o'clock in the afternoon we arrived at Salto, and found our little special waiting for us. I speak of this as if it was a complete train, but, to be accurate, it merely consisted of a small steam trolly, with seats for two persons, which is used in the winter months to convey people up and down from Salto to Los Andes, the mail train going but once a week. We had a quick run down, covering the twenty miles in fifty-nine minutes. On the route we ran over a cock, and nearly dashed into a calf. This, I fear, would have been as fatal to ourselves as to the animal, for the little trolly had but small wheels and was very light. If it had struck anything as large as a calf it would have surely been derailed, and as we were rushing along at a rate of about twenty-five miles an hour, this trifling cause would have brought our doings to a full stop, just as well as any of the more imposing dangers we had luckily survived.

At Los Andes we were in the heart of Chilian civilisation and luxury, so I may say that here ends our narrative of work in the Andes. It was, however, seven months before we reached England, and the reader may perhaps be interested to know of the misfortunes which overtook us in the meantime, for they were many and severe.

CHAPTER XXVII

CONCLUSION

WITH the heavy snows that fell in the early part of June, I considered my work in the Andes to be at an end. As the reader is already aware, my disappointment was very great at being so prematurely interrupted when I was convinced that I had at least three weeks before me in which to complete one or two points in the survey, and take duplicates of those photographs the result of which might be doubtful. From Los Andes we went to Valparaiso, where we were the guests of Mr. Ball for three weeks. During that time Lightbody and I developed many hundreds of the photographs taken, and roughly printed off the majority of them. The percentage of good results was very large, but, as will so often happen, some of the views which were particularly important to me had suffered in one way and another. We had dreaded more than anything trouble from the unsteadiness of the camera, caused by the wind, and injury to plates and films by dust. Our surmises were correct, for we found a great many plates and films spotted and scratched by sand, but as Lightbody had made his exposures as short as possible, without being instantaneous, the plates had suffered less from shaking than was expected, and the detail was in most cases clear and distinct. We had not anticipated, however, that our double-backs would have suffered so severely from the dryness of the climate and shaking by continual transport: in many cases where we had looked forward to good results our picture was scarred with white fog-marks. So much for the full-plate results: the views taken with the Lea Bridges camera were more for surveying purposes, and not feeling so anxious about them, I

LIGHTBODY'S CAMP IN TUPUNGATO VALLEY

TYPHOID FEVER

did not develop them. The long spools of the panoramic photographs, taken with the cycloramic camera, I had no means at Valparaiso for developing. The results of Vines's quarter-plate work at great heights were on the whole satisfactory.

In ten days or a fortnight we were going to sail by way of the Magellan Straits for Southampton—in fact our berths were already secured—so I never imagined for a moment that I should have time to put in finishing touches to my work. Little did I think that the opportunity was already being created; for having completed our work of development, we went to Santiago, and within a week I was down with typhoid fever—that scourge that attacks every European sooner or later in these parts. It was now the middle of July; by the end of August I was again well enough to think of sailing. Berths were secured once more, but as so often happens in typhoid, I suffered a relapse. By the end of September I was convalescent, and Lightbody and Vines strongly urged me, as the spring and summer were again approaching, to allow them to go once more to the scene of our labours, complete the list of photographs and add a little to the survey work, whilst I proceeded by sea through the Magellan Straits and met them at Monte Video. This was therefore arranged, but again the unforeseen happened; Vines also fell a victim to typhoid, so that it was not until 4th November that Lightbody started alone for the mountains, with the intention of doing some three or four weeks' additional work. He set out with several small instruments and a full-plate camera with telephoto attachment. In addition to the completion of a few points in the survey of the Vacas and Tupungato Valleys, he intended if possible to make his way up the eastern branch of the Horcones Valley and take an entirely new set of photographs of the great southern wall of Aconcagua, for the wind had so shaken the camera during the taking of the first set of photographs that, on developing them in Valparaiso, I found them to be almost useless for the purposes of illustration. Lightbody also intended to ascend the mountain known as the Penitentes,[1] or Iglesia, with a full-plate camera, and take a panorama and numerous views from the summit. One of the great objects he had in view was to take a series of photographs, first with the ordinary lens, and then, where it was possible, with the telephoto objective, without moving the camera between the two processes.

He first made his way, starting on 10th November, up the eastern branch of the Horcones Valley to the foot of Aconcagua. He says in his diary:—

" . . . We proceeded on our mules and at last had Aconcagua in view from base to summit. The face appeared perpendicular, with strata of rock showing between masses of ice of immense thickness. We were at a height of nearly 13,000 feet: I saw no animal life, and of vegetation there was nothing visible. I was as fully impressed with the awful grandeur of my surroundings as FitzGerald and Vines had been when they first penetrated this valley in the previous autumn. Clouds began to collect on the summit and the wind howled fiercely though the day was bright. Two hours' work saw me through with my ten plates, but during the taking of the views I fear the camera was vibrating with the wind, and the head-cloth flickered and cracked like a jib with the sheets carried away in a squall."

The illustration opposite p. 222 gives the view looking south from this point, and that opposite p. 224 shows the wall of rock and ice with the summit of Aconcagua in cloud. I should like to call attention to several illustrations of the work done by Lightbody with the telephoto lens. Opposite p. 30 we have a view taken from the mouth of the Horcones Valley of the mass of Aconcagua, some fifteen miles distant. The reader should observe the shadows on this face of ice and rock, and the outline of the two peaks and saddle between. On 2nd November Lightbody ascended to a point of over 11,000 feet, a little to the south of the Penitentes mountain, and took a photograph of this

---

[1] I feel I ought to apologise for the frequent occurrence of this word. Güssfeldt called a valley and mountain to the north of Aconcagua by this name. This mountain here mentioned lies to the south of the Inca Valley. See Map.

Ibelesa from Las Vacas. Telephoto View.

PHOTOGRAPHIC RESULTS

same face with the telephoto objective at a distance of about twenty-four miles. This view is reproduced in the photogravure opposite p. 114: though the shadows and outlines are seen greatly magnified, yet the distance is almost double that referred to in the previous view. Of other work done in this way are two views of Torlosa from twenty miles to the east, near Vacas, both taken from much the same point, the wide-angle on an afternoon in early June, midwinter, (see opposite p. 291); and the long focus on a November morning of the same year, on the opposite page.

In order to give some idea of the troubles of a photographer working with a full-plate camera in the high valleys of the Andes, I will quote Lightbody's words with regard to the illustration opposite p. 43. He was at the time up the higher reaches of the Vacas Valley. He says: "In about an hour I arrived at a place where there was a very fine view of the eastern side of Aconcagua. I had never before beheld the mountain from this point of view, and, much impressed by its outlines, I took nearly half a dozen photographs of it without changing the position of the camera. My reason for doing this was that the sudden blasts of wind that came first up the valley and then down made me feel certain that each view as I took it was a failure. I hoped, however, from so many, to obtain at least one good result. I shortened the legs of the tripod, put them far apart, and tied a stone of some thirty pounds' weight to steady them. Sebastian and I were nearly blown from the ledge on which we had secured the camera."

Perhaps the most successful of all his views was that of Tupungato, opposite p. 157, taken from the valley some thirty miles distant with the telephoto objective. The sprigs of yareta in the foreground give a very characteristic touch to the picture. This should be compared with one taken with the wide-angle lens opposite p. 158, showing the level reaches of the Tupungato Valley in the foreground. These two photographs are taken almost from the same spot.

Lightbody eventually, after some three weeks' work, made his headquarters again at Inca, and ascended that picturesque mass of cliff—the Penitentes, or Iglesia. To all who cross the Andes by the Uspallata route the Penitentes are pointed out as one of the wonders to be seen. This great wall of rock, cut by time and water, presents the shapes of perpendicular pillars and buttresses some two thousand feet high, and is in the imagination of the beholder the "Iglesia," or monastery. On the steep red slope of debris leading to its base stands a long line of black pinnacles of rock—the "Penitents," the monks, toiling in solemn procession up the steep slope to the portals above. I have heard many people who have crossed the Andes say — "I saw the boasted marvels of the Penitentes, and I frankly confess I do not appreciate them." Now, had I not myself had the advantage of seeing them on more than one occasion and in different lights, I should probably have carried away the same impression. The effect is to a great extent produced by the light. In the morning or evening when the shadows are long, the effect is particularly striking. I saw it once by moonlight, when the procession was both real and lifelike, and I thoroughly entered into the feelings of my imaginative arriero, who, standing quite still and beckoning to me to do the same, whispered, "Stay a moment, señor, listen, and you will hear the monks chanting." Lightbody first of all climbed the Iglesia, 14,000 feet, with a full-plate camera, and took a panorama,[1] beginning at the north with Aconcagua and going round westward to the south, and taking in Torlosa, Juncal, Pollera, Navarro, and Tupungato. He describes his ascent in the following words :—

"On Monday, 21st November, I received news that Vines was really convalescent, and that FitzGerald intended leaving Valparaiso by the S.S. *Oravia* on the 23rd. I therefore prepared to start the next day and finish my work by making the ascent of the Penitentes, as I wished to join the ship on its arrival at Monte Video on 3rd December. Leaving Inca at daybreak, I reached the summit at 1 p.m., having ridden all but two hours. My mule took me farther than most people would care to ride, and not every animal could have

[1] See panorama at end of book.

THE IGLESIA OR PENITENTES

INCA INSCRIPTIONS 303

ascended to such a height. We had to pass along several snow ridges and fields before reaching the summit, but the top itself was clear of snow and constructed of rock of a crumbly nature, precipitous towards the north, and having two points of rock at the eastern and western extremity with a somewhat deep depression between. Our line of ascent was from the south, where a rolling tableland gives an easy approach to the rock above. From this isolated position, for it was the centre of a circle of great peaks, I gained the finest possible view of all the country we had covered in our work of exploration amongst the mountains. Before me lay the noblest panorama I had ever beheld. Aconcagua was magnificent, and the distance which separated me from it—twenty-three miles—was an ideal one for examining its vast proportions.[1] I passed a very busy two hours taking photographs and bearings from this point of vantage. The cold was bitter, and quite windy enough to render photography, etc., difficult and unpleasant. I had a particularly fine view of the Cerro de las Rejas, that massive and precipitous ridge of black rock and ice, the continuation eastwards of the Almacenes, and also down the main valley of the Rio Mendoza as far as Zanjon Amarillo. A bank of white clouds rolled over Mendoza and the lower lands. After my photographs were taken I had hardly sufficient time to get bearings of the different peaks before their tops were enveloped in cloud. I was interested to find on the saddle, between the two highest points of rock forming the summit, the remains of four stone-built walls which had formed a corral,—some twenty feet by twelve in dimension. To me it had the appearance of the ordinary walls built by the Indians to protect themselves from the weather, but the position of this very substantial erection on the top of such a conspicuous mountain pointed to it as a centre of the ancient Indian worship. I had, unfortunately, little time to spare, having many more photographs and bearings to take, otherwise I should have examined the stones for traces of Indian writing so frequently to be found on such ancient ruins. I discovered a specimen of these

[1] See illustration opposite p. 114.

carved signs while doing some railway levels on the Transandine Railway, at a spot not far from the Zanjon Amarillo.[1] I do not know to what period they belong, but there is a record that the early Incas came down as far as these passes, and it is their supposed treasure that draws many a gaucho to a lonely grave.

"We led our mules the greater part of the descent, and arrived at Inca at half-past six in the evening.

"Somewhat late on the day of the 23rd I took the camera with the telephoto attachment down the valley some three miles below Inca, and took several views of the Penitent Monks beneath the Iglesia at a time when the shadows cast by the sun accentuated their outline.[2]

"On the 25th I descended to Mendoza, and joined FitzGerald on 3rd December at Monte Video."

This last entry in Lightbody's journal is our final word on the Andes of Argentina. But before drawing my narrative to a close I should like to quote a few notes from Philip Gosse's diary, written in Mendoza a few months previously, when, as the reader will no doubt remember, he had left me amidst the winter snows at the little Andine railway station at Vacas.

Phillip Gosse writes:—

"On my arrival at Mendoza, after leaving Inca, in May, I had a very kind invitation from Mr. Norton to stay at his *finca* or vineyard, until I was well enough to go to Chile. This I readily accepted, as Mendoza is a dead and alive place at the best of times, and to a stranger and an invalid unbearable. Mr. Norton's finca is about fifteen miles to the south of Mendoza, near to the village of Lujan. We set out in a snowstorm, and Mr. Norton had no easy task managing three very fresh horses in the light buggy, with his hands stiff with the cold. For a 'gringo' like me, it was an exciting drive, as we went galloping through the deep sand, the broad road now and then becoming so narrow where it crossed a river by a bridge that there was only just room for the buggy to cross, with six inches to spare on

[1] See illustration on opposite page.   [2] See illustration opposite p. 302.

INCA CUTTINGS ON A ROCK

either side between the wheels and the edge of the bridge, which in this part of Argentina have no walls, or any kind of protection whatever. We arrived at the finca an hour after dark, and as we drove into the patio or courtyard, a pack of all sorts and conditions of dogs surrounded the buggy, barking in a most formidable way. But as soon as they heard Norton's voice they became quiet, only now and then growling when one of them came near me. A boy came and took the buggy, and we entered a cheerful room with a large fire burning, where Mrs. Norton, a charming Argentine lady, awaited our arrival, with a good supper ready on the table. The next day Norton showed me over the finca, which consists of several thousand acres of cultivated land, given up entirely to vine-growing. The chief and quickly growing industry of the two provinces of Mendoza and San Juan is this vine-growing. Almost all the men on Norton's estate were Italians, gangs of whom go about together and get engaged by contract. The chief enemy is the locust, clouds of which come and destroy a whole vineyard in a few hours. The vineyards are irrigated by the government canals, and receive a stated amount of water daily. It did not rain here during the whole of my visit, lasting six weeks, but snowed twice. The birds most common round Lujan are the *chingolos* or song sparrows (*Zonotrichia pileata*), also there are a great number of the *Sycalis lutea*, pretty yellow birds. Of condors I saw a great many. In the vineyards there are large numbers of kites, which the natives call *chimangos*. These birds seem to eat almost anything, and are great friends to the vine-growers. One day I shot a chimango, which I found had a large live toad in its beak. They are also said to catch rats and mice. Carrion is perhaps their chief diet. A curious sight is to watch these birds when there is ploughing going on. The plough as it moves along is followed by a flock of sometimes one hundred or more chimangos, who utter shrill cries while they scramble for the worms turned up by the plough ; in fact, so eager are they to get these luxuries, that they will dive between the ploughshare and the ploughman. When a chimango has got a worm, he will often go a little way ahead, and station himself on one of the vine-poles in front of the plough, where he can eat his worm at his ease and wait the arrival of the plough.

"In a field near the house there was a stunted prickly tree, where a great many small birds used to roost, and often I found a heap of feathers in the morning underneath it. I couldn't think what creature it could be that fed on the birds, so one evening I set a gin baited with a dead bird. Early next morning I went to make my round of the traps, but when I was quite one hundred yards from this trap I suddenly became aware of the most disgusting smell imaginable. This got worse and worse until I really felt quite ill; so I made a detour and got on the windward side of the trap, and on approaching found a dark fluffy animal with a head very much like that of a small pig, caught by one of its legs. Then it suddenly occurred to me that this, of course, was a skunk. Contrary to my rule I had come without my gun, and it wasn't safe to get too near the animal if I wanted to go near a human habitation for some weeks, so I returned to the house for the gun. Just at the moment I was going to shoot, the bull-terrier, who had followed me without my noticing her, rushed at the skunk and killed it, and then returned to me, very pleased with herself. But when she was just going to jump up at me, I got a whiff of the choking smell of the skunk which had got on to the dog, and I had to drive her out of range with stones. I was alarmed to see her galloping for home. I followed, but before I got there I saw her reappear at the gate in a tremendous hurry, followed by a regular storm of sticks and stones. We couldn't let her come near the house for over a week after. I had heard that the Indians buried the skunks for a while and then skinned them under water, so I dug a hole and put it in, having carried it at the end of a stick at arm's length holding my nose with the other hand. After ten days I dug it up again, and skinned it under water in a little stream, and only smelt of it a little. I did not try trapping any more skunks after that. All the livestock I had tried to bring for the Zoological Gardens had died except one large mouse. I tried my hand at trapping small birds, and managed to get some chingolo sparrows and some chimango kites (*Milvargo chimango*) alive, which are now in London. One of the kites I shot in the wing and the leg, both of which were broken, another shot passing through its crop, but about half an hour after I quietly approached its cage and found it eating some raw meat. Another one I caught in a gin, baited with a dead rat.

"A serious enemy to the grapes, Norton told me, are the foxes. These will come at night and go down a whole row of vines, just tearing down a branch here and there, and eating a few off each. Now and then a dog develops a craving for grapes also, and the only thing to prevent it is to shoot the dog.

"All the fields are separated by broad walls of hard mud, which are the homes of no end of burrowing owls and guinea-pigs (*Cavia aperea*). There was one ruined mud hut, I remember, which was turned into a kind of flat for these little animals, as they had made little terraces all about the walls, and often I have seen one appear at one hole, run along the terrace or balcony and disappear at another hole.

"I must not cease without a word about the spur-winged or Cayenne plovers, as they are called. These birds go about in flocks of two or three hundred, and prefer marshy ground for feeding; when a meadow is flooded, you may be sure of finding the plovers there. I tried eating one, one day, but it was very hard and stringy. It is a wonderful sight to see the plovers wheeling round and round high up in the sky, separating into regiments and reforming again, like an army manœuvring at the orders of some unseen general.

"The guinea-pigs I found such good eating that we often had our dinner off them. They much resemble a very tender rabbit. One day when we were driving home after visiting some friends in Mendoza, Norton, who was driving, suddenly drew up sharp, and called to me, as I was sitting in the back, to get out quick, as there was an addition to the Zoo swearing at the horses. I hurried round and found a small black ferret-like animal standing facing the three horses, and evidently in a terrific rage. Luckily I had a large wire rat-trap with me, into which I rather unceremoniously bundled the small fury. He turned out to be a young Giron (*Galictis vittata*). I kept him for a few days, and he became very tame, and used to follow me about. But he was really too young to keep, and one morning I found him dead at the bottom of his cage. About this time I had two large chinchilla-like mice (*Phyllotis darwini*) in a cage; not thinking it necessary to separate them as they looked so peaceful, I was horrified to find one day that one of them, now in the Zoological Gardens, had eaten his comrade."

APPENDICES

APPENDIX A

NOTES ON SPECIMENS COLLECTED IN THE CHILIAN ANDES BY MEMBERS OF MR. FITZ GERALD'S EXPEDITION

BY PROFESSOR T. G. BONNEY, D.SC., LL.D., F.R.S.

(a) IN the description of these specimens it will be most natural and advantageous to commence with those collected at the greatest distance from the axis of the Andean Chain and at the lowest level. The first specimen (22) was obtained in the Horcones Valley, some distance east of Aconcagua; on the left bank of the river bearing the same name, to west-south-west of, and rather more than two and a half miles in a straight line from Mr. FitzGerald's base camp. It is a reddish limestone with part of the whorl of an ammonite.

(b) 23, collected a little more than a mile farther up the valley, and on the opposite bank of this stream is a similar specimen. For description of these two, see Mr. Crick's Note on the Fossils (p. 333).

(c) 12 (bis), comes from the same bank of the river, above three and a half miles farther up, and (9) from the slopes above on the same side. This bears the label "K2 Camp, loose (7th April, Gosse)." The specimen is about two inches in diameter, purplish or blackish in colour, apparently coated with iron-oxide, with a little of a whitish mineral and traces of malachite. It is not likely to repay a more intimate examination, being either a vein product or rock impregnated with metallic deposits.

(d) 1. "K3 District, 12,000 feet, foot of mountain south of Aconcagua, large slabs appearing above sands and mud" nearly two miles beyond the last described (c), and on the left bank of the Horcones River. It is a piece, about a foot long, of Gypsum "marbled" with darkish lines, one face also being incrusted with a secondary deposit of the mineral of which the specimen is composed; it is stained a reddish colour.

We come next to the specimens connected with the Torlosa Valley. Taking these in the order of lettering, we find on the left bank near the mouth of the valley (barely a mile from the last locality):—

(*a*) "Found loose (Vines)." A flattish triangular piece, not quite three inches in vertical height. Apparently a sedimentary rock consisting of a grey silty material, which effervesces moderately with hydrochloric acid, and is traversed by small veins of calc-spar; there is a reddish stain on the exterior. It was probably once a silt, possibly containing much volcanic dust.

(*b*) "Stone found in springs north-east base of Torlosa (22nd April, Gosse)." A flattish specimen, with rounded edges about three inches in longest dimension, coated externally with an ochre-brown film, under which is a reddish-grey deposit; perhaps showing some indications of sulphur. These coatings conceal the actual material of the rock. The spring is probably chalybeate, and possibly may also contain sulphides or sulphates. It is added that the water was bad to drink, and the information is not surprising.

(*c*) "Found just above water-line near springs, base of Torlosa; all the stones covered with the same white deposit." A rudely triangular piece, a little more than two inches in greatest length, of a rather hard compact grey rock, resembling a fine quartzose grit, but with some specks of felspar. The rock itself appears insensible to hydrochloric acid, but the white incrustation effervesces briskly. Without more minute examination (which would be wasting time) I cannot be quite certain of the nature of this rock, but it is not improbably an indurated volcanic dust.

(*d*) "North-west side of dried-up spring (23rd April, Gosse)." Four specimens of calcite evidently deposited by water. All consist of two layers: one showing remnants of a third (at bottom). This seems to be a muddy limestone (the calcareous constituent being doubtless a precipitate). The next layer (about half an inch thick) has a rather cellular structure; over this is a slightly mammillated outer coating (about one-fifth of an inch thick) of calcite or aragonite in small crowded prisms. Both these layers are no doubt precipitates. A fifth specimen is a little lump of a yellowish-grey colour, about three-quarters of an inch in diameter, with some resemblance to the concretions called "race," in the brick earth of the Thames Valley.

(*e*) "All the stones in water at mouth of spring like this (23rd April, Gosse)." A subangular stone, so thickly coated with rust that the rock itself is not visible. The water evidently is chalybeate; the stone is not likely to repay further examination.

(*f*) See Mr. Crick's Notes, p. 335.

(*g*) In springs, under water (25th April, Vines)." The specimen seems to be bounded by natural joint faces, which are covered with

DESCRIPTION OF ROCK SPECIMENS 313

rust, the water being probably chalybeate. A cut surface discloses a compact dark rock with paler greyish spots. Microscopic examination shows a glassy base thickly crowded with lath-like microliths of plagioclase felspar, minute pyroxenes, ferrite and opacite. Scattered in this are larger grains of iron-oxide, some being hematite, and several, not so large, of a pale green mineral. Of this three types are noted; some irregular in shape, are aggregates of a fibrous mineral, in parts very dense, which has low polarisation tints, and resembles a serpentine. These are occasionally bordered with a thin layer of a clear mineral, and may occupy minute vesicles; others, more regular in form, show parallel cleavage planes. In the better preserved parts of these some exhibit straight extinction, others that of diallage, and slight differences in aspect may be noted. Hence I conclude that both diallage and a variety of enstatite have been present, and that the rock is a rather altered enstatite-andesite. A crack in it is filled with hematite.

(h) See Mr. Crick's Notes, p. 335.

(j) "South-east side, found below spring in quantities." Apparently a chip of a dark limestone or a calcareous mudstone, almost covered with a thin film of carbonate of lime.

(k) "The north-west side of the valley in this rock (Vines)." Small fragments, of a purplish-grey rock, resembling a rather altered andesite. A green tint in some of the fragments suggests the presence of minute epidote; felspar can be distinguished; dark spots probably indicate pyroxene; some calcite is deposited on one side (a joint face); on the surface (probably similar) of a second chip is a group of small radiating crystals of a colourless transparent mineral, not effervescing with hydrochloric acid, and apparently rather too hard for a sulphate. Possibly it is a zeolite, but it seemed needless to carry the investigation further.

(l) "Loose in bed of stream (17th April, Lightbody)." Four specimens of a rather platy or foliated selenite, showing the clinodiagonal cleavage faces. Apparently it has been formed in a yellowish-grey clay.

(m) "Pure gypsum in quantities, mouth of valley, in debris and in sand." The label sufficiently describes the specimen, which evidently is a precipitate.

(n) "Mouth of valley in quantities (22nd April, Vines)." A slab of darkish limestone (fairly brisk effervescence with hydrochloric acid). Weathered surfaces are a pale reddish grey, showing a subconchoidal fracture and a rather platy jointing; no signs of fossils. Not very unlike one of the darker Carboniferous limestones of England, but it might be of any age, from late Palæozoic to early Tertiary.

Near to it occurs (19) "Shingle behind K3 (22nd April, Vines)." A small lump of gypsum, enclosing deep reddish-coloured bits,—apparently of indurated mud.

(On the right bank of the stream come in succession (*m*) with some more of (*n*), (*f*), (*l*), (*a*), (*j*), (*e*), and then nearly on a line up the slope (*g*), (*b*), (*c*); on the left bank in the same order is (*h* and *k*), with (*d*) roughly opposite to (*e*)).

16. The next two specimens come from high up on the east side of the ridge bounding the Torlosa Valley on the west. "Whitish-yellow streak running east to west through brown rock (17), same colour throughout Torlosa." This is an elongated specimen (about three and a half inches in length), defined by irregular joint faces. It is of a pale pinkish-grey colour, with yellowish (felspathic) spots, and is of a redder tint on the exposed surfaces. On microscopic examination it appears doubtful whether any base remains; probably that is now devitrified: if not it is very thickly crowded with felspar microliths, some of which are more like sanidine than plagioclase. Both these minerals appear to occur among the larger crystals. All however are rather decomposed, numerous microliths of sericitic aspect being developed, which are often about one-tenth of an inch in diameter. There are grains of iron-oxide (? hematite), and several rudely outlined prisms—less than half the length of the felspar—consisting of a pale brown micaceous mineral, with opacite and ferrite. The cross-section of one or two suggests that these aggregates replace hornblende. A few small crystals of a nearly colourless mica are present, and two or three of apatite (?). The rock has been an andesite, probably with hornblende, possibly also with biotite.

17. *A*. This is a slab of fine-grained sandy mudstone of a rather dark reddish-brown colour. Under the microscope the rock is seen to be composed of small rather angular fragments of quartz and felspar, the latter being the more abundant, and some of them certainly plagioclase, with less angular fragments of felspathic lava, devitrified or crowded with microliths, not often scoriaceous. Cavities and the interstices of the ground-mass are occupied with a deep brown material, probably largely composed of iron-oxide. There are no signs of cleavage; the rock is probably an indurated stratified volcanic dust.

3. "K2 Camp. From solid rock; also lying in debris on Col, Buenavista Valley; seen also in many other places in Horcones Valley at 11,000 and 12,000 feet (7th April, Gosse)." Seven lumps of ore, the dominant material being a purplish-brown colour, inclining

DESCRIPTION OF ROCK SPECIMENS 315

to reddish. The ore probably is a mixture of iron and copper oxides; here and there are thin films of malachite. On the exterior of some we find one or two crystals of a white mineral (? monoclinic). These specimens throw no light on the general geology of the region, and are very probably vein products; they are only interesting as indicating the presence of copper.

E. "In Horcones Valley, at foot of steep western base of Aconcagua—in large quantities everywhere standing up amid the rock debris a little higher up the slope than the last." (2) A rather wedge-shaped piece of gypsum, from about three to four inches long, two and a half inches wide, and one and a half at the thickest part, faintly tinged with red and slightly darker coloured on the outside. The general form and the small hemispherical lumps on one surface suggest that the rock is a precipitate. A second smaller fragment is not materially different, except that it is harder than the thumb-nail, so that probably some anhydrite is mixed with the gypsum.

F. (1) "Western side of Horcones Valley, opposite to Aconcagua, from rock *in situ* on right bank of glacier stream, between 12,000 and 13,000 feet above sea-level." Two specimens of a warm grey-coloured limestone, stained reddish externally, with impressions of ammonites. (See Mr. Crick's Notes, p. 334.)

(2) "South-west base of Aconcagua, 13,000 feet, in great quantities; breaking through surface and also in masses; found loose in snow-bed (24th April, Lightbody)." A large block about one foot long; either curiously worn by stream action or else a deposit hardly less singular, for it forms narrow ridges parted by deep furrows, both very irregular; colour white, no effervescence, hardness about 3 in the scale; anhydrite; possibly with a slight intimate admixture of gypsum.

18. "Large boulders of this at foot of Aconcagua, in Horcones Valley, 13,500 feet (28th April, Vines)." A specimen, about three and a half inches in greatest length, of a dull purplish-grey rock, having a rather rough surface, spotted with whitish felspar, and with some extremely small filled-up vesicles. On examining a thin slice it appears possible that a base remains, but it is thickly crowded with felspar microliths, mostly plagioclase, and with specks, grains, or rods, of deep brown iron oxide. The larger constituents (besides the last named) include felspar, somewhat decomposed, but mostly plagioclase, and a secondary pale green mineral with low polarisation tints, one variety replacing a pyroxene, another filling tiny cavities. Of the former one or two suggest a member of the enstatite group. Though it is difficult to determine the species of the pyroxene, the rock itself is indubitably an andesite.

Aconcagua

We turn at this point away from the Horcones River at no great distance below its glacier source, and on the north-west base of Aconcagua, low down near bed of valley, find G and L. The former occurs "in solid blocks, generally darker on outside; associated with large round pieces of L." The specimen measures from two to three inches each way, is of a dull purplish colour, speckled with whitish felspar crystals, up to about one-tenth of an inch long, and subangular dark spots, the largest being about one-eighth of an inch. The other specimen, labelled "Same position from rock *in situ*," is a compact grey rock, with a few minute cavities and very small felspar crystals (up to about one-twentieth of an inch in length), and some of a dark pyroxenic mineral, occasionally nearly one-fifth of an inch long; it is also speckled with a pale green mineral. Both specimens have been examined under the microscope. In L the more conspicuous minerals are: (*a*) plagioclase felspar (species uncertain but resembling andesine), variable in size, sometimes rounded or broken in outline. (*b*) Hornblende, also variable in size, the largest specimen containing small enclosures of felspar. This constituent is often darkened by opacite, has the crystalline form badly preserved, and shows traces of a corrosion border. (*c*) Granules of iron-oxide. These lie in a glass which is nearly colourless itself, but contains some opacite and many minute microliths of plagioclase. The section exhibits numerous small irregularly shaped vesicles, filled with aggregates of a chloritic mineral, giving rather bright polarisation tints, together with one or two enclosures of a slightly different rock; one of which appears to be almost holocrystalline, though the constituents are small. Probably these are portions of a slightly different and better crystallised magma which has been caught up by the lava in its upward course.

Specimen G is not so well preserved; the felspar, as above, being largely replaced by a granular mineral, which affords fairly bright polarisation tints, and in part at least appears to be dolomite, though probably a silicate is also present. The mode of replacement is a little remarkable; sometimes, while part of the crystal is thus replaced, the remainder is fairly fresh-looking. The hornblende shows corrosion borders of opacite, and is often darkened by the same material. There is possibly a flake or two of biotite. The ground mass differs but little from that of L, and the glassy base shows less sign of decomposition than might have been expected, but there are no vesicles. The specimens are varieties of hornblende-andesite.

DESCRIPTION OF ROCK SPECIMENS 317

M and *O*. "On moraine above the last two specimens, fallen from masses with stratified aspect in cliffs above, which reach to the western peaks." These seem to be different coloured varieties of the same kind of rock. *M* is a piece, approximately four inches long and one-third of this measurement in other directions, of a pale pinkish-grey colour, but weathering externally to a slight yellowish brown. It is compact in structure, the felspar crystals scattered in it being so small that they are only just visible to the unaided eye; there are a few little darkish spots. The specimen *O* somewhat exceeds three inches in its longest measurement, and has a rather irregular and rough surface of slightly scoriaceous aspect. It is a darkish grey colour, speckled with numerous crystals of a glassy felspar, ranging up to about one-tenth or even one-eighth of an inch in diameter, and with some running up to about one-quarter of an inch, of a dark pyroxene, apparently hornblende. I thought it unnecessary to have slices cut from these rocks, since they were neither obtained *in situ* nor in a promising condition, but they are obviously andesites, and probably represent the variety containing hornblende.

N. "Higher up than the last two, from solid rock, very brittle." A specimen of a rather pale grey andesite, containing felspar crystals, generally less than one-tenth of an inch long, but in two or three instances rather larger, and many crystals of a pyroxene, which run a little bigger than the felspar, and in a few cases reach about one-quarter of an inch, when they seem to enclose some impurity towards the middle part. A few small cavities are visible. These felspars under the microscope appear to be mainly plagioclastic, but one or two may be sanidine. The hornblende has sometimes crystal outlines, but generally a corrosion border, and occasionally a second and inner black band. There are also larger grains of iron-oxide. These minerals are included in a base of pale coloured glass crowded with felspar microliths, apt to be rather square in form; augite microliths may also be present, and a pale green mineral, the nature of which is uncertain. Without chemical analysis it is difficult to say whether hornblende-andesite or hornblende-sanidine-trachyte would be the more accurate name for this rock.

K. "At 17,000 feet, on north-west flank of Aconcagua, in great quantities from solid rock." A parcel of a fine sandy dust with harder lumps of a yellowish colour, representing a very decomposed trachytic lava or ash, probably the former. I expect that the condition of this rock is the result of solfataric action, and that a "blow-hole" of steam once existed at this place.

A and *C*. "Northern slope of Aconcagua, 18,000 feet, close to our camp." *A* is described as "a soft caking powder, dry, in large quantities on the surface." It appears to represent a trachytic rock, like the last, in an extreme stage of decomposition. *C* is "found in veins in the solid rock; also among loose decomposed rock." These are fragments of a dull grey andesite, with small scattered whitish crystals of felspar, up to about one-eighth of an inch in length. Some of the fragments are partially encrusted with a whitish mineral, which does not effervesce with hydrochloric acid, and varies in hardness, being both less and greater than that of the thumb-nail (? a mixture of anhydrite and gypsum). Some small black rather lustrous grains or granules are visible, of moderate hardness, and one or two brownish-black stripes (? produced by iron-oxide). Possibly this rock may form intrusive veins in the other, but both seem to have suffered from solfataric action. They appear to be hardly worth slicing.

H. "At 18,700, about one mile to north of our camp. Loose, not in great quantities." These are small pieces of selenite, showing crystalline structure, seemingly in rudely parallel flakes. When scratched by the thumb-nail a slight "grating" is perceptible, as if some harder particles (possibly anhydrite) were mingled with the dominant mineral.

J. "Northern side of Aconcagua, at 19,000 feet—in great quantities at this level and higher over this face of the mountain." This is a small lump of white, rather crystalline, gypsum, slightly stained on one side with iron-oxide, and on the other with a green material, perhaps of vegetable origin.

These two specimens must, I think, be products of mineral springs, and the memoranda indicate that the latter must formerly have been rather plentiful on this part of the mountain.

R. "Between the highest camp and the summit, about 1000 to 1500 feet below the latter, lying loose among debris at mouth of the couloir leading into amphitheatre, in which I saw nothing like it." A subangular specimen, just over an inch long and rather more than half an inch in greatest breadth and thickness, greenish black in colour, with a roughened surface due apparently to small constituent crystals. This rock under the microscope is found to be holocrystalline, and to consist almost wholly of not quite perfectly developed hornblende crystals, generally not exceeding one-fiftieth of an inch in length, which are green and pleochroic as usual, and speckled with opacite. The slice, however, contains a few larger grains of iron-oxide, and occasionally interstitial felspars of small size, but in one or two cases just large enough to show twinning, so probably it is plagioclase. This specimen obviously is not a lava but almost a hornblendite, and must have been broken from some more deeply

DESCRIPTION OF ROCK SPECIMENS 319

seated solidified rock, more basic in composition than the ordinary effusive materials of Aconcagua. Fragments of crystalline and more or less altered sedimentary rocks are not unfrequently ejected among volcanic products, but they are usually partly or wholly embedded in scoria or lava, except when, as sometimes in the Eifel, they represent the materials of the uppermost part of the crust in which the orifice has been opened; hence the occurrence of this specimen of a rather uncommon rock in such a position is remarkable.

S. "Found on the summit plateau of Aconcagua." A rather triangular flattish chip of rock, slightly over two inches in its longest dimension; compact in structure and greyish to yellowish-green in colour (suggesting the presence of epidote), but slightly speckled and mottled with a darker green, and traversed by a thin whitish vein. There are a few small elongated cavities, apparently lined with minute crystals of epidote. On microscopic examination a number of grains of this mineral are recognised, often about 0.03 inch in diameter, of a greenish-yellow colour; some being dusty and of composite aspect, others clearer and with more regular crystal outlines. The ground-mass is micro-granular and is speckled with opacite, parts of it having a pale yellowish-green tint like that of epidote, the whole being spotted with rather larger clear granules, somewhat resembling fragments of felspar. The more colourless, and on the whole predominant part of the ground-mass (in which the darker tinted epidotes are rather more common), seems to be composed of minute colourless granules and dusty opacite, so as to resemble some speckled glasses, but on applying high powers this is found to consist of granules (some rather scaly in aspect), among which I think both epidote and felspar may be recognised, set in a uniform base. This, however, is not isotropic, and affords with crossing nicols low tints, more or less reddish grey, so that it also appears to be composite and crystalline. The yellower part of the ground-mass, when thus examined, is also found to be composite, some granules being a pale but duller green than the others, and these in extinction and other respects seem more probably hornblende than epidote.

I am not able to arrive at any definite conclusion as to the history of this rock. I suspect that most, if not all, of its constituents, are secondary in origin. The original rock evidently must have contained a fair amount of lime and iron, with some alumina and a little magnesia, besides silica, and must, I think, have been either a pyroxenic andesite or a fine ash of similar composition. Had it been the former I should have expected to find clearer traces of well-formed felspar crystals, and so I incline to the latter view; for pyroxenes seem to be less injured than felspars by explosions. The present condition of the rock may be the result of solfataric action, but its position on the mountain is not very easily explained.

Q. "Loose specimen from near the summit." A lump rather pyramidal in form, of a dull red colour, with a rough surface and a slightly scoriaceous aspect. The removal of a slice proves this tint to be more than superficial, besides disclosing many minute vesicles and small crystals of whitish felspar, up to about one-twentieth of an inch in diameter, and a few black specks, the largest of which measure nearly one-eighth of an inch. The rock under the microscope is seen to be rather vesicular. In consequence of this structure a very thin slice has not been obtained, but a glassy base of a ruddy sienna-brown colour is almost certainly present, which is studded with microliths of plagioclase and some granules of iron-oxide. In it are embedded : (*a*) larger grains of the last-named mineral, probably magnetite; (*b*) plagioclase felspar with rather large extinction angles (measured from the composition line); some are regular shaped, some zoned ; some are clear, others contain enclosures probably of glass; most of them, I think, are labradorite; (*c*) augite, pale olive-brown in colour, and with a slightly corroded exterior, besides the "ruins" of a crystal, apparently once distinctly larger than the rest ; (*d*) hornblende, with a much more markedly corroded exterior, the colour, with transmitted light, varying from a burnt sienna to a burnt umber-brown ; strongly pleochroic, and changing from a pale raw umber to a rich sienna-red, the darkest tint occurring when the vibrations are parallel to the vertical axis of the prism. The rock is a scoriaceous hornblende andesite, but is probably rather more basic than those already described, or, as will be seen, than the next specimen.

B. "Loose fragment from the summit of Aconcagua, all the neighbouring rock of the plateau, about seventy-five yards square, appears to be the same." A rather triangular piece of rock, measuring from five to six inches along the side, and about two and a half inches in the thickest part. It is a warm purplish grey in colour; the old surfaces are rather speckled, and have weathered to a reddish or yellowish-brown colour; small whitish felspars and a black pyroxenic mineral, with possibly some iron-oxide, can just be detected by the unaided eye. A few minute vesicles are present. These larger minerals prove on microscopic examination to be :—

(*a*) Felspars rather variable in size, often about one-fifteenth of an inch long, much as already described, probably andesine; (*b*) hornblendes, fairly regular in outline, but occasionally with blunted angles or a corrosion border, sometimes even rounded ; pleochroic, changing from pale greenish brown to a deep sienna-brown ; in one or two cases forming a kind of skeleton, owing to the inclusion of small

DESCRIPTION OF ROCK SPECIMENS

irregular-shaped felspar crystals; (c) a few grains or crystals of augite of a pale brown tint inclining to green; (d) iron-oxide. The base in which these crystalline grains are embedded is sprinkled with opacite and clouded with ferrite, being apparently a slightly decomposed glass; it is crowded with microliths of plagioclase, which give rather small extinction angles. Hence the summit rock of Aconcagua is a hornblende-andesite. This determination is fully confirmed by a chemical analysis, which has been made for me in the Chemical Laboratory of University College (London), by R. W. Gray, Esq., to whom I return my sincere thanks. The following is the composition:—

$$
\begin{aligned}
SiO_2 &= 60.32 \\
Al_2O_3 &= 17.10 \\
P_2O_5 &= 0.05 \\
Fe_2O_3 &= 4.74 \\
FeO &= 1.12 \\
MnO &= \text{trace} \\
CaO &= 3.51 \\
MgO &= 2.89 \\
K_2O &= 2.11 \\
Na_2O &= 5.06 \\
H_2O &= 1.99 \\
\text{Loss on heating to } 100° C. &= 0.81 \\
\hline
& 99.70
\end{aligned}
$$

Specific gravity . . 2.609

Returning from the peak to the foot of Aconcagua, and resuming the examination of specimens collected around the upper portion of the principal (Horcones) valley, we have the following rocks:—

20. "West side between Buenavista Valley and Catedral. Patches of this all over the sides of the valley from 14,000 to 15,000 feet (18th March, Lightbody)." A large rather heavy lump, about six inches in greatest length, varying in colour from a light reddish grey to dark brown, moderately hard, and with slight effervescence locally. I have not made a more minute examination, as the specimen appears to have no real interest. It is probably a mineral precipitate connected with springs or solfataric action.

21. "West side between Buenavista Valley and Catedral. From solid rock occurring frequently (18th March, Vines)." An elongated specimen, fully five inches in length, thickly coated with iron-oxide, and showing traces of sulphur. From examination of a freshly broken surface we see that the rock is a rather compact grey andesite, speckled somewhat sparsely with small felspars and minute pyroxenes.

CATEDRAL

"Height 18,000 feet, seven miles due west of Aconcagua."

(1) A fragment of an andesite, of a slightly darker grey colour than (3), which see; difference only varietal.

(3) A darkish grey rock, containing a rather large amount of whitish glassy-looking felspar (the biggest grain being rather more than a quarter of an inch across) and sundry spots of a dark green pyroxene. On one side of the specimen is a whitish incrustation, which effervesces rather briskly with hydrochloric acid, and in which are scattered a few quartz crystals, variable in size, but all small. The exterior of the specimen is generally stained with hematite. A slice examined with the microscope shows a ground-mass consisting of a slightly ferrite-stained material, studded with felspar microliths, and a little opacite. On crossing the nicols these microliths give low polarisation tints, and the surrounding material is seen to be an aggregate of rather bright-coloured granules, indicating that secondary products have replaced the original glass. The following minerals belong to an early stage of consolidation: (*a*) plagioclase felspars (perhaps andesine), fairly idiomorphic, showing albite twinning, and in the larger also a zonal growth; varying much in size, the biggest being about 0.15 inch across. These include granules and microlithic streaks of a rather fibrous mineral similar to that observed in the ground-mass. (*b*) Ferromagnesian silicates; these are present in considerable quantity, but are all greatly altered; they have apparently belonged to more than one species. Some suggest biotite in their shape and in traces of a close cleavage, and in one some remnants of this mineral seem to occur; others, however, are more like hornblende, and in some of them a few tiny brown flakes represent this mineral or biotite. Corrosion borders occur, the opacite of which often seems to granulate into the ground-mass, and the interior is more or less darkened by the same substance. (*c*) A third mineral, now consisting of a little opacite and a granular mixture of a pale green mineral, giving low polarisation tints (apparently a variety of serpentine) and of that with bright tints (already mentioned); perhaps this represents an augite. The rock is a hornblende or hornblende-biotite-andesite, but prior to its final consolidation the ferromagnesian silicates were much injured, and since then the whole rock has been attacked by water (? solfataric action).

(4) Loose specimens. A rather flat piece, a little more than three inches in greatest length, of a dark reddish ferruginous rock, in which are vein-like cracks filled with a white mineral. The rock as a

DESCRIPTION OF ROCK SPECIMENS 323

whole is rather heavy, and seems in one part to contain some black iron ore. The white mineral has a hardness approaching 4, and does not effervesce with hydrochloric acid, though in one place it shows a good cleavage suggestive of calcite. Hence it is more probably a sulphate, possibly anhydrite. The rock seemed so much affected by secondary changes as not to be worth cutting.

(2) "Summit rock; but the whole mountain seems composed of a generally similar rock." The specimen, which in greatest length is about 4.5 inches, breadth 3 inches, and thickness not exceeding 2 inches, is a darkish grey andesite, weathering reddish, containing felspar crystals, generally less than one-eighth of an inch, and dark pyroxenes, sometimes slightly larger, differing only from the others in the greater abundance of visible crystals. In this specimen the microscope reveals distinct traces of a glassy base, speckled with a pale green mineral, which also occurs in spots of greater size. The larger ferromagnesian silicates are corroded, much as in the last case, but the clear part is green, and shows bright polarisation tints; probably it is only another variety of serpentine. The same mineral also occurs in small independent spots, with little or no opacite. One or two grains of brown hornblende still remain. It is doubtful whether biotite has been present. The felspars (plagioclase) are much changed, being partly replaced by a mineral resembling an impure calcite. The rock is hornblende-andesite, and its history has been generally similar to that of the last one, but perhaps its original composition was slightly more basic.

Buenavista Valley

B. "Buenavista Valley (28th April, Gosse)." An incrustation of a colourless but slightly iron-stained mineral occurring in minute parallel prisms, no effervescence with hydrochloric acid, and softer than the finger-nail: hence gypsum. A second specimen shows two layers and apparently traces of sulphur. These probably are solfataric in origin.

14. "A great deal of this below Col. (28th April, Gosse)." A rather irregular-shaped piece, a little more than two inches one way and a little less the other, somewhat heavy, and looking as if impregnated with hematite. On one side is a rather mammillated crust of a whitish mineral, of secondary origin, which also seems to have filled some cracks. On microscopic examination we find an extremely dark brown ground-mass, barely translucent in any part, in which are several spots of clustered granules looking like a ferrite-

stained carbonate, together with fairly well-defined crystals of a water-clear mineral, idiomorphic, and occurring in elongated prisms (probably monoclinic), and extinguishing up to angles of over 30° with edges in the prism zone; it has a moderate basal and a fairly good prismatic or possibly orthopinacoidal cleavage; is rather like a felspar in general appearance, but I think is more probably one of the zeolites. On the edge of the slice is part of a vein of calcite (probably with some magnesian carbonate). I believe that secondary action has quite obscured the original structure of the rock.

15. "Specimens of shingle in Buenavista Valley (28th April, Vines)." Two of these have been sliced for microscopic examination, with the following results:—

A is a dark purplish-red compact rock, with subconchoidal fracture and a slight banding apparently due to stratification. Under the microscope it appears to be composed of little granules of a clear mineral and (?) some glass, together with specks of ferrite, traversed by irregularly outlined bands darkened with the latter mineral, one or two dark specks suggesting scoria. Rather larger angular or sub-angular bits of felspar are scattered about, which sometimes seem to have received secondary enlargement, the very narrow border including some ferrite. As the constituents are very minute, it is difficult to be sure about this rock; possibly it is a devitrified glass, but I think it more probably fragmental, *i.e.* a volcanic dust, largely composed of broken felspar.

B. Specimen (about $3 \times 2\frac{1}{2} \times 1\frac{1}{2}$ inches) of a mottled purplish to pinkish-grey rock, resembling a rather stratified volcanic ash. Under the microscope the greater part of the slice looks like a glass (in colour a light dull brown, owing to the presence of minute ferrite), which includes grains, usually small, of iron-oxide, and a number of crystals, most of which evidently have been almost entirely replaced by secondary minerals. The rock apparently was once irregularly vesicular. The cavities, however, are now filled; first a coating of mammillated structure was deposited, consisting of a mineral in minute prisms, acting fairly well on polarised light, then came a less regularly ordered prismatic or fibrous mineral, with brighter polarisation tints—possibly chalcedony. The included minerals are replaced by similar microlithic products, with more or less included earthy matter. Some of them resemble felspar; two or three of larger size have been hornblende, one having the original characteristic lozenge structure indicated by dark lines, and the replacing materials in them seem not quite identical with those in the last named. I think the fragmental aspect of the hand specimen is illusory, and that the rock has been a vesicular hornblende-andesite,

DESCRIPTION OF ROCK SPECIMENS 325

which has been greatly altered by infiltration, probably from solfataric action. Chalcedony may be among the secondary products, but as some of the better defined prisms give an oblique extinction, a zeolite is likely to be present.

4. "Spur between valley of Buenavista and tributary valley, debris below cliff of it (28th April, Vines)." One of these is an irregular lump, roughly three inches in diameter, of badly developed and crowded crystals of selenite; in another and smaller one the crystals are rather more regular in direction. Also three pieces of rather platy selenite, one about $4\frac{1}{2} \times 3\frac{1}{4}$ inches, and a fourth, small, of satin spar.

I. Under the microscope this presents a general resemblance to No. 3 of Catedral (p. 322).

II. A specimen of a purplish rock, nearly three inches in greatest length; colours stronger on cut surface; apparently fragmental; slickensides on one surface, and three smaller fragments of the same, also showing slickensides, but less perfectly. Under the microscope the structure is rather obscured by decomposition and by deposit of a secondary mineral, apparently a carbonate, approaching dolomite or ankerite; this also occupies cracks which are rather numerous in places. The rock is composed of fragments, some are andesitic lava, others (small) blackish or brownish, more or less scoriaceous; some possibly are a decomposed pyroxene; one or two small zircons are present. The whole mass is well cemented. I have doubted whether this rock might not be a lava which has included fragments of its own crust, but I think these are too numerous and various to allow of such an explanation, and so regard it as an indurated andesite-ash.

TUPUNGATO

XIV. "Rock *in situ* forming cliff by river, in valley north of Tupungato, not part of the mountain itself." It has a fragmental structure, the materials are volcanic, and the aspect is rather ancient. Under the microscope it is seen to consist of subangular to angular fragments of volcanic rock, with a few minerals. There have been considerable secondary changes, by which the more minute interstitial materials are obscured. A yellow-green filmy mineral has been produced, which is present more or less all over the slice, and in the fragments themselves; it affords rather bright polarisation tints, and is probably a hydrous mica. The bigger fragments are devitrified, in fact every part of the slice affects polarised light. The larger minerals represent: (*a*) quartz (small and scarce—perhaps chalcedonic); (*b*) plagioclase; (*c*) an altered pyroxene (rare); (*d*) iron-oxide;—none being really common. Among the rock fragments are: (*a*) three or four clear angular bits, no doubt a devitrified glass, the largest showing a distinct fluxional structure; (*b*) two or three varieties of microporphyritic andesite or trachyte, in one of which is a grain of quartz; (*c*) three or four darkish dusty-looking specimens, perhaps representing rather decomposed bits of scoria; small amygdales possibly occurring in one. Thus the rock is an andesitic ash, and if it has not been exceptionally affected by some local agent, I should conjecture it to be distinctly more ancient than those on the upper part of Tupungato itself.

Two specimens with a general resemblance. VI. bears this label, "opposite base camp in valley north-east of Tupungato, 11,000 feet; whole mountain side seems of this." X. is as follows: "On route from the base camp up Tupungato, 15,000 to 19,000 feet; small aiguilles of this breaking out of broken loose material. Frequent all over north-east side of mountain." The shape of VI. is partly due to joints which follow a rather irregular course, as we often see in a dyke near its edge. The rock is compact, of a dull red colour, a little mottled, spotted, and streaked with black; the latter being slightly dendritic at the edge, and apparently determined in its distribution by the presence of minute cracks. The specimen is sparsely speckled by felspars of a paler colour, not generally exceeding one-tenth of an inch in length. X. is a rudely wedge-shaped specimen, nearly five inches long, with a general resemblance to the last rock, but paler in colour, and not stained with black; showing a fluxional structure, and indications of free quartz, besides containing a small enclosure of a slightly different rock. Under the microscope the minerals of anterior consolidation in VI. are seen to be felspar and quartz. The former are the less numerous, generally imperfect in their crystalline outline, sometimes distinctly fragmental, and once or twice rounded; affected by decomposition or possibly by heat, and to some extent ferrite stained; so far as can be ascertained they are orthoclase. Of the quartz grains (which are the more numerous) some retain, wholly or in part, their crystal outlines; in others these have been removed by corrosion. They have few enclosures, even cavities being minute and not abundant. Some larger grains of iron-oxide (? hematite) are present. The ground-mass for the most part is microcrystalline, being a mosaic of quartz and ferrite-stained granules, probably representing felspar, in which are irregular streaks and patches of the same mineral in a different state of development; sometimes small idiomorphic crystals of the felspar occur in a ground-mass of quartz; sometimes the two assume a slightly micrographic structure, and sometimes they form a coarser mosaic. In one or two

DESCRIPTION OF ROCK SPECIMENS

cases they are associated with grains of felspar apparently of earlier consolidation. It is difficult to determine whether these little patches are enclosures of rock in a slightly different crystalline condition, which have been partially melted down by a later magma, or whether they formed while the rock was in process of consolidation. On the whole I incline to the latter view, for they seem to pass so gradually into the ordinary ground-mass, but I think they may indicate slight original differences in the composition of the magma.

The microscopic structure of X. is so generally similar to that of VI. that a detailed description is needless. The two or three felspars present in the slice seem to be replaced by a pinite-like aggregate: the devitrification structure of the ground-mass is more minute, and the fluxional structure is very distinct. These two rocks appear to be quartz-felsite (quartz-porphyry of some authors) rather than quartz-porphyrite, but I should not be surprised if in chemical composition they were intermediate between rhyolites and dacites.

VII. "At 15,000 feet, north of Tupungato, very far from the summit. Loose specimens, on a (?) moraine." A rather subangular lump, in volume from two to two and a half cubic inches, showing white felspars from one-eighth inch diameter downwards, and some smaller pyroxenes set in a dark purplish compact matrix, in which are many small irregularly distributed vesicles. Microscopic examination reveals a brown glass as base, which shows fluxion structure, and is crowded with very minute lath-like felspars; possibly one or two rutiles are present. Scattered in this as a ground-mass are larger crystals of the following minerals: (*a*) iron-oxide, generally rather small; (*b*) felspar, mostly plagioclase, some idiomorphic and water-clear; others, not quite so regular in outline, enclosing more brown glass, which occasionally forms almost half the grain; but such a one is now and then surrounded by a zone of clear plagioclase. Some are about ·06 inch in the longer diameter, but they range down to as small as ·006 without any very definite break, though for general purposes they may be grouped as large and small; (*c*) hornblende, brown and pleochroic; sometimes fairly idiomorphic, sometimes with a corrosion margin, occasionally with enclosed granules of (?) felspar; (*d*) augite — only one fair-sized crystal (though this mineral is probably represented by several small grains)—clear, of a very pale green tint, associated with some brown hornblende in such a way as to suggest that the latter may be of paramorphic origin. The rock may be named a hornblende-andesite.

IX. and XII. "From the great northern ridge of Tupungato at 19,000 feet." The former (which has assumed a redder but lighter tint in weathering) is a rather subangular piece about 3 × 2 × 1 inches, showing whitish felspar, a blackish pyroxene and a little (?) biotite, all running up to about one-eighth inch diameter, and set in a grey, somewhat vesicular matrix with a rather rough exterior. On one side is a superficial deposit of a white mineral. The latter, a small piece of similar rock, is coated on one side with hematite. On microscopic examination IX. is seen to consist of a colourless glassy base, crowded with lath-like microliths of plagioclase, belonites of (probably) another mineral, and some opacite. In this ground-mass are scattered: (*a*) larger crystals of plagioclase, which in some cases include the microliths just mentioned, or fluid cavities; (*b*) a fair amount of hornblende, the edges of the crystals not being corroded; and (*c*) two or three flakes of biotite. The rock accordingly is a variety of hornblende-andesite.

XI. "Great couloir leading up from ridge to the dome. About 21,000." This specimen is a grey compact igneous rock, speckled with small white felspars, no doubt an andesite.

III., IV., V., XIII. These four specimens, together with II., which represents the rock of the highest point, come from the summit dome or plateau of Tupungato.

I. "Centre of dome of Tupungato, between two of the peaks." A lump from three to four inches in diameter, not very vesicular, inclining to be slaggy, in colour a very dark purplish brown, almost black, speckled sparsely with small white crystals of felspar. On the outside, and sometimes apparently occupying a small cavity, are little spots of a white mineral, perhaps a zeolite. The rock evidently is a scoriaceous andesite.

III. "Loose on top of dome of Tupungato, but solid blocks are seen to appear above the surface." A specimen, measuring roughly 3 × 2 × 1 inches, of a whitish or cream-coloured rock, in which are a fair number of small vesicles, partly occupied by a white mineral, and felspar crystals of about the usual size (two or three cobalt-coloured small patches on the exterior are probably accidental). On microscopic examination this rock is seen to be in a very peculiar condition. At the first glance one would take it for a slightly vesicular andesite, not well preserved, containing in the first stage of consolidation some iron-oxide, with crystals of felspar, and possibly of a pyroxenic mineral; the second of these having a curious granular aspect, and the third a very muddy one. On closer examination we find that the ground-mass, except for a rather small number of lath-like or flaky microliths, produces no effect on polarised light, and the larger minerals, just named, prove to be in almost the same condition. Those identified as felspar contain a few enclosures

DESCRIPTION OF ROCK SPECIMENS 329

of ground-mass, and show traces of the original planes of cleavage, the material being in places clear, in others stained with a brownish dust. The former acts very feebly on polarised light, rotation of the stage just making the difference between darkness and a very faint twilight, but bringing into view some brighter lines corresponding in position with those of cleavage. The other material is less translucent and has about as little effect on polarised light. The altered pyroxenic mineral resembles hornblende rather than augite, but biotite may also be present in one or two instances. The rock most probably was once an hornblende-andesite, and evidently has been much altered, probably by solfataric action. I should suggest infiltration by opaline silica, were it not that the vesicles are empty.

IV. "In quantities lying loose on the summit." A rather irregularly formed lump, about $4 \times 3 \times 2$ inches, of a slightly vesicular rock, which might have been ejected among scoria. For its general appearance we may refer to the description of the summit rock given below. This one, however, is slightly paler in colour than it, being a dull lavender grey inclining to purplish; the scattered felspar crystals are perhaps a shade larger, and so are those of pyroxene, which occasionally attain to one-eighth of an inch. It exhibits some fulgurites, which will be described below with those of the summit rock.

V. "Centre of dome, between two of the peaks." Very dark scoria like I., but distinctly more vesicular; about two and a half inches in greatest length; one or two very small pyroxenes visible. Under the microscope the minerals of early consolidation are found to be: (a) iron-oxide; (b) hornblende; (c) augite, as in VII., but more abundant; (d) plagioclase, but here without glass enclosures. The last mineral occurs of many sizes, though the majority may be distinguished into those approximating to a tenth of an inch and microliths. The extinction angles of many of the former correspond most nearly with those of labradorite; (e) a clear mineral, imperfect in outline and cleavage, much resembling olivine, but as the extinction measured from any promising line is oblique, I conclude it to be another variety of augite. The ground-mass is so much darkened with opacite that it is difficult to ascertain whether a glassy base is present, but dimly outlined crystals can be seen with crossed nicols, like ghosts of felspar (which may possibly indicate partially melted crystals) and crowds of lath-like microliths. The rock is a scoriaceous hornblende-andesite.

XIII. "Summit of Tupungato in large quantities." A rather irregularly shaped piece of rock, about a cubic inch in volume, consisting of felspar (perhaps more than one species), a blackish pyroxene and biotite (all often about one-tenth inch in diameter) set in a pale reddish compact matrix, with a rather rough exterior, but apparently not vesicular. No fresh broken surface. An andesite, with some biotite and probably hornblende.

II. "Found loose in quantities on the top of highest of the three heaps or peaks at summit of Tupungato." A block rather irregular in shape, one surface being somewhat convex and the corresponding one concave, but the dimensions may be very roughly given as 6 × 6 × 4 inches; slightly weathered on the older surfaces (some being fresh fractures). The rock is compact, except for a few minute vesicles; in colour it is a dull purplish-brown or madder, and is spotted with small white felspar, the largest of which vary from about one-tenth to one-sixth of an inch in diameter. Under the microscope this rock presents the same general characters as VII. The minerals of early consolidation are: (*a*) iron-oxide; (*b*) brown hornblende, not seldom fairly idiomorphic (much as before, but no corrosion borders), very variable in size, and sometimes including grains of felspar and of iron-oxide; (*c*) biotite, only in a very few ill-developed flakes; (*d*) one or two small grains of augite. The felspar, plagioclase, is variable in size, inclusions are inconspicuous; some of the larger grains are broken; these in extinction agree best with andesine, but possibly oligoclase may be also present; a small zircon is seen, and a few little vesicles. The base is a glass, crowded with microliths, probably felspar, and tinted with ferrite, though less strongly coloured than VII. Thus the rock is a hornblende-andesite.

In this block fulgurites are abundant, commonly perforations, but occasionally forming channels on the surface. The tubes not seldom branch irregularly, and vary in size. When fairly circular in shape the diameter ranges from about one-fifth to one-third of an inch, but the latter measurement of course is exceeded at a fork. The irregularity of their course makes a precise statement impossible. Where the tube shows on a broken surface we see that it is coated at first with a film, hardly so thick as the finger-nail, of a reddish-white or warm grey tint, over which is a layer of glass of a greenish colour, not unlike some of the lighter coloured varieties of common bottle glass, and occasionally presenting in this respect and in fracture a superficial resemblance to some varieties of olivine. This glass appears not to form a perfectly regular coating, for sometimes it is almost absent, at others it occurs in patches, the thickness of which is about one-eighth of an inch; while at others the tubes are almost choked by it, but in the last case it forms an aggregate of separate clots rather than a solid mass; the interstices, in many instances at

DESCRIPTION OF ROCK SPECIMENS 331

least, being due to bubbles. In a section of one branching tube the aggregated glass extends for about two inches inwards from the surface, and for about one inch in a transverse direction at a short, thick offshoot.

On careful examination of this material I came to the conclusion that a thin slice could not be made, and that the attempt to obtain it might seriously damage the specimen, so that I have studied the glass by crushing some small fragments and examining the powder under the microscope. The fragments vary in form, but flattish chips are not uncommon, and occasionally they have a rather fibrous structure; curved surfaces are visible, probably indicating the former presence of bubbles. The glass is of a very pale yellow tint, clear, containing but few enclosures. These are either minute bubbles or very small flaky microliths of ferrite and opacite.

In the fulgurites of IV., the tubes run slightly smaller than in the last specimen, the glass is similar in appearance but just a shade darker in colour. With a strong lens many minute vesicles, or their broken surfaces, can be seen. Under the microscope the glass is almost the same as in the other case, except that it seems slightly more strongly coloured; bubbles and definite flakes are perhaps rather less numerous, but here and there are tiny brown patches. The white film, mentioned above, occurs in specimens from both; it appears to be a layer of imperfectly fused rock; the transition from this to the perfect glass being very rapid. It is more or less opaque, but signs of felspar microliths can be detected. Evidently the rock was not materially affected by the lightening for more than about a hundredth of an inch beyond the fused part.

By way of conclusion, I may call attention to the following points in these notes: (1) the generally uniform character of the volcanic rocks in this rather extensive region; all the specimens, except in one place on Tupungato (p. 326), representing closely related varieties of andesite. To a certain extent this was true of the collection made in the Ecuadorian Andes by Mr. E. Whymper, but I think that his specimens exhibited a little more variety. (2) The general absence of cellular materials. This collection does not contain one piece of true scoria, and hardly any lava that is more than slightly vesicular. The rocks from the summit of Aconcagua are all but solid; of those from the same position on Tupungato only one includes some small cavities. On the first the crateral part of the cone seems to have entirely vanished, and on the second almost as completely. These facts are in accord with the testimony of the photographs, that denudation has taken place, probably still continues, on an enormous scale. To this the great quantities of loose debris on the slopes, the huge combes and precipices beneath the summit, the terraced walls of lava and the rugged outlines of the peaks, all bear witness. Not only so, but Aconcagua, at any rate, seems to have been built up by successive flows of lava, like Mauna Loa in Hawaii, rather than by explosive eruptions of scoriaceous material, for the photographs of its cliffs recall, though on a vastly grander scale, those of Snowdon above Glas Llyn or those beneath the summit of the Puy de Sancy.

I may add that Professor Roth has described, in Dr. P. Güssfeldt's *Reise in den Andes* (p. 465), three specimens brought by that explorer from the north-west flank of Aconcagua, and collected at from 18,000 to 20,000 feet. They are (1) a much altered rock, probably a "felsitporphyr," ; (2) a dark tuff, also altered, (3) a whitish rock, probably a decomposed trachyte, impregnated with sulphur and gypsum, indicative of solfataric action. A few rocks from other parts of the Chilian Andes are described on pages 462 to 464.

APPENDIX B

NOTES ON THE FOSSILS FROM THE CHILIAN ANDES COLLECTED BY MR. FITZ GERALD'S EXPEDITION

BY G. C. CRICK, F.G.S., OF THE BRITISH MUSEUM
(NATURAL HISTORY)

THE fossils which form the subject of the following notes were sent to Dr. Woodward, F.R.S., etc., who has kindly handed them over to me for examination. They were collected by the members of Mr. FitzGerald's party during their expedition to Aconcagua towards the end of the year 1896.

There are only six specimens. Two are labelled, "Torlosa Valley"; two "Horcones Valley"; and two marked "F" come from the western side of the same valley. The two last mentioned were *in situ* on the right bank of the glacier stream at an elevation of from 10,000 to 11,000 feet above sea-level; the others were found loose on the ground. Five of the fossils are in a reddish limestone, but one, labelled "Torlosa Valley," is in a greyish crystalline limestone, and has been very much rolled.

Only a very few fossils have been recorded from this locality. The first specimens to be obtained were collected by Mr. Pentland near the Puente del Inca, and determined by L. v. Buch[1] to be of Upper Jurassic age. Darwin[2] visited this spot in 1835, and gave a detailed description of the section near the Puente del Inca. Traces of fossils were observed in two beds which lithologically were very distinct from each other, one near the base of the section being "a stratum, eighty feet thick, of hard and very compact impure whitish limestone, weathering bright red;" the other, higher up in the section, being a "yellow, fine-grained, thinly-stratified, magnesian (judging from its slow dissolution in acids) limestone." Numerous

---

[1] As consisting of :—*Trigonia*, resembling in form *T. costata* ; *Pholadomya*, like one found by M. Dufresnoy near Alençon ; and *Isocardia excentrica*, Voltz, identical with that from the Jura. See L. v. Buch, *Descrip. des Iles Canaries*, 1836, p. 472 ; and C. Darwin, *Geol. Obs. S. America*, 1846, p. 193.

[2] C. Darwin, *Geol. Obs. S. America*, 1846, p. 190 *et seq.*

fragments of limestone, containing fossils, were scattered on the ground, and from the nature of the matrix Darwin had no difficulty in deciding that they were derived from the stratum near the base of the section. D'Orbigny determined these fossils as *Gryphæa*, near to *G. Couloni*; and *Arca*, perhaps *A. Gabrielis*, and regarded them as of Neocomian age. The few fossils obtained near the Puente del Inca by Dr. Stelzner during his journey at the end of 1872 and in the early part of 1873 were determined by Gottsche[1] as *Gryphæa*, cf. *calceola*, Quenst., and *Pecten* (sp.), and considered to be of Lower Oolitic age. So far as I am aware only Pelecypoda have hitherto been recorded from near the Puente del Inca; the present collection therefore, although small, possesses considerable interest, as it reveals the presence of Ammonites at this locality.

The six specimens (I.-VI.) constituting the present collection are labelled as follows:—

I. "*F*"
II. "*F*"} These are portions of one fossil.

III. "*f*" Torlosa Valley. On right-hand side going up to spring, loose in bed of valley. 12,000 feet (23rd April, Vines).

IV. "*h*" Torlosa Valley. (?) (Gosse).

V. "22" Horcones Valley. Found loose in Horcones Valley, 10,000 to 11,000 feet (11th April, Lightbody).

VI. "23" Horcones Valley. Found loose in Horcones Valley, 10,000 to 11,000 feet (11th April, Lightbody).

Specimens I. and II. are fragments of the same block of limestone, each bearing the impression of a portion of the same Ammonite; VI. is a portion of the whorl of an Ammonite; III. and V. are Pelecypods; and IV. is indeterminable.

Cephalopoda.—This group is represented by the specimens I., II., and VI., all belonging to the genus *Perisphinctes*. Two of these (I. and II.) are merely impressions of the opposite sides of the same Ammonite on the surface of small blocks of limestone. This Ammonite closely resembles Neumayr's figures[2] of *Perisphinctes polyplocus* (Reinecke) from the beds with *Aspidoceras acanthicum*, but it is not sufficiently well-preserved for exact determination. The other example (VI.) is a portion (about one-fifth) of the whorl of a slowly-increasing, widely-umbilicated species of *Perisphinctes*. The principal ribs are fairly close together, and usually divide on the lateral area into three branches; there is an occasional intermediate

---

[1] *Palæontographica*, 1878, Suppl. Bd. iii. Lief 2, Heft 2, S. 40; *Beiträge zur Geologie und Palæontologie der argentinischen Republik*, Herausgegeben von Dr. Alfred Stelzner; *II. Palæontologischer Theil*, Abth. 3; C. Gottsche, "Ueber jurassische Versteinerungen aus der argentinischen Cordillere."

[2] M. Neumayr, "Die Fauna der Schichten mit Aspidoceras acanthicum," *Abh. d. k. k. Geol. Reichsanst.* Wien, Bd. v. S. 182, Taf. xxxiv. Fig. 2.

single rib; two ribs near the posterior end simply bifurcate, and between these two ribs there is a constriction. The whorl is somewhat crushed, and there is no trace of the suture-line. Almost precisely similar forms occur in the Kimmeridge clay of Dorset.[1] It also comes very near Neumayr's *Perisphinctes selectus*[2] from beds with *Aspidoceras acanthicum*, and Michalski's *Perisphinctes Nikitini*[3] from the uppermost part of the Lower Volgian of Russia.

All the Cephalopoda therefore appear to be of Upper Jurassic (Upper Oolitic) age.

Pelecypoda.—To this group belong the two specimens V. and III. Specimen V. is merely the impression of two valves on the surface of a small block of limestone; these probably did not belong to the same individual, one being somewhat larger than the other. A cast of this impression shows that the fossil is probably a *Trigonia*, very closely resembling, if not identical with, the species which Castillo and Aguilera[4] have described as *Goniomya Calderoni* from Upper Jurassic rocks (Kimmeridgian and Portlandian) of Mexico. The more nearly complete valve is 30 mm. long and 17 mm. high. The other is more imperfect, and seems to have belonged to a larger individual.

Specimen III. consists of two valves, probably belonging to the same shell, that have been displaced during fossilisation. They are in a greyish crystalline limestone. Unfortunately the hinge cannot be seen, and therefore the exact determination of the specimen is not possible; the fossil, however, agrees fairly well with the figures of *Astarte andium* given by Gottsche[5] and by Tornquist,[6] so we refer it with some doubt to that species. *Astarte andium* occurs at the Espinazito Pass, in beds which Tornquist considers to be of Bajocian age.

Five of the fossils (two from the "Horcones Valley," one from the "Torlosa Valley" and the two portions of the specimen marked "*F*") are, as already stated, in a reddish limestone; these are apparently of Upper Jurassic (Upper Oolitic) age. The other specimen (from

---

[1] See Damon's Geol. Weymouth, 1888, Suppl. pl. xiii. fig. 3.

[2] M. Neumayr, "Die Fauna der Schichten mit Aspidoceras acanthicum," *Abh. d. k. k. Geol. Reichsanst*, Wien, Bd. v. S. 183, Taf. xxxiv. Fig. 3.

[3] A. Michalski, "Die Ammoniten der unteren Wolga-Stufe," *Mém. Com. Géol. St. Pétersbourg*, 1890 and 1894, tome viii. No. 2. pp. 232, 459, pl. xii. fig. 5-7; pl. xiii. figs. 1-3.

[4] Castillo and Aguilera, "Fauna fosil de la Sierra de Catorce San Luis Potosi," *Bol. Com. Geol. Mexico*, No. 1. p. 9, pl. v. figs. 17, 18.

[5] C. Gottsche, "Ueber jurassische Versteinerungen aus der argentinischen Cordillere," *Palæontographica*, 1878, Suppl. Bd. iii. Lief 2, Heft 2, S. 29, Taf. vii. Fig. 9.

[6] A. Tornquist, "Der Dogger am Espinazito Pass, nebst einer Zusammenstellung der jetzigen Kenntnisse von der argentinischer Juraformation," *Pal. Abhandl.* Dames & Koken, Bd. viii. Heft 2, S. 170 (38), Taf. xx. (vii.), Fig. 11.

the "Torlosa Valley"), which is in a greyish crystalline limestone, may possibly be of Bajocian age.

Although but few Jurassic and Cretaceous fossils have been recorded from near the Puente del Inca they have been observed at other places in this portion of the Andes. Darwin[1] has described the section at the Penquennes Ridge, some sixty miles south of Inca. Here the road crosses the ridge at a height of 13,210 feet above sea-level. "The lowest stratum visible in this ridge is a red stratified sandstone. On it are superimposed two great masses of black, hard, compact, even having a conchoidal fracture, calcareous, more or less laminated shale, passing into limestone." Between these masses a bed of gypsum about 300 feet thick is interposed; these three beds being estimated at a thickness of 3000 feet. The fossils from these black calcareous shales were few in number and in a very imperfect condition; they were determined by M. D'Orbigny as of Neocomian age.

Dr. F. J. F. Meyen,[2] who ascended the valley of the Rio Volcan, on the western side of the mountain chain and a little to the south of the Penquennes Pass, found a nearly similar, but apparently more calcareous formation, with much gypsum. The beds were vertical, and at a height of 9000 feet above sea-level abounded with fossils of Upper Jurassic age.[3] Rather more than one hundred miles still farther south, in the Sierra de Malargue, on the eastern side of the Argentine Cordillera, between the Rio Diamante and the Rio Grande, beds of Lower Oolitic age rest upon a Liassic conglomerate, and are conformably overlain by limestones containing a rich Tithonian fauna, that pass continuously upward into rocks of Neocomian age.[4]

The fauna of the Jurassic rocks at the Espinazito Pass, some thirty-five or forty miles north of Aconcagua, is one of the best known in South America. Detailed descriptions of the section have been given by Stelzner[5] and by Bodenbender,[6] and the fauna of the beds has

[1] C. Darwin, *Geol. Obs. S. America*, 1846, p. 175 *et seq.*

[2] Dr. F. J. F. Meyen, *Reise um Erde*, 1834, Th. 1. S. 357; Dr. F. J. F. Meyen, "Einige Bemerkungen über die Identitat der Flotzformation in der alten und in der neuen Welt," *Nova Acta Leopold-Carol.* 1835, Bd. xvii. pt. 2, S. 647–656; C. Darwin, 1846, *Geol. Obs. S. America*, p. 181.

[3] L. v. Buch, *Descrip. Phys. des Iles Canaries*, 1836, p. 471.

[4] O. Behrendsen, "Zur Geologie des Ostabhanges der argentinischen Cordillere," *Zeitschr. deutsch. Geol. Gesell.* 1891, Bd. xliii. S. 369–420, Taf. xxii.–xxv. and *ibid.* 1892, Bd. xliv. S. 1–42, Taf. i.–iv.; A. Steuer, "Argentinische Jura-Ablagerungen, Ein Beitrag zur Kenntniss der Geologie und Paläontologie der Argentinischen Anden," *Pal. Abhandl.* Dames & Kayser, 1897, Bd. vii. Heft 3.

[5] A. Stelzner, "Ueber die argentinische Cordillere zwischen 31° and 36° s. Br.," *Neues Jahrb.* 1873, S. 726; A. Stelzner, "Beiträge zur Geologie und Paläontologie der argentinischen Republik," 1885, Th. 1, S. 106.

[6] Bodenbender, in A. Tornquist, *op. cit. infra*, S. 137 (5).

been carefully worked out by Gottsche,[1] and quite recently by Tornquist.[2] The last-named author distinguishes at that locality a Liassic conglomerate, succeeded by Lower Dogger and Middle Bajocian beds, upon which rest Lower and Upper Callovian strata, these being followed by a Tithonian conglomerate. Tornquist also gives a summary of our present knowledge of the Jurassic formation in the Argentine Cordillera.

[1] C. Gottsche, "Ueber jurassische Versteinerungen aus der argentinischen Cordillere," *Palæontographica*, 1878, Suppl. Bd. iii. Heft 2.

[2] A. Tornquist, "Der Dogger am Espinazito Pass, nebst einer Zusammenstellung der jetzigen Kenntnisse von der argentinischen Juraformation," *Pal. Abhandl.*, Dames & Koken, 1898, Bd. viii. Heft 2.

APPENDIX C

NOTES ON THE NATURAL HISTORY OF THE ACONCAGUA VALLEYS

By PHILIP GOSSE

Naturalist to the FitzGerald Expedition

WHEN Mr. FitzGerald so very kindly appointed me naturalist to his expedition in the Andes, he was aware of my entire inexperience with regard to everything connected with South America. More than that, with the exception of having given some little study to birds, I had no special knowledge of any one department of zoology, and a complete ignorance of botany. I went out simply as a collector. Before I started, Professor E. Ray Lankester was kind enough to give me the practical piece of advice, not to attempt to select, but to bring back at least one specimen of every form, small and great, which I was able to observe. By an accident I was deprived even of any help which books could give me, but I endeavoured to act strictly upon Professor Lankester's counsel. I am perfectly conscious that, as the majority of the specimens I brought back were quite commonplace, so the notes I made of the habits and habitats of animals and plants must in the main be already familiar to naturalists. Nevertheless, I tried to collect everything and to note down everything I saw, in the hope that, as all was independently observed, something might possess a little novelty and freshness.

The first appearance of the Aconcagua valleys was discouraging. At a first glance, the eye detected no signs of life,—no mammals, no birds, and scarcely any vegetation except a prickly shrub (*Adesmia trijuga*), which appeared to cover everything with its miserable growth. So empty of life did the whole landscape seem, that, when I began to be used to it, and came back into camp with my birds and insects and plants, Mr. FitzGerald playfully accused me of having brought them from England with me in bottles, since he and the others, having other things to think about, saw absolutely nothing that was alive in any direction. I believe, however, that the empty dreariness of the valleys was really a very useful discipline for a young and inexperienced naturalist, as it obliged one to keep one's attention always concentrated. There was no temptation to wait for the creatures to come to me, for in that case I should have collected nothing at all.

Those who have read Mr. FitzGerald's book will know what the general character of these high Andean valleys was. They were desolate, monotonous, and dreary in the highest degree. A feature of the life which was most discouraging to a naturalist was the hot gale which blew every day from about 10 a.m. to sundown, burying everything in a wind of dust. There was very little to be effected in the way of collecting, except from sunrise to 10 a.m. Most of my skinning of birds and mammals and pressing of plants had to be done in the daytime, out of doors, because of the intense heat, and sheltered as well as possible from the driving dust, since I could not spare for this work any of the precious hours of the early morning.

A reference to the map will show where my specimens were taken and my observations made, namely, between Punta de las Vacas, which is 7546 feet above the sea-level, and the camp 14,000 feet up the Horcones Valley. While Mr. FitzGerald and the rest of the expedition were in Chile, in June and July 1897, I was staying in the remote *finca* de "Los Inglises," near Lujan, in the province of Mendoza, Argentina. As this is a district which had not been visited by a naturalist, and as the character of it is sub-Andean, I made collections there also, but in the following notes I have always distinguished between my Aconcagua and my Lujan specimens.

I have only further to express my sense of the kindness which I have met with from eminent naturalists since my return to England, a kindness which my inexperience is not worthy of, but which I shall always remember with deep gratitude. I name, in the following pages, those to whom I am indebted, but I must particularly mention here Mr. P. L. Sclater, F.R.S. Mr. Arthur E. Shipley, of Christ's College, Cambridge, has been so extremely kind as to revise my proofs. I should like here to thank Mr. FitzGerald once more for his goodness to me, and for all his patience and help. I wish I could have been more worthy of the honour he did me when he entrusted me with this responsible post in his expedition.

PHILIP GOSSE.

1st July 1899.

I

MAMMALIA

The native mammalia of this part of the Andes are very scanty. The largest quadruped is the guanaco (*Lama huanacus*), which resembles the Bolivian llama, except in having much shorter wool. In the Vacas Valley these animals are plentiful. At first they are very difficult to see, as they are exactly the same colour as the shingle. They sometimes make a curious neigh, very shakily. This sound is, I think, not solely used as a warning, because, once, when I was concealed behind a rock, two guanacos came within forty or fifty yards of me, and they made the noise as they strolled along, as if conversing with each other. When walking, these guanacos seem to glide about like shadows. If frightened, they will start off galloping uphill at a great rate. One day I sent the porter who was with me up the valley to see if he could drive the guanacos down to me, and as he was doing this, I noticed that they simply trotted behind a rock above him, to hide, and when he had passed, slipped out again and went on feeding. They use their long necks to reconnoitre, and see if any danger is in sight. The slot in the sand on the level is like the mark which two long eggs might make at an acute angle, the front of the toes being wedged further apart when the track goes downhill.

It has hitherto been supposed that the puma (*Felis concolor*) does not inhabit the high Andes so far south as Aconcagua. I found, however, that the Indians consider that this animal is to be met with on the low spurs of the mountain, at about 6000 feet above the sea or even higher. One day, when I was riding with Dr. Cotton above the Horcones Lake, suddenly a large yellow quadruped, with rather short legs, leaped out from behind a rock, and slipped over the very steep side of the cliff, above the lake. The mules, in a truly mulish spirit, refused to move an inch further when we spurred them in the direction where the animal disappeared. We therefore jumped down, loading our rifles as we ran, and went to the edge of the cliff, but when we got there, we could see nothing. This was the more extraordinary as there was no cover for an animal to hide in. What we had seen could have been nothing else than a puma, but unfortunately this was the only occasion on which I met with one. A great many of the mules and horses we saw had their ears torn, which, the peons assured me, was done by pumas springing on the animals' heads while they were feeding. The truth of this statement

I cannot vouch for, but I can think of no better reason for the mutilated state of the animals' ears.

The only other large mammal of which there was any trace in the Aconcagua valleys was the Patagonian fox (*Canis azaræ*). The highest altitude at which I saw a specimen of this animal was far up the Vacas Valley (9000 feet). Here Lochmatter killed a fox which was feeding on the body of a guanaco which I had shot the preceding day. An account of my adventures with a fox which haunted our camp at Inca at night will be found on p. 96. The same species occurred plentifully at Lujan.

There seem to be only two species of mice in the Horcones and Cuevas Valleys. The larger is *Phyllotis darwini* (Waterhouse), first discovered by Darwin at Coquimbo, but of which I was fortunate enough to bring home the only good specimens which have as yet reached this country. This rare species has a long tail, large ears and eyes, with a soft, almost chinchilla-like fur. I often observed that, when I was trying to capture these mice, they would spring against a wall or rock, which they very much resembled in colour, and cling to it, motionless, in the hope of escaping notice. At all times, they are much more sluggish than the European house-mouse. The other species, rather like a vole, *Akodon andinus* (Philippi), is much smaller than the former, the tail being quite short. This latter species I found very common throughout this district—the Horcones Valley, the Vacas, and the Tupungato and Cuevas Valleys.

This list of mammals is very meagre, but I am almost inclined to think that it is exhaustive. The whole character of these barren and exposed high Andean valleys is unfavourable to mammalian life, and I did not hear even from the natives of any other striking forms. At the K3 camp (13,500 feet), however, I should mention that I saw, sitting under a rock, a rodent of a light brownish-red colour, with a long snout, and tail of moderate length, which unfortunately escaped me. For the identification of the two species I brought home, I have to thank Mr. Oldfield Thomas, of the South Kensington Museum.

At the Lujan *finca* I secured a young specimen of the grison (*Galictis vittata*), of which an account is given from my diary on p. 308. I believe these animals to be somewhat rare in the Mendoza district. On the other hand, the skunk (*Conepatus chilensis*) abounds at Lujan, where it is an object of the greatest detestation to the rearers of chickens. On p. 306 will be found an account of the painful results of catching a skunk in a trap. I was not so fortunate as to secure a living armadillo (*Tatusia hybrida* or *Dasypus villosus*) while I was in Argentina, but that they are not uncommon is proved by the fact that on market-days scores of them are exposed for sale. The flesh should be cooked in the "shell," and is considered a great luxury. I tried it on several occasions, and was reminded of sucking-pig with the addition of a "gamey" taste. The natives have a gruesome belief that the most succulent armadillos are those which are found in graveyards, and there is a special value set on *peludos*, as they call them, which are warranted to have been caught among the tombs.

II

BIRDS OF THE ACONCAGUA VALLEYS

The birds of which I offer the following notes were collected by me at Puente del Inca and other spots in the Aconcagua valleys between December 1896 and May 1897. I have also added some account of the birds I obtained near Lujan, in the province of Mendoza, in June and July 1897. My warmest thanks are due to Mr. Philip Sclater, F.R.S. and Secretary of the Zoological Society, for the extreme kindness with which he enabled me to identify the species.

Fam. Vulturidæ. (*Sub-Fam. Sarcorhamphinæ*)

GREAT CONDOR (*Sarcorhamphus gryphus*)

Condors are very abundant in this part of the Andes. If an animal dies they seem to appear at once on the spot, although a little time before there were none in sight. We shot one which measured ten feet from wing to wing. The natives call the condors with the white on the back of their wings Oetres,[1] but they are really condors. A Scandinavian in Los Andes in Chile told me that he had seen the condors feeding on dead seals far down the Chilian coast, which shows that the popular idea in the country that condors cannot live in low altitudes is incorrect. I saw several in Mendoza, and in Lujan during the winter. There always seemed to be several condors hovering about the rock above Punta de las Vacas, perhaps because there were large herds of cattle generally passing through into Chile in the summer, and the meadows also were usually full of cattle.

[1] Pronounced "Weetree."

BIRDS

Fam. Falconidæ. (Sub-Fam. Polyborinæ)
CHIMANGO KITE (*Milvargo chimango*)

These birds are very common in Mendoza, and I have seen them up the Horcones Valley as high as 13,000 feet. They live on carrion principally. When ploughing is going on in the vineyards, these kites may be seen by the score, sitting on the posts, and flying down as the plough passes, to get the worms that are turned up. They utter a harsh cry. I caught two chimangos alive, one in a rat-trap. The other I shot, breaking its wing and leg, another shot passing through its crop, but he soon recovered, and may now be seen in the Zoological Gardens. These birds seem to have very little blood. I shot one through the heart with a Winchester rifle, and scarcely a drop of blood appeared. They seem to eat almost anything. Sometimes they kill young chickens, while insects (beetles, etc.) and vegetables form a common diet. One evening, at dusk, I saw one of these birds with something in its beak, which turned out to be a large toad.

Fam. Falconidæ. (Sub-Fam. Buteoninæ)
CHILIAN EAGLE (*Buteo melanoleucus*)

Above the hotel at Inca I found a large nest made of sticks, in a cliff, my attention being drawn to it by the shrill cries of the young ones. These were about the size of an ordinary domestic fowl. Although I was near the nest for three or four days, I failed to secure an old bird. The nest was on a ledge of a cliff, measured about four feet across, and was lined with dry grass.

Fam. Strigidæ. (Sub-Fam. Buboninæ)
MAGELLAN'S OWL (*Bubo magellanicus*)

One specimen was shot and given to me at Punta de las Vacas. Another, a live one, was also given me by a Scandinavian in Los Andes, and I kept it for about four months. It came to an untimely end, being killed by a peon with a stone.

Fam. Hirundinidæ. (Sub-Fam. Hirundininæ)
BANK SWALLOW (*Atticora cyanoleuca*)

I have seen these swallows as high as the marsh at the second ford up the Horcones Valley, about 11,000 feet. These birds nest in the cliffs, and leave the higher altitudes as soon as the frosts come.

Fam. Trochilidæ. (*Sub-Fam. Polytminæ*)
HUMMING-BIRDS—TROCHILIDÆ
WHITE-SIDED HUMMING-BIRD (*Oreotrochilus leucopleurus*)

I shot only one species of humming-bird in the mountains. There were three nests, one under the Inca bridge, another against a cliff higher up the river, and the third on a boulder overhanging the river. One morning, on waking a little before sunrise, having slept out in the open, I heard a whirring sound, and saw one of these birds hovering in front of me. It immediately perched on the brim of my soft hat, flew away, and then perched there again for a moment. These birds are most common round Puente del Inca in December and January. I saw another species of humming-bird. One morning, 25th March, Mr. FitzGerald and I were getting ready to start up the Horcones Valley from the Inca camp when suddenly a large brown humming-bird, nearly the size of the Patagonian earthcreeper, and about the same colour, flew about in the camp for a few seconds and then flew away again. It had a long curved beak. It had a much clumsier flight than the white-sided variety, and was far larger. It was probably the Patagonian humming-bird.

Fam. Anabatidæ. (*Sub-Fam. Furnariinæ*)
COMMON MINER (*Geositta cunicularia*)

These birds utter a very shrill cry, generally when flying, and run rapidly when on the ground. They nest in holes in walls and between stones, etc.; and feed apparently on insects, for I found a small black beetle in the throat of one of them.

Fam. Anabatidæ. (*Sub-Fam. Furnariinæ*)
ISABELLINE MINER (*Geositta isabellina*)

This bird, which closely resembles the common miner, *Geositta cunicularia*, is fairly abundant at Puente del Inca, although not so common as the latter. It seemed to prefer living near our camp. It builds its nest amongst the loosely-built walls and stone heaps.

Fam. Anabatidæ. (*Sub-Fam. Furnariinæ*)
WHITE-RUMPED MINER (*Geositta fasciata*)

The habits and general appearance of this bird are much the same as those of the two former species, *Geositta cunicularia* and

BIRDS

Geositta isabellina. I have seen all these as high as 12,000 feet in the Horcones and Cuevas Valleys, though the specimens collected were from Puente del Inca.

Fam. Anabatidæ. (*Sub-Fam. Furnariinæ*)

BROWN CINCLODES (*Cinclodes fuscus*)

This, the commoner species of the two, I found up to 12,000 feet. Almost under the Puente (bridge) del Inca, I found on Dec. 14 a nest with three white eggs. The nest was made of horse-hair, and placed under a large boulder near the river. These birds stop at Inca during the winter, when all the other birds are gone. It may be owing to the warmth of the hot springs, as I saw them nowhere else during the winter; in fact they seemed to have collected round the bridge as if to take up their winter quarters there. Their habits closely resemble those of our British Water-dipper, the nest and eggs also bearing a striking resemblance.

Fam. Anabatidæ. (*Sub-Fam. Furnariinæ*)

WHITE-WINGED CINCLODES (*Cinclodes bifasciatus*)

I only saw these interesting birds in the marsh between Inca and Vacas. They are larger and handsomer than *Cinclodes fuscus.* Collected in April.

Fam. Anabatidæ. (*Sub-Fam. Furnariinæ*)

PATAGONIAN EARTHCREEPER (*Upucerthia dumetoria*)

These birds are fairly common at Inca. I saw them as high up as the second ford in the Horcones Valley, about 11,000 feet. They very often nest in holes in the banks of the roads. These holes, which vary in length from three to six feet, they dig out for themselves with their long curved beaks. The nests, of which I brought home a specimen, are made of bits of dry grass, with a depression in the middle for the eggs. I never saw more than three eggs in one nest. The eggs are pure white, smooth, and rather varied in shape. These birds are solitary except during the breeding season. I saw a few of them also in Lujan in the winter.

Fam. Anabatidæ. (*Sub-Fam. Furnariinæ*)

RED-TAILED EARTHCREEPER (*Upucerthia ruficauda*)

Two specimens collected at Puente del Inca in March. During the summer months I saw none of these birds lower than 10,000 feet. They are very inquisitive and tame. The natives call this bird the "carpenter," probably on account of its habit of jerking its body backwards and forwards, and also jerking its tail at the same time as though in the act of sawing. When doing this, the end of the tail comes within an inch of the bird's head. It also utters a shrill, grating cry, like the squeak of a saw. In the winter-time these birds lived close round the Inca; and I also saw one or two of them in Lujan during the winter.

Fam. Anabatidæ. (*Sub-Fam. Synallaxinæ*)

TIT-LIKE SPINE-TAIL (*Leptasthenura ægithaloides*)

I saw this quiet little bird two or three times between Inca and Vacas. It seemed to be very shy, and was generally hopping about at the base of a thick shrub.

Fam. Anabatidæ. (*Sub-Fam. Synallaxinæ*)

SORDID SPINE-TAIL (*Synallaxis sordida*)

These birds are quiet and shy, and fly with a jerky motion, spreading out their red fanlike tails as they go. They feed on insects, and soft buds, etc. They are rather scarce at Inca; those brought home were collected at Puente del Inca in January.

Fam. Tyrannidæ. (*Sub-Fam. Elaineinæ*)

WHITE-CRESTED TYRANT (*Elainea albiceps*)

This bird lives in the Adesmia scrub, and feeds on the seeds of the same. They disappeared altogether in the winter, nor did I see any round Mendoza at this season. Male and female seem to be closely alike. In dissecting one of these rare birds I had the fortune to discover a hitherto entirely unknown parasitic worm, coiled up close to the bird's heart. This parasite, of which a description will be found on page 361, has been named *Filaria elaineæ*. Collected 9th December, Punta de las Vacas.

BIRDS

Fam. Tyrannidæ. (*Sub-Fam. Tæniopterinæ*)

WHITE-TAILED TYRANT (*Agriornis maritima*)

These birds are rather scarce at high altitudes, but I am told by Mr. Smyth, the engineer of the Transandine Railway, that about 6000 feet they are more plentiful. I also saw them in Lujan in the winter. The highest point at which I saw these birds was about 11,000 feet. In the summer they are shy, but in the winter they used to live around the posada at Puente del Inca. I only once heard one utter any sound, and that was at Inca in the winter. It was one note, four or five times repeated, sounding like "Kank-kank-kank-kank," fairly loud. The flight is heavy, awkward and jerky, but quite noiseless. I often saw them chasing smaller birds. They feed on carrion. In the winter I have seen these birds tapping a hard piece of meat on the roof of the posada to soften it.

Fam. Fringillidæ. (*Sub-Fam. Fringillinæ*)

GOLDEN SISKIN (*Melanomitris uropygialis*)

I have never seen these siskins alight on the ground; they were usually hopping about, head or tail downwards, creeping and pecking in the bushes or shrubs. They live in flocks varying from five to twenty or even as many as thirty. Their food consists of seeds. These birds seem to be of a roving disposition. Even during the breeding season I never saw a pair singly, but always in flocks; their flight is very jerky. They do not sing a continuous song, but only a few melodious notes, like those of our goldfinch. One cannot call these birds shy, but they would never come and feed in the neighbourhood of our camps. Their habits resemble those of the British siskins. Collected at Vacas in December.

Fam. Fringillidæ. (*Sub-Fam. Passerellinæ*)

GAY'S FINCH (*Phrygilus gayi*)

These brilliantly coloured birds are fairly common in the summer at Inca, and I have seen them as high as 11,000 feet in the Horcones Valley. I saw a few also during the winter months in Lujan, which is fifteen miles south of Mendoza. The female is similar to the male, only the colours are not so bright. They feed on seeds, insects, etc. They nest in the Adesmia scrub, about five feet from the ground, and five speckled eggs form the full clutch.

Fam. Fringillidæ. (*Sub-Fam. Passerellinæ*)

MOURNING FINCH (*Phrygilus fruticeti*)

This is a quiet retiring bird in habits, and sober in appearance, the female being of a dark brown colour, whilst the male is absolutely black in places. For a long time I had heard its song without seeing the bird, as it is very shy. The song is a very sweet warble. Some of the notes are almost harsh, and this contrasting pleasantly with the more harmonious notes, gives the song a peculiar fascination. At Vacas this species is fairly common, but I have seldom met with it above Inca. They all disappear when winter sets in. They sing mostly in the evening, when they become less shy, and I have heard them singing on moonlight nights. The adjective "mourning" is very appropriate, as the plumage in the male is mostly black, and its song extremely sad. Collected 11th December.

Fam. Fringillidæ. (*Sub-Fam. Passerellinæ*)

PILEATED SONG-SPARROW (*Zonotrichia pileata*)

These little birds were quite the commonest both round Mendoza and higher up about Inca. Their general appearance and habits reminded me very much of our common house-sparrow in England. The native name for them is "chingolo." I found quite a number of their nests, which generally contained four or five speckled eggs. The nest is built of hay and lined with horse-hair. One nest I found under a big stone, several others in the Adesmia shrubs, quite five or six feet from the ground. I have heard these little birds singing during the clear moonlight nights. The song consists of a series of disconnected little runs of notes, not at all unpleasing. I succeeded in bringing some of these sparrows home, and they are now thriving well in the Zoological Gardens. I very seldom saw them far from some habitation, but they were always plentiful in the cultivated fields or near houses or camps.

Fam. Columbidæ. (*Sub-Fam. Peristerinæ*)

BLACK-WINGED DOVE (*Metriopelia melanoptera*)

These doves began to arrive at Puente del Inca from about the 15th to the 20th of December 1896, and soon after that became very common. Flocks of sometimes fifty or more might be seen feeding on the seeds of the shrubs that grew along the banks of the river. They all disappeared when the cold weather came. They are seen as high as 12,000 feet. A little way below Inca I came across a flock of them which must have numbered five or six hundred.

Fam. Thinocorythidæ. (Sub-Fam. Thinocorinæ)

D'ORBIGNY'S SEED-SNIPE (*Thinocorys orbignyianus*)

A male and female were procured in the upper part of the Horcones Valley, 23rd April, about 12,000 feet. I have since seen these snipes several times in the Andes; but not lower than 11,000 feet. They are never found far from water, but always near a damp marshy spot; and are very difficult to see when on the ground, being much the same colour as the shingle. They will sometimes come within a foot or two of where one is standing before they can be seen. One day I had been following a flock of these birds for about an hour without getting a shot when at last I discovered one sitting on a boulder. I shot it, and on going to pick it up could not see it anywhere, but only blood and feathers. After a search of several minutes I found two dead specimens close together, having failed to see them before, so closely did their tints assimilate with the surroundings. When they are flushed, they generally utter a short sharp cry several times in succession. They look like moths with their quiet, jerky flight. I saw one pair in the Horcones Valley as high up as 14,000 feet.

Fam. Thinocoridæ. (Sub-Fam. Thinocorinæ)

COMMON SEED-SNIPE (*Thinocorus rumicivorus*)

These birds live only where the ground is damp and marshy. Before I was able to shoot a specimen, I often heard the bird flying round and round the camp (at least so it seemed to me) in the middle of the night, and uttering a noise rather like the croak of a frog, only without the rough notes. When these birds are calling, it is very difficult to ascertain where they are, although perhaps they are quite close to you all the time. Near the lake above Inca, I found two old birds, with three little ones, all sitting in about half an inch of water. They are fairly common in the marshy parts of all the Aconcaguan valleys.

Fam. Pteroptochidæ. (*Sub-Fam. Pteroptochinæ*)
SCYTALOPUS MAGELLANICUS

This specimen is the only one I saw in the mountains, and was found near a waterfall. It had hitherto been supposed to be confined to the Chilian side of the Andes. Collected at 11,500 feet, Horcones Valley, in April.

Fam. Anatidæ. (*Sub-Fam. Anatinæ*)
CRESTED DUCK (*Anas cristata*)

These ducks were sometimes seen during the summer on the little lake in the Horcones Valley. When we first saw them, we mistook them for geese on account of their size. They seemed to use the lake as a halting-station when crossing the Andes, as they never stopped more than a day or two.

BIRDS COLLECTED AT LUJAN, FIFTEEN MILES SOUTH OF MENDOZA

Fam. Falconidæ. (*Sub-Fam. Polyborinæ*)
CÁRACARA CARRION-HAWK OR CARANCHO (*Polyborus tharus*)

These birds are pretty common in the Mendoza district, but I never came across them in the mountains. When seen from a distance they look uncommonly shabby and disreputable, but on a close inspection they prove to be quite handsome birds, with a kind of crest. They are nearly as big as a good-sized turkey. I shot one as it flew off the carcass of a dead donkey, and broke its wing. It began to run across the meadow, I chasing it, until it was "cornered." Seeing escape was impossible, it suddenly stopped running, and, throwing its head far back, produced the most weird cries, I suppose calling to its friends for help. In doing this the back of its head almost touched its shoulders. These buzzards have very strong talons, as I found to my cost when trying to catch one alive, having as usual the "Zoo" in my mind.

Fam. Falconidæ. (*Sub-Fam. Falconinæ*)
CINNAMON KESTREL (*Tinnunculus cinnamominus*)

These kestrels were extremely common at Lujan. They seemed to follow the flocks of chingolo song-sparrows (*Zonotrichia pileata*), which often consisted of over two or three hundred birds.

BIRDS

Fam. Falconidæ. (Sub-Fam. Circinæ)

CINEREOUS HARRIER (*Circus cinereus*)

I think this harrier feeds mainly on the cavies, which are very common in the neighbourhood of Mendoza; but it also hunts and kills small birds. I often, during the winter at Lujan, saw these birds hunting in pairs; they are very destructive in the chicken-runs. Collected in June.

Fam. Troglodytidæ. (Sub-Fam. Troglodytinæ)

BROWN HOUSE-WREN (*Troglodytes furvus*)

There were usually two or three of these little birds round Mr. Norton's house at Lujan; and one in particular that lived in an outhouse. They often came into the rooms, where they would catch the small insects on the ceiling, and were not particularly alarmed if we came in. They are busy little birds, ever on the move, and very inquisitive.

Fam. Icteridæ. (Sub-Fam. Agelaeinæ)

PATAGONIAN MARSH-STARLING (*Trupialis defilippii*)

These birds are very common about Mendoza. I saw strings of them for sale in the markets, the natives considering them a great delicacy. During the winter these birds lived in flocks varying in size from five to twenty. I often saw one sitting on the topmost bough of a small tree and singing a sweet little song, in some ways resembling that of our English starling; in the sun they look very handsome with their scarlet breasts. They are usually to be found in the long grass, and do not often come near a house. The natives call this bird the "Pecho colorado."

Fam. Icteridæ. (Sub-Fam. Agelainæ)

SILKY COW-BIRD (*Molothrus bonariensis*)

This specimen was shot by Mr. Smyth of Mendoza. I have seen flocks near this town consisting of as many as a hundred birds; but they never came into the neighbourhood of Lujan.

Fam. Tanagridæ. (Sub-Fam. Tanagrinæ)

BLUE-AND-YELLOW TANAGER (*Lamprotes bonariensis*)

The only specimen I secured was given to me by Mr. Smyth of Mendoza. I also saw one sitting on the top of a tree near Lujan.

Fam. Tanagridæ. (Sub-Fam. Pitylinæ)

MANY-COLOURED GROUND-FINCH (*Saltatricula multicolor*)

This specimen was shot for me by Mr. Smyth, at Mendoza. He tells me that the natives call the bird the "siete cuchillos" or "seven knives," on account of the damage it does to the buds of the vines. I saw only one, in the orchard at Lujan.

Fam. Fringillidæ. (Sub-Fam. Fringillinæ)

YELLOW SEED-FINCH (*Sycalis lutea*)

I have seen these little finches usually in flocks of ten to twenty. They do not come near the towns or villages, but live in the waste and uncultivated land, feeding on the seeds of various plants.

Fam. Psittacidæ. (Sub-Fam. Arainæ)

AYMANE PARRAKEET (*Bolborhynchus aymara*)

One specimen was given to me by Mr. Smyth, which he shot a little way above Mendoza in the Sierras.

Fam. Cuculidæ. (Sub-Fam. Crotophaginæ)

GUIRA CUCKOO (*Guira piririgua*)

I did not see very many of these birds at Lujan in the winter. The few that there were lived in flocks of eight to fifteen in number. But in the spring I saw a great number in the Eucalyptus avenues at La Plata. The peons are fond of getting these birds quite young; they soon become very tame, and run about the house, as though the whole establishment belonged to them.

23

LIOLÆMUS FITZ GERALDI, natural size.

III

REPTILES

BY G. A. BOULENGER, F.R.S.
Zoological Department, British Museum

LIZARDS

1. *Phymaturus palluma*, Molina. Puente del Inca, 8930 feet.
2. *Liolæmus fitzgeraldi* (sp. n.).

Nostril latero-superior. Upper head-scales small, convex, smooth; a small azygos frontal shield; a series of four to six transverse supraoculars; interparietal smaller than parietals; a single series of scales between the labials and the subocular; temporal scales smooth; anterior border of ear not distinctly denticulated. Sides of neck granular, strongly folded; a curved antehumeral fold. Dorsal scales moderate, rhomboidal, pointed, strongly keeled, the keels forming continuous longitudinal lines; lateral scales smaller than dorsals; ventrals nearly as large as dorsals, rounded, smooth; 48 to 56 scales round the middle of the body. The adpressed hind limb reaches the axil in the female, the shoulder in the male; hinder side of thighs uniformly granulate. Male with three anal pores. Tail once and a half as long as head and body; caudal scales as large as dorsals. Pale brownish or bronzy above, with a more or less distinct light dorso-lateral stripe, and with or without dark transverse spots or bars across the back; throat bluish; lower surface of tail orange.

	Male.	Female.
Total length .	144 mm.	140 mm.
Head .	12 ,,	11 ,,
Width of head	8 ,,	8 ,,
Body .	48 ,,	44 ,,
Fore limb .	20 ,,	18 ,,
Hind limb .	33 ,,	28 ,,
Tail .	84 ,,	85 ,,

Several specimens were obtained by Mr. Gosse at Puente del Inca, at an altitude of 8930 feet.

This species is closely allied to *L. darwinii*, Bell, from which it differs in the absence of enlarged scales on the back of the thighs, and in the coloration, the black spots in front of the arms and above the shoulder, as well as the white black-edged streak on the back of the thighs, characteristic of *L. darwinii*, being absent.

3. *Liolæmus nigromaculatus*, Wiegm. Tupungato Valley.

SNAKES

4. *Philodryas burmeisteri*, Jan.   Lujan, province of Mendoza.

FROGS.

5. *Bufo spinulosus*, Wiegm.   Puente del Inca and Tupungato Valley.

IV

SCORPIONS AND SPIDERS

BY R. I. POCOCK
Zoological Department, British Museum

Although owing to difficulties of transport and other causes, Mr. Philip Gosse was only able to bring home a small number of species of spiders and scorpions, these have proved to be of considerable interest from a scientific point of view. The large scorpion (*Bothriurus d'orbignyi*), of which Mr. Gosse collected several specimens of both sexes at Lujan, was previously represented in our national collection by a single small example. The second scorpion (*B. coriaceus*), taken at Punta de las Vacas at an altitude of 7858 feet, is also a rarity; and the third species, taken at a still higher altitude, has not previously been described.

The large spider is also worthy of special mention on account of its being the second known species of the genus *Citharoscelus*, the latter being remarkable, though not unique, amongst South American Theraphosidæ in possessing a stridulating organ consisting of modified bristles lodged between the basal segments of the palpus and of the first leg.

The Solpuga (*Cleobis andinus*) belongs to a genus which ranges from the West Indies and Central America along the chain of the Andes as far as the Argentine. This new species procured by Mr. Gosse is, with *C. morsicans* of Gervais, the most southern representative of the group hitherto discovered.

SCORPIONS

Order *Scorpiones*; Genus *Bothriurus*

(1) *Bothriurus d'orbignyi*, Guer.

Scorpio d'orbignyi, Guerin Meneville, *Icon. Regne An. Arachn.* 1843, p. 12; *Gerv. Ins. Apt.* 1844, vol. iii. p. 58.

SCORPIONS

Bothriurus d'orbignyi, Thorell, *Atti Soc. Ital.* 1877, vol. xix. p. 170; Kraepelin, *Mt. Mus. Hamb.* 1894, vol. xi. p. 224; id. *Das Tierr. Scorpiones*, 1899, p. 196.

Loc: Several specimens, both male and female of this species, were procured by Mr. Gosse at Lujan, fifteen miles south of Mendoza. The largest measures 84 mm. in length.

(2) *Bothriurus coriaceus*, Poc.

Pocock, *Ann. Mag. Nat. Hist.* (6) vol. xii. pp. 95, 96.
Loc: Punta de las Vacas in the Argentine.

(3) *Bothriurus alticola* (sp. n.). (Fig. 1)

Colour a tolerably uniform reddish yellow, the body and the digits darker than the limbs and tail; tergites with paler posterior border; inferior surface of tail with longitudinal darker bands.

Carapace finely granular at the sides, its anterior border convex, ocular tubercle sulcate. Dorsal plates smooth and punctured, with the exception of the last, which is somewhat coarsely granular, and provided on each side with a pair of granular crests. Sternal plates smooth, punctured, the last closely granular in the middle, the granular area bounded on each side by a curved crest or series of granules.

Tail slender, nearly parallel sided: the fifth segment a little wider than high; segments 1-4 with distinct superior and superolateral granular keels, the first segment with ten granular keels, the inferior median and lateral keels being distinct and granular, with the spaces between them also more or less granular. Similar keels are also traceable on the second segment, but the third and fourth segments are smooth and punctured below, fifth segment without superolateral keel, the superior keel represented by a series of granules, its lower surface furnished with three distinct granular keels, the area between them sparsely but coarsely granular, the granules externally assuming a linear arrangement; no "area" at the extremity of the lower surface of this segment; vesicle granular and punctured below, forming a long oval; aculeus very short, not half the length of the vesicle.

Chelæ smooth and polished, except for the anterior crests on the humerus and brachium, which are granular; width of hand about one-third less than length of hand-back; movable digit slightly exceeding the length of the "hand-back" and a little less than the carapace in height. Pectinal teeth 15.

Male differs from female in having its dorsal surface finely shagreened; in having the tail thinner and a spike on the inner surface of the hands. Pectinal teeth 20.

Total length female . 36 mm. = carapace 4.5 = tail 21.
" " male . 31 mm. = " 3.5 = tail 19.5.
Loc: Inca, 8930 feet. Adult male and female.

Allied to *B. burmeisteri* (Kraepelin, *Mt. Mus. Hamb.* 1894, vol. xi. p. 217; *Das Tierr. Scorpiones*, 1899, p. 196), from the Argentine, in having the under surface of the first caudal segment and in a lesser degree of the second granularly keeled. In *burmeisteri* there is no trace of median and lateral keels on these segments. Moreover, the superior and superolateral caudal keels in *burmeisteri* are described as being developed as in *B. d'orbignyi*, and provided with very coarse granulation. In *B. alticola* these keels are not nearly so strong as in *B. d'orbignyi*, especially the superolateral crest of the fourth, which is weak. Lastly, the carapace of *burmeisteri* is said to have the ocular tubercle entire, in *alticola* it is sulcate, and in the female of the former there are 21–22 pectinal teeth as opposed to 15 in the latter.

SPIDERS

Order *Araneæ*; Family *Theraphosidæ*; Genus *Citharoscelus* Poc.[1]

(4) *Citharoscelus gossei* (sp. n.). (Fig. 2–2*b*)

Colour a tolerably uniform yellowish brown above and below; legs without distinct longitudinal pale bands, but with little tufts of pale hair set transversely at the extremity of the segments.

Carapace shorter than patella and tibia of first, of second, and of fourth leg; a little longer than those of third and than protarsus of fourth. Patella and tibia of fourth leg slightly shorter than of first, about equal to those of second; tibiæ and protarsi, especially of third and fourth legs, strongly spined; protarsi with one median and usually a second lateral spine at the apex beneath; protarsi of first and second with two or three spines at base of scopula, a distinct scopula at apex of fourth protarsus. Stridulating organ on posterior side of coxa of palp consisting of perhaps about one hundred close-set characteristically modified bristles, with some short black spines below, and on the anterior aspect of the coxa of the first leg by a large number of similar bristles both above and below the suture, and some black spines below the bristles.

Inferior tibial process of male tipped with a spine, a spine lying along the under edge of the upper process; protarsus strongly bowed in its basal half (Fig. 2*a*); palpal organ piriform attenuate at its end, with a spiral twist and two keels (Fig. 2*b*).

Measurements in millimetres. Total length about 40, carapace 19,

[1] *Ann. Mag. Nat. Hist.* (7) vol. iii. p. 347.

width 16, patella and tibia of first leg 21.5, of fourth 20.2, protarsus of first 13.2, of fourth 17.

Loc: Lujan.

This species and *C. kochii*, Poc., which occurs at Valparaiso and other places in Chile,[1] may be readily distinguished as follows:—

(*a*) Carapace covered with silky hairs of a pink or rosy hue; lower side of thorax and abdomen jet black; legs with distinct pale bands and clothed with red bristles; protarsus of first leg less strongly bowed; stridulating organ both on maxilla and on coxa of first leg consisting of a few bristles not accompanied by spines—*Kochii*, Poc.

(*b*) Carapace and limbs above and below a tolerably uniform brownish colour: protarsus of first leg much more strongly bowed, stridulating bristles very numerous and close set and accompanied by spines both upon the coxa of the first leg and of the palpus.

Gossei (sp. n.).

In addition to the large spider described above, Mr. Gosse procured an example of *Argiope argentata*, Fabr., and immature or dried and indeterminable examples of *Sparassus*, *Lycosa*, and *Gayenna*.

SOLPUGAS

Order *Solifugæ*; Genus *Cleobis* Sim.

(5) *Cleobis andinus* (sp. n.). (Fig. 3)

Colour: head-plate fuscous with a median yellow line or patch, ocular tubercle black, mandibles flavous with thin fuscous bands above; dorsal plates of abdomen furnished with three fuscous bands, one median and one on each side; legs and palpi uniformly fuscous throughout, except the coxa and trochanter and in part the base of the femora which are flavous.

Head-plate not quite equalling the length of the tibia (penultimate segment) of palp in width, and only a little more than half the length of patella of this appendage, about half the length of the patella of the fourth leg and three-fourths the length of its tibia; studded with setiferous tubercles, its anterior border only lightly convex.

On the upper fang of the mandible there is no superior crest; the first, third, and fifth teeth large, the fifth a little larger than the third, the third than the first, the second and fourth noticeably smaller, the sixth, *i.e.* the first of the external basal series, smaller than the fifth.

Femur of palp armed below with about four or five pairs of long spines, those of the anterior series longest; patella and tibia

[1] *Ann. Mag. Nat. Hist.* (7) vol. iii. p. 347; see also F. Cambridge, *Journ. Linn. Soc.* 1899, vol. xxvii. p. 16, pl. ii. fig. 13, 15.

also armed below with about four pairs of long spines; tarsus of fourth legs armed below with about four pairs of spines, tibia also armed with a few spines; femora of fourth leg but little dilated.

Male resembling female in colour. Legs and palpi very much longer. Width of carapace less than half the length of the patella of palp, and about two-thirds the length of its tibia; less also than half the length of the patella of the fourth leg. Upper fang of mandibles more curved than in female, with superior crest, flagellum membranous with incurved edges, broader and rounder behind.

Measurements in millimetres. Female, total length (excluding mandibles) 12.5, width of head 2.3, length of palp 12.5, of fourth leg 16 (measured from base of femora).

Male, total length 13, width of head 2.8, length of palp 19, of fourth leg 22 (from base of femora).

Loc: Inca, 8930 feet, (*Type*) Punta de las Vacas, 7856 feet, and Vacas Valley. Found under stones.

Differs from the Chilian species, *C. morsicans*, Gervais (v. Gay's *Historia de Chile, Zoologia*, 1854, vol. iv. p. 16, pl. 1, fig. 1 (not fig. 2), sub *Galcodes*), in its longitudinally banded dorsal plates and greater length of legs. In the figure of *C. morsicans*, the upper surface of abdomen, carapace, and mandibles is a uniform brown, and the width of the head is represented as slightly exceeding the tibia and tarsus of the palp, and is only a little shorter than the patella of this appendage.

The more northern species, *C. cubæ* of Lucas, from the West Indies, *C. stolli* (Poc.) from Guatemala, and *C. gervaisii* (Poc.) from Columbia, in addition to being differently coloured from *C. andinus*, have the palpi shorter, and in the female at least no spines on the femur and tibia.

EXPLANATION OF PLATE (*facing this page*)

FIG. 1. *Bothriurus alticola* (sp. n.).
,, 2. *Citharoscelus gossei* (sp. n.).
,, 2a. ,, ,, extremity of first leg of male.
,, 2b. ,, ,, palpal organ of ditto.
,, 3. *Cleobis andinus*, sp. n.

A NEW PARASITE

BY DR. VON LINSTOW

A new Nematide was found by Mr. P. Gosse on the 7th of December 1896, at Punta de las Vacas, 7858 feet above sea-level, in the Argentine Republic, in the Andes, South America. It was coiled up close against the heart of a small bird, the size of a chaffinch,

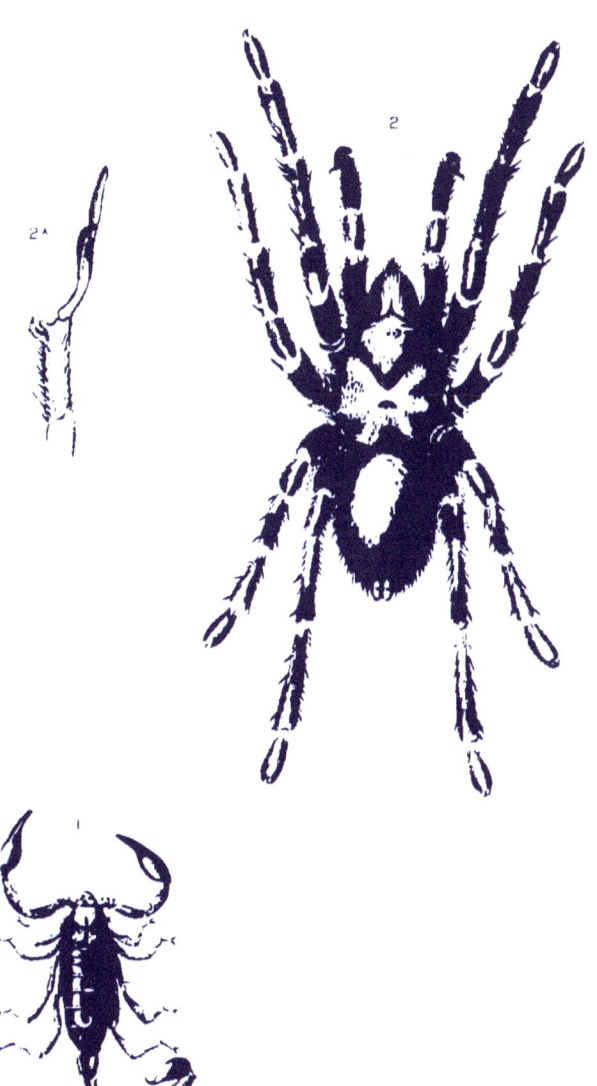

i.e. Elainea albiceps (a small tyrant bird). This parasite has been named by Dr. von Linstow, and is described by him as follows:—

Filaria elaineæ (sp. n.)

"The specimen is a male, probably immature. The length is 27.7 mm., the breadth 0.97 mm. The anterior end is rounded. There are no lips or papillæ. The skin is smooth and without rings. The œsophagus takes up $\frac{2}{15}$ of the total body length, the intestine has a blackish-brown colour. The very short tail is pointed like a skittle, and measures $\frac{1}{231}$ of the total length. The two spicules differ greatly, the left is 0.26 mm., the right 0.83 mm. long. The tail bears no papillæ, which in other species of the genus are always found on the male, so that it is possible that the specimen in question is immature."[1]

V

NOTES ON PLANTS COLLECTED
IN THE ACONCAGUA VALLEYS BY PHILIP GOSSE

By I. Henry Burkill, M.A.

"Little can be seen," wrote Charles Darwin,[2] when describing his journey across the Cumbre Pass, "beyond the bare walls of the one grand flat-bottomed valley which the road follows up to the highest crest. The valley and the huge rocky mountains are extremely barren : excepting a few resinous bushes scarcely a plant can be seen." This is the impression which Darwin received from crossing the Andes in April, ascending the Valley de las Cuevas from Punta de las Vacas (7858 feet) to the crest which is reached at 12,800 feet. From the north the Rio Horcones enters this valley, its head-waters rising from the melting snows and glaciers of Aconcagua, and pouring down in variable turbulent torrents difficult to cross and of uncertain level. The waters of these rivers are icy cold, and consequently inimical to vegetation. Away from their banks stretch sands of variable depth overlying the bed-rock, and for ever shifting, as inhospitable to vegetation as the glacial river banks, but from other causes. Their surface is alternately hot and cold, and usually very dry, the heat quivering up in the sun: all that grows there risks being parched, and risks, too, being buried by the shifting of the sand which the wind produces. Here and there are springs, and

---

[1] Translated by Mr. A. E. Shipley, of Christ's College, Cambridge.
[2] *Naturalist's Voyage Round the World*, 1889 ed. p. 334.

these are the spots most favourable to vegetation. Along the course of a stream arising in a little spring near Puente del Inca were found plants not seen elsewhere; its banks were gay with a monkey-flower and a calceolaria, both of which well merit the introduction into European gardens which they obtained early in this century; and here, too, the evening primrose (*Œnothera biennis*) had established itself. Such a situation is undoubtedly the most favoured of any in these bleak and barren regions. Here and there at higher levels than Puente del Inca, springs supply so constant a store of water that a variety of plants obtain an asylum. One such—a bog of small extent—was dotted over in April with the yellow flowers of *Werneria pygmæa*, and supplied a moderate bite of uninviting grass to the mules. On the banks of this marsh, near enough to be within the zone of influence of the spring, grew another yellow-flowered composite (*Haplopappus densifolius*). Yet both the *Werneria* within and the *Haplopappus* beside the marsh have the firm rather leathery leaves which we find in desert regions, and which imply a difficulty in obtaining water. It is well to explain this here. Water is necessary for the plant's growth; but the plant cannot absorb it at a temperature almost that of melting ice. For this cause all the vegetation which has but ice-cold water to hand has almost as great a need of economy as that which lives in the dry sand. Leaves are the great evaporating organs of the plant, and dry-climate plants need to reduce them to economise their small store. Thus it comes about that the same character of narrow and reduced leaves occurs alike in the *Haplopappus* and *Werneria* as in the *Oriastrum* and *Verbena* of the dry sand—of which a short description presently.

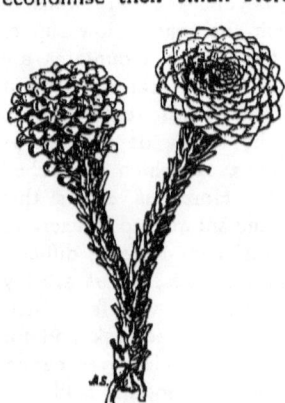

VIOLA SEMPERVIVUM, one-half natural size.

A great feature of these plants is the abundance of their flowers. At the junction of the Horcones Valley and the Valley de las Cuevas the ground was covered with a Nasturtium (*Tropæolum polyphyllum*), whose yellow flowers of various shades made quite a feature in the landscape. Almost a flower to every leaf was the rule with this plant. The little pansies in the sand were thickly studded with small flowers of the deepest purple with a yellow eye, and a handsome Gentian high up the Horcones Valley produced far more flowers than leaves.

CALYCERA VIRIDIFLORA, one-half natural size.

PLANTS 365

The seeds ripen freely, and some of the plants exercise a special care in guarding them. The little sand-pansies hide them amongst their leaves, and fragments of old dehisced capsules may be found among the broken bases of the old leaves held against the ground by the newer leaves above them. The succulent *Calycera* which was found about Puente del Inca has formidable spines amongst the flowers, and by appearance forbids a bite to any but the hungriest animal.

Many of the seeds of the vegetation of these regions are adapted for dispersal by wind. Those of *Anemone*, *Stipa*, *Deyeuxia*, and many of the composites, are furnished with a more or less perfect parachute of hairs. *Hexaptera* has winged seeds. In some others the fruits are bladdery; and one never-to-be-forgotten shrub (*Acæna lævigata*) has a troublesome burr.

Acæna lævigata grows to the height of eighteen inches, and its small flowers are crowded together, each furnished with four barbed prickles. The accompanying figure illustrates the burr which covers the legs of the mules when the seed is ripe and adheres to one's clothes in a most aggravating manner.

ACÆNA LÆVIGATA, single fruit enlarged, and burr formed of a number of such fruits.

As in all Alpine or Arctic situations, annual plants are very few; for into a region where the climate is so adverse, plants whose existence depends on a perfectly regular fruiting as well as growth are more or less forbidden an entry.

Ascending the Rio Mendoza we gradually leave behind the bushy *Larrea* and *Proustia* which characterise its lower part, and before we get to Punta de las Vacas they have disappeared. This, according to F. Kurtz[1] is the lowest Andine zone which we have left behind, and none of the plants to be enumerated in the following list belong to it. Still ascending, between Punta de las Vacas and Puente del Inca a stinging plant, *Blumenbachia coronata*, becomes the most noticeable object. Its large flowers are very pretty, and peep out from under the green-foliage like small eggs, gaining for the plant the name of "hen and eggs," as well as the indirectly

---

[1] F. Kurtz, "Informe preliminar de un viaje botánico ... en las provincias de Cordoba, San Luis y Mendoza, 1885-86," Buenos Aires, 1887.

complimentary one of "devil's beauty." The sting is more severe than that of our English nettle. This plant Kurtz makes the mark of his second Andine zone. With it is associated abundantly a

BLUMENBACHIA CORONATA.

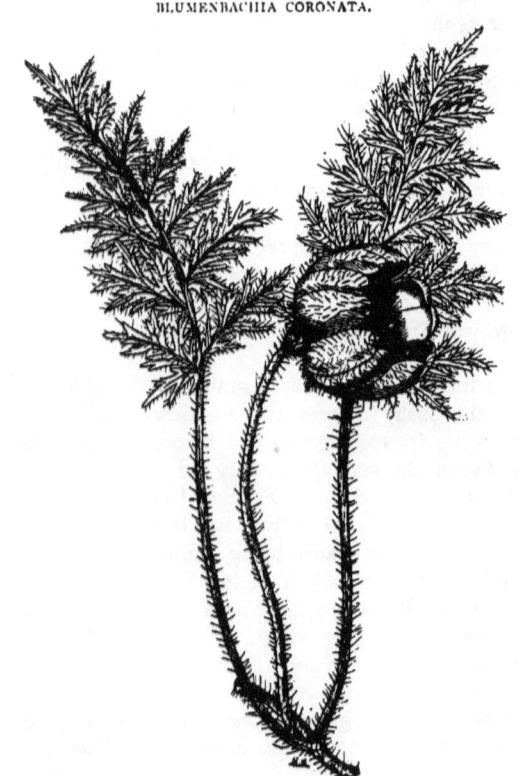

BLUMENBACHIA CORONATA, flower and leaves, one-half natural size.

PLANTS

small tobacco (*Nicotiana lychnoides*)—sticky from innumerable dark-coloured glands, and, equally conspicuous, *Acæna lævigata*, whose burrs have been mentioned, an *Astragalus* and the spiny *Adesmia*, which apparently most of all attracted Darwin's notice. Here at Puente del Inca the *Ephedra* tails out. This plant, with its stiff broom-like appearance and spiny branches, has no inviting aspect.

In irrigated fields at this place grows with the greatest luxuriance Lucerne (*Medicago sativa*). It is a plant well calculated to resist considerable drought, and roots at a great depth; indeed it is on record that in Switzerland its roots have been traced to a distance of sixty-six feet from the surface of the soil. Yet here unirrigated it must fail, for it needs a distributed rainfall of not less than thirty-two to thirty-six inches per annum. With the Lucerne our common English bindweed grows, appearing here at 9000 feet, while in our own islands it does not ascend beyond 1200 feet.

Gradually, after leaving Inca, we get into the zone of dwarf groundsels and dandelion-like plants. The woody plants disappear, and the vegetation which remains is chiefly noticeable for the proximity of the leaves to the ground. The following are some figures, referring to plants found at 12,000 feet and above.

Name.	Height in inches above ground.	
	A. of upper leaves.	B. of flower.
Anemone major	3 –3½	3 –3½
Hexaptera cuneata	1½–2	2 –2½
Viola Montagnei	1 –1¼	0 –1½
Viola cano barbata	1 –1½	0 –1½
Viola Sempervivum	1 –1½	0 –1½
Calandrinia arenaria	1½–2	0 –2
Malvastrum compactum	½–1	0 –1
Phaca arnottiana	3 –3½	2 –3½
Senecio crithmoides	1½–2	½–2

Among the strangest of plants of the region is *Barneoudia major* or more correctly *Anemone major*, for we place the genus *Barneoudia* as a section of the larger genus *Anemone*. From a solid little body underground — a corm — spring up in the early Spring two or three stems terminating in a flower, and under the flower a ring of foliage.

Visitors to the Alps are familiar with the way in which *Soldanella alpina* springs up through the snow, being the first thing to blossom as the snow melts. Just such a habit have some of these South Andine Anemones. It is not certain that *Anemone major* itself springs up through the snow, but such a habit is attributed to *Anemone chilensis*. The plant lives in little colonies in the sand, and when the fruit is ripe and the leaves withering is very inconspicuous.

Hardly less strange is *Verbena uniflora*. In the tropics Verbenas grow to bushes of some height; but this little plant forms a cushion scarcely an inch above the surface of the soil. The leaves are about a line to a line and a half long, and the flowers rise singly just above them. Every leaf is rolled back on itself—a protection of the more delicate under surface against drought.

Oriastrum pulvinatum is a small composite of the same habit;

ANEMONE MAJOR, one-half natural size.

its stems, each terminated in a fairly conspicuous flower, rise about one to one and a half inches, and are invisible by reason of the crowded heath-like woolly leaves which coat them.

Another very humble plant is *Malvastrum compactum*, whose soft woolly leaves form a little rosette on the ground, above which the flowers hardly rise.

A situation close to the sand is of advantage in fruit-ripening, for the surface of this is the warmest spot; hence perhaps it is that the sand-plants so often ripen their seeds on it. The little pansies have been mentioned; *Blumenbachia* and *Tropæolum* may be cited as other examples. And, further, the difficulty of maintaining existence prevents among the most Alpine plants any lavish expenditure of material upon the formation of flower-stalks. About Puente del Inca, however, we have not reached so high an elevation that this is forbidden; for we see conspicuous stalks in the *Calycera* figured, in a *Sisymbrium*, in *Mimulus, Calceolaria, Phacelia, Gilia, Nicotiana*, and some others whose names appear in the following list.

A glance must be given at the composition of the flora, and the question asked whence it came. What part can the extensive mountain chains of the Northern Hemisphere have contributed, and what part owes its origin to local development or to the peculiar antarctic flora? Every plant noticed was gathered, and the vegetation is represented as completely as possible in the collection made.

The higher plants (*Phanerogams*) are enumerated in the list, which follows, under forty-six generic names, but from this we must deduct four, two—*Medicago* and *Œnothera*—as belonging to introduced plants, and two—*Eutoca* and *Phaca*—because they equal *Phacelia* and *Astragalus* respectively.

Of the remaining forty-two genera the following are confined to South America, chiefly to the southern parts and within the tropics to the mountains.

>   *Hexaptera.*   *Oriastrum (Chætanthera).*
>   *Adesmia.*   *Leuceria.*
>   *Blumenbachia.*   *Trechonætes.*
>   *Calycera.*   *Melosperma.*
>   *Nassauvia.*   *Arjona.*

The following are centred in South America and extend to the north of the Isthmus of Panama.

>   *Tropæolum.*
>   *Haplopappus.*
>   *Calceolaria.*

Again widening the range the following extend to New Zealand, Australia, or the Cape, or at least are excluded from the parts of the Old World in the Northern Hemisphere.

>   *Colobanthus.*   *Malvastrum.*
>   *Calandrinia.*   *Acæna.*

Nicotiana, Verbena, and *Werneria* might almost be added to these, for their range is only a very little wider.

The genera enumerated so far are southern types, which do not occur (*Werneria* excepted) in the mountains of the northern parts of the Old World.

Now for the northern type, which is not absent by any means.

We have amongst the genera of these valleys the following whose home appears to be in the north:—

Anemone. *Convolvulus.*
Sisymbrium. *Gentiana.*
Viola. *Plantago.*
Lotus. *Festuca.*
Astragalus. *Ephedra.*

They make a little set whose ancestors, perhaps having reached North America from the Old World, may well have spread southwards along the great chain of mountains which joins north temperate to south temperate America, and are somewhat familiar in general appearance to one who knows the flora of Europe. Yet while it may be thought that the Gentian, Anemones, and Pansies, etc., came of a stock which had thus spread round the Northern Hemisphere and down the Andes from their home in the north, in their new-found home they developed into new species. As species they are of a southern-developed Alpine flora, although as genera of a northern type. Still more of southern type are the plants which represent the genera named in the first three lists, whose appearance is for the most part so distinct that they emphasise on the European traveller's mind the remoteness of these Andine Alps from his own home.

PLANTS COLLECTED BY PHILIP GOSSE IN THE LAS CUEVAS AND HORCONES VALLEYS

Identified at Kew by I. H. BURKILL, M.A.; *the Algæ by* W. WEST, F.L.S.

RANUNCULACEÆ

Anemone major (Reiche); *Barneoudia major* (Phil.), 10,000–12,000 feet above Inca and in B Valley. Underground there exists a tuber from which shoot up in spring 1–4 flowering branches, each bearing a ring of leaves (involucre) under the solitary flower. It is one of the most curious forms in these mountains. The plant exists in little colonies in the bare sand. The specimens obtained had fruited, and the yellowish-green leaves were very inconspicuous.

CRUCIFERÆ

Hexaptera cuneata (Gill. & Hook.). Above Puente del Inca about 12,000–13,000 feet. A low hairy plant, some 4–6 inches high.

Sisymbrium canescens (Nutt.); *Descurainia canescens* (Prantl.). Inca, at 9170 feet (27th Dec. 1896). The leaves are woolly and the stem glandular-hairy. Fruit was ripe at the end of December, and the plant still in flower.

VIOLACEÆ

Viola Montagnei (C. Gay). About 12,000 feet, 29th Dec. 1896, opposite Inca. A dwarf tufted plant, less succulent and more hairy than *V. Sempervivum*, with deep purple flowers, flowering and fruiting most profusely. The stems had elongated 2½–3 inches since the last flowering, probably an effect of sand accumulating over them.

Viola cano barbata (Leybold). About 12,000 feet, Horcones Valley. A dwarf plant, much like the last, with flowers lighter in colour. Found under the shelter of a rock. Flowering and fruiting most profusely.

Viola Sempervivum (C. Gay). Above Puente del Inca at 10,000 feet and in the Horcones Valley at 13,000 feet, in sand. A dwarf stone-crop-like plant of most curious appearance. The leaves suggest the scales of a lizard, so do they overlap. The seed-pods are almost lost among the older leaves which have grown over them.

CARYOPHYLLACEÆ

Colobanthus quitensis (Bartl.). Camp, second ford, Horcones Valley. A plant of the habit of a Plantain (*Plantago*), with leaves close to the ground, forming a little cushion.

PORTULACACEÆ

Calandrinia potentilloides (Barn.). 27th Dec. 1896, Inca, 9170 feet. A very silky plant, with stems arising from a strong rootstock.

Calandrinia arenaria (Cham.), about 12,000 feet. A somewhat succulent plant.

MALVACEÆ

Malvastrum compactum (A. Gray). A very small and very hairy plant, which is found in the Andes as far north as Sorata.

GERANIACEÆ

Tropæolum polyphyllum (Cav.). Inca, and above it at the junction of the Horcones and Cuevas Valleys, creeping on the sand, and flowering most profusely. Flowers of several shades of yellow.

LEGUMINOSÆ

Medicago sativa (L.). Punta de las Vacas. An introduced fodder-plant, grown in irrigated fields from 3000 to 11,000 feet.

Lotus capitellatus (C. Gay). Horcones Valley, 11,000 feet. A little silky-leaved plant with a small flower.

Astragalus Cruikshankii (Gris.). Inca, and above it in the Cuevas Valley, very common up to 11,000 feet. A plant with snowy-white and pale mauve flowers.

Phaca anottiana (Gillies & Hook.). About 12,000 feet. A little blue-flowered, silvery-leaved plant.

Adesmia trijuga (Gillies). This shrub attains a height averaging 6 or 7 feet. It grows on both the east and the west slopes of the Andes up to 12,000 and 13,000 feet.

Adesmia (sp.), near *A. pauciflora* (Vog.). Inca, 8930 feet.

ROSACEÆ

Acæna lævigata (Ait.). About Puente del Inca to 13,500 feet; and elsewhere, common. A coarse woody plant with a burr.

ONAGRACEÆ

Œnothera biennis (L.). Inca, 2nd January 1897. A plant long naturalised in Chile, and probably thence introduced to the Cuevas Valley.

LOASACEÆ

Blumenbachia coronata (Hook. & Arn.). Inca and above and to 11,000 feet below it, but hardly found in the Horcones Valley, 2nd January 1897. A characteristic plant of the valley in this part, with pretty white flowers, and leaves covered with stinging hairs. "Devil's Beauty," and "Hen and Eggs" of the inhabitants.

CALYCERACEÆ

Calycera viridiflora (Miers); *C. nudicaulis* (Phil.). Inca. A curious succulent.

COMPOSITÆ

Haplopappus densifolius (Rémy). D camp, Horcones Valley. At 11,000 feet, on a bank a few feet above a marsh.

Senecio glandulosus (Don). Puente del Inca, 10,000 feet. A coarse groundsel, with a dense coat of glandular hairs and some wool. The leaves with the margins recurved.

Senecio uspallatensis (Hook. & Arn.). Puente del Inca, 10,000 feet. A shrubby groundsel, with much-cut rather fleshy leaves, not very common.

Senecio erithmoides (Hook.). About 12,000 feet.

Senecio donianus (Hook. & Arn.). A species described in 1841 by Sir William Hooker, and Professor Walker-Arnott in Hooker's *Journal of Botany*, iii. p. 332, from the material now in the Herbarium of the Royal Gardens, Kew. But their specimens contain intermixed two fragments which doubtless belong to another species, and which by their thick covering of woolly hairs have caused the introduction of an error into the too meagre description. With excellent material now to hand a fresh description may well be drawn up.

Senecio deserticola, radice primaria longe sub terram penetrante, ramis lignosis cæspitosis 6-10 poll. longis. *Rami* juniores leviter lanati, foliis dense obtecti, flores 1-3 ad apicem gerentes. *Folia* oblanceolata, margine conspicue serrata vel pinnatipartita, apicem versus plus minusve rotundata, sessilia, juniora sublanata, dein glabra, subcarnosa, $\frac{1}{2}$-1 poll. longa, $\frac{1}{6}$-$\frac{1}{4}$ poll. lata. *Involucri* bracteæ biseriatæ; exteriores paucæ, subulatæ, perbreves; interiores pedicellis longiores, lineares, margine scariosæ, apice subacutæ, dorso pilis glandulosis luteis brevibus scabræ, 6 lin. longæ. *Flores* omnes tubulosi, involucrum paululum excedentes, lutei. *Staminum* filamenta dimidio superiore conspicue tumescentia; appendices subproductæ. *Ovarium* glabrum.

In one example upwards of thirty branches arise from the surface of the soil. These are woody and leafless; while the lateral branches, borne on these, carry a number of leaves and terminate in 1-3 flowers. When young the branches and leaves are more or less covered with a white felt of hairs, but not enough to justify the adjective "albolanati," which the authors of the description, judging by their mixed material, applied to the plant. These leaves soon lose their hairs, and the margins curve back, increasing the prominence of the teeth along them. The distinction of the Chilian species of this genus is difficult, and it is quite possible that *S. donianus* may be identical with one of the many species described by Philippi, who, possibly misled by the error in the description, has failed to recognise it. *S. mouttianus*, Rémy, is a near ally. The plant was gathered at 9450 feet. Station 8.

Senecio wernerioides (Wedd.). Second ford in Horcones Valley. A plant very like a dandelion. Most of the abundant specimens collected differ from the type in the deeper division of the leaves. From the more typical oblanceolate slightly crenated condition they become so deeply cut as to be almost pinnatisect. When freshly gathered it has the smell of green celery.

Werneria pygmæa (Hook. and Arn.). D camp. At the bottom of a waterfall in a marsh (20th April) among grasses.

Nassauvia glomerata (Wedd.). B Valley, 11,000 feet. In very dry places, its little pungent leaves forming a cushion on the soil.

Oriastrum pulvinatum (Phil.). Above Inca hotel, a tiny plant with the stems buried in short leaves.

Leuceria hiercioides (Cass.). A coarse weedy plant of the river bank at Inca.

CONVOLVULACEÆ

Convolvulus arvensis (L.). Inca. Common.

POLEMONIACEÆ

Eutoca pinnatifida (Phil.). River bank in Horcones Valley (20th April 1897). A low glandular plant with green flowers turning to purple.

Phacelia circinnata (Jacq. f.). Around Puente del Inca up to 10,000 feet, fairly common.

Gilia crassifolia (Benth.). Inca. A low glandular plant very common about Inca, the largest specimen about 8 inches high.

GENTIANACEÆ

Gentiana multicaulis (Gillies). B Valley, and at Puente del Inca, 2nd January 1896. A very pretty Gentian, 6–7 inches high.

SOLANACEÆ

Nicotiana lychnoides (Rémy). Puente del Inca. Common. Excessively glandular everywhere.

Trechonætes laciniata (Miers). D camp, Horcones Valley, 11,000 feet, and by the lake in Horcones Valley. A plant of singular aspect, its leaves spreading close to the ground, and amongst them rather large greenish-purple flowers.

SCROPHULARIACEÆ

Calceolaria plantaginea (Sm.). Inca, bank of fresh-water stream.

Mimulus cupreus (Regel). Bed of fresh-water stream, Puente del Inca, with the last.

Melosperma andicola (Benth.). Inca, at 9170 feet. A low creeping plant, with rather small purple flowers.

VERBENACEÆ

Verbena uniflora (Phil.). Above Inca, at 13,000 feet. A very low plant, forming dense cushions on the surface of the soil.

PLANTAGINACEÆ.

Plantago pauciflora (Lam.). Second ford, Horcones Valley, in marshy ground. In fruit in April 1897.

PLANTS

SANTALACEÆ
Arjona patagonica (Humb. and Jacquinot). K3 river, at 11,000 feet, Horcones Valley. A plant with rigid, rather spiny leaves.

EUPHORBIACEÆ
Euphorbia portulacoides (Spreng.). Inca. A succulent plant.

JUNCACEÆ
Juncus andicolus (Hook.). By bed of stream, Puente del Inca, and Horcones Valley. A very coarse, wiry rush spreading underground by stout runners.

NAIADACEÆ
Potamogeton pectinatus (L.). Horcones Valley, in the lake at 11,000 feet.

CYPERACEÆ
Eleocharis albibracteata (Nees). Second ford in Horcones Valley.

GRAMINÆ
Stipa chrysophylla (E. Desv.). Second ford in Horcones Valley, K3 river.
Agrostis araucana (Phil.). Puente del Inca up to 10,000 feet, by fresh water.
Deyeuxia eminens (Presl). K3 river, Horcones Valley.
Festuca (sp.), near *F. scabriuscula* (Phil.). Second ford in Horcones Valley, K3 river.
Bromus macranthus (E. Desv.). K3 river, and second ford in Horcones Valley.

GNETACEÆ
Ephedra americana (Humb. and Bonpl.), var. *andina* (Stapf). Inca to 10,000 feet. A low bush.

CHARACEÆ
Chara contraria (A. Br.). The lake in Horcones Valley.

CONJUGATÆ (determined by W. West, F.L.S.)
Spirogyra (sp.). The lake in Horcones Valley.
Mougeotia (sp.). With the preceding, and in the marsh at the second ford in Horcones Valley.

DIATOMACEÆ (determined by W. West, F.L.S.)

Denticula tenuis (Kuetz.). In the marsh at the second ford in Horcones Valley, and at 12,000 feet at Zurbriggen's camp.

Epithemia gibba (Keutz.). In the lake in Horcones Valley.

Cocconema cymbiforme (Rabh.). With the preceding.

Cocconema parvum (W. Sm.). In the marsh at the second ford in Horcones Valley.

Synedra acus (Keutz.), var. With the preceding.

Achnanthes (sp.) With the preceding.

APPENDIX D

THE BOUNDARY DISPUTE BETWEEN CHILE AND THE ARGENTINE REPUBLIC

WHEN in South America we frequently found, on both sides of the Andes, indications of the dispute that has continued so long between Chile and the Argentine Republic on the boundary question.

The controversy has at length entered on what everyone trusts will be its final stage. It has been laid for decision before Her Majesty the Queen as arbitress, and at the moment when I write, commissioners from both Republics are in London for the purpose of presenting their case.

The dispute has been going on for many years, and has more than once brought the two States to the very brink of war. It depends upon two main issues—the true configuration of the mountainous part of South America between the acknowledged territory of the Republics, much of which has still been most imperfectly explored, and the precise interpretation to be put upon the terms of existing treaties. The difficulty has really been pending ever since the independence of those countries was recognised by Spain. In the old days when both alike were governed from Madrid, it was understood that all territories to the east of the Andes were under the control of the Viceroy of Buenos Aires, all territories to the west under that of the Captain-general of Chile. In the settled parts of the country the great mountain chain was supposed to be a sufficient boundary, and as the immense district of Patagonia was still unsettled and even untraversed, the necessity for a strict settlement of limits there was unfelt.

When the southern part of the continent had been divided between two independent powers, rivalry between the authorities of Buenos Aires and Chile naturally became much keener, and the extent of their jurisdiction required to be more definitely fixed. The gradual opening up of Patagonia made the question more acute. Both parties could claim with some plausibility to be the successors of Spain in that region. And as it came to be recognised that

Patagonia was by no means an inhospitable waste, but a territory of value and ready for settlement, each country was naturally anxious to secure for itself as large a portion of this debatable land as possible.

For many years the controversy lingered on ; one draft treaty after another being proposed and rejected by either side. A general agreement, however, was worked out, under which the superior claim of the Argentine to much the greater part of Patagonia was recognised ; while, on the other hand, the possession of the Strait of Magellan was secured for Chile. Considering the immense importance of the Strait in the communication between Valparaiso and Europe, this was a claim which the Chilians could hardly have given up without war. In 1881 a treaty between the two Republics was signed at last, after negotiations carried on on their behalf by the American Ministers in Santiago and Buenos Aires respectively.

This Treaty of 1881 is the classical document in the case. Under its provisions the boundary between Chile and the Argentine down to the 52nd parallel—a point a little north of the Strait of Magellan—is stated to be the Cordillera, *i.e.* the chain of the Andes. On meeting the 52nd parallel, the boundary is to turn almost at right angles and run about due east and west to Point Dungeness, where the Strait enters the Atlantic. Tierra del Fuego fell to Chile, except the Atlantic coast of the island, which was reserved, with a small strip of territory behind it, for the Argentine. Chile was not to fortify the Strait, but it was to remain open to the flags of all nations for ever. Finally, it was provided that each country should appoint a commissioner by whom the boundary should be marked out on the spot, all disputed points being referred to the arbitration of a friendly Power.

After the lapse of eighteen years, however, the boundary still remains unmarked. The treaty, which was supposed to have settled everything, became one of the most disputed documents in recent history. So much ingenuity and perverted acuteness have been applied to its interpretation that the problem with which it deals remains as perplexing as ever.

When two countries are separated by one of the highest mountain chains in the world, and both have agreed that the mountains shall be their boundary, it would appear at the first glance that no further difficulty could arise. It is accepted on both sides that the dividing line is the Cordillera of the Andes, or rather in the Cordillera of the Andes. But in fixing a frontier in a range of mountains, two principles can be followed which may give very different results. In the first place the boundary may be fixed at the water-parting, all rivers on one side, with their tributaries, being assigned to one

THE BOUNDARY DISPUTE 379

country, all those on the other side to the other. Every stream that rises on the Andes, every drop of water that falls on their slopes, finds its way ultimately to the Atlantic or the Pacific; and even at the highest well-springs there can be no doubt in an explored country as to the direction it takes. On the other hand, the boundary may be fixed by the highest ridge, or, where there is a succession of isolated peaks, by an imaginary line joining their summits. Naturally, it may easily happen that in a mountain range these two lines coincide, the ridge where the waters divide and the highest ridge of all being in fact one and the same. In the Andes, however, this is not the case. The highest summits are not upon the water-parting: the water divides on its way to the Pacific or the Atlantic at a lower range some distance to the west of that which attains to the greatest elevation. Aconcagua is not on the water-parting, but stands wholly and entirely to the east of it. The streams that are fed from its western side do not continue in that direction to the Pacific, but, curving round the base of the mountain, they fall into the Rio Mendoza or the Rio de los Patos, which both flow downward through the pampas of the Argentine. Thus the melted snows of Aconcagua have their destination in the Atlantic, and not a drop of them ever enters the Pacific. The watershed is actually at the much lower elevations of the Cumbre and the Boquete del Valle Hermoso, while the highest peaks stand to the east of the ridge that divides the waters in the district between Santiago and Mendoza. As we go farther south the relationship changes. The highest ridge of the Cordillera trends towards the Pacific, and the water-parting changes to the other side. In the far south the parting of the waters is somewhere in the lower and central lands, as yet imperfectly explored, of Patagonia, whilst the summits that attain the greatest elevation are close to the western shore of the continent, and some are even said to be upon the islands off the coast. According to Señor Moreno, the Argentine expert, "it is shown in an irrefutable manner that in latitude 52° S. the Cordillera of the Andes sheds all the water from its slopes into the Pacific." It is needless to say that in these regions the Andes have been broken into a number of isolated mountains, sometimes divided by arms of the sea, between which the rivers coming down from the interior have no difficulty in flowing.

The difference of opinion that divides the representatives of the two countries may now be briefly stated. The Chilians stand out for the water-parting, the Argentines for the line of highest summits. The frontier proposed by the former, "leaves within the territory of each of the two nations, the peaks, ridges or ranges, however elevated they may be, which do not divide the waters of the river systems belonging to each country." Aconcagua thus belongs entirely to the Argentine, as, although it is the highest mountain on the continent, it stands wholly within the Argentine river system; whilst the lofty mountains on the Pacific coast to the south would fall completely inside Chilian territory. The boundary claimed by the Chilians "is no other than the natural and effective dividing line of the waters of the South American continent." This principle would give to Chile a very much larger share of Patagonia than a division according to the line of highest summits would do. The latter would leave to Chile little more than the coast-line of the Pacific. But by adopting the water-parting as the frontier, Chile would be entitled to the complete river basin of every stream emptying into the Pacific, right up to the remotest source of its tributaries in the heart of the continent. By adopting the highest mountain line, on the other hand, the Argentine Republic would become possessed of the greater part of these river basins, and in places would push Chile right back to the Pacific itself.

It is stated by the Argentine explorers that in some parts of Patagonia the water-parting is excessively indistinct. Streams change their courses, says Señor Moreno, and flow now to the Atlantic and now to the Pacific. In the flat land in the heart of Patagonia, rivers frequently form new channels. A heavy storm, or a flood which washes away an old gravel bank or piles up a new one, will divert the drainage of many square miles of territory from one ocean to the other. In one instance, Señor Moreno found that a river which formerly flowed eastward, had now taken a westward direction, but by employing the labour of his party for about a week, he diverted it into its old channel, and sent its waters down once more through Argentine territory to the Atlantic.

A boundary fixed by highest summits would, however, present many difficulties. It would upset what in the central districts has long been the acknowledged frontier. The ridge of the Cumbre is accepted as the boundary by everyone who crosses the pass; so is the Boquete del Valle Hermoso, farther to the north, where another pass road crosses the mountains. Between the province of Mendoza and Chile, the frontier is perfectly well known and established; and that frontier is the water-parting.

Accept the principle of highest summits, and everything is thrown into confusion. The boundary shifts from the Cumbre to the top of Aconcagua. But it is by no means obvious how it is to run from there. Clearly it must also pass over the top of Tupungato. Yet it is less certain how the line shall be drawn. As Aconcagua and Tupungato are the highest points in the neighbourhood, it might

THE BOUNDARY DISPUTE 381

be argued that the boundary should be a mathematically straight line drawn between their summits. But then Juncal, though not so high as either, is undoubtedly one of the "highest crests" in the Andes. Should not the line be deflected at an angle, on its way from Aconcagua to Tupungato, so as to touch Juncal as well? And if Juncal, why not also Torlosa? Everything depends upon the definition of highest summits. It seems hardly possible to fix a height in feet or metres above which a summit shall count for the purposes of delimitation, and below which it may safely be ignored. And according to the list of highest crests which anyone may choose to draw up, the boundary might be shifted indefinitely, and made to go through a curious variety of bends and loops, zigzags, and tacks.

The highest peaks of the Andes have not been arranged by Nature in a neat line running north and south. They occur irregularly, some on one side of the main ridge, some on the other. Their heights have been determined only in a few cases. When two mountains of an approximately equal height stand near together, it is difficult to say which shall be selected for delimiting purposes. A great number of trigonometrical measurements must first be undertaken before such questions can be settled. It may also be remarked that a frontier so arranged would present quite an artificial character when applied in the valleys, where, and not among the mountain tops, a definite boundary is needed. It is easy for every traveller and arriero to understand that up to the ridge of the Cumbre the Cuevas Valley is Argentine territory, and that the slopes on the farther side of the Cumbre are Chilian; that the Valle Hermoso, through which flows an Argentine river, the Rio de los Patos, is Argentine, and that the crest of the Boquete del Valle Hermoso, where one begins to descend towards the Pacific, is the point beyond which Chilian soil also begins. According to the theory of highest crests, many valleys would be divided between both countries; and in order to determine the point of demarcation, it would be necessary to find the highest mountains on each side and observe where the valley is intersected by an imaginary straight line drawn from one summit to the other.

The natural geographical difficulties presented along the borders of the two Republics are considerable, and demand very discriminating and impartial treatment. They are as nothing, however, when compared with the complications which diplomatic subtlety has contrived to pile up. The Treaty of 1881 is the most authoritative document in the case. When Chile insists on the water-parting as the boundary and the Argentine Republic claims the line of highest crests, each side professes to do no more than interpret the Treaty according to its obvious meaning and the intention of those by whom it was signed. It might be supposed that an instrument so variously construed was one of some ambiguity. Yet to anyone approaching it for the first time without prepossessions, its purport seems unmistakable. The important and vital words of the first clause may therefore be quoted literally from a translation of the document which lies before me.

"Clause 1.—The boundary between Chile and the Argentine Republic is from north to south, up to the fifty-second parallel of latitude, the Cordillera of the Andes. The boundary line within these limits shall pass along the highest crests of said Cordillera which divide the waters, and shall pass between the slopes down which the waters flow on the one side and the other. The difficulties which may arise owing to the existence of certain valleys formed by the bifurcation of the Cordillera, and in which the line dividing the waters may not be clear, shall be amicably settled by two experts, one to be named by each party."

It will be observed that the Treaty does not merely speak of the highest crests. The words expressly are—"the highest crests of said Cordillera which divide the waters." Aconcagua is the highest crest in the Cordillera; but it does not divide the waters. Therefore it does not come within the class of summits contemplated by the Treaty. As if to make matters absolutely definite and final, the Treaty adds that the frontier "shall pass between the slopes down which the waters flow on the one side and the other." This seems quite explicitly to exclude the Argentine interpretation. In the telegrams exchanged at the time when the Treaty was concluded, by the American Ministers whom both parties had authorised to conduct the negotiations, it was also stated that "the boundary between Chile and the Argentine Republic shall be the *divortia aquarum* of the Cordillera of the Andes up to the fifty-second parallel."

It should be noticed, however, that in such expressions the term *divortia aquarum* does not stand alone. It is always spoken of as the *divortia aquarum* of the Cordillera of the Andes. It would appear that in the extreme south of the continent, the water-parting and the Cordillera of the Andes are two distinct and separate things. The parting of the water lies in the lower ground inland, while the Cordillera runs nearer to the western coast, and does not really part the waters at all. The Chilians therefore, abandoning the strict reference to the mountain chain, take their stand upon the water-parting alone. It is, they maintain, the general line, where the waters divide in opposite directions for the Pacific and Atlantic, that was contemplated as the boundary in the Treaty of 1881. They stand upon "the natural and effective dividing line of the waters of the South American continent." The Argentines incline to ignore the water-parting altogether, and hold fast to "the Cordillera of the Andes." In the discussion between the experts of both countries which took place at Santiago in September 1898, the Argentine representative laid down these principles:—

(1) That the general line which he proposes to his colleague is wholly comprised within the Cordillera of the Andes.
(2) That in its entire extent it passes between the slopes which descend on one side or the other of the main range.
(3) That he considers the said main range is constituted by the predominating edge of the principal and central chain of the Andes, considered such by the first geographers of the world.
(4) That the principal chain is the most elevated, the most continual, with most uniform general direction, and its flanks shed the largest volume of water, thus presenting the conditions established, both by the Treaty of 23rd July 1881 and the Protocol of 1st May 1893, to constitute, with the crest line of its slope, the general frontier line between the Argentine Republic and the Republic of Chile.

In this declaration it will be observed how carefully the question of the water-divide is hidden out of sight behind "the predominating edge of the principal and central chain of the Andes." On the same occasion the Argentine representative used words even less easy to reconcile with the Treaty of 1881. "At that time," he said, "the general watershed of the Cordillera was considered inseparable from the latter's central or prevailing chain; and the coast thereof—that is to say, the snow-capped chain of the historians and geographers of all times—was for the signatories of the Treaty of 1881, and for those who accepted it, the only international boundary; although they knew that the chain was crossed, not only in one but in several cases, by rivers having their sources to the east of the same."

This statement, an ardent Chilian might almost say, is not the interpretation of the Treaty: it is a repudiation of it.

EDW. A. FITZGERALD.

INDEX

ACONCAGUA, its attraction for the explorer, 2; no literature relating to, 4; route of the expedition, 4; Dr. Güssfeldt's attempt, 4, 7, 8–14; Habel's name for the mountain, 14; its situation, 22, 28; mystery regarding summit, 23, 34, 40; wrongly described as volcano, 30; difficulty of access, 34; terribly uncertain weather, 35; dust and temperature, 35; storms, 36; highest mountain outside Asia, 37; first sight of, 43; first attempt of the expedition, 52; Mr. FitzGerald at 14,000 feet, 53; a view at 19,000 feet, 57; Zurbriggen reaches the summit, 83; thermometer at 19,000 feet, 89, 92; no snow at 22,000 feet, 113; Mr. Vines makes the ascent, 115; thermometer at the summit, 116; the scene, 118, 207; a colossal ruin, 121; considered as a volcano, 121; a sublime view, 124; as seen from the Catedral, 136; view from Tupungato, 208; verifying the height, 220; the great precipice, 224; the south side, 263; Mr. Lightbody takes photographs, 300; the east side, 301; rock specimens, 316; natural history of the valleys, 338; relation to the boundary dispute, 380 *et seq.*
Aconcagua River, 228.
Air, stagnation of the, 199.
Almacenes, 14, 120.
American carbines in Chile, 292.
American explorers in 1849–52, 5.
Anæmia of the brain, 67, 112.
Andes, previous books on, 4; southern Cordilleras, 5; ascents by Humboldt, Boussingault, Whymper, Reiss, Stübel, Wolf, and Thielmann, 5, 6; a track into the Pampas, 9; San Martin's crossing, 30; desolation of the valleys, 33; geology, 33, 194, 203, 311; snowline, 33, 235; atmosphere, 35, 199; storms, 36, 223, 242; vegetation, 36; the highest mountain, 36; denudation, 121, 143, 209; the people and their character, 129, 235, 261; a magnificent view, 207; absence of food and shelter, 229; the ranges in their winter dress, 249.
Antisana, 6.
Arctic expeditions and mountain expeditions, 3.
Armadillo, 341.

Arrieros, 17, 43, 262 (*see* Mules and mule-drivers).
Astronomical expedition of 1849–52, 5.

BALL, Mr., 219, 298.
Baths at Cachenta, 23.
Bell mares, 17, 272, 274, 277.
Bell of Quillota, 120.
Betting on the success of the expedition, 154, 205, 218.
Birds round Lujan, 305.
Birmingham spurs, 18.
Blanco River, 228.
Blood, circulation, 67, 112.
Boca del Rio, 22.
Bodegas, 233.
Bodenbender, 336.
Bolivian herb, 178.
Bonney, Professor, 33; 122*n*, 194, 311.
Books about the Andes, 4.
Boquete del Valle Hermoso, 9, 30, 32, 380, 381.
Boulenger, Mr. G. A., 355.
Boundary Commission, 238.
Boundary dispute between Chile and the Argentine Republic, 22, 208, 234, 238, 377.
Brain, anæmia of the, 67, 112.
Breathlessness, 198.
Buch, L. von, 333.
Buenavista Valley, 314, 321, 323, 324, 325.
Buenos Aires, 15, 16.
Burkill, Mr. I. H., 361, 370.
Büsserthor, 11.
Buzzard, 350.

CABLE COMPANY, 228.
Cachenta, 23.
Cannon, Dr., 178.
Cañon del Volcan, 10.
Cape route, 17.
Cáracara Buzzard, 350.
Carrion-hawk, 350.
Carrying trade on Cumbre Pass, 270.
Caste among arrieros, 17, 43, 292.
Casuchas, 33, 294.
Catedral, ascent of the, 134; a dangerous ledge, 139; Mr. Vines at the summit, 142; rock specimens, 322.
Cattle, 194, 207.
Cauldron, the, 98.

386 INDEX

Cayambe, 6.
Cayenne plovers, 307.
Cerillos, 21.
Cerro de la Plata, 22, 23, 207.
Cerro de las Rejas, 303.
Cerro de los Almacenes, 14, 120.
Cerro del Plomo, 119, 232.
Cerro del Roble, 120.
Chacabuco, 32.
Chaca coma, 178.
Chicha, 232.
Chile and Argentine boundary, 22, 208, 234, 377.
Chile and Spanish power, 32.
Chilenos with Dr. Güssfeldt, 12.
Chilian "huasos," 7.
Chimango kites, 305, 343.
Chimborazo, 5, 6.
Christmas at 17,000 feet, 56.
Cinclodes, 345.
Circulation of the blood, 67, 112.
Climate, 21, 35.
Climber's dangers and joys, the, 248.
Clothing taken by the party, 4.
Commission de Limites, 238.
Condiment, a popular, 26.
Condor, 42, 305.
Congratulations from British residents, 85.
Conway, Sir Martin, 36.
Cooking at high levels, 56, 66, 75, 87, 90, 101, 180, 214, 255.
Cordilleras, 5, 22.
Correspondents of *La Union*, 219.
Cotocachi, 6.
Cotopaxi, 6.
Cotton, Dr., 21, 244 258, 264, 282.
Cow-bird, 351.
Crested duck, 350.
Cuckoo, 352.
Cuerno, 143.
Cuevas, 47, 269.
Cumbre Pass, 5, 32, 47, 129, 270, 284.
Customs officials, 269, 288.

DALTON, Mr., 23.
Darwin, Mr., in the Andes, 5; 120*n*, 162, 209, 333, 361.
Dedos, 137, 152.
Denudation, 121, 209.
Desolation of Andine valleys, 33, 137, 249.
D'Orbigny, M., 336
D'Orbigny's seed-snipe, 349.
De Trafford, Mr., 110, 117.
Dinnigan, Mr., 130, 133.
Distances, deceptive, 173.
Dove, 348.
Drinking festival, 232.
Drinking-houses, 25.
Driving adventures at Vacas, 26.
Duck, 350.
Duel between officers, 229.
Dust in the upper valleys, 29.

EAGLE, 73, 343.
Earthcreeper, 345, 346.
Earthquake at Mendoza, 19.

Egg-boiling, 101.
Engineering feat, 287.
Equipment, 3, 38, 106, 248.
Espinazito Pass, 9, 10, 336.
Explosion, 64.
Express Company, 25, 153.

FAIR VALLEY, 10.
Finches, 347, 348, 352.
FitzGerald, Mr., prospecting for Aconcagua, 29, 38; surveying under difficulties, 35; first attempt on Aconcagua, 52; a night at 16,000 feet, 53; mountain sickness, 55; rescuing Zurbriggen, 69; surveying during Zurbriggen's illness, 72; taken ill at 20,000 feet, 77; reaches 21,000 feet, 79; a great disappointment, 81; sends Zurbriggen to complete the ascent, 81; starts with Mr. Vines, 84; rescued from the snow, 92; obliged to turn back, 92; a sprained ankle, 93; another attempt, 96; horse's narrow escape, 99; disappointment again, 102, 103; receiving Mr. Vines, 127; fifteen nights at 19,000 feet, 128; fever on the way to Chile, 129; rough walking and a wet crossing, 147; out of condition, 148; surveying in Horcones Valley, 148, 152, 220, 223, 227; the last of Aconcagua, 222; another visit to Horcones Valley, 241; in a great gale, 242; back to Inca, 243; at Vacas and Mendoza, 246; climb back for the instruments, 248; overtaking Mr. Gosse in the snow, 250; horses better than mules, 254; death of pony, 260; dealing with José, 265; at Mr. Gosse's bedside, 264; welcome to Mr. Vines, 279; removing Mr. Gosse, 290; José's threats, 291; an encounter in the snow, 292; departure from Inca, 293, settling accounts with José, 295; typhoid fever in Santiago, 299; on the boundary dispute between Chile and the Argentine Republic, 377.
FitzGerald expedition, genesis, 1; party, and the preliminary experiments, 2; equipment, 3; departure, 15; hiring mules at Mendoza, 17; meeting with Mr. Lightbody, 20; bound for Vacas, 20; at 6000 feet, 24; Mr. Vines' loss and Pollinger's fears of conspiracy, 25; first camp, 26; Mr. Vines' driving adventure, 27; wind and dust, 29; the only way to deal with a native, 38; Andine ponies, 39; first day in the mountains, 40; unwholesome water, 41; steep slopes for the horses, 43; meagre pasturage, 44; a new camp, 45; buying horses, 47; ascending the Cumbre Pass, 48; Zurbriggen's four days' absence, 49; first attempt on Aconcagua, 52; cold nights in the heights, 54, 57; Christmas and Irish stew at 17,000 feet, 56; back to 12,000 feet, 59; restart, 60; poor firewood, 60; treat-

INDEX 387

ing Zurbriggen's feet, 62; 20,000 feet, 64; loose footing, 65; a view across the Pacific, 65; direct route abandoned, 65; intense suffering causes retreat at 22,000 feet, 68; fresh attempt, 74; failure, 77; Mr. FitzGerald's disappointment, 81; Aconcagua ascended, 83; congratulations from Valparaiso, 85; Mr. FitzGerald and Mr. Vines begin ascent, 84; snowed in, 91; they turn back, 92; Mr. Gosse's Zoo, 95; another attempt on the mountain, 96; twelve minutes to boil an egg, 101; night at the high camp, 101; moving the camp, 102; heliographing, 110, 116, 122, 130, 132; Mr. Vines and Lanti on the summit of Aconcagua, 115-123; the mountain as volcano, 121; a sublime view, 124; Lanti Nicola, 125; descent, and trip to Chile, 129; character of the Andine people, 129; suspicious-looking companions, 130; porters attend missionary service, 131; Mr. Vines climbs the Catedral, 134; miraculous escape of Joseph Pollinger, 140; Mr. Vines on the summit of the Catedral, 142; José's views on camping, 149; Mr. FitzGerald traversing the Horcones Valley, 149; sufferings of Mr. Lightbody, 151; Mr. Vines off to Tupungato, 155; the dog Paramillo, 159; a fox-hunt, 166; mules at high altitudes, 171; under-estimating the distance, 173; driven back by the storm, 174; Villa Sieja's farewell, 177; another attack on Tupungato, 177; herb medicine, 178; a frolicsome wind, 179; Lanti breaks a bottle of wine, 181; new route, 181; a muddy brown "lake of gold," 182; Lochmatter paralysed, 183; a retreat, 184; fresh plans and tea, 185; terrible night at 17,000 feet, 187; Tupungato now or never, 191; food at high altitudes, 192; a new volcano, 195; 20,000 feet, 196; Pollinger collapses, 197; stagnation of the air, 199; the summit attained, 202; memorial cairn and record, 203-5, unprecedented weather, 206; view from top of Tupungato, 206; a half-way crater, 210; the hardships of pioneers, 211; a reluctant descent, 212; a magnificent sunset, 214; betting on the result; 218; interviewers in the Horcones Valley, 219; Mr. Vines returns, 219; the party in Horcones Valley, 220; sagacity of the ponies, 225; back to Inca, 227; search for a volcano, 225; news of a duel on the frontier, 229; to Santa Rosa by rail, 231; a saint's day in Chile, 232; *Tierra del FitzGeraldo*, 234; the Yeso Valley, 234; an arriero runs away, 237; row between Chileno mule-drivers and Argentine passengers, 240; great gale, and retreat from Horcones camp, 242; the Jonah of the expedition, 244; building a sledge, 244; the mules reduced to eating chairs, 245; return to Vacas, 246; saying good-bye at Mendoza, 246; the journey to rescue the instruments, 248; grandeur of the mountains, 249; horses in the snow, 250; the tents at last, 253; horses better than mules, 254; a mouse-hunt, 254; safe return to Inca, 256; the Queen's birthday, 258; departure of the guides, 259; a journey to the base camp, 259; an unfeeling peon, 261; José chastised by Mr. Lightbody, 262; an afternoon's photographing, 263; removing the luggage to Vacas, 264; Mr. Gosse attacked by fever, 264; native porters fascinated by the putties, 268; Mr. Vines arrives at Cuevas, 269; the carrying trade and postal service over Cumbre, 270; transport and new fodder, 273; the arrieros get drunk, 276; mules die of starvation, 280; Mr. Lightbody's adventure in the Cumbre Pass, 283; the land pirates of the snow, 283; the guides, 285; heavy loads, 286; novel tobogganing, 286; Mr. Lightbody arrives at Los Andes, 288; José takes his revenge, 289; the crime of horse-stealing, 289; Mr. Gosse removed to Mendoza, 290; José threatens Mr. FitzGerald, 291; their meeting in the snow, 292; a precaution for travellers, 293; departure from Inca, 293; settling with José, 295; passage over the Cumbre, 296; the best meal for a long time, 296; the "special" from Salto to Los Andes, 297; work at Valparaiso, 298; Mr. FitzGerald and Mr. Vines down with typhoid fever, 299; Mr. Lightbody returns to the mountains, 299; photographing in the Andes, 301; the Penitentes, or Iglesia, 302; Mr. Lightbody's ascent, 302; Indian ruins, 303; last word on the Andes of Argentina, 304.

Flora, 369.
Food, 3, 4, 63, 110, 180, 189, 192, 237, 255.
Footgear of native porters, 268.
Fortunato the arriero, 154; unpunctuality and fears, 155; 158, 160, 161; falls into a bog, 164; 166, 167, 170, 176, 184.
Fossils, 333 *et seq.*
Foxes, 96, 166, 307, 341.
Fox-hunt, 166.
Freshfield, Mr., 199.
Frost-bite, 61, 128, 129, 212.
Furnace, Russian, 63.

GAMBLING spirit among arrieros, 217.
Gay's finch, 347.
Genesis of the expedition, 1.
Geology of the country, 33, 194, 203, 311, 331.
German Athletic Club and Aconcagua, 49, 85, 94.
German tramp, a, 260.
Gilliss in the Andes, 5.
Gosse, Mr., chasing an eagle, 73; his Zoo, 95; lying in wait for a fox, 96; parrakeets,

INDEX

131, 352; on the porters and the missionary, 131; hunting in Vacas Valley, 155; in Horcones Valley, 220, 241; difficulties in the snow, 250; a mouse-hunt, 254; dangerous falls, 256; fever, 264, 285; removal to Mendoza, 290; notes on natural history, 338.
Gottsche, C., 337.
Grass for mules, 44.
Gravel, terraces of, 162.
Gray, Mr. R. W., 321.
Gringos, 20.
Grim sentinel, a, 10.
Grison, 308, 341.
Ground-finch, 352.
Guanaco, 42, 164, 340.
Guides, character of, 285.
Guinea-pigs, 307.
Guira cuckoo, 352.
Gunther, Dr., 142.
Güssfeldt, Dr., his attempt to climb Aconcagua, 4, 7, 8-14; ascent of Maipo, 8; our obligation to him, 14; his card at 21,000 feet, 51, 58; 122*n*, 332.

HABEL, Herr, 14.
Harrier, 351.
Heights of some mountains, 37.
Heliographing, 110, 116, 122, 130, 132.
"Hen and eggs," 365.
Herb medicine, 178.
Hermoso Valley, 9, 10, 13, 380, 381.
Highest mountains of South America, 36.
Horcones Valley, 10, 14, 52, 120, 137, 148, 220, 223, 311, 333.
Horses in the mountains, 47, 48, 160, 250, 254, 275.
Horse-stealing, 289.
Hot springs, 23.
House-wren, 351.
Huasos of Chile, 7.
Humboldt's attempt on Chimborazo, 5.
Humming-birds, 344.
Huts in Yeso Valley, 235.

IGLESIA, or Penitentes, 300, 302.
Inca, 33, 47, 52, 163, 227, 243, 258.
Indian ruins, 303.
Inn at Inca, 258.
Inscriptions at Inca, 303.
Interviewers, 219.

JONAH of the expedition, 244.
Juncal, 32, 208, 209, 228, 239, 286, 297, 381.

KENNEDY, Mr., 234.
Kestrel, 350.
Kites, 305, 343.
Knee, cure for a bruised, 172.

LAGUNA SECA, 236, 238.
"Lake of gold," 182.
Las Cuevas, 47.
Legs, paralysis of the, 183.
Leones, 119.

Lightbody, Mr., 20, 23; sings Spanish ballads, 28; meeting at Inca, 129; a triangulation completed, 131; sufferings at 19,000 feet, 150; in Horcones Valley, 220; takes photographs, 224; another visit to Horcones Valley, 241; at Mendoza, 247; ill, 247; summary dealing with José, 262; negotiating with porters at Cuevas, 271; crossing the Andes, 281; marvellous results in photography, 282; adventures in the Cumbre Pass, 283; a quick ascent, 284; arrival at Portillo, 285; character of guides, 285; novel tobogganing, 286; at Juncal, 287; arrival at Los Andes, 288; printing photographs at Valparaiso, 298; goes back alone to the mountains, 299; at 13,000 feet on Aconcagua, 300; ascent of the Penitentes, or Iglesia, 302; Indian ruins, 303; arrival at Mendoza and Monte Video, 304.
Lightning in the Andes, 36.
Limache, 129.
Linstow, Dr. von, 360.
Literature of the Andes, 4.
Lizards, 355.
Locusts, 305.
Los Andes, 129, 130, 288, 297.
Lujan, 305, 350.

MADRINAS, 272.
Magellan's owl, 343.
Magellan Strait, 16, 378.
Maipo, 8, 32, 207.
Malargue, 336.
Mammalia, 340.
Marsh-startling, 351.
Martin, General, 30.
Mendoza, 15, 17, 21, 22, 304.
Mendoza old town, 19.
Mendoza River, 22.
Mercedario, 22, 32, 37, 118, 209.
Meteoric phenomenon, 214.
Meyen, Dr., 336.
Mice, 254, 307, 308, 341.
Military pack-saddles, 45.
Mineral springs, 33.
Miners, 344.
Missionary service, 132.
Monastery (Iglesia), 302.
Mountaineering, dangers and compensations, 248.
Mountain expeditions and Arctic expeditions, 3.
Mountain sickness, 55, 67, 77.
Mourning finch, 348.
Mud avalanches, 23.
Mules and mule-drivers, 17, 21, 43, 44, 46, 48, 69, 97, 150, 155, 161-3, 171, 210, 239, 240, 245, 253, 262, 274, 280, 292.

NATURAL History, 338.
Naval astronomical expedition of 1849-52, 5.
Navarro, 32, 119, 208.
Neamayr, M., 334.
Nieve Penitente, 10, 34, 60, 138, 172.

INDEX 389

Norton, Mr., 290, 304.
Nourishment at high altitudes, 192.

OLD MENDOZA, 19.
Outfit, 3, 38, 106, 248.
Owl, 343.

PACK saddles, 45.
Paramillos, 47, 268, 274.
Parasite, a new, 360.
Parrakeets, 131, 352.
Paso Malo, 97, 226.
Pasturage for mules, 44.
Patagonia, 208, 377.
Patagonian earthcreeper, 345.
Patagonian fox, 341.
Penitent friars, 34.
Penitente gateway, 11.
Penitente Valley, 10, 30, 120.
Penitentes, or Iglesia, 300, 302.
Pentland, Mr., 333.
Peons, 26, 261, 283, 294.
People, and their character, 129, 235, 261.
Photographing in stormy weather, 224, 282, 298, 299–301.
Pioneers, hardships of, 211.
Pissis in the Andes, 5, 37.
Placilla, 120.
Plants, 361, 370.
Plata, 22, 23.
Plomo, 119, 232.
Plovers, 307.
Pochero, 180.
Pocock, Mr. R. I., 356.
Pollera, 32, 119, 159, 208, 217.
Ponchos, 18, 177, 191.
Ponies, 39, 223, 225, 260.
Porters on the Cumbre Pass, 271, 283, 286.
Portezuelo del Penitente, 11.
Portillo, 5, 207, 238, 285.
Posadas, 25, 258, 282.
Postal service, 16, 263, 267, 269, 270, 273, 293.
Predecessors in the Andes, 5.
Puente Alto, 232.
Puente del Inca, 33, 47.
Puma, 340.
Puna, 90.
Punta de las Vacas, 25.
Putaendo River, 9.
Putties for the natives, 268.

QUEBRADAS, 160.
Queen Victoria, 377.
Quillota, Bell of, 120.

RAILWAYS, 16, 231, 287, 290.
Ravines or quebradas, 160.
Reclus, M., on Aconcagua, 35.
Reiss, Dr., 6.
Rejas, 303.
Reptiles, 355.
Revellers in a Chile town, 233.
Riding on a precipice, 43.
Rio Aconcagua, 228.
Rio Blanco, 228.

Rio de las Cuevas Valley, 14.
Roble, 120.
Rock specimens collected, 311 *et seq.*; Professor Bonney's conclusions, 331.
Roth, Professor, 332.
Route of the expedition, 4.
Routes to South America, 16.
Russian furnace, 63.
Ruwenzori ranges, 37.

SADDLES, 40, 45.
Sagacity of ponies, 225.
Salto del Soldado, 129, 130, 231, 287, 297.
San José, 32, 207.
San José de Maipu, 232, 234, 238.
San Martin, General, 30.
Santa Rosa de los Andes, 15, 228, 232.
Santiago, 49, 129.
Santiago interviewers, 219.
Sara-urcu, 6.
Scorpions, 356.
Seca, Laguna, 236, 238.
Seed-finches, 352.
Seed-snipes, 349.
Shelter in the Andes, 228, 256.
Shoeing mules and horses, 156.
Sickness, 55, 67, 77.
Sierra de Malargue, 336.
Sierra del Penitente, 10.
Signalling, 116.
Siskin, 347.
Skeleton in the mountains, 10.
Skunks, 306, 341.
Sleeping, 2; precaution, 293.
Snow-grass for mules, 44.
Snow-line of the Andes, 33, 235.
Snow, "penitent," 10, 34, 60, 138, 172.
Snowstorms, 35, 91, 242, 272, 274.
Solpuga, 356, 359.
Song-sparrow, 348.
Sosa, Tomas, 17, 18, 69, 236.
South America, routes to, 16.
South America, travelling in, 16, 231, 238, 240.
Spaniards defeated by San Martin, 32.
Sparrows, 305, 348.
Spider's web for theodolite, 72.
Spiders, 356.
Spine-tails, 346.
Springs, 23, 33.
Stagnation of the air, 199.
Starling, 351.
Stelzner in the Andes, 5, 334, 336.
Stephen, Mr. Leslie, 105, 211.
Storms, 36, 179, 187, 242, 274.
Stübel in the Andes, 5, 6.
Suez Canal route, 16.
Surveying outfit, 3.
Surveys, rough, 227.
Swallows, 343.
Switzerland, 2, 192.

TANAGER, 352.
Telegram, a friendly, 85.
Telephoto lens, 300.
Theodolite, 72, 223, 255.

Thornton, Mr., 21.
Toboganning, novel kind of, 286.
Tomas, 17, 18, 69, 236.
Torlosa, 156, 301, 311 *et seq.*, 333 *et seq.*
Tornquist, A., 337.
Transandine Railway, 15, 23, 25, 231, 287, 290.
Travelling in South America, 16, 231, 232, 239, 288.
Trees, absence of, 35.
Tuffield, Mr., 228, 231, 232, 239, 288.
Tunnels, 287.
Tupungato, first sight of, 22; height, 37; a road to treasure, 154; Mr. Vines begins ascent, 155; Fortunato's dread of the mountain, 155; rough paths, 157; a difficult *quebrada*, 161; terraces of gravel, 162; a troublesome mule, 163; Fortunato falls into the bog, 164; memorable scene, 168; at 14,000 feet, 171; deceptive distances, 173; storm causes retreat at 19,000 feet, 174; another start, 177, 181; a frolicsome wind, 179; Zurbriggen's new route, 181; a muddy brown "lake of gold," 182; another retreat, 184; fresh plans, 185; terrible night at 17,000 feet, 187; now or never, 191; another route, 194; a new volcano, 195; 20,000 feet, 196; the highest point at last, 202; stones on the summit, 203; leaving cairn and record, 205; a magnificent view, 207; Darwin on the crater, 210; the base camp, 215; Mr. Lightbody's photographs, 301; its relation to the boundary dispute, 380.
Tyrants, 346, 347.

UNITED STATES expedition of 1849-52, 5.
Uspallata Pampa, 22, 24.
Uspallata Pass, 5.

VACAS, 25, 246, 289.
Vacas Valley, 39, 43, 120.
Valle Hermoso, 9, 10, 13.
Valle Penitente, 10.
Valparaiso, 15, 16, 85, 130.
Vegetation in the valleys, 36, 159, 229.
Vicuña, Señor Morla, 234.
Villa Longa Express Company, 25, 153.
Vines, Mr., loses revolver and gold, 25; driving accident, 27; brings provisions to 12,000 feet, 59; begins ascent of Aconcagua with Mr. FitzGerald, 84; accident at a bad corner, 87; rescues Mr. FitzGerald from the snow, 92; falls into a stream, 93; another attempt on the mountain, 96; turns back, 92; heliographing, 110, 116, 122, 130, 132, 133; patience and endurance, 111; on the summit, 115-123; a gorgeous sight, 124; return to camp, 125; nose frost-bitten, 128, 129; starts for Chile, 129; again at the high-level camp, 132; climbing the Catedral, 134; geological specimens, 136; a dangerous ledge, 139; at the top, 142; climbing Tupungato, 155; cure for a bruised knee, 172; forced to retreat at 19,000 feet, 174; second attack on Tupungato, 177, 181; a frolicsome wind, 179; a terrible night, 187; Tupungato now or never, 191; breathlessness, 198; the summit, 202; hard work, 210; fingers frost-bitten, 212; meeting with Mr. FitzGerald, 219; in Horcones Valley, 221; search for a volcano, 228; at Puente Alto, 232; in Yeso Valley, 235; ride to Vacas, 261; leap through a window, 266; arrival at Cuevas, 269; a fight with the snow, 275; swimming across Rio Mendoza, 278; Mr. FitzGerald's words of welcome, 279; laid up with cold, 290; squaring accounts with José, 295; typhoid fever, 299.
Vineyards, 21, 305.
Volcan Cañon, 10, 336.
Volcano, 195, 228, 240.

WALKING, and loss of caste, 17, 43, 292.
Water, unwholesome, 41.
Water-dipper, 345.
Weather, 35, 94, 153, 188, 206, 241.
West, Mr. W., 375, 376.
West Coast Cable Company, 228.
Whymper, Mr. E., 6, 331.
Wine, an unfortunate breakage, 181.
Winter dress of the Andes, 249.
Wolf's ascent of Cotopaxi, 6.
Wren, 351.

YARETA, 168.
Yellow Gorge, 16, 24.
Yeso Valley, 234.

ZANJON Amarillo, 16, 24, 303.
Zoo, inhabitants of, 95.
Zurbriggen Mattias, without a gun, 42; he sees Aconcagua, 43; buying horses, 47; in the Horcones torrent, 49; falls among the snow, 51; discovers Dr. Güssfeldt's card, 58; frozen feet at 20,000 feet, 61; boiler explosion, 64; nearly drowned, 68; superstition and accident, 70; sent forward to complete the ascent, 81; reaches the summit of Aconcagua, 83; betting on the ascent of Tupungato, 154, 205; buys a horse, 176; taken ill on Tupungato, 183, 189; at the top, 205; a fall, 212; ill at San José de Maipu, 234.

www.ingramcontent.com/pod-product-compliance
Lightning Source LLC
Chambersburg PA
CBHW021423300426
44114CB00010B/619